Expert CARD Technique

CLOSE-UP TABLE MAGIC
WITH 318 ILLUSTRATIONS
BY DONNA ALLEN

JEAN HUGARD AND
FREDERICK BRAUE

DOVER PUBLICATIONS, INC.
NEW YORK

Published in Canada by General Publishing Company, Ltd., 30 Lesmill Road, Don Mills, Toronto, Ontario.

Published in the United Kingdom by Constable and Company, Ltd., 10 Orange Street, London WC 2.

This Dover edition, first published in 1974, is an unabridged and unaltered republication of the second (1944) edition of the work originally published by the authors, in Brooklyn, New York, and Alameda, California, in 1940.

International Standard Book Number: 0-486-21755-8
Library of Congress Catalog Card Number: 74-82208

Manufactured in the United States of America
Dover Publications, Inc.
180 Varick Street
New York, N.Y. 10014

DEDICATION

THIS BOOK IS DEDICATED to all who love the art of conjuring with cards; to the most skilful adept as well as the youth yet to explore the heady mysteries of the art; to the man who comprehends the abracadabraish nomenclature of the craft as well as to those to whom such knowledge offers an open sesame to a new and exciting world; to the experienced in guileful trickery and to the tyro still experiencing the intoxicating excitement of thumbing through the textbooks of the craft; to the rich and poor, wise and foolish, young and old; to all the present generation of card conjurers as well as to the generations to come; in the sincere hope that they may find in its pages a knowledge which will enable them to add to the prestige and the dignity of the art of conjuring with cards.

FOREWORD

~~~~~~

THE AUTHORS WISH TO EXPRESS their appreciation of the friendly spirit in which many of the tricks and sleights printed in this book were contributed by Bert Allerton, Theo Annemann, Cliff Green, Gerald L. Kaufman, Harold Lloyd, Jack McMillen, Jack Merlin, Paul Rosini, Dai Vernon and Luis Zingone.

They are particularly indebted to Charles Miller, who generously and freely gave of his favorite methods that this book might be that which the authors can only hope it will be—a comprehensive and lucid source book of expert card technique.

It was indeed a happy circumstance that Carl W. Jones of Minneapolis. accepted the manuscript for publication. Mr. Jones has endeared himself to magicians the world round for his editing and publishing of John N. Hilliard's notable book, *Greater Magic*, a book that has established an all time record in popularity with magicians. It is Mr. Jones' prediction and the authors' wish, that *Expert Card Technique* will also become a standard book of card magic.

<div style="text-align: right">

JEAN HUGARD　　　　FREDERICK BRAUE
New York　　　　　　San Francisco

</div>

November 14, 1940

CONTENTS

~~~~~~

CONTENTS

CONTENTS xiii

INTRODUCTION

IN NO OTHER BRANCH of the art of conjuring has such progress been made as in sleight of hand with cards. Beginning with the half-dozen basic sleights known to the magician of a hundred years ago, there have slowly been evolved new methods of performing these sleights, and new sleights the purpose of which is to achieve results never dreamed of by the earliest experts. The progress of the art is milestoned by the great conjuring classics—*Secrets of Conjuring and Magic*, Sachs' *Sleight of Hand*, the great Hoffmann trinity, *Modern Magic*, *More Magic* and *Later Magic*, and Lang Neill's *The Modern Conjurer*. These were supplemented at the turn of the century by *The Expert at the Card Table* and *The Art of Magic*, two fine books which recorded the newer improvements in the art, the former of which even today will be found in the library of every card conjurer; perhaps no other book in all the list of conjuring books has been so avidly read, so affectionately regarded.

For three decades these books were the textbooks of the aspiring card conjurer, no new and important titles making their appearance. Then, during the middle thirties, the literature of magic was enriched by such valuable treatises as *Greater Magic*, by John Northern Hilliard; *The Encyclopedia of Card Tricks*, edited by Jean Hugard; *Card Manipulations* and *More Card Manipulations*, by Jean Hugard; and the publications of Theo Annemann, Laurie Ireland and Ralph Hull. Once again it became apparent that the art of conjuring is not static; that it is constantly moving forward in an era in which sleight of hand with cards has reached its greatest development, with new refinements, new techniques and new subterfuges displacing the older artifices. It has become apparent that there is a need for a book which would exclusively record the changes which have taken place in card manipulation since publication of the Downs and the Erdnase books, and the present volume has been written to fill that need.

The dissemination of knowledge almost invariably results in an increase in knowledge, and this is as true of conjuring as it is of science. It is nothing less than fascinating to perceive how a trick or sleight is improved by the many intelligences which leave their mark upon it, each mind shaping and improving the original concept. Always there is one goal: simplicity, which means ease of execution and increased deceptiveness. This simplicity is not easily achieved, although in retrospect a simple idea always seems absurdly easy of attainment; if the sleights of today are nearing perfection it should be remembered that this is only because of the thought of the preceding generations of magicians which passed along their efforts for the good of the fraternity.

In the following pages will be found the simplest methods of performing the sleights which play a part in the performance of feats with cards, as well as a number of tricks which have been found to be effective and entertaining. The sleights range from improved methods of performing the elementary and basic procedures, such as the pass, the change, the glide, the crimps and the palms, to the more pretentious and little known methods of the gambling fraternity, including the false deals, shuffles and cuts, and the perfect shuffle. The tricks include easy and surprising self-working feats as well as those dependent upon skill. All of these have been chosen with but one criterion in mind: They must be entertaining and mystifying to those who witness them.

As much as anything else, this book champions a *style* of card conjuring. The card expert commands the respect and admiration of those who watch him because apparently he does not manipulate the cards. His every effort is centered on presenting his feats with a minimum of handling of the cards. He attempts to present each trick exactly as though it were performed by true magical means. Under such conditions, the pack would be handled simply and naturally, without ostentation. The performer who constantly riffles the ends of the pack, who rushes through his feats as though Beelzebub were hard on his heels, whose movements are quick and jerky, is defeated before he starts, for his spectators always are conscious of the fact that he is employing sleight of hand; his every action betrays this fact.

The true expert is impressive because he achieves his results apparently without sleight of hand. It is as though the pack of cards in his hands had magical properties and the conjurer is simply the personality entrusted with the duty of showing these feats of which the pack is capable. It is this *style* of card conjuring which is offered in this volume; the sleights and tricks have been crafted with this end in view, that they may be performed wholly imperceptibly. As a case in point, although the simple crimping of a card may seem to be the easiest of all sleights, there still remains a right and a wrong method. The expert crimps the corner of the card in the natural action of picking it up for a moment; nothing could be more innocent of guile. The tyro makes of the crimp an arduous task in which the corner is bent almost at right angles to the card. Where the expert's technique is that of the rapier, the tyro's is that of the bludgeon.

Amongst card conjurers there is the belief that the expert achieves his results by means of prodigious skill, that his methods call for extraordinary application and tedious practice. The authors cannot stress too strongly that it requires no more practice to perform a sleight correctly than to perform it badly. Where the expert shines is that he has gone through the hard work of thinking out the correct *method;* he has experimented by the hour in searching for the easiest and best technique. For him it is a labor of love, rewarded by the inner glow which comes when at last he sees how to improve the sleight, or when he devises a clean-cut method of attaining a result required in a given trick. It is this secret knowledge which makes him the craftsman he is.

To prove this, let the reader study the chapter dealing with the false deals, supposedly the most difficult of all sleights. He will find that once he understands the correct method the various false deals may be had with a tenth the effort he may have expended in *searching for a method that would work.*

The reader will find on the following pages many methods which are new to him. He will find the perfect shuffle, the use of which will enable him to perform feats not possible by any other means. The rear palm, known and used by only a very few top-notch conjurers, is an excellent expedient when used as a *coup de grace.* The various gamblers' false deals will be found to be invaluable and are well worth the effort required for mastery; they represent the finest handling yet conceived. These methods are amongst those in the higher flights of card magic; there will also be found improved methods for almost every other subterfuge employed by the card conjurer—changes, crimps, peeks, glimpses, jogs, reverses and flourishes.

Of particular interest are the methods given for the various lifts, the side slip, the pass and the palms; these sleights are the very backbone of modern conjuring. Although the pass, in which two packets of cards are transposed, has fallen into disuse amongst many present-day experts, it is still a requisite if many excellent feats are to be attempted.

Amongst the tricks will be found something for every taste. Many of these feats are favorites of ranking card men; all of them are effective in the sense that they will entertain audiences.

The authors deem it advisable to include a complete compendium of the shakedown sleights employed by gamblers and card sharkers. Erdnase in his excellent and unique book did this for another generation but it has never been brought up to date and simplified. *Expert Card Technique* presents the work of this gentry as of 1941, illustrated and diagrammed so that the novice at card games may be forearmed as well as forewarned. Most of these *moves* are now employed in card magic and here they become excellent accessories in the legitimate art of entertaining deception.

Finally, chapters on technique, presentation and misdirection have been included. The experienced card conjurer may find that these chapters contain little that he has not already learned in the school of experience; it is hoped, however, that the neophyte may obtain from these pages a knowledge which will make smooth the path he must follow.

NOMENCLATURE

~~~~~~

THE FOLLOWING TECHNICAL TERMS have been used in the text throughout this book. Most of them were originated by S. W. Erdnase to describe the procedures given in *The Expert at the Card Table* and have become a part of the conjurer's lexicon.

Break: A minute division held in the pack to mark the position of a number of cards or of a single card. In conjuring the break is usually employed when the pack is held in the left hand as for dealing. The flesh at the outermost phalange of the little finger is pressed against the division at the right side at the inner corner (the finger tip is not inserted between the packets) and the remaining fingers are held together at the same side, concealing the subterfuge.

This break is often taken by the ball of the right thumb at the inner end of the pack, prior to an overhand shuffle, the fingers being at the outer end. The cards are shuffled into the left hand until those above the break have dropped; the remaining cards are then *thrown* upon those in the left hand. This is an easy method much used to bring a desired card to the top of the pack.

Bridge: To press the sides or ends of half the pack together so that the packet is made convex, if it be the upper half, or concave if it be the lower half. This is done to mark the position of a card or a number of cards. If a bridged pack is cut, this cut almost invariably will be at the bridge.

Crimp: To bend a part of a card, usually a corner, upward or downward, so that its position in the pack may be determined by sight. It is used to locate a single card or a *stock* which may be above or below the crimped card. It is possible to cut to such a card without glancing at the pack.

Cull: To secure certain cards at the top or bottom in the act of mixing the cards with the overhand shuffle.

Jog: A card extending for a fraction of an inch from any part of the pack. It marks the position of a desired card or of a *stock* of cards. When it is at the inner end of the pack the right hand in taking the pack for an overhand shuffle applies pressure with the ball of the thumb, turning the *jog* into a *break*, after which the cards are shuffled to this break and *thrown*, bringing the desired card or cards to the top.

A *jog* at the right side of the pack, when it is held by the left hand as for dealing, may be turned into a *break* by pulling down on the protruding edge with the tip of the left little finger, after which the pass may be made, or the card may be shuffled to the top.

Injog: A card protruding beyond the inner end of the pack. During an overhand shuffle a card is *injogged* by moving the right hand, with its packet, inwards towards the body. The left thumb draws off the top card of the right packet, thus causing it to protrude beyond the inner end. The remainder of the cards are then *shuffled off*.

Outjog: The same procedure, but the right hand moves outwards, causing the card to extend beyond the outer end. In the course of certain tricks, the *outjog* and *injog* may be employed during a single shuffle.

Joints and Phalanges: The joint or phalange nearest the palm is the first, or the innermost; the second is at the middle; the third is the outermost, that at the nail.

Run: During an overhand shuffle, to draw cards one at a time off the packet held by the right hand with the left thumb.

Stock: A number of cards, which may or may not be in an arranged sequence, which have been placed in some particular place in the pack, usually the top or bottom.

Shuffle Off: A genuine overhand shuffle, in which the cards are dropped from the right hand indiscriminately, in small packets.

Throw: During an overhand shuffle, to drop from the right hand packet onto the cards held by the left hand a number of cards in one packet, these cards retaining their order. Cards are usually thrown from above a *break*.

Undercut: To draw out a packet of cards from the bottom of the pack prior to an overhand shuffle.

Part 1
SLEIGHTS

AT THIS LATE DATE it should not be necessary to emphasize the fact that sleights should never be used except as *secret* processes in the course of a trick. To demonstrate one's ability in making the pass or changing a card, for instance, is simply to destroy the mystery of such tricks in which these sleights are used later on.

The many new processes revealed herein for the first time have been thoroughly tested by practical magicians and will be found indispensable by all who aspire to the title of finished performers.

Chapter 1
THE SECRET LIFTS

~~~~~~

The Double Lift

THE DOUBLE LIFT—that is to say, the lifting of two cards as one—is one of the most useful of modern card sleights. Many methods have been devised but all of them entail a certain preliminary movement for the purpose of getting ready, or "set," for the sleight, and this movement must be covered by misdirection.

The ideal double lift is the simple pushing off of two cards, as one, with the left thumb in exactly the same manner as in dealing, and such a method is given elsewhere. The following method, however, is the nearest approach to such perfection which can be had by purely mechanical means. A preliminary "get-ready" movement is still necessary but the gesture covering it is so casual and natural that the keenest eye cannot detect it and the practice necessary to master the sleight is negligible in comparison with its value. This method, hitherto unknown to the fraternity, represents the very finest handling, enabling the operator to lift two cards as one in such a wholly natural manner that even the most skeptical of spectators finds nothing suspicious in the procedure.

The Triple and Quadruple Lifts

A new and very important technique is also being introduced in this volume for the first time for the triple and quadruple lifts, which have previously been believed to be impracticable and dangerous of execution, chimeras which would never become realities.

As with the old methods of performing the double lift, the two elements which have prevented deceptive use of the triple and quadruple lifts have been the lack of a certain and easy method of controlling the cards during the push-off of the left thumb, holding the cards without any tell-tale overlap of their edges, and a certain and easy method of inserting the left little finger under the cards prior to the push-off: the old method of picking up cards at the inner end with the right thumb, dangerous with the double lift, is wholly impracticable with the triple and quadruple lifts.

Upon examination of these problems it will be found that the method

3

of preparing for the lift, and of making the lift, which is given here, when applied to the triple and quadruple lift make these sleights entirely practical and deceptive. These methods are given hereunder:

THE LIFT GET-READY

1. Hold the pack in the left hand as for dealing, the thumb lying flat against the left side, the four fingers at the right side, the tip of the second finger at the middle of the side. The first, third and fourth are held slightly away from the pack.

2. Press the second finger to the left against the right side of the pack, beveling it to the left. Press the left inner corner of the deck firmly against the base of the thumb, Fig. 1.

3. Bring the right hand over the pack, place the fingers at the outer end, the thumb at the inner end, and lightly square the cards.

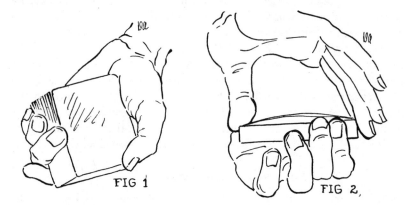

FIG 1   FIG 2

4. Press inwards lightly on the ends of the top cards with the thumb and second finger, causing the top cards to bend upwards breadthwise at the middle, Fig. 2.

5. Allow cards to escape one at a time from under the tip of the left second finger as they buckle upwards, and with this finger tip hold a break under the desired two, three or four cards which have passed, the number of cards being governed by whether a double, triple or quadruple lift is being made. The pack being beveled to the left aids greatly in enabling the second finger tip to allow only one card at a time to slip past it as the right finger tips apply the buckling pressure at the ends.

6. Drop the ball of the left thumb upon the top of the outer half of

the deck and raise the right thumb at the inner end. This action levers up the inner end of the cards, the second finger tip acting as a fulcrum. Insert the left little finger tip in the break thus transferred to the inner right corner.

7. Again run the right thumb and second finger lightly over the ends of the pack, squaring it.

In this manner you have quickly and indetectibly prepared for the lift, whether a double, triple or quadruple turnover.

THE LIFT

1. Hold the pack in the left hand, the little finger, which holds a break of two, three or four cards, being even with the inner end. Press the inner left corner of the pack firmly into the flesh below the base of the thumb by an inward pressure of the left little finger; when the thumb is moved, the flesh at the base of the thumb must swing freely over the top of the pack, Fig. 3.

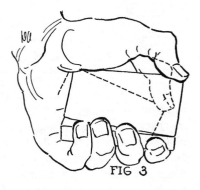

FIG 3

2. Bend the thumb at the joint inwards and place the side of its tip at the extreme edge of the left outer corner, resting upon the top surface with sufficient pressure to force a tiny fold of flesh over the side of the second card. This flesh fold later serves to draw with the top card the cards to be secretly lifted with it.

3. Move the thumb to the right and inward, describing a small segment of an arc, taking with it the cards to be lifted as one card, Fig. 3. Note that the finger tips are above the top of the pack; as the thumb moves the cards to the right in an inward arcing action these fingers tip to the right to allow the cards to pass over them, the remainder of the pack being held firmly in place by the inward pressure of the left little finger tip. The inner left corner of the cards pivots under the base of the thumb, the inward arcing pressure of the thumb tip forcing this corner into the flesh of the palm, thus holding the cards in perfect register.

4. Turn the right hand palm upwards and seize the cards at the outer right corner between the right thumb, above, and the first and second

fingers below, Fig. 3a. Turn them face upwards and place them squarely on the deck.

5. Slip the tip of the left little finger under the cards at the inner

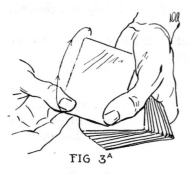

right corner during the last action as the cards are placed face upwards on the deck, thus preparing to turn the cards face downwards without any further get-ready. Square the cards at the ends with the right fingers and thumb.

6. Turn the cards face downwards in exactly the same manner. You have apparently shown the spectators the top card of the pack; actually you showed the second, third or fourth card.

FIG 3ᴬ

The Double Lift in Action

With only two cards to control, the double lift is made with the hands in almost any position, before the body or at the left side, with the pack in regular dealing position or with the outer end pointing obliquely downwards. The cards being turned over are grasped either as given in the previous instructions or may instead be grasped at the outer right corner with the thumb below and the fingers above, the turnover then being similar to the deal in stud poker. The hands may be held motionless or kept slightly in motion to the left as the turn-over is made.

All these are matters for the individual performer to decide for himself; the control of the two cards is so complete that variations in handling are matters of personal choice. The action in all instances, however, should be smooth and continuous, approximating a natural turnover; there is no real reason why the performer should watch the cards and this he should refrain from doing as this indifference towards the turn-over gives to it the naturalness which is absolutely vital to successful conjuring.

A glaring fault of many card conjurers is the overuse of the double lift. If one has to show that a chosen card is not at the top or bottom of the deck, for instance, it can be sent second from the bottom by the overhand shuffle and the bottom card shown, also several of the top cards. A repetition of the shuffle will bring the card back to the top naturally and unsuspiciously. The double lift should be kept in reserve for tricks in which it is indispensable.

Nor should the double lift be a plaything with which to show your skill with cards; it cannot be emphasized too strongly that it is a secret subterfuge which should be used only as a legitimate sleight with which to obtain results not otherwise possible. The conjurer who makes a series of lifts—six or eight in a row—and believes that the average spectator will not reason out what is being done grossly underrates the intelligence of laymen.

The Triple and Quadruple Lifts in Action

As will have been seen, the method of making the triple and quadruple lift is exactly the same as that used for the double lift. However, since the extra cards make the edges thicker and thus make the sleight more vulnerable, the triple and quadruple lifts cannot be made with the same disregard for sight angles which characterizes the double lift.

The following should be kept in mind in making these lifts:

1. Exert a greater pressure downwards at the outer left corner with the left thumb in pushing off the cards than is used in the double lift.

2. Hold the pack squarely facing the spectators, to the left or directly in front of the body a little below the waist, as though to permit a clear view of the operation. This position places the cards at right angles to the onlookers' line of vision and prevents the extra thickness of the edges of the cards from being noticed.

3. Turn the cards face upwards, or downwards, with the right hand without hesitation in the least possible time: in other words, naturally.

4. Move the outer end of the pack obliquely downwards as the right hand turns the cards, enabling them to be turned in less than the half-revolution which otherwise would be required.

5. Move both hands six inches to the left during the turnover, making it difficult for the spectators to focus their gaze upon the edges of the cards. This movement of the hands is a leisurely, normal action.

If these conditions are observed, the conjurer will find that an entirely new vista of card conjuring lies before him, making possible some of the most effective of card tricks.

The Double Lift Turnover

a. The orthodox manner of turning the two cards face up in the double lift by seizing the lower right corners with the right hand, turning them face up on the pack with the lower ends protruding and then turning them face down in the same manner, has become hackneyed. All who dabble in card tricks and, unfortunately, many who do not, know at once what is taking place the moment this movement is made. Adepts have found it advisable to change the handling of the two cards. The following method of displaying them as one card will be found to be not only natural but completely deceptive to lay audiences and will puzzle well informed magicians.

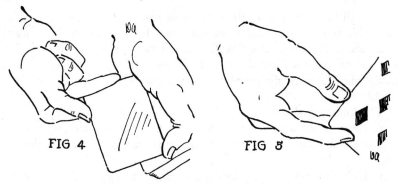

FIG 4   FIG 5

1. Push off the two top cards, as one, with the left thumb (page 5).
2. With the right hand, palm upwards, clip the two cards between the forefinger at the face of the cards and the second finger on the back at that part of the card where the innermost pip of a ten spot is printed. Let the cards slide between the two fingers to the outermost joints.
3. Press the extreme tip of the right thumb against the right sides of the two cards just above the two fingers which grip them, and the side of the third finger tip against the bottom, the little finger remaining free. Buckle the cards slightly downwards to ensure that the two cards will remain in perfect alignment, Fig. 4.
4. Show the face of the second card by turning the wrist inwards, Fig. 5, after which turn the cards down again and put them on the pack. The action is the same as that used by many card players when turning the top card of a pack face upwards.

It is advisable to use this method of handling when you turn a single card at any time in the course of a trick.

b. In spite of the fact that the handling of the cards in this method may be considered rather fanciful, it is very useful as a variation of the usual method. In spite of the twisting and turning of the cards there is no danger that they will come apart.

1. Push off the two cards with the left thumb as explained in the first method and take them between the tips of the right thumb and second finger at the right hand corners.

2. Move the left hand and the pack a little to the right and with the tip of the left thumb press on the left sides of the two cards making them describe a semi-revolution with the right thumb and finger tips as pivots, bringing them face upwards under the right palm. The right hand now has

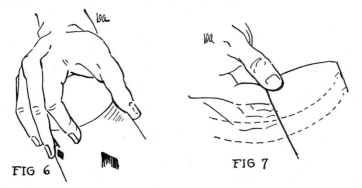

FIG 6   FIG 7

its back outwards, the thumb being upwards and the cards facing outwards.

3. Grip the sides of the two cards near the lower ends between the first joints of the right first and fourth fingers and remove the thumb.

4. Twist the two cards upwards until the right thumb can rest against the right sides, opposite the first finger, and release the little finger. Move the hands to the right bringing the backs of the cards outwards and at the same time let the right second finger take the place of the forefinger, Fig. 6.

5. Press the forefinger on the middle of the back of the two cards, release the grip of the second finger, turn the hand to the right and grip the cards, face outwards, between the tips of the thumb and forefinger with a snap, Fig. 7.

You have shown both the back and the front of the supposed single card. Replace the cards on the top of the pack.

The One Hand Push-Off

The secret move to be described is one for which the cleverest card men in America have sought—a move which opens up an entirely new field of expert card work. It is the pushing off of two cards, as one, with the left thumb in exactly the same manner as in dealing. Heretofore it has been believed that such a sleight called for an inexhaustible patience in practice and an uncanny skill. Actually the move is very easy, although we cannot pretend to explain why the method proves to be workable.

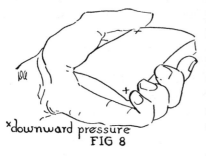

First of all it must be explained that only a description of the action involved can be given, along with an accurate description of the position of the fingers, and of the secret move itself.

xdownward pressure
FIG 8

Place the pack in the left hand, the inner left corner pressing into the flesh under the heel of the thumb, so that the thumb can move freely above the deck. Place the left little finger at the opposite side, barely above the corner, with the third finger next above it, the second finger a little above the third, and the forefinger above all. Since this last finger takes no part in the sleight, hold it slightly off the side of the pack. Place the tips of the left fingers flush with the top card of the pack, and hold the pack firmly by pressure between the left little finger and the flesh of the palm under the heel of the thumb.

To obtain the correct position, use a pack with a border, place the left thumb exactly at the outer left corner of the inner design of the top card. Hold the thumb nail at right angles to the card so that the flesh at the side of the thumb (or, more properly, the flesh just under the cuticle of the nail) touches the top card. To take this position, the thumb must be bent at the first joint. (If the pack were held face upwards, the thumb would rest at that point where the numeral of a card's index would be.)

With the left thumb press the left outer corner of the pack downwards; at the same moment, press the inner right corner downwards with the tip of the left little finger, slipping it slightly onto the top of the pack. Thus the diagonally opposite corners of the pack are bent downwards at the same moment, Fig. 8.

Without altering the position of the left thumb move it, still bent, lightly to the right. For some reason which the authors do not pretend to understand, the second card will move with the top card, remaining so perfectly in alignment that the dealer himself will often be deceived.

The positions outlined above are for a man with a medium-sized hand; however, each reader will have to experiment to determine exactly the placement of the left thumb in order to secure the desired result.

It should be emphasized that the left thumb, in pushing the two cards off as one, does not bear down on the top card. No conscious effort must be made to take the second card with the top card; pushing the latter lightly to the right will automatically carry the second card with it.

Chapter 2
FALSE DEALS

~~~~~~

THE SECOND DEAL

THE SECOND DEAL is generally conceded to be the most difficult of all card sleights to master, a statement the ambiguity of which has clouded the fact that it is not the action of *dealing* second which is difficult, but the method of gripping the pack with the left hand.

Because of this misunderstanding many card conjurers have spent endless profitless hours toiling to perfect the action of the sleight, heedless of the old axiom that, while practice may make perfect, no amount of improper practice can be of value. Once, however, the proper grip is taken, and the underlying principles of the deal are understood, dealing seconds can be mastered with a minimum of effort.

The literature of magic is singularly devoid of any really comprehensive instruction in the art of dealing second. Erdnase has given a detailed description of the sleight, but the methods, and more particularly the grips, which he gives have long since been discarded by the front rank card men. Walter Irving Scott in his manuscript gives considered and detailed instructions for the strike method, but unfortunately this booklet is not available to the mass of conjurers, both because of its scarcity and its cost. Furthermore, the strike method he gives cannot compare, for general utility, with the method employing the two card push-off. This latter method has been treated by Laurie Ireland in his excellent booklet, *Lessons in Dishonesty*, which the reader will do well to study, if only to compare the method with that to be given here and to decide for himself which of the two is best suited to his particular needs.

The sources mentioned complete the list of worthwhile instructions in second dealing. The reason for this remarkable reticence on the part of authors of conjuring textbooks is not far to seek; very few of the authorities on card conjuring have an intimate knowledge of the deal. Those gamblers who have perfected the sleight have a natural and understandable reluctance to reveal their secrets, even if they could describe the action clearly; in most instances, gamblers have acquired the "feel" of the deal and can perform it skilfully but are totally oblivious to the principles, and even the grip, which they utilize. Often, when asked to describe their grip, they are at a complete loss for words and summarize by saying, "Just place the deck in your left hand and deal." Excellent advice, but difficult to follow.

Amongst those experts who handle cards purely for entertainment purposes, there are hardly more than a dozen who can deal absolutely perfect seconds and these have not described their methods, usually because an incentive was lacking. Because of this cloud of mystery which has surrounded the second deal, the action will be described here in the fullest detail, even at the risk of prolixity. At best a difficult sleight to explain, it is hoped that this treatment will make clear the principles of the two best methods.

I. The Push-Off Second Deal

In this method the first and second cards are pushed off the deck as one card by the left thumb. The right hand draws off the second card as the left thumb draws back the first card onto the deck.

This method has the great virtue of providing a deal in which the cards are dealt in a manner approximating the standard deal used by most card players. The demands for perfect timing are less exacting than in the strike method but, as in that method, the grip of the left hand must be absolutely correct.

The procedure to be described here for the first time is a further improvement over other similar deals in that the grip has been simplified, the four right fingers being at the side of the pack as in a regular deal with the top card always under absolute control.

a. The Left Hand Grip

First of all, hold your left hand out flat before you with the fingers pressed tightly one against the other. Bend the four fingers, as a unit, at the innermost joints, placing them at right angles to the palm of the hand. Note that the point of the right angle thus formed is marked by the crease from which both the so-called life line and head line stem. When a reference to the palm is made hereafter it will signify that portion of the palm above the head line crease—that portion of the palm which forms the upright arc of the right angle. To secure the correct grip of the pack, proceed as follows:

1. With the left hand held in the above position, place the deck in it, its left side pressing flat against the palm of the hand above the head line crease. The top of the pack thus falls just below the base of the thumb; the inner left corner is pressed into the palm an inch from its inner side, and the outer end extends half an inch beyond the side of the first finger,

the end of the pack and the length of the palm being parallel. The left fingers, pressed closely together, are grouped at the right side of the pack, their tips flush with the top, the little finger being at the inner right corner.

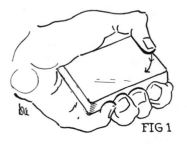

2. Grip the pack by an inward pressure of the joints of the left third and fourth fingers. If the position is properly taken, the left first and second fingers can be removed completely and the pack will still be held firmly by the third and fourth fingers pressing its left side flat against the palm of the hand. The fingers now arc slightly under the top of the pack, Fig. 1.

FIG 1

3. Place the right thumb and second finger at the right ends of the cards and bevel them approximately a quarter of an inch inwards, Fig. 2. This action is of great importance since it materially aids in the action of pushing off two cards as one.

FIG 2

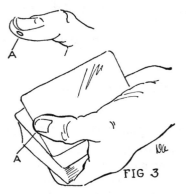

FIG 3

4. Place the left thumb tip upon the edge of the top card at the middle of the end. To do this it will be necessary to bend the top joint so that the point of contact with the card is the side of the thumb tip, as marked A in Fig. 3.

5. Move the left thumb three-quarters of an inch to the right in an arc which is a segment of an imaginary circle, the center of which would be a point midway between the tip of the thumb and the inner left corner of the top card, which is pressed into the flesh of the palm, Fig. 1. Again, it is important that the left thumb should not push the card straight off the pack to the right but should describe the small inward arc as stated; the nature of this action will be more fully explained in item 2 of the actual

deal. The reason for this arcing push-off is that the card pivots at its inner left corner against the flesh of the palm and is at all times under the control of the left thumb, whether it is being pushed off the pack or drawn back onto it.

b. The Deal

With the grip taken as described in the preceding section, the tip of the left thumb, at its side, rests upon the extreme edge of the middle of the top card as in Fig. 1. To make the deal:

1. Press downwards very lightly with the thumb tip forcing a minute segment of flesh far enough over the edge of the top card to engage the edge of the second card. This is not nearly as difficult as it may seem and a minimum of experiment will teach the amount of downward pressure re⁻ quired.

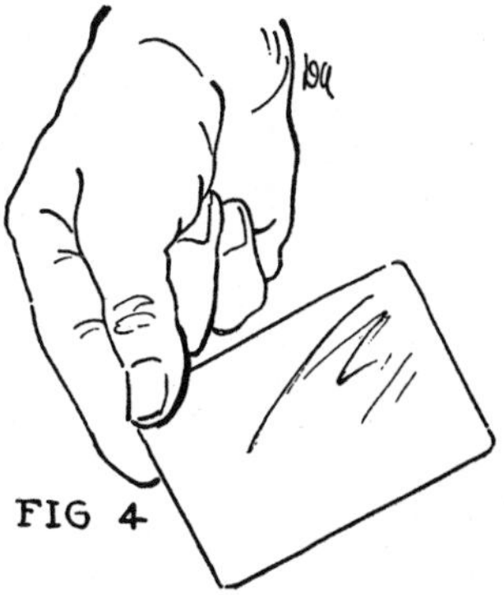

2. Move the thumb to the right in an arc, taking with it the top and second cards, the latter being drawn along by the tiny fold of flesh. Because of the pivoting action at the inner left corner, as has been explained, the two cards swing outwards towards the right as one card and remain always in

FIG 4

perfect register. They should not be pushed off the pack more than three-quarters of an inch, Fig. 3.

It should be noted particularly that, because of the bent position of the first joint of the left thumb, the pressure on the edges of the two cards is an inward pressure which forces their inner left corners into the flesh of the palm. In other words, the pressure is exerted from beyond the end of the pack and inwards towards the right; it must not—and this cannot be stressed too strongly—be merely a pressure to the right since this would give no control of the cards.

3. With the cards thus pushed off the deck, place the tip of the right second finger upon the face of the second card. By a slight upward pressure to the right draw this card away to the right at the same moment that the left thumb, now pressing lightly on the top card, draws it back to the left squarely on the pack. Drop the right thumb upon the second card the instant the first card is out of the way and deal it as the top card, Fig. 4.

The entire action has been described in the fullest detail but it must be remembered that one hand differs from another in the width and length of the palm, in the length of the thumb and fingers and, because of this disparity in individual anatomy, these instructions should be studied more for the basic principles than for exact measurements.

c. The Push-Off Stud Poker Deal

In this method of dealing, in which the cards are dealt face upwards, the cards are pushed off the pack exactly as in the preceding method.

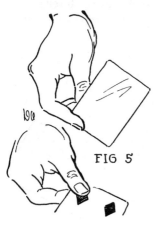

FIG 5

However, the right hand approaches to take the second card with its palm towards the body. The first and second fingers slide over the two projecting cards, the upper side of the second finger pressing against the face of the lower card at the index at the right outer corner. At the same moment the left thumb draws the top card back upon the pack, the second card being drawn to the right, face down, between the right first and second fingers, Fig. 5.

The right thumb presses upwards on the face of the card and turns it face upwards as it is dropped on the table, Fig. 5.

d. As a False Table Count

This method makes an excellent subterfuge for dealing extra cards secretly on a table pile. For each extra card required a two-card push-off is made and these two cards are dealt as one in the usual manner.

For small numbers, when special care must be taken, a good plan is this: Assuming that a four ace trick is being performed and that the operator wishes to deal, apparently, three cards on the table, whereas four cards are dealt in reality:

1. Deal one card on the table.
2. Deal a second card.
3. Push off the next two cards as one, grasp both at the outer right corner and thrust the two, as one, under the tabled cards.

Finally, it is earnestly suggested that the student bear these main principles in mind at all times:

1. The principle of the right angle grip, with the left side of the pack resting against the palm above the angle thus formed.

2. The grasping and the control of the whole pack by pressure of the third and fourth fingers at the inner right side, this pressure holding the left side flat against the entire width of the palm.

3. The beveling inwards of the cards at the right corners.

4. The inward pressure to the right of the thumb arcing to push off the two cards.

5. The pivoting of the inner left corners of the two cards against the flesh of the palm.

With these points thoroughly understood, experiment should be made until the right grip of the pack for the reader's hand is secured. This should be marked at once upon the palm and the fingers and all phases of the grip noted. It cannot be too strongly stressed that the difficulty in second dealing does not come from the action but from the placing of the pack in the hand. Two hours spent in acquiring the correct grip will prove more valuable than a hundred hours of aimless dealing of the cards.

II. THE STRIKE SECOND DEAL

In this method the thumb pushes the top card to the right as the right thumb strikes the surface of the second card, drawing it off to the right as the left thumb draws the top card back squarely onto the pack.

The great defect in this method is that very few card players deal cards in this fashion; the action is abnormal and hence open to suspicion, no matter how excellent the technique. Moreover, the student must have the expert's willingness to work upon a sleight, for the strike deal calls for absolute dead certainty of execution, for perfect timing and for perfect gripping of the cards.

Nevertheless, the student will not be satisfied until he has tried his hand at this method and it must be confessed that there are excellent uses for it. Some experts use it for pseudo-exposés of gamblers' subterfuges, explaining the method used to attain the result and reserving the push-off method as a secret weapon for use against onlookers who, satisfied that they now know how second dealing is accomplished, are completely hoaxed by the change of method.

The action for the strike method follows:

1. Grip the pack exactly as for the push-off deal, but extend the left thumb diagonally across the pack so that its tip rests as shown in Fig. 6.

2. Move the left thumb a quarter of an inch to the right, taking the top card with it. This card slides over the tips of the left fingers which are flush with the top of the deck. The pressure of the thumb downwards on the top card is light, being just sufficient to move the card. As in the previous deal the inner left corner pivots on the palm.

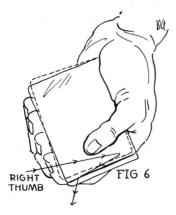

RIGHT
THUMB   FIG 6

3. Bring the right thumb over the pack at the outer end, its ball paralleling the surface of the card, the second, third and fourth fingers being curled tightly into the palm. Strike lightly and diagonally outwards with the thumb upon the exposed surface of the second card, drawing it away and dealing it, Fig. 6.

4. As the right thumb deals the second card, move the left thumb back to the left and draw the top card squarely back on the pack.

Essentially, this second deal is very simple, yet it calls for the finest coördination. The timing is this: The right hand moves over the deck, the length of the thumb being parallel to the end of the deck, the ball of the thumb being in the same plane as the top surface of the pack and its tip being brought approximately to a point three-quarters of an inch from the left corner. It thus masks the outer end of the deck for most of its length.

The left thumb pushes to the right* and inwards in an arc a quarter of an inch (with practice, the push-off can be so small that it seems incredible that the second card can be pulled out) and the right thumb immediately strikes to the right. This is in the smallest degree a dipping movement, that is to say, as it moves to the right, the thumb drops a fraction of an inch bringing its ball upon the exposed sur-

---

* The time element is considered here in fractions of a second. Actually, the left thumb does not push the top card to the right until after the right thumb has begun its return sweep to the right; if both movements are started at the same instant, the top card will be out of the way when the right thumb strikes at the second card, and an instant later, when the right thumb has moved away with the second card, the left thumb draws back the top card. The knack of coördinating these movements comes with practice; until the knack is acquired the instructions given in the body of the text should be followed, slowly at first and with increasing rapidity as the technique is understood and facility is acquired.

face of the second card and continues its movement to the right drawing this second card with it, the right forefinger moving up, pincer-like, to pinch it from below against the thumb. It is this action which gives the method its name; the right thumb is already in motion when it comes in contact with the second card and strikes it, the friction of its movement drawing off the second card, much as a card placed on a smooth flat surface may be moved by striking it with the flat of the thumb. The ball of the thumb must be held parallel to the top surface of the pack to prevent an inopportune "miss."

When the second card has been drawn no more than half an inch outwards to the right, the left thumb moves back to the left, drawing the top card back squarely upon the pack before the second card is clear of the pack.

FIG 7

Mastery of this method is attained by performing the various actions in a smooth flowing sequence with the different moves virtually being made at the same moment—or rather, a fraction of a second one after the other. Lightness of touch should prevail throughout, in the action of the left thumb, in controlling the top card and in the striking of the right thumb as it whips the second card from the deck.

Figure 7 depicts an excellent covering action for the deal. As the right hand approaches to deal a card the left hand tips the outer end of the pack upward and slightly to the right in a wrist action in which the inner end of the pack barely moves. The right thumb strikes out the second card as the outer end of the pack points obliquely upwards; as the card is dealt the pack drops back into a horizontal plane. The action is repeated for each successive deal.

Before commencing the deal it is sometimes wise to push the top card off to the right with the left thumb, which then draws it back squarely upon the pack. This serves as an assurance that the grip is properly taken and "loosens" the top card so that the lightest touch of the left thumb will push off and draw back this card smoothly.

In the hands of an expert it is absolutely unbelievable that the second card can be drawn off the deck when no movement of the top card is perceptible. A beautiful method of dealing second, it is, as has been remarked before, marred only by the fact that the almost universal method of dealing cards is first to push off the top card with the left thumb.

<h2 style="text-align:center">THE BOTTOM DEAL</h2>

There are at least two good brochures devoted to second and bottom dealing available today, as has already been mentioned. Ireland's *Lessons in Dishonesty* and Eddie McGuire's *The Phantom of the Card Table* in which are given the methods of the wraith-like Walter Irving Scott. To the excellent accounts of bottom dealing in these booklets we have one vastly important point to add: A method of withdrawing the bottom card swiftly and certainly with the right second finger, an action which heretofore has proved a stumbling block to those desiring to learn the sleight.

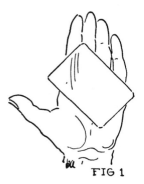

FIG 1

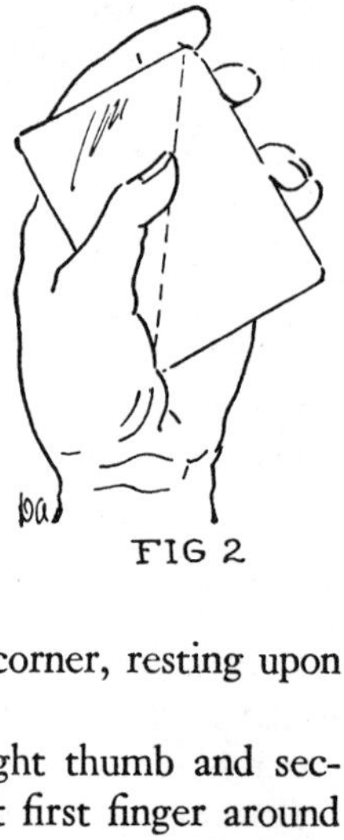

Before explaining the actual deal it is necessary to set forth clearly the positions of the hands:

a. The Left Hand

1. Place half the pack diagonally across the flat left palm so that the right side, near the outer corner, rests upon the second joint of the second finger, the right side, near the inner corner, resting upon the innermost joint of the little finger, Fig. 1.

FIG 2

2. Raise the right side of the pack with the right thumb and second finger at the ends and hook the ball of the left first finger around the right outer corner. In this position the pack is supported by diagonal pressure between the first finger at the right outer corner and the heel of the palm at the inner left corner. The left second, third and fourth fingers curl at the right side of the pack, their tips flush with the top, taking no part, however, in supporting the pack, Fig. 2. The left thumb points towards the outer right corner and rests lightly on the top of the pack.

As Mr. Ireland has pointed out, all hands differ but, once the principle of the grip is understood, experiment will give the exact points of the first finger tip and the heel of the hand at which the grip **is** made.

Once this exact position has been found, we would suggest that these points be marked in ink upon the flesh at the heel of the hand, the side of the palm nearest the thumb and the tip of the first finger. An hour or two devoted to placing the pack in the proper position will then make the procedure automatic and it will become second nature.

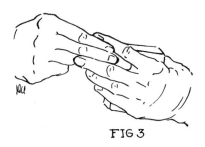

FIG 3

b. The Right Hand

The action of the right hand in taking the bottom card in lieu of the top card has never been fully described. It is most important.

1. Curl the right third and fourth fingers against the palm and retain them in this position throughout.

2. Hold the right first and second fingers rigidly together. During the subsequent actions these fingers must hold this position and must act as a unit. Any movement is from the innermost joints, they are never bent at the outer joints.

c. The Deal

1. Push off the top card with the left thumb.

2. Bring up the right hand and place the first and second fingers, always acting as a unit, under the left forefinger so that this finger rests in the groove formed by the juncture of the right first and second fingers, Fig. 3. The tip of the left first finger rests at the outer joint of the right first finger; the right second finger is in the gap between the left first and second fingers. The flat surface of the right fingers is always parallel to the surface of the pack.

If this position is taken correctly, the flat first phalange of the right second finger presses lightly against the face of the bottom card at the right outer index, and the right thumb on the outer right corner of the top card which projects diagonally off the pack some three-fourths of an inch.

3. Draw the right hand to the right, simultaneously snapping the first joint of the second finger inwards, taking the bottom card with it. This card is then grasped between the right second finger and thumb, the right first finger still being held rigidly against the second finger,

Fig. 4. In this figure the top card is being drawn back onto the pack by the left thumb as the bottom card is removed. The pack is shown face upwards for clarity.

This snapping action of the right second finger can be likened to the schoolboy's action of snapping his fingers to attract the teacher's attention; it is a quick sideways action of both right fingers with the bottom card playing the part of the thumb. This card is whipped out to the tips of

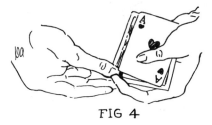

FIG 4

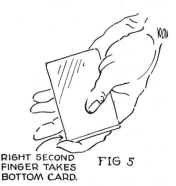

RIGHT SECOND   FIG 5
FINGER TAKES
BOTTOM CARD.

the right fingers, passing over the left second, third and fourth fingers.

Up to the moment when the deal is begun these three left fingers have been curled gently at the right side of the pack; once the deal is started they are extended rigidly, the fingers being straight from the palm to the tips, Fig. 5. As the bottom card is withdrawn to the right, they drop as a unit a fraction of an inch to allow its passage; this movement is negligible and passes unnoticed if the fingers are held rigidly straight. If the fingers are not straight this dip becomes very noticeable; some work is required to get the knack of the flat fingers but it quickly becomes automatic.

4. The bottom card is dropped on the table to the right as, simultaneously, the left thumb draws the top card back squarely onto the pack. Some operators make the deal without any movement of the top card, the movement of the hands in dealing being considered sufficient cover for the sleight. Others, again, move the thumb to the right and back without disturbing the top card.

The reason for holding the right first and second fingers tightly together becomes apparent as soon as the procedure is followed; the forefinger masks the placing of the second finger at the bottom of the deck and, furthermore, makes the deal more natural in appearance. This latter point also applies to the curling of the right third and fourth fingers tightly against the palm.

A covering movement is made with the left wrist by some card conjurers, upwards to the right as the hand approaches to take a card, downwards as the card is taken, while others move both hands together as the card is taken, apart as the card is dealt. The object in each case is to conceal the movement of the left thumb in drawing back the top card.

Another method is to draw the right hand away with a long stroke instead of drawing back the left hand with the pack. Still another is that wherein the left hand, holding the pack, always follows the right hand, the deal apparently being made slowly. Each expert has evolved his own particular method of covering the action but the method explained above will be found easy to acquire and completely satisfactory.

THE MIDDLE DEAL

Here is a will-o'-the-wisp that has had the super card experts agog for years. The first rumors of such a sleight being in existence naturally came from the gaming table. Certain top-notch gamblers were said to be using the swindle and, quite naturally, keeping the details a closely guarded secret. In spite of this, or rather because of this, several methods have been worked out for performing the sleight but it is problematical if these duplicate those used by the very few gamblers who are skilful enough to use the middle deal in actual play.

The first question that the reader will probably ask is—what is the use of the middle deal? To the gambler it is almost an indispensable accomplishment for this reason: The easiest place to set any desired cards in a game is at the bottom of the deck from whence the expert dealer can secure them at will. The trouble is that after the cards have been placed in this position the pack is cut and, when the cut is completed honestly, the desired cards are lost in the middle. In a loose game the gambler can overcome this inconvenience by simply picking up the lower portion and dealing directly from it. This would never pass in fast company, therefore the cut is completed in regular fashion and the gambler falls back on the middle deal to secure the desired cards.

On the other hand the sleight is of little use to the conjurer in the performance of tricks with cards with the one exception of the exhibition of an exposé of gamblers' methods. It is for the individual performer, therefore, to decide whether it is worth his while to devote the hours of practice necessary to master this sleight merely for this one display.

We give several methods of working the sleight, the first being one that is actually in use by the less skilful gamblers who work their wiles in the less sophisticated circles. Here are the moves:

a. 1. Hold the pack as for the regular deal, with the four left fingers at the right side of the pack, flush with the top card. The third finger holds the break after the cut has been completed. Push the top card off with the left thumb keeping its sides parallel with those of the pack at the end of this push-off.

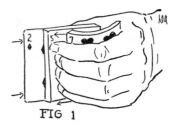

FIG 1

2. Move the tip of the second finger inwards until it presses against the right side of the card above the break. This action is concealed by the card pushed half-way off the deck. Insert only the tip of the second finger and let it touch only enough of the card above the break to give it a purchase.

3. Push upwards and outwards towards the right with the second finger tip. At the same moment draw the top card back with the left thumb, Fig. 1. These two actions coincide, the second finger pushing outwards as the thumb draws the top card back; this double action, the second finger pressing upwards and the thumb pressing downwards upon the top card, serves to control the cards between them and hold them squarely in place above the lower half of the pack.

4. The right hand, which has approached to take the card pushed off by the thumb, takes in its place the card pushed out from the center of the pack and deals it to the right.

b. This method is used by some conjurers in their so-called exposé of gamblers' chicaneries.

The deck is held very much in the same way as for the push-off second deal (page 13), the left little finger holding a break between the two packets after the cut has been made. The left little finger pulls the lower packet well down, extending the break along the side of the deck, the right second finger tip goes into the break and pulls out the bottom card of the upper packet. The right forefinger shields this action by curling in front of the outer end of the deck and the left thumb pushes forward and pulls back the top card as usual.

For exhibition purposes this method can be made to serve with comparatively little practice, particularly if the operator faces towards the right in the action.

c. This method is claimed to be that used by expert gamblers, though we cannot vouch for this by personal knowledge. It is much cleaner in execution and no doubt if sufficient practice were devoted to it a perfectly deceptive middle deal would result.

1. Place the cut well down in the fork of the left hand and the other packet on top in a slightly diagonal position so that there is a small

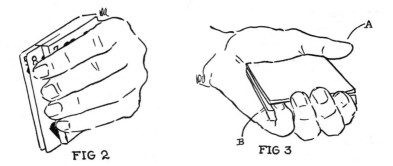

FIG 2   FIG 3

step on the right side, the outer corner of the lower portion projecting.

2. Press down on this projecting side with the left third finger and press the tip of the left little finger on the face of the bottom card of the upper packet, pushing it out sideways, Fig. 2.

3. Seize the upper right corner of this card between the right thumb and second finger, bending the right forefinger in front to shield it. The left thumb pushes the top card off and draws it back in the usual way.

d. 1. Hold the pack in the left hand as for dealing, with the fingers at the right side of the pack, but with the thumb pressing down on the top at the left outer corner, Fig. 3. The little finger holds a break at the inner right corner. The first, second and third finger tips project well above the top of the deck in an entirely natural grip.

2. Deal cards by taking them between the right thumb and first finger at the inner right corner. Draw these cards inwards for an inch and then remove them to the right, a perfectly natural action since the tips of the fingers prevent them from being drawn directly towards the right.

3. To deal from the middle: Press down with the left thumb upon the outer left corner of the pack at A in Fig. 3, at the same time pressing down with the tip of the little finger upon the lower packet at B in the same figure. This double action opens a large break at the inner right corner which is wholly concealed by the left fingers curling up at the right side.

4. Place the tip of the right first finger upon the face of the lowermost card of the upper packet at the right inner corner; rest the ball of the right thumb upon the edges of the cards at the right inner corner, pressing to the left against the edges of the upper packet as the forefinger draws the face card of the packet to the right and inwards; this double pressure in opposite directions keeps the upper packet in good order and greatly facilitates the removal of the desired card by the right forefinger. The card drawn from the middle is whipped inward and to the right at exactly the same speed that cards previously have been dealt from the top of the pack; and, particularly if all-over backs are used, it takes a very keen eye to determine that the card does not come from the top of the pack. Moreover, the left first, second and third fingers remain immovable at the right side of the pack, their tips extending above it, and it therefore seems impossible for the operator to have drawn off any card other than the top card, since these fingers should, logically, obstruct the passage of any other card.

During the sleight the left thumb remains at its place at the outer left corner; its only function is to press downwards on its corner when it is desired to open the break at the inner right corner to admit the tip of the right forefinger.

This deal, surprisingly, is the easiest of all gamblers' moves to master.

This method of opening a break at the inner right corner of the deck is so satisfactory that it should be noted that it can be used for a second deal. The left little finger holds a break under the two top cards; as the right hand approaches, apparently to remove the top card, the left thumb presses down on its corner, the break at the inner right corner is opened and the second card is whipped away inward and to the right. The move is almost indetectible, extremely easy of execution and can be mastered in a matter of minutes. It will be found useful in any number of card tricks.

The move can also be used as a substitute for the double lift push-off. As the right hand approaches to take the top card, the left thumb presses downwards on its corner and the break is opened at the right inner corner. The two cards are grasped by the right thumb above, and the second and first fingers below, at the corners; the two cards are turned face upwards as one and placed between the left thumb, first and second fingers at the left side, the end and the right side respectively.

The move has value since it can be made in a split-second, without fumbling and gives the natural handling that spectators expect of a person who supposedly is showing but a single card. It is, however, solely a substitute for the double lift push-off which remains the superior handling.

e. This method is exactly the same as the preceding one except that the break between the two packets is maintained by the flesh grip at the heel of the thumb and that the pack is held in the Mechanics' Grip, Fig. 4.

1. Hold the pack in the left hand, the second, third and little fingers at the right side, the first finger curling at the end of the pack, the thumb pressed upon the top of the pack at the outer left corner, Fig. 4. A small mound of flesh at the heel of the thumb is pressed into a break between the two packets, the bottom cards of the upper packet being the desired cards. It should be noted that when the pack is held in this manner all the finger tips are exposed and apparently no break could be held.

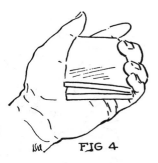

FIG 4

2. Relax the grip of the left fingers and draw the left thumb, the ball of which has bent inwards to press upon the top of the pack, to the left. This action will shift the upper packet a quarter of an inch to the left. Press the tip of the left little finger down upon the exposed quarter inch of the lower packet at the inner right corner, and move the thumb back to the right with the upper half of the deck. The little finger now holds a break at the inner corner.

3. Press the thumb downwards against the outer right corner once more and make the deal exactly as in the preceding method.

4. Stop the deal at any point, remove the left little finger and press down upon the top of the pack with all the left fingers; the pack will appear to be in perfectly regular condition although the break is still maintained by the flesh grip at the heel of the thumb.

In this method, as in the preceding one, it is important that the fingers of the left hand should not move as the card is being dealt from the middle; they remain pressed against the side of the upper packet and it is this fact as much as any other which makes any false dealing seem impossible.

THE DOUBLE DEAL

In this deal the top and bottom cards of a small packet are dealt as one card. One of the specialties of Jack Merlin, it was suppressed by him when writing his booklet, . . . *and a Pack of Cards.*

A method of duplicating the deal, not necessarily Merlin's, follows:

a. 1. Hold a small packet of cards, face upwards, in the left hand in position for the bottom deal, page 20. Push the top card diagonally off the pack with the left thumb, the inner end pivoting upon the flesh at the base of the thumb.

2. Place the outermost phalange of the right second finger upon the

FIG 1

FIG 2

back of the bottom card, exactly as in removing this card in the bottom deal. From this point onward, however, the deal differs from the bottom deal.

3. Place the ball of the right thumb upon the outer right corner of the top card. Drop the rigid left fingers a little lower than in the bottom deal, allowing the right second finger to move freely inward, over them, during the following action:

4. Draw the bottom card inward to the right with the right second finger, this card also pivoting upon the flesh at the base of the thumb, until it is directly under the top card at the face of the packet, Fig. 1.

5. Pinch these two cards tightly together between the ball of the thumb and the outermost phalange of the second finger and deal them as one card upon the table, Fig. 2. If there happens to be any overlap of the two cards, let it be on the right-hand side, for the cards should be dealt directly under the right hand, which is two or three inches above them, obscuring them from view immediately as the hand moves with a wrist action upwards to remove another card.

The double deal should not be made until a number of single cards have been dealt from the top, when the presence of an overlap in the two cards when placed on the table pile will not be noticed.

This deal can be used to show that a single card has vanished from a packet, or to effect a set-up of cards stocked at the top of the packet in dealing them. Many other uses will suggest themselves. Merlin's *Lost Aces* trick, in another part of this book, is an excellent example of the use to which the sleight can be put.

Second Method

b. This method of double dealing employs the Erdnase bottom deal, page 52, *The Expert at the Card Table.* As with the preceding method, it is for use with a small number of cards.

1. Hold the cards in the left hand, the first and second fingers curled up and pressing against the outer end at the right corner, the third and fourth fingers resting against the right side, the thumb lying diagonally across the pack with its tip pointing to the outer right corner. The pack is supported by the inward pressure of the outermost phalange of the second finger at the outer right corner which, exerted diagonally, presses the inner left corner into the flesh of the palm below the base of the thumb. When

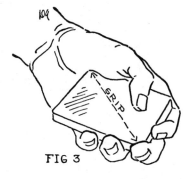

FIG 3

this grip is taken the left first, third and fourth fingers can be removed from the packet and it will remain supported between the second finger and the flesh of the palm. Note, in Fig. 3, that the outer right corner is pressed into the flesh of the first phalange of the second finger.

This grip is a modification of the Erdnase method which is preferred by some; the grip as described by Erdnase may, however, be used for this deal with equally satisfactory results should the reader prefer it.

2. Push off the top card of the packet with the left thumb, the card pivoting at the left inner corner on the flesh of the palm, and bring the right hand up to the packet to remove this card in the same grip used in the preceding method. The ball of the thumb and the side of the second finger press lightly against the outer right corner of the card from above and below; the first finger presses against the tip of the left second finger and helps to screen the next action, in which the bottom card is pushed from the pack, Fig. 1.

3. Concealed by the card which has been pushed over the right side of the packet, press the tip of the left third finger inward and to the right against the bottom card near the outer right corner, Fig. 4. This action

buckles this card and enables the third finger easily to release it from the inward pressure of the second finger and to move it directly under the top card, the bottom card also pivoting at the inner left corner upon the flesh at the base of the thumb.

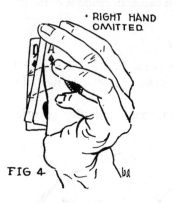

· RIGHT HAND OMITTED

FIG 4

4. Move the tip of the right first finger inwards, pressing it against the outer ends of the two cards at the corner in order to place them in alignment, grasp the corners between the right thumb and second finger and deal the two cards as one, as shown in Fig. 2.

The deal is made similarly, so that the right hand and wrist mask the dealt packet as much as possible; and again if there is to be an error in alignment, it should be on the right side of the dealt cards, not the left.

A clean deal can be had with very little practice.

Chapter 3
THE SIDE SLIP

THIS SLEIGHT IS GENERALLY used to bring to the top of the pack a card, the index of which has been peeked at by a spectator. We give two methods; the first is as follows:

a. 1. Hold the pack in the left hand as for dealing, the little finger holding a break under the desired card at the inner right corner.

2. Place the right hand over the pack, the first and second fingers at the outer end, the thumb at the inner end resting against the break at the inner right corner.

3. Press the right thumb against the end of the upper packet, insert the tip of the left little finger in the break and press upwards and outwards against the bottom card of the upper packet (that is to say, the card to be brought to the top) causing it to protrude diagonally from the pack, Fig. 1.

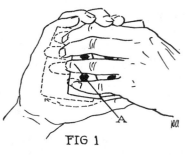

FIG 1

4. Place the tip of the left third finger on the face of this card near the inner right corner and straighten the finger, carrying the card with it to the right as shown by the ghost card in Fig. 1. The outer right corner, striking against the right side of the right little finger, causes the card to pivot into the correct palming position as the left third finger continues pressing the inner end to the right. Thus the card is placed directly under the right palm, being completely concealed by the back of the hand as in the orthodox palm.

5. Grip this card at its right corners between the first joint of the right little finger and the flesh of the palm at the right side.

6. Under cover of an unhurried movement of the body and hands towards the left, first move the left hand a little faster than the right until the gripped card is free of the pack, then move the right hand a little faster than the left bringing it over the pack, Fig. 2. Deposit the card on the top and square the pack with the right hand. A swift action at this point would betray the sleight.

An excellent method of guiding the slipped card to the top of the pack is this: Before slipping the card, move the right thumb and second finger along the ends of the pack squaring it. Note particularly how the ball of the thumb, which is almost parallel with the pack, brushes the inner end. Now, in slipping the card to the top, at all times maintain a light contact between the ball of the thumb and the inner end of the pack. This action has two advantages; it appears that you are continuing the squaring of the pack and, more important,

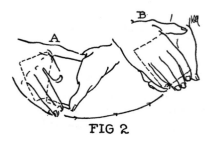

FIG 2

it controls the slipping of the card to the top. If the right thumb is removed from the inner end, the hand may raise the stolen card half an inch higher than is necessary to bring it to the top; whereas with the thumb maintaining contact with the inner end, the card will be lifted only enough to slide it onto the pack. The thumb strokes the inner end, moving to the right as the card is drawn from the center of the deck, back again to the left as it is brought to the top. With the card at the top, repeat the squaring movement once or twice, then lightly square the sides with the left fingers.

If it is desired to palm the card, you have merely to curl the right fingers on it as the left hand carries the pack away in the swing towards the left.

b. 1. Hold the pack in the left hand as for dealing, the little finger holding a break under the desired card, the thumb lying along the left side, A in Fig. 2.

2. Place the right hand over the pack, the thumb lying along the inner end, the second, third and fourth fingers at the outer end and the forefinger curled tightly on the top. Hold the wrist low so that the palm of the hand is in the same plane as the top of the pack, Fig. 2.

3. Insert the tip of the little finger in the break and with it push the desired card diagonally to the right about three-quarters of an inch.

4. Grasp the jogged card at the right corners between the first joint of the little finger and the flesh of the palm at the right side.

5. Move the body and the hands to the left, the left hand moving more quickly than the right, and thus drawing the pack away until

the card is freed. Turn again to the front, moving the hands in the reverse direction, the left hand moving faster than the right, and so place the desired card on the top of the pack. During the action the right first finger remains curled at all times, until the hand strokes the ends of the pack in squaring it. B shows the right hand depositing the palmed cards squarely on the pack, afterwards moving back to the right.

The curling of the right forefinger and the low position of the right wrist and hand are the features of this method, making it an excellent one for use under adverse conditions with spectators surrounding the performer.

Two Covers for the Side Slip

The legendary strolling conjurer, Max Malini, brought to its apogee the natural and audacious concealment of a vital sleight by covering it with a characteristic and deliberate action. For instance, with a card pushed from the pack in readiness for the side slip, he often paused to converse with the spectators and, perhaps a minute later, brought the card to the top effortlessly in an unhurried action which superimposed the card on the pack as he turned to an onlooker and illustrated how the pack was to be opened for the spectator peek. The action, a legitimate one, gave a tacit reason for the right hand moving over the pack.

Another favorite subterfuge of this expert card handler was the following cover for the same sleight, the side slip. Immediately before slipping the card to the top, he would request the spectator to concentrate on his card. As if to emphasize the request, he would raise both hands until the back of his right hand rested against his forehead, his right fingers grasping the pack by the ends and the left fingers by its sides. The hands, grasping the pack, seemed only to dramatize the request, actually the side slip was made as the hands rose, perfect cover for the sleight being thus afforded.

It is not suggested that readers adopt these actions, for, while they suited perfectly Malini's personality and style of presentation, they may be wholly unsuited to others. They are given as examples of the type of covering actions which card conjurers should seek—actions which are natural, unhurried and apparently predicated upon necessity.

Malini's Side Slip

1. After the spectator peek, retain a break with the left little finger as in the methods previously given.

2. Place the right hand over the pack and under its cover push the peeked card three-quarters of an inch to the right with the tip of the left little finger, which presses up against the face of the card at the right inner corner. The left third finger aids in this action.

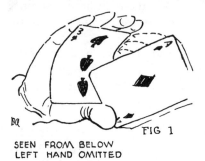

SEEN FROM BELOW
LEFT HAND OMITTED

3. Place the outermost joint of the right little finger upon the outer edge of the card, at the right corner, and drop the right thumb upon the inner end of the pack at the middle.

4. Move the fingers of the right hand to the right in an inward arc, thus swinging the card diagonally outwards from the deck, the inner end pivoting upon the ball of the right thumb which has remained against the inner end of the deck, Fig. 1.

5. Rest the right forefinger against the right edge of the pack. Hold the hands motionless for at least ten seconds; move the hands slowly to the left and quietly and very leisurely draw the card, which is held between the outermost joints of the fingers and the ball of the thumb, with its face bent concave, entirely free of the deck, replace the right thumb at the inner end and place the card at the top of the pack by swinging the fingers in an outward arc to the left until the card is squarely upon the deck.

6. Lightly square the ends of the pack, or indicate to another spectator how he is to peek at a card, either operation providing a logical reason for having brought the hand over the deck.

The leitmotif of the sleight is an almost absurd deliberation of action.

The Delayed Side Slip

In the first published explanation of the side slip, immediately after the peek was made a break was secured by the tip of the left first finger and the left arm dropped rapidly to the side. As the left hand was raised again, the right hand covered the pack and the left first finger pushed out the required card swiftly into the right hand which placed it on the top of the pack. There are two drawbacks to this method, the dropping of the arm to the side to hide the break held by the forefinger and the swift extraction of the card in the upward motion of the two hands which inevitably produces a telltale click as the card leaves the pack.

This procedure, which has been abandoned by experts, is still, unfortunately, used widely. A trial of the two preceding methods will prove instantly their great superiority. The application of the delaying principle is a still further improvement on the original sleight.

1. Proceed as in the foregoing descriptions until the desired card is pushed partly out of the pack and is gripped by the right little finger and the right side of the palm.

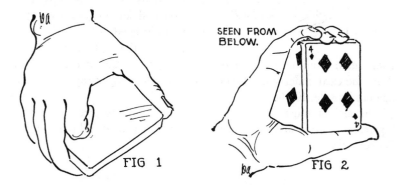

SEEN FROM BELOW.

FIG 1   FIG 2

2. At once grip the pack between the right thumb, which lies along the inner end, and the second, third and fourth fingers at the outer end, the first finger doubled on top, Fig. 1. The same grip is seen from below in Fig. 2.

3. Square the sides of the pack with the left thumb and fingers below and remove that hand.

4. A few moments later, with some appropriate remark, take the pack with the left hand, drawing it away horizontally to avoid any sound as it leaves the card behind. Let the right hand drop to the side naturally, bending the fingers in a little and securing the card in the orthodox palm.

The Bottom Side Slip

After a spectator has peeked at a card and a break below it has been secured by the left little finger, proceed as follows:

1. Cover the deck with the right hand and square the ends several times.

2. Insert the left third finger into the break and push the bottom card of the upper packet, the card peeked at, diagonally outwards by

straightening the finger; extend the other three fingers of the left hand at the same time, covering the action with the right hand.

3. Bend the right little finger on the outer right corner of this card, and press its lower right corner into the flesh of the palm on the right side, thus gripping the card firmly.

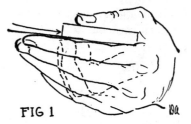

4. Turn slowly towards the left, moving the hands in the same direction, the left hand moving first until the pack is drawn away from the gripped card and the card rests on the outstretched left fingers under cover of the right hand.

FIG 1

5. Move the right hand over the pack again, continuing the action of squaring it and at the same time draw the card underneath the deck with the left fingers by closing them against its side, Fig. 1.

The sleight must be executed smoothly with no attempt at speed. Squaring the pack and turning towards the left provide all the cover that is necessary.

Chapter 4
THE PASS

~~~~~~

THE INVISIBLE TURN-OVER PASS

THIS PASS IS WORTHY of the practice required for its mastery and for this reason has been described in completest detail. It has been tested exhaustively before one of America's finest card experts, under close-up conditions and at a distance of twenty feet, under a brilliant light, with the operator turning slowly so that the pass might be observed from every angle. Under these conditions, with the hands at rest and without any covering motion, this authority pronounced it the first invisible pass he had ever seen.

The transposition of the packets is made under cover of a smooth and orderly action which exactly simulates the turning of a pack face upwards, and in studying the actions the reader should strive for smoothness, with one movement following the other without any hesitation or awkwardness, until the sleight, to all intents and purposes, does become the simple action of turning a pack face upwards. This is not nearly so difficult as it may appear once the nature of the pass is understood, for the various actions blend and the movement of the two packets is at all times screened by the position of the hands and the pack. Here are the moves:

1. Hold the pack in the left hand as for dealing, with the single exception that the thumb lies along the left side until the last movement of the sleight. With the little finger hold a break above the card to be brought to the top, this card lying somewhere near the middle of the pack.

2. Place the right hand over the deck, the middle phalange of the first finger resting on the end at the left corner, the ball of the thumb resting on the inner edge at the left corner. Press the flat ball of the left thumb against the side of the right first finger at the left outer corner. The outer right corner of the pack rests at the root of the right third finger, the right wrist being dropped to bring the palm of the hand on the same level as the top of the pack. In this position the fingers of the right hand screen the outer end of the pack, Fig. 1.

3. Curl the left first finger under the pack, its nail resting on the face of the bottom card.

4. Drop the right side of the lower packet half an inch and insert the tip of the left second finger between the two packets. Grip the lower packet between the left first finger, at the bottom, and the left second finger at the top.

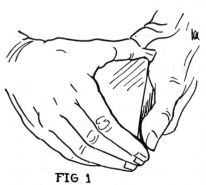

FIG 1

5. Straighten these fingers, thus moving the lower packet into a vertical position still gripped between the fingers. This action is concealed by the screening fingers of the right hand, Fig. 2.

6. The moment the edges of the two packets clear one another, turn the upper packet, A, down to a vertical position behind B by pulling upwards on its left outer corner with the first joint of the right forefinger. Do this by bending the first joint of the forefinger inwards, allowing the packet A to pivot at the ends near the left corners between the ball of the right thumb and the side of the right second finger at the middle joint. As the first finger bends inwards the second finger straightens rigidly and presses outwards, the double action serving to whip packet A from a horizontal to a vertical position, Fig. 3.

FIG 2

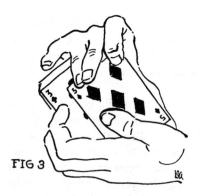

FIG 3

7. Bend the left thumb bringing its tip against the middle of the face card of A and press sharply outwards, snapping the pack into a horizontal position, face upwards, and resting on the top joints of

the left fingers. The pack will now be face upwards with the desired card at the top.

The following points should be kept in mind:

a. With the right fingers forming a screen at the end of the pack, it is impossible for the onlookers to see the movement of the lower packet when it is extended to the right.

b. The moment the lower packet clears the upper packet, the right first finger must bend inwards, pivoting its packet into a vertical position without the loss of a fraction of a second.

c. Similarly, immediately thereafter the left thumb and fingers snap the assembled pack face upwards without hesitation.

The pass can be made without the slightest telltale sound; however, if the proper timing is not maintained, there may be a small whisper of card on card. Once perfect coördination is established, this is eliminated.

In making this pass it should be clear to the onlookers that the pack is turned over and there should be a self-evident reason for having turned it. Commenting upon the favorable import of having a certain card at the face of the deck may be used, but the following is an even better procedure:

Immediately upon terminating the pass grasp the pack at the inner sides from underneath between the left thumb and second, third and fourth fingers, with the first finger curled at the bottom. Place the right thumb, second and third fingers at the right ends and make a pressure fan. After a brief glimpse at the fan, close it and square the deck upon the left palm.

By this procedure you have given a tacit reason for turning the pack and you have further amply demonstrated that you have turned the face-down pack face upwards, and vice versa.

The Zingone Perfect Table Pass

Referring to the pass, or shift as it is sometimes called, Erdnase in his book, *The Expert at the Card Table*, writes: "The shift has yet to be invented that can be executed by a movement appearing as coincident with card table routine." Jack Merlin agrees with this statement and writes that he has spent many weary hours trying to devise an invisible pass without success. The following pass, invented by Mr. Zingone, fulfills the requirements. In his hands, performing at the table, the pass is imperceptible. Here are the moves:

1. The pack having been cut, pick up the original lower portion by the ends between the right thumb and second finger, the other three fingers resting on the end but taking no part in the grip.

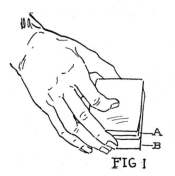

2. Place this half of the pack on the original upper half and, in drawing the pack off the table, secure a break between the two packets by pressing a minute portion of the flesh of the ball of the second finger between them.

3. Place the third finger against the outer end of the lower packet and hold it against the thumb at the inner end, Fig. 1.

FIG 1

4. Bring the left hand, palm upwards, over to the right hand and, in the act of placing the pack in it and moving both hands towards the left, grip the outer left corner of the upper packet with the left thumb and draw the lower packet towards the right with the right thumb and third finger, Fig. 2.

5. Raise the right side of the lower packet and press downwards on the upper packet with the left thumb until the packets clear one

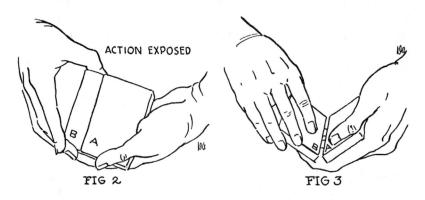

ACTION EXPOSED

FIG 2   FIG 3

another, Fig. 3. Bring the packets together, remove the right hand, continue the motion of the left hand to the left and deal the top card with the left hand.

The moves are not difficult but a good deal of practice will be required to execute them with the deftness of the originator.

THE FLESH GRIP PASS

The striking feature of this pass is that, with all the fingers of the left hand visible and the pack held in a perfectly natural position, no such sleight seems to be contemplated or even possible.

1. Place the pack vertically on its side in the left hand, the thumb at the upper side, so that it lies somewhat diagonally across the fingers with the outer corner resting on the middle phalange of the forefinger, the inner corner resting on the innermost phalange of the little finger. Let the four fingers curl over the side and their tips rest upon the back of the pack. The position is a natural one, all the fingers being exposed to the spectators' view.

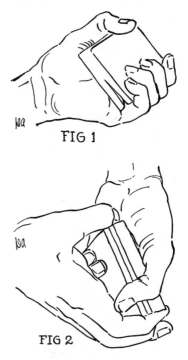

FIG 1

2. Place the right hand over the pack and break it with the thumb at the inner end. Press the little finger upwards forcing the soft flesh of its first phalange up into the break at the lower side near the inner corner. Remove the right thumb and the two packets will snap shut on the little pillow of flesh, which retains the break, Fig. 1.

3. Relax the pressure of the left fingers against the back of the upper packet and lower the left little

FIG 2

finger very slightly, causing the two packets to fall a little apart; at the same moment grasp the ends of the lower packet, near the upper corners between the thumb and first and second fingers of the right hand. Alter the position of the left thumb from the top side of the pack to the middle joint of the right forefinger, Fig. 2. When the right hand is held in the position shown the two packets must always remain parallel to one another and thus must be transposed in a minimum of space. Note particularly that the two outermost joints of the right first and second fingers are at right angles to the remainder of the side of the hand.

4. Transpose the two packets by bending the right second finger inwards, causing the lower packet to pivot on the left forefinger and thumb; at the moment that the two packets clear one another, press the tips of the left fingers against the back of the upper packet thus completing the pass which is made very swiftly and well-nigh invisibly.

When a break is held by the tip of the left little finger in the usual fashion and a pass must be made, the right hand takes the pack at the ends, the thumb holding the break at the inner end. The pack is placed in the vertical position, on its side, in the left hand, the flesh of the little finger is forced into the break and the pass is made as described above.

The Jog Pass

This fast and very deceptive pass is so named because its best use is with a card jogged at the inner end of the deck.

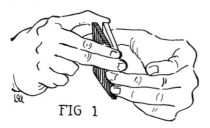

FIG 1

1. Hold the pack vertically in the left hand, the thumb at the middle of the upper side, the forefinger curled at the middle of the face card, the second, third and middle fingers being at the inner end of the lower side. A card is jogged at the inner end.

2. Place the right hand over the deck·and take it between the

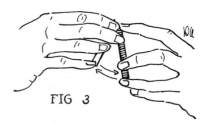

FIG 2

FIG 3

first and second fingers at the upper outer corner and the thumb at the upper inner corner, making a break with the thumb above the jogged card.

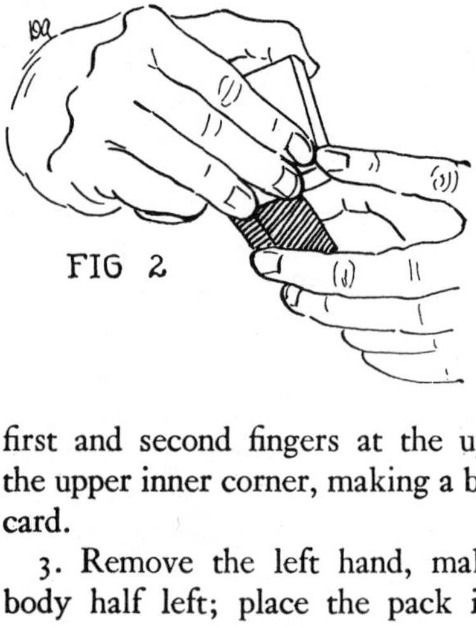

3. Remove the left hand, making a casual gesture, and turn the body half left; place the pack in the left hand, grasping it by the

ends between the second and third fingers at the lower outer corner
and the thumb at the lower inner corner, retaining the break, the forefinger and the little finger free, Fig. 1. Make a gesture with the right
hand.

4. Bring the right hand over the pack and grasp the lower packet at
the top corners between the thumb and second and third fingers, Fig. 1.

5. Draw the upper packet downwards a quarter of an inch with the
left thumb and second and third fingers and press inwards with the tip
of the right second finger, causing the packets to pivot in opposite directions and forming a V lying on its side, the apex of the V being towards the right, Fig. 2.

6. The moment the edges of the packets clear one another, pull the
left hand packet inwards with the tip of the left second finger and let
the two packets slide together in a vertical position, Fig. 3. Square the
pack with the right hand.

The action transposes the two packets with a minimum of clearance.
It is noiseless and very fast; the back of the right hand must be kept towards the audience, concealing the pack.

THE BRAUE PASS

Countless conjurers have attempted to devise a method of performing the pass, that is to say, to transpose the two halves of the deck
imperceptibly with the hands at rest; but all such efforts have failed.
We have the confessions of such experts as Erdnase and Merlin that
they have spent many fruitless hours wrestling with the problem. The
survival of the method of making the classic pass through the centuries proves that the basic principles are correct and the best yet
evolved. The following method uses these principles but applies
them in a slightly different way, with the result that the two
packets are transposed with less movement and, therefore, more
rapidly. The directions should be followed with the pack in hand.

1. Hold the deck vertically in the left hand, the little finger being
inserted between the upper packet, which we will call No. 1, and the
lower packet, No. 2.

Press the first phalange of the left first finger firmly upon the top of
the upper packet, No. 1. The sides of the cards rest upon the innermost
phalange of this finger.

Rest the left thumb upon the upper side of the pack and extend the
second and third fingers so that they do not touch the deck at any point.

Throughout the subsequent actions these two fingers are held away from the cards at all times.

The position of the two hands is as in Fig. 1. Fig. 2 shows the nature of the left hand grip of its packet, the cards being controlled mainly by the left first finger.

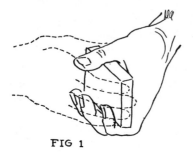

FIG 1

2. Bring up the right hand and cover the deck, seizing the top corners of No. 2 between the thumb and forefinger and keeping all the fingers close together. In this position, the tip of the left thumb presses against the side of the right forefinger at a point between the second and the innermost joints.

3. Pressing lightly downward with the first phalange of the left first finger against the top of packet No. 1, lift the No. 2 packet slightly upward by moving the right hand to the left and upward in a very small arc; at the same moment, with the right thumb and forefinger acting as pivots, draw No. 2 to the right by bending the right second finger inward. This action forces the upper side of No. 1 also to the right, its lower side pressing against the first phalange of the left first finger, which relaxes sufficiently to allow the packet to make its small movement to the right, Fig. 3. The tip of the left thumb remains pressing lightly against the side of the right forefinger.

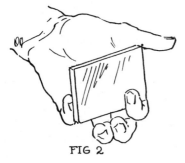

FIG 2

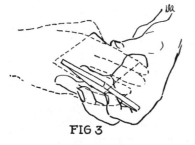

FIG 3

4. When the two packets clear one another, swing No. 1 to the left by bending the top joint of the left forefinger inwards and let No. 2 drop on top of it, Fig. 3. Note particularly that the left little finger remains curled under packet No. 1, supporting the now assembled pack. Again, for clarity, the position of the left thumb tip against the right forefinger has been omitted.

The striking feature of this method is the heretofore unappreciated fact that a single left finger, the first finger, can fulfill the duties which heretofore have been performed by the left first, second and third fingers in controlling the No. 1 packet. This eliminates to a surprising degree the fatal dipping of the left fingers during the transposition of the packets which has been one of the great flaws of the pass.

In actual practice the pack should be held in a slanting position with the right side downwards. The pass is made noiselessly, very swiftly, and practically at the fingertips; but it requires a great amount of practice to accomplish the sleight perfectly. As with all sleights, the positions must be taken accurately and the action performed slowly until the fingers become accustomed to the necessary movements.

THE CHARLIER PASS

The shift that goes by this name is credited generally to that mysterious personage, Charlier, though this is disputed by French writers. The sleight has been the vortex of a controversy which has raged for many years: Can it, or can it not, be performed imperceptibly? Merlin, in his book, has written that the transposition of the packets invisibly by this pass is impossible; on the other hand the senior collaborator of this volume has seen Charles Bertram use it as an instantaneous color change with perfect success. Although Bertram disclaimed any special dexterity with the sleight he was able to do it eighty times a minute. When he used it as a color change he applied the pass in this way:

a. Color Change

1. Hold the pack vertically in the left hand, face outwards, with the thumb at the upper side, the second, third and fourth fingers at the lower side and the first finger curled at the bottom of the deck.

2. Move the hand outwards about six inches and call attention to the face card, naming it.

3. Bring the hand back to its original position at the same time dropping half the pack onto the left palm, transpose the two packets in the usual way by pushing upwards with the first finger and letting them fall onto the left palm upon which the packet controlled by the first finger is dropped. In making this movement turn the hand

over rapidly to the right, bringing it momentarily back upwards, and drop the thumb to the inner end of the face card, Fig. 1. Instantly turn the hand up again, Fig. 2, and quickly move the thumb over the

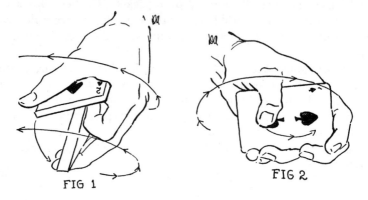

FIG 1

FIG 2

face card from the bottom to the top, Fig. 2. Accompany the action with some such remark as this: "You see, I merely rub my thumb over the card and it changes completely."

The illusion depends upon the rapid twist of the wrist downwards and upwards and the passage of the thumb over the face of the card which conceal the smaller movements of the cards completely.

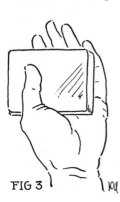

FIG 3

b. To Control a Card

It must be conceded that this pass cannot be made invisibly with the hand at rest and without cover, but this can be done under cover of the right hand when the pack is hidden momentarily in taking it by the ends between the right thumb and fingers.

Perfect cover can also be provided, without the intervention of the right hand, in this way:

After you have split the pack and a selected card has been placed on top of the lower packet, quickly raise the hand above your head, saying: "Who'll shuffle the deck?" Make the pass as the hand is raised, the upward motion making the transposition of the packets easy. At the end of the action let the pack rest on the left thumb, the fingers pointing upwards, Fig. 3.

This method of bringing a card to the top, when combined with the one-hand top palm in handing the pack out to be shuffled, is one of the best methods of controlling a chosen card yet devised.

THE FINGER PALM PASS IMPROVED

This pass, although fairly well known to expert card men, has never, to our knowledge, appeared in print. With the modifications now made in it, revealed here for the first time, the pass becomes a very valuable one. The misdirection is perfect and the execution easy.

1. Hold the pack in the left hand as for dealing, the little finger holding a break at the point at which the pass is to be made.

2. Bring the right hand over the deck and grasp it between the right thumb at the inner end, accepting and retaining the break, and the second, third and fourth fingers at the outer end, the first finger being curled on the top.

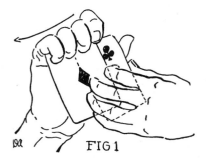

FIG 1

3. Curl the left forefinger on the face of the bottom card and with the right hand move the pack forward a little to enable the left thumb and little finger to grasp the upper packet firmly at the inner corners; release the left second and third fingers.

4. With the right thumb at the inner end, push the lower packet, below the break, a quarter of an inch outwards and press upwards with the left forefinger, supporting this packet and keeping it against the upper packet. This outward projection of the lower packet is hidden by the right second, third and fourth fingers.

5. Slide the right hand outward and grip the projecting end of the lower packet by curling the middle and top joints of the second, third and fourth fingers downwards and inwards.

6. Move the right hand directly to the right, carrying with it the lower packet, the inner end of which barely clears the left little finger at the inner right corner; there must be no outward motion of the right hand, Fig. 1. Immediately press the packet against the right palm with the last three fingers, concealing it with the back of the hand, and point with the forefinger to the packet in the left hand. Replace the second and third fingers of the left hand on the side of its packet.

7. Move the right hand over the left hand packet and deposit the palmed packet on it in the action of squaring the pack.

The sleight must be performed under cover of a movement to the left by both hands with the different moves taking place almost simultaneously.

Chapter 5
PALMING

~~~~~~

THE BRAUE DIAGONAL TIP-UP PALM

THIS METHOD is much the same as that of the one-hand top palm of a single card; the action is so subtle that it is impossible for an expert even to detect whether or not cards have been palmed.

1. Hold the pack in the left hand as for dealing, but with the thumb lying flat along its left side, the fleshy ball pressing against the corner and thus forcing a fold of flesh upon the top of the pack. The tip of the little finger holds a break under the cards to be palmed.

FIG 1

2. Place the right hand over the deck as if to square it, the fingers at the outer end, the thumb at the inner end.

3. Move the tip of the little finger, which presses against the face of the lowest card of the packet, upwards and to the right about half an inch, carrying the packet with it and causing it to pivot against the ball of the left thumb at the outer left corner, diagonally opposite. This action raises the inner ends of the cards to be palmed and places them diagonally across the remainder of the pack, Fig. 1.

4. Place the right thumb at B, pressing it against the pack proper, and press downwards at A with the tip of the right little finger, levering the packet up into the right palm.

5. The instant the cards are secured in the palm, run the fingers and thumb along the ends of the remaining cards, squaring them. Then seize the pack between the tips of the first finger and thumb at the outer right corners and hold it thus for a few moments before placing it on the table or disposing of it as may be necessary for the trick in hand. Be careful not to raise the right thumb at the moment the palm is made, a common fault in palming cards.

THE SWING PALM

This palm is very fast, easy of execution and indetectible.

49

1. Hold the pack in the left hand as for dealing, then move the thumb to the left side. Place the right hand over the pack, the fingers at the outer end and the thumb at the inner end.

2. Lift the cards to be palmed with the tip of the right little finger at the outer right corner of the pack.

3. Move the right fingers a quarter of an inch to the right, the little finger carrying its cards with it, the packet pivoting on the right thumb at the center of the inner end. Place the tip of the left forefinger against the extreme outer right corner of the packet directly under the tip of the right little finger.

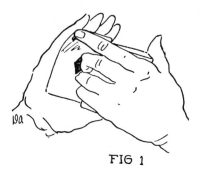

FIG 1

4. Press the left forefinger and the right little finger together, clipping the corner of the packet to be palmed between these two finger tips, Fig. 1.

5. Straighten the left forefinger to the right, moving the little finger with it, thus moving the packet to the right and causing it to swing up against the right palm in perfect position for palming, Fig. 1. Twist the left wrist upwards and outwards to bring the remainder of the pack into view as much as possible.

6. Finally square the ends of the remaining cards with the right thumb and fingers and grip the pack by the right hand corners with the right hand.

Note that when the left little finger holds a break and it is desired to palm the cards above the finger, the break is allowed to move down to the outer right corner of the pack so that the right little finger can instantly secure the cards desired.

The Thumb-Count Palm

This is a quick and easy method of securing any desired number of cards in the right hand. The procedure is as follows:

1. Hold the pack in the left hand vertically, face outwards, in position for the top thumb count (page 183), the left arm bent to bring the hand about opposite the second vest button.

2. With the left thumb count off the desired number of cards and slip its tip into the break.

3. Bring the right hand over the pack, the fingers at the outer end, the thumb at the inner end, and, under cover of a half turn to the left,

palm the separated packet in the right hand, the left thumb aiding the action by pressing upwards, Fig. 1.

4. Immediately square the ends of the pack with the right thumb and fingers and then grip it between them at the right corners.

5. Square the sides of the deck with the left thumb and fingers, then remove the left hand, leaving the pack gripped between the right thumb and first finger at the extreme right corners.

The fact that the moment the back of the pack comes into view, the left thumb is seen pressing down on it, seems to preclude any possibility of palming.

FIG 1

FACE CARD PALM, RIGHT HAND

a. The purpose of this sleight is to provide a method of palming the face card of the deck in the right hand indetectibly.

1. Hold the pack face down in the right hand at the ends near the right corners between the first and second fingers and the thumb.

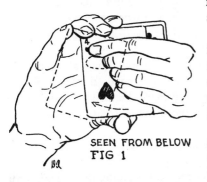

SEEN FROM BELOW
FIG 1

2. In the act of placing the pack in the left hand let the tip of the left forefinger press on the outer index of the face card, causing it to protrude on the right side of the deck, Fig. 1.

3. When the motion of the right hand has caused the card to be jogged about half an inch, curl the left second finger and press its tip on the face card about half an inch to the left of the first finger tip. Straighten this second finger causing the lower end of the face card to twist outwards and bringing it into the position most favorable for palming, Fig. 1.

4. Grasp the pack with the left hand and at the same moment palm the card in the right hand by slightly contracting the second, third and fourth fingers and the thumb, the forefinger remaining extended, pointing towards the pack, at the completion of its transfer to the left hand.

The action must be accompanied by a slight turn to the left, bringing the back of the right hand towards the spectators. It can be done in an instant and without disarranging the rest of the cards in the slightest degree.

b. This method of palming is used in most cases for a color change. The curling of the right forefinger on the top of the pack seems to pre-

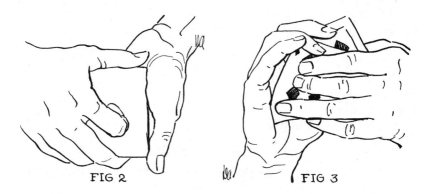

FIG 2   FIG 3

clude any possibility of palming and also exposes a great part of the back of the pack. The low position of the right wrist prevents the spectators on the operator's right from observing the movement of the face card. Here is the method:

1. Hold the deck in the right hand, the thumb lying along the inner end, the outer end grasped between the second, third and fourth fingers, and the first finger curled on the back. Hold the wrist low so that the palm of the hand is on the same plane as the top of the pack, Fig. 2.

2. Place the deck upon the left palm, much as for dealing, but with the left thumb lying along the left side, Fig. 2.

3. Draw back the left fingers under the pack, holding them rigid, until the tip of the third finger rests against the right side of the face card near its inner corner, and with it push the card to the right until it extends diagonally from the pack about an inch, Fig. 3.

4. Grasp this card between the top joint of the right little finger and the right side of the palm.

5. Carry the pack away in the left hand, bend the right second, third and fourth fingers, curling the card up into the palm and straighten the right forefinger, pointing with it to the pack.

The Crosswise Palm

This sleight is an innovation; heretofore cards have always been palmed from a pack the length of which paralleled the length of the palming hand. This new action steals the cards from a pack held breadthwise, a fact which apparently makes a palm impossible as will be seen from the description following:

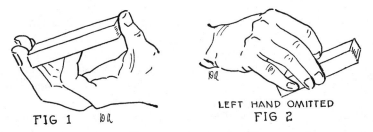

FIG 1

LEFT HAND OMITTED
FIG 2

1. Hold the pack by the ends between the left thumb at one end, the second, third and fourth fingers at the other, the first finger being curled in with its tip resting against the bottom card, Fig. 1.

2. Place the right hand over the pack, the thumb at the center of the inner side, the second finger at the center of the outer side and the forefinger curled on top of the pack, Fig. 2.

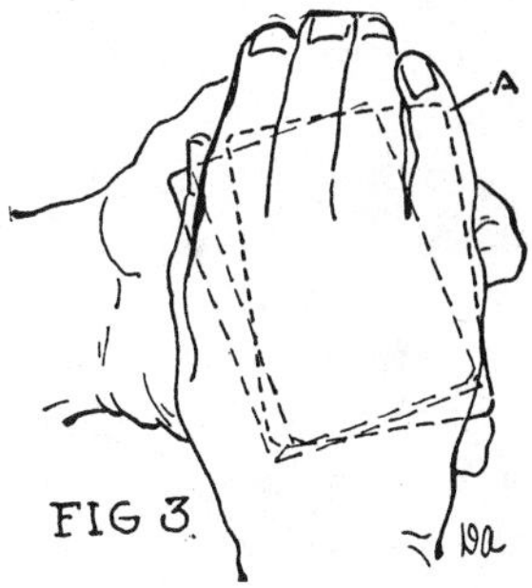

3. Lift the cards to be palmed with the tip of the right thumb; raise and straighten all the other fingers so that they extend over and above the left end of the pack.

4. With the right thumb push the packet outwards so that it pivots on the tip of the left second finger and swings diagonally half an inch across the pack, Fig. 3. The right end of the packet remains pressed against the left second finger until, at the completion of No. 5, the packet is palmed.

5. Press downwards with the right little finger at the outer right corner of the packet, A, levering the cards directly up into the right palm, Fig. 3. Close the fingers, gripping the cards, turn the hand towards the right and move it slowly downwards, squaring the sides of the pack between the thumb and fingers.

6. Finally, grip the deck at its lower end between the right thumb and fingers and hold it thus for a few moments at least.

New Vertical Palm

This sleight will be found especially useful when, in the trick of passing a number of cards from the left hand into the trousers pocket, the conjurer finds himself with the last three, four or five cards (de-

FIG 1

pending upon the routine used) to send upon their invisible journey. To execute this special palm:

1. Display the last few cards in a fan in the right hand. Square the cards with the left fingers and, holding the packet face out with the sides horizontal, grasp it between the left thumb and first and second fingers near its lower left corner, Fig. 1.

2. Place the right palm over the face of the packet, in the same position one would use to actually palm the cards, and swiftly draw the hand upwards. This action should be quick and casual, as though merely squaring the ends of the packet, and immediately afterwards the right thumb and fingers must be drawn along the sides in a similar squaring action. This gesture is a feint to prepare the spectators for that in the course of which the cards actually will be palmed.

3. Fan the cards once more in the right hand, requesting the spectators to remember them, and again take the packet horizontally between the left thumb and first and second fingers at the lower left corner, exactly as before. Place the right hand over the packet lengthwise and palm it, but in drawing the hand upwards, re-

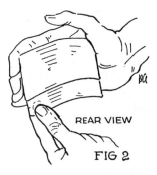

REAR VIEW

FIG 2

tain the face card with the left fingers and carry away the cards behind it, the left thumb aiding in the action by pushing these cards upwards, Fig. 2. Turn the right hand downwards immediately to square the sides of the remaining card as in the feint.

With a minimum of practice, it will be found that the cards behind the face card can be palmed in a flash, the right hand merely moving upwards over the face of the packet to square the ends and then lengthwise to square the sides.

The one remaining card (supposedly several cards) is then placed in the left hand against the palm and the cards palmed in the right hand are carried to the right trousers pocket to be produced therefrom in due course.

THE GAMBLERS' SQUARING PALM

This is another subtle sleight which has come to us from the gaming table and it is, therefore, designed for use when seated at a table. The mode of execution is as follows:

1. Hold the pack in the left hand between the top joints of the

FIG 1

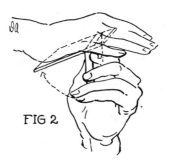

FIG 2

thumb, at the middle of the left side, and the second and third fingers at the middle of the right side, the first finger doubled in against the bottom card and the little finger holding a break below the cards to be palmed.

2. Place the right hand over the pack so that the joint of the thumb and the first joint of the little finger will be at the sides of the pack near the outer corners and

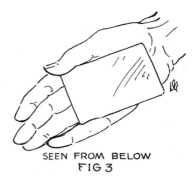

SEEN FROM BELOW
FIG 3

the first joints of the first, second and third fingers rest on the outer end, Fig. 1.

3. Grasp the packet to be palmed at its outer end, between the side of the thumb and the side of the little finger, and lift it half an inch, at the same time move both hands towards the table top to tap the inner end of the pack against it.

4. Move the right hand forward, apparently to square the top end of the pack and by this action lever the packet to be palmed up against the right palm, Fig. 2, where it is retained by the pressure of the thumb and little fingers on its sides, Fig. 3. The hand, with the cards palmed, can then be placed flat on the table.

The sleight can also be executed in tapping the pack on the left hand. The angles of vision must always be studied during the action.

The Gamblers' Flat Palm

a. By the use of this method of palming the hand can be placed flat on the table and can be lifted again, retaining the card, with perfect freedom.

With a card in the regular palm, the flat palm is made in this manner: Hold the card at the outer index corner by a slight contraction of

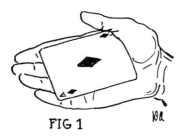

FIG 1

the top joint of the little finger. Hold the upper index corner in the fold of flesh which is formed when the thumb is moved backward and pressed tightly against the side of the palm, in this action taking with it the corner of the card and thus forcing it to buckle outwards slightly from the palm, Fig. 1. It is the thumb action which buckles the card, not that of the little finger, although the latter aids to some small extent at its corner.

It will be found that the grip on the corners holds the card with perfect security and it can be transferred from the orthodox palm to the flat palm, and vice versa, with ease.

This special palm will also be found very useful in many forms of the color change.

b. Another extremely useful, and for some purposes a better, palm is to transfer the packet of cards to the flat palm by catching its right inner corner in a fold of flesh near the crotch of the thumb, Fig. 1. The corner does not actually press into the crotch of the thumb, but is caught in a fold of flesh by moving the thumb outwards, as though to touch the tip of the second finger, and then moving it up against the hand. This action folds a crease of flesh over the corner of the packet sufficient to hold it in position when the hand is placed flat on the table with all the fingers straightened out, and to bring it back to the regular palm when the hand is drawn along the table towards the body in removing it.

FIG 1

This grip will not support the cards if the hand is lifted straight up from the table since they are held by one corner only. There is, however, a sufficient grip for the purpose desired, that is to say, to place the hand flat on the table, to slide it off the table and to bring with it the concealed cards and take them again into the regular palm.

This is another of the stratagems which have been transferred from the armory of the gambler to that of the conjurer.

THE HUGARD TOP PALM

This method of palming the top card can be executed with either hand and is ideal for use in such tricks as the Card in the Wallet in which the left hand is thrust into the inside coat pocket immediately after the card has been palmed. We will describe the action for palming the top card with the left hand:

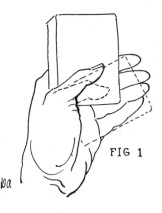

FIG 1

1. Hold the pack face downwards by its inner end in fork of the left thumb, the thumb lying across the end and its tip touching the tips of the first and second fingers which press against the side of the pack just above the inner end. The tips of these two fingers must be held flush with the top of the deck so that one card only can be pushed off without spreading any of the other cards.

2. Raise the thumb, press it against the middle of the top card and move it to the right and downwards in an arc, carrying the top card with it and making this card revolve on its inner left corner which remains firmly pressed into the crotch of the thumb.

3. Straighten the left fingers momentarily to receive the card, Fig. 1, then bend them and grip the card.

4. Remove the pack with the right hand, taking it by the sides between the thumb and fingers.

The action takes place in bringing the left hand across the body to place the pack in the right hand and is completely covered by the turning of the left hand which brings its back towards the spectators.

The Flip-Over Palm

At first sight this method may seem to be too audacious to be successful, but in its very boldness lies its safety. Its execution adds a little extra to that inward glow so dear to the heart of the wizard when he succeeds in barefacedly deceiving his victims.

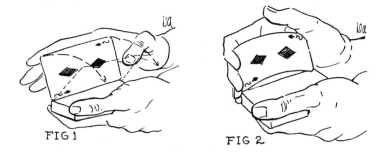

FIG 1   FIG 2

We will suppose that in the course of a trick you have had occasion to turn the top card face upwards several times. You have done this by pushing the card off the pack a little with the left thumb and then striking it with the side of the right forefinger as the right hand is brought upwards in a vertical position, the fingers and thumb pointing straight to the front, Fig. 1.

When you wish to palm the card:

1. Turn it face upwards on the pack in the manner just described and bring the right hand over the pack, close the fingers and thumb on the ends and draw the hand back to the right in the action of squaring the cards.

2. Turn the card face downwards in the same way but, this time, bend the first joint of the right forefinger on the outer corner of the card as it turns over, pressing the inner corner of the same side of the card against the root of the thumb. Turn the right hand completely

over the pack as before and draw the fingers and thumb back along the ends, squaring the cards.

The bending of the fingers will place the card against the inside of the right hand in the regular palming position. After pushing the card over the right side of the pack, the left thumb must move to the left side, Fig. 2.

In the action the right side of the body must be to the front so that the back of the right hand is towards the spectators.

The Hofzinser Bottom Palm

This bottom palm was a favorite of that storied master card manipulator of the last century, Johann Nepomuk Hofzinser. It is prac-

FIG 1

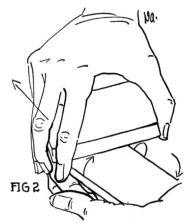

FIG 2

tically unknown in this country.

1. Hold the pack in the left hand as for dealing, but rather more into the crotch of the thumb and with the left forefinger even with the outer end of the deck, Fig. 1. Form a break with the tip of the left little finger above the cards to be palmed.

2. Place the right hand over the pack, press the first finger against the left side just below the outer corner, and rest the other fingers against the outer end.

3. Move the pack to the right with the right hand; the cards to be palmed pivot between the left little finger at the inner right corner and the right forefinger at the outer left corner, moving into position for palming, Fig. 2. In the illustration the right packet has been lifted to show the action.

4. Take the pack with the left fingers.

The Braue Bottom Palm

Up to the present time there have been only three methods of palming the bottom card of any value to card manipulators, the Erdnase, Hofzinser and Hugard methods. That to be described here for the first time is new in conception and entirely practical, and, for some purposes, particularly those of the poker genre, is of greater utility than those just mentioned. It is very fast, easy and deceptive, and it can be made with one or a score of cards; it can be used for legitimate palming purposes or as a color change. The method follows the explanation hereunder:

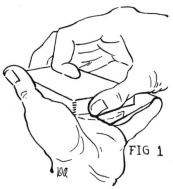

FIG 1

1. Hold the pack in the left hand, the first finger curled at the face, the other fingers at the right side and the thumb extended flat against the left side of the pack. Insert the left little finger above the cards to be palmed from the bottom by the right hand.

2. Place the right second, third and fourth fingers at the outer end, the thumb at the inner end, the first finger being curled at the top of the pack exposing as much of its surface as possible. Rest the left little finger tip at the bottom of the pack at the end, on the curved outer right corner, and press the tip of the right thumb into the break at the inner end, retaining it.

3. Move the left little finger, pressing its side against the edge of the packet to be palmed at the inner end, near the right corner.

4. Swing the little finger to the right, carrying the inner end of the packet with it, the outer end pivoting on the tip of the right little finger at the outer right corner. This action causes the packet to project diagonally, Fig. 1.

5. Remove the right thumb from the inner end and lower the right wrist until the inner left corner of the packet to be palmed presses against the inner surface of the right thumb at its root, the pack being supported by the curled left first finger pressing up against its face.

Lift the left thumb and place it slantwise across the left outer corner of the deck, thus gripping it between the thumb and the side of the first finger, the right fingers supporting the pack meanwhile. Grip the packet between the tip of the right little finger at the outer right corner and the root of the right thumb at the inner left corner. Exert an inward pressure with the thumb and finger as the left hand withdraws the pack to the left, the right thumb moving inwards as though to touch the tip of the second finger and thus curving the packet up into the right hand where it is palmed.

Note particularly that the right hand must remain stationary as the left hand carries the pack away, otherwise the illusion is destroyed.

If it is desired to palm cards from the bottom into the left hand, the procedure is simply reversed: The right hand grips the pack as for dealing and the left hand covers it.

Delaying the Braue Bottom Palm. The series of actions from No. 1 to 4 having been made, an extremely effective use of the palm is the following:

1. Grasp the diagonally jogged packet between the tip of the right forefinger and the base of the palm, extending the thumb straight along the inner end of the pack. The packet is now to all intents and purposes already palmed, for if the pack is removed not another action need be made to bring the cards up against the right palm. Figure 2 shows the right hand, seen from below, with the pack and packet in the correct positions. The right first finger is curled tightly at the top, its nail pressing upon the back of the top card, exposing as much of its surface as possible. The deck is held in a vertical position.

FIG 2

2. Transfer it to the left hand, grasping it at the left side. A moment before the pack is removed to the left the right first finger straightens and the palmed packet is perfectly concealed, the right hand remaining motionless as the left hand moves away.

To the onlookers, the pack is transferred to the right hand, which holds it naturally as the left hand is used for any purpose, such as moving cards previously tabled, or tugging at the right sleeve, or gesturing. The cards are taken from the right hand and, the packet having long since been effectively gripped in the right hand, it seemingly is impossible for a palm to be effected. The impression created here is that the two hands are not together long enough to permit sleight of hand.

THE ZINGONE BOTTOM PALM

This very ingenious method of palming cards from the bottom of a deck can be used with a full deck but it is most useful in cases where it is necessary to steal a few cards from the bottom of a small packet.

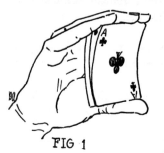

FIG 1

We will take the latter case first and suppose that three cards are to be palmed from the bottom of a packet of ten cards. The moves follow:

a. 1. Hold the packet of ten cards face outwards in the right hand between the thumb at the lower left corner and the four fingers on the upper end, the little finger holding a break between the three cards to be stolen and the packet of seven cards above them. Press on the ends of the cards bending them inwards towards the palm, Fig. 1.

FIG 2

FIG 3

2. Spread the first and little fingers in opposite directions, the first finger towards the left, the little finger towards the right, carrying their respective packets with them, and move the second and third fingers to the right until the side of the top joint of the second finger rests against the side of the upper packet just below the upper right corner, Fig. 2. These two fingers with the little finger cover the removal of the three bottom cards.

3. Slide the first finger along the top edge of the upper packet and clip the seven cards by their right upper corners against the first joint of the second finger, Fig. 3.

4. Let the inner end of the upper packet slip free from the thumb, leaving the seven cards held only by the top joints of the first and second fingers. Bend the thumb inwards, pushing the three cards into the hand, and palm them by bending the second, third and fourth fingers on them and, at the same moment, press the point of the thumb against the upper index corner of the other packet, turning it upwards into a vertical position, face inwards, Fig. 4.

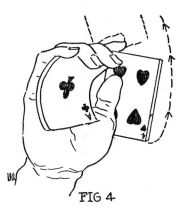

FIG 4

The action of the palm takes place in moving the right hand a little downwards and towards the left, for example, in placing the packet in the left hand or in giving it to a spectator to wrap up in a handkerchief.

b. With a Full Deck

1. Hold the pack in exactly the same manner as in *a*, the little finger holding a break between the cards to be palmed and the remainder of the deck.

2. Move the second, third and fourth fingers towards the right, the little finger carrying the lower packet with it, until the side of the first joint of the second finger rests against the side of the upper packet at the right upper corner, Fig. 2.

3. Slide the first finger along the top edge of the upper packet to join the second finger as in Fig. 3 but without clipping the outer corner of the packet between the fingers.

4. Place the upper packet in the left hand, at the same moment bending the right thumb inwards carrying the lower packet into the right hand. Let the corner of this packet slip off the thumb and bend the right fingers inwards palming the bottom packet as the right hand drops naturally to the side.

The action takes place as the right hand moves towards the left and places the pack in the left hand. The removal of the bottom packet is completely concealed by the back of the right hand.

Three Cards Across

In his version of this popular trick Mr. Zingone uses his one-hand bottom palm with quite startling effect. The moves follow:

1. Have the pack shuffled by a spectator and then have him deal ten cards onto your left hand.

2. Have three of these cards initialled by different spectators and collect them on the top of the packet. Check the number by counting the cards into your right hand and secure a break between the three bottom cards (the initialled cards) and the remaining seven. Take the packet in the right hand by the ends in exactly the same way as for the bottom palm.

3. Again hold out your left hand to the spectator and have him deal ten more cards onto it.

4. Holding your hands well separated, ask another spectator to take out his handkerchief and hold it up by two corners. Bring your right hand to the middle of the handkerchief at the same time executing the one-hand bottom palm with the three cards (the initialled cards). Thrust the packet of seven cards against the handkerchief and have the spectator wrap them in it and hold them.

5. Immediately remark that you haven't checked the second packet of ten cards and count these cards from the left hand into the right, face upwards, on top of the palmed cards.

6. Take the thirteen cards with the left hand by turning it back upwards and thrusting the thumb under the palmed cards thus adding them imperceptibly to the cards just counted.

7. Hand the packet to a spectator on your left to hold between his two hands and finish the trick in the usual manner but with special emphasis that the cards that pass across are the very cards which were initialled by the spectators themselves.

This method of palming will also be found very useful in securing the first cards to be passed from the left hand in the popular trick of passing cards into the trousers pocket.

Chapter 6
FALSE SHUFFLES

~~~~~~

THE PERFECT RIFFLE SHUFFLE

THE MASTER MINDS of card conjuring, those who aspire to the heights of virtuosity in the handling of cards, have sought for years to master the perfect riffle shuffle; that is to say, to make the shuffle by interweaving the two packets card for card. By dint of incessant practice some performers have attained sufficient skill to make the perfect shuffle some four times out of five but, in spite of all attempts they cannot acquire an absolute certainty of success. By resorting to a subterfuge, however, not only is all this tedious practice eliminated, but success is assured every time. The following very easy method, which exactly simulates the movements of the riffle shuffle, is actually an application of the principle of the weave. With it, as with the Perfect Faro Shuffle, a pack can be brought back to its original condition after eight shuffles.

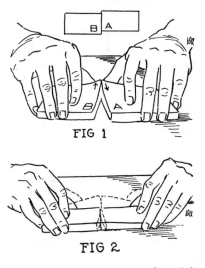

FIG 1

FIG 2

a. 1. Place the hands over the tabled pack, the second and third fingers at the outer side close to the corners, the first fingers resting on the top, the thumbs at the inner sides near the corners.

2. Cut the pack into two packets, A and B, placing the upper half (B) to the right, the inner ends of A and B parallel and touching but with B three-eighths of an inch beyond A, as shown in the small drawing, Fig. 1.

3. Place the tips of the little fingers against the ends at the outer corners. Both packets are boxed in at these corners by the second, third and little fingers, the extreme tips of which press firmly against the table top and maintain the same position throughout the action to follow, Fig. 1.

4. Lift the inner sides with the thumbs, retaining the position of the fingers and thus mooring the outer corners of the pack in the two right-angle vises formed by the three fingers of each hand. Press firmly with the first fingers against the backs of the packets. By means of an outward pressure of the thumbs at the inner sides, swivel the two packets a quarter of an inch outward, the inner corners of A and B now making the only contact between the two packets, Fig. 1.

5. Remove the first fingers of both hands and relax the pressure of the thumbs at the sides, holding the packets very lightly. This relaxation of pressure will cause the two packets to commence weaving together at the bottom.

6. Move packet A outward, packet B inward, as indicated by the arrows in Fig. 1. The change of position of the inner corners of the two packets makes the meshing of the cards, swiftly and exactly, a complete certainty. At the end of the mesh the packets are still supported by the thumbs, save for the few at the bottom which, interweaving, may have dropped to the table.

7. Immediately run the thumbs of both hands up the sides of the cards, producing the riffling sound associated with the riffle shuffle, the cards dropping off the thumbs to the tabletop, Fig. 2.

The entire action is made possible by the peculiar grip at the corners with the second, third and little fingers, this boxing of the outer corners producing a tension at the inner corners when the packets are moved into the position shown in the figure, this tension making the perfect mesh possible.

b. Another method is to make the shuffle as follows:

1. Cut the pack, placing the two packets with their ends parallel and touching, as in Fig. 2.

2. Place the tips of the little fingers against the ends at the outer corners. Both packets are boxed in at these corners, as in the preceding method, by the second, third and little fingers, the tips of which press on the table top and maintain the same position throughout the shuffle. The thumbs, as shown in the illustration, are at the middle of the inner sides.

3. Lift both packets with the thumbs and press outwards, as shown in the ghost illustration in Fig. 2. The touching inner corners press against one another.

4. Relax the pressure of the thumbs, allowing the cards to mesh at the corners, at the same time moving the thumbs upwards to simulate the usual action of the riffle shuffle. The interwoven cards, dropping

off the thumbs, produce the characteristic riffling sound of the regular shuffle.

This method is used by Charles Miller.

THE STRIP-OUT FALSE SHUFFLE
Charles Miller Method

Mr. Miller has made some modifications in this shuffle which make it not only more deceptive but easier to do.

1. Divide the pack, taking the top half in the right hand, place the inner corners together, and seize both packets at the sides close to the adjoining ends between the second finger and thumb of each hand, the third and fourth fingers curling in with the first joints resting on the packets and the first fingers pressing down on the backs.

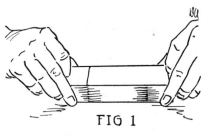

FIG 1

2. Raise the thumb corners and release a half dozen cards from the right thumb, then continue the action with both thumbs until all the cards have been riffled in. When the corners are interlaced, move the hands to the outer ends, grasping the sides near the corners between the thumbs and second fingers, and telescope the two packets about two thirds, Fig. 1.

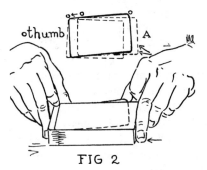

FIG 2

3. Shift the position of the fingers at the outer ends, placing a second finger at the middle of each end and resting the ball of each thumb upon the inner side opposite the inner corner of a packet, Fig. 2.

4. Press the tip of the right second finger upon the table to hold the right packet motionless during the following actions. Push the left packet to the right with the left second finger, pressing it diagonally inwards. This forces its inner right corner against the ball of the right thumb, which prevents it from breaking through the inner side. The packet continues to slide diagonally into the right packet, the ball of

the right thumb moving along with it at the inner side and always pressing back upon the corner as it seeks to break through.

Note in A that the left thumb remains motionless on the inner corner of the right packet, but that the right thumb moves with the inner corner of the left packet, as indicated by the small circles.

Thus during this action the outer side of the pack, which the onlookers can see, always presents a regular appearance. When the action is completed the pack appears as in B. The diagonal jog at the inner side, exaggerated for the sake of clarity, is in practice no more (and sometimes less) than a quarter of an inch.

5. Place the thumbs and third fingers at the end corners, Fig. 3,

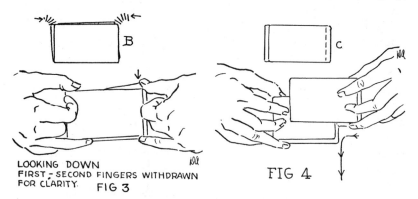

LOOKING DOWN
FIRST - SECOND FINGERS WITHDRAWN
FOR CLARITY.   FIG 3

FIG 4

and apparently push the packets flush, but actually apply a pressure with both thumbs as indicated in B. This serves to move the pack into the condition shown in C, in which there is shown an extension of each packet of a quarter of an inch. Grasp this extension at each end with the thumbs and third fingers, draw the right hand packet half an inch towards the right, then move the hand outward so that the packet slides free from the outer side of the left hand packet, at the same time drawing both hands inwards towards the body, Fig. 4.

6. Drop the right hand packet on top of the left hand packet, returning the pack to its original condition.

Note that when the two packets have been telescoped, as in C, prior to the strip-out action, the hands may be removed from the pack and the spectators will find nothing unusual or suspicious in its appearance.

Hindu Shuffle Variation

It is many years since this shuffle was introduced to American conjurers; in those years it has become immensely popular since it is an easy and showy method of controlling a chosen card. The following new handling will be found to baffle even those who know the regular Hindu shuffle. Here is the procedure after a card has been drawn:

FIG 1

1. Hold the pack in the regular position for executing the Hindu shuffle, pull off about one-third of the pack with the left thumb and second finger, letting the packet fall into the left hand.

2. Have the selected card replaced on top of the cards in the left hand.

3. Pull off a small packet with the left fingers letting it fall on the first packet about half an inch inwards; that is to say, you injog the packet, Fig. 1.

4. Continue as in the regular Hindu shuffle but let all the following packets fall with their outer ends slightly irregular, thus covering the projecting packet.

5. Pick up the whole pack with the right thumb and second finger, first lifting the jogged packet slightly with the tip of the right third finger, making a break, and hold this break with the thumb and second finger.

6. Make the regular Hindu shuffle by pulling off packets from the top and letting them fall into the left hand until the break is reached, then let the last packet drop on top intact, thus bringing the chosen card to the top.

The formation of the break is completely covered by the action of putting the pack in the left hand to repeat the shuffle.

False Shuffle Retaining Top Stock

By means of this shuffle any small number of cards which need not be in any particular sequence can be kept intact at the top of the pack. For instance, let us assume that you wish to retain the thirteen cards of a suit at the top, in any sequence, for such a trick as The Mind Mirror, page 223. Here is the procedure:

1. Undercut somewhat less than half the pack, injog the first card and shuffle off the remainder of the cards.

2. Undercut at the injog and run the first six cards of the undercut, these being desired cards.

3. Throw the undercut on top of the other packet, making it project half an inch outwards.

4. Make a break at the point of junction of the two packets in squaring the pack by placing the right thumb at the inner end and pushing the upper packet inwards with the fingers. Hold the break with the right thumb.

5. Take the pack in the right hand, the fingers at the outer end, the thumb at the inner end retaining the break.

6. Riffle the lower half, up to the break, onto the left fingers, rest the outer side of this packet on the right finger tips, grasp its ends between the left thumb and fingers and make an end riffle shuffle. The top six cards of both packets are cards of the original stock and, by taking care to riffle these top cards together, the original stock will be returned to the top of the assembled deck.

GAMBLERS' FALSE SHUFFLE

This very easy method of making a false riffle shuffle is so bold that it is hard to believe that any gambler respecting the integrity of his person would attempt it in any kind of game in fast company, and yet it is reported to be so used in certain card games south of the border.

For conjuring purposes, it serves well enough if done in a matter-of-fact manner, although it is not to be compared with more advanced methods. The moves follow:

a. 1. With the pack before you, grasp the sides of the upper half of the pack near the left corners between the right thumb and second finger, cutting the pack and placing this upper half to the right.

2. Immediately grasp the remaining packet at the sides near the right corners between the left thumb and second finger. Cover the packets as much as possible with the hands and press down with the forefingers at the middle of each end, Fig. 1.

3. Allow the cards to riffle off the left thumb and immediately afterwards riffle the cards off the right thumb so that the packet overlaps the other.

4. With the hands still covering the packets, push them together with the outer sides of the palms, simulating the action of telescoping

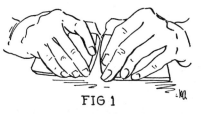

FIG 1

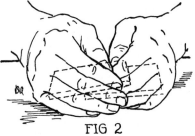

FIG 2

the packets by exerting the proper amount of pressure, Fig. 2.

The entire shuffle should be made without hesitation and while the operator converses with the spectators.

Retaining Top Stock

b. As with other sleights developed at the gaming table this false shuffle defies the closest scrutiny. By its means a top stock is sent to

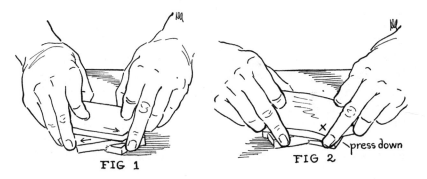

FIG 1

FIG 2

press down

the middle of the deck and yet remains under perfect control. The sleight is an easy one and can be applied advantageously to any trick in which it is necessary to retain a small packet of cards at the top of the pack.

We will suppose, for example, that five cards have been selected, brought to the top and that a shuffle is to be made to strengthen the belief that they are lost in the pack. Proceed thus:

1. Undercut about two-thirds of the deck with the right hand and place the inner corners of the two packets together to form an inverted V.

2. Begin the riffle by dropping cards from the left hand packet first. Then let the cards from this packet drop faster than those in the right hand packet so that the five card stock will fall together under the last dozen or more cards of the right hand packet. Take care that no cards

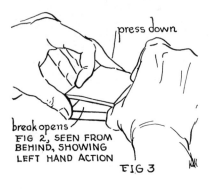

FIG 2, SEEN FROM
BEHIND, SHOWING
LEFT HAND ACTION

FIG 3

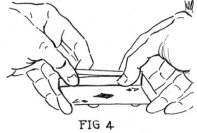

FIG 4

are interwoven into the stock.

3. Grip the ends of the two packets between the thumbs and second fingers, press the third fingers against the middle of the ends and rest the tips of the forefingers on the backs of the cards. Keep the hands well over the cards and push the packets together at an angle as in Fig. 1.

4. When the packets have coalesced, press the tip of the left second finger on the projecting corner of the right hand packet at X, lifting the inner side of the packet above the stock. Fig. 3 shows this action as seen from behind. Press downwards and inwards with the left thumb to secure this break and at the same moment push the packets square with the thumbs and third fingers, Fig. 4.

5. Lift the pack, keeping the hands in the same positions, and pressing downwards with the tips of the first fingers on the back so that the outer side of the pack presents a perfectly regular appearance, Fig. 4.

6. With the right hand make a running cut, pulling off a few cards at a time from the top and dropping them on the table until the break held by the left thumb is reached. Finally drop all the remaining cards on top of the pile thus formed. The stock is again on the top of the pack.

After the left thumb secures the break above the stock, a straight cut can be made instead of the running cut, or a packet with the stock on top of it can be pulled out of the middle and dropped on top. Again a small packet can be undercut with the right hand, the pack then divided at the break and the shuffle repeated. These are matters for individual taste.

A System of Stock Shuffling

The only means of stocking cards with an overhand shuffle heretofore published has been the Erdnase method, given in his book on page 68 et seq. While it possesses the merit which he claims for it, his method has the decided drawback that varying calculations must be made in dealing different numbers of hands, and this can be very confusing to the operator since there is no definite pattern to the shuffles. It is for this reason that the Erdnase shuffles are so little used, even amongst the experts.

The method to be given here has one great advantage; the runs of cards during the shuffles are always governed by the number of hands to be dealt, and there is no further calculation to be made or any odd number of cards to be run. If four hands are to be dealt, the number 4 governs and controls the shuffle throughout and this is the only number which need be kept in mind.

Moreover, the shuffle is considerably less involved than the Erdnase shuffle and, once its nature is understood, it cannot be easily forgotten. We would suggest that the reader compare, in actual practice, the Erdnase method of stocking two cards with that given below. The far greater facility of the latter will be appreciated at once. The various movements of the cards in the action will be greatly clarified in the reader's mind if he will reverse the desired cards when practicing the shuffles; thus he will be enabled to watch each card and note how the stock is made. There is a definite pattern in the shuffles and this is repeated for each card; once this is noted the shuffles are made with swiftness and certainty that only comes from full comprehension of the material with which one works.

Two Card Stock

One desired card on the top, the other on the bottom.
To stock the cards to fall to the fourth hand.

1. Undercut half the pack, run three cards, injog the next card, the 4th, and shuffle off, bringing the card originally on the bottom to the top.

2. Undercut at the injog and run four cards; run three more cards and injog the next, the 4th, and shuffle off.

3. Undercut at the injog and throw on top.

The two desired cards now lie fourth and eighth in the pack, in position to fall to the fourth hand in a four-handed deal.

If it were desired to stock the two cards to fall to, say, the sixth hand, the above procedure would be followed but in place of using 4 as the controlling figure on the runs, 6 would be used. Thus, the first item would read: "Undercut half the pack, run five cards, injog the next card, the 6th, and shuffle off, bringing the card originally at the bottom to the top."

THREE CARD STOCK

One card at the top; two cards at the bottom.
To stock the cards to fall to the fourth hand.

To stock three cards, the actions in the preceding shuffle are carried one step farther:

1. Undercut half the pack, run 3 cards, injog the next card, the 4th, and shuffle off, bringing the two cards originally at the bottom to the top.

2. Undercut at the injog, and injog the top card of the left hand packet. Run 4 cards; then run 3 cards and outjog the next card, the 4th, and shuffle off.

3. Undercut at the outjog, retaining a break at the injog with the right thumb; and throw the cards above the break onto the top of the left hand packet.

4. Run 4 cards, injog the next card and shuffle off.

5. Undercut at the injog and throw on top of the left hand packet.

The three cards are now at 4, 8 and 12, in position to fall to the fourth hand.

FOUR CARD STOCK

One card at the top; three cards at the bottom.
To stock the cards to fall to the fourth hand.

To stock four cards, the actions in the preceding shuffle are once again carried a step farther:

1. Undercut half the pack, run 3 cards, injog the next card, the 4th, and shuffle off, bringing the three cards originally at the bottom to the top.

2. Undercut at the injog, injog the top card of the left hand packet; run 4 cards; run 3 more cards and outjog the next, the 4th; and shuffle off.

3. Undercut at the outjog, retaining a break at the injog with the right thumb, and throw the cards above the break onto the top of the left hand packet. Run 4 cards, injog the next card and shuffle off.

4. Undercut at the injog, run 3 cards and injog the next card, the 4th; run 4 cards; run 4 more; run 3 more and outjog the next card, the 4th; and shuffle off.

5. Undercut at the outjog, retaining a break at the injog with the right thumb, and throw the cards above the break onto the top of the left hand packet. Run 4 cards, injog the next card and shuffle off.

6. Undercut at the injog and throw on top.

The cards are stocked at 4, 8, 12 and 16 in position to fall to the fourth hand.

Five Card Stock

One card at the top; four cards at the bottom.
To stock the cards to fall to the fourth hand.

Again the action is carried another step farther:

1. Undercut half the pack, run 3 cards, injog the next card and shuffle off, bringing the four cards originally at the bottom to the top.

2. Undercut at the injog, injog the top card of the left hand packet; run 4 cards; run 3 more cards and outjog the next, the 4th; and shuffle off.

3. Undercut at the outjog, retaining a break at the injog with the right thumb, and throw the cards above the break onto the top of the left hand packet. Run 4 cards, injog the next card and shuffle off.

4. Undercut at the injog, run 3 cards and injog the next card, the 4th; run 4 cards; run 4 more; run 3 more and outjog the next card, the 4th; and shuffle off.

5. Undercut at the outjog, retaining a break at the injog with the right thumb, and throw the cards above the break onto the top of the left hand packet. Run 4 cards, injog the next card and shuffle off.

6. Undercut at the injog, run 3 cards and injog the next card, the 4th; run 4 cards; run 4 more; run 4 more; run 3 more and injog the next card, the 4th; and shuffle off.

7. Undercut at the outjog, retaining a break at the injog with the right thumb, and throw the cards above the break onto the top of the left hand packet. Run 4 cards, injog the next and shuffle off.

8. Undercut at the injog and throw the packet on top.

The five cards are stocked at 4, 8, 12, 16 and 20, in position to fall to the fourth hand. A complex stock, this is little used.

OFF THE TABLE FALSE RIFFLE SHUFFLE

This false riffle shuffle, as its name indicates, is for use when it is not convenient to place the pack on a table for the riffle shuffle. It will be found very deceptive.

1. Hold the pack in the right hand at the ends between the thumb and second, third and fourth fingers. Split the pack by riffling off the

FIG 1

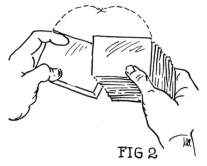

FIG 2

right thumb onto the fingers of the left hand until half the pack has fallen.

2. Grip both packets as shown in Fig. 1 and riffle the outer corners, first letting some six cards slip off the left thumb. Continue the riffle, barely interlocking the cards at the outer corners. Let the last six or so cards from the right thumb slip off last.

3. Spread these cards to the left and bring the outer ends of the two packets together, as indicated in Fig. 2, and so twist the locked corners free. The packets are now parallel to one another and their free condition is masked by the fan of cards pushed off by the right thumb.

4. Lift the inner end of the right packet, place it on the left packet and push the packets together, dropping the left thumb upon them as the right hand pats the right side of the pack square.

5. Square the ends with the right thumb and fingers.

The shuffle should be made at the same tempo as that of an ordinary shuffle and the cards should be squared with the same amount of effort required in the honest procedure.

Chapter 7
FALSE CUTS

～～～～～～～～～～～～～～～～～～～～～～～～～～～

THE FALSE RUNNING CUT

THIS SLEIGHT WILL BE FOUND very useful in secretly bringing together several cards which have been openly placed in different parts of the pack. It can be used with three, four or even five cards, but for the sake of illustration we will suppose that the four aces are used. The moves follow:

a. 1. Hold the pack face downwards in the left hand between the top joints of the thumb on one side and the second, third and fourth fingers on the other; insert the aces, one by one, in different places in the outer end, allowing them to project an inch.

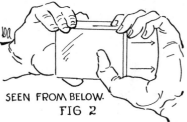

FIG 1

2. With the left forefinger secretly push the bottom card outwards until it is even with the projecting cards.

3. Place the right hand over the deck, the thumb at the inner end, the fingers over the ends of the five projecting cards and apparently push them flush with the pack,

SEEN FROM BELOW.
FIG 2

really press them to the left, as shown in 2 of Fig. 1 and press them through the pack diagonally, Fig. 2. Press on the projecting corners with the left little finger, straightening the five cards and jogging them for about half an inch at the inner end of the pack, as shown in 3 of Fig. 1. The whole action, which takes but a second, should be covered by the right hand.

4. Turn the left hand over, bringing its back upwards with the pack face upwards, and grip the five jogged cards between the second joint of the left little finger and the flesh at the base of the thumb. Seize the pack by the sides near the right end with the thumb and second finger, Fig. 2, and strip the five cards from the pack with the left hand, dropping them

face upwards on the table with the indifferent card at the face of the packet concealing the aces.

5. In like fashion strip small packets of cards from the face of the deck with the left hand in a running cut until the entire pack has been dropped onto the table.

When the pack is picked up and turned face downwards the four aces will be together on the top and available for disposal as may be necessary.

b. In this case you hold the pack face upwards and insert the aces, following the action in *a* but without pushing an indifferent card forward. After pushing the four cards through diagonally and jogging them at the inner end, proceed as follows:

1. Immediately turn the left hand over, holding the pack between the left fingers and the crotch of the thumb. Press the jogged cards firmly between the second joint of the left little finger and the base of the thumb, this condition of the pack being concealed by the back of the hand.

2. Make a running cut by stripping small packets of cards from the bottom of the pack with the right thumb and second fingers, grasping them by the sides near the outer ends and dropping them on the table.

3. Continue the action until the four jogged cards only remain in the left hand. Seize them in exactly the same manner and drop them on the top of the tabled pack.

The action in both cases is easy and completely deceptive.

Gamblers' False Cut

This extremely deceptive false cut, whereby the entire deck is retained in its original order, is another gamblers' device. It is called, appropriately enough, "Up the Ladder."

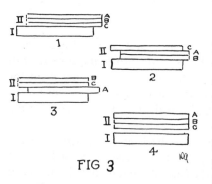

FIG 3

1. Grasp the pack with both hands between the thumbs and third fingers at the sides near the ends. Divide the pack at approximately the middle.

2. Draw the lower half, which we will call packet II, to the right holding it between the right thumb and third finger, and drop it upon packet I, jogging it half an inch to the right. See the first drawing, Fig. 3. The left thumb and third finger retain their grasp of packet I.

3. Draw out a small packet of cards, C in the figures, with the right

thumb and third finger and drop it upon A and B, flush with packet I, as in the second drawing, Fig. 3. Hold the break thus automatically formed between the small packet C and the large bottom packet I with the left thumb; this will be utilized later.

4. Draw out another small packet B from packet II and drop it on top of C, as in the third drawing in Fig. 3.

5. Repeat this action with A, as in the fourth drawing in Fig. 3.

6. Repeat this same running cut with packet I, the break held by the left thumb under packet II ensuring a correct final cut, which will complete the return of the pack to its original condition.

Figures 1 and 2 show how the fingers of both hands grasp the packets during these running

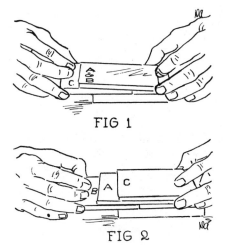

FIG 1

FIG 2

cuts. In Fig. 1 the right thumb and third finger are stripping out C as left thumb and second finger retain A and B. In Fig. 2 C has been placed at the top, directly above the bottom packet I, and B is being stripped out in turn by the right hand. Note that the left thumb and second finger now control both packets A and C. B is dropped directly upon C and A is then stripped out by the right hand in the same manner. The left thumb holds a break between packets II and I in readiness for a repetition of this running cut with I, after which the pack will be in its original order.

This particularly illusive false cut can be used with excellent effect after the Strip-Out False Shuffle given on page 67. Take the upper half of the pack in the right hand, riffle it into the left hand packet and immediately strip it out with the right hand as described. Drop it on top of the left hand packet and make the Gamblers' False Cut with these cards. Thus the cards are apparently fairly shuffled and cut.

The reader will find that, of all false cuts, this is perhaps the best; and, for all practical purposes, the only one he need know.

Gamblers' False Cut
Retaining Bottom Stock

This is another ruse lifted from the gaming table which can be put to good use in many card tricks, since with it the bottom stock is retained after a genuine cut by a spectator. We will suppose that the four aces are at the bottom of the pack and that you desire to keep them in that position. Here is the working:

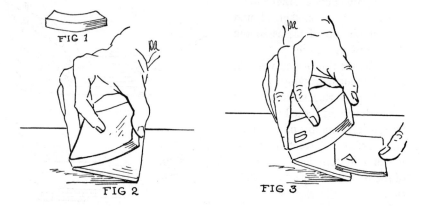

1. Execute a riffle shuffle, interlacing the corners giving the sides of each packet an upward bend by pressing down with the forefingers, and letting the four aces drop first. Square the cards which will then have a lengthwise crimp making their backs slightly concave, and hand the pack to be cut, Fig. 1.

2. After the cut, A, has been tabled, pick up the lower packet, B, with the right thumb at its left side, the fingers at the right side; let half a dozen cards at the bottom slip off the right thumb, gripping them with the right fingers on the right side only, Fig. 2; the left sides of these cards rest on the table.

3. As you sweep B towards A, press the left thumb on the left side of A, thus lifting its right side about an eighth of an inch off the table.

4. In sliding the two packets together let the six separated cards at the bottom of B pass under A while the remainder go on top, Fig. 3.

5. Pick up the pack, square it and, in doing so, take out the crimp with the left hand. The four aces are still on the bottom ready to be dealt with as you may desire.

Chapter 8
CHANGES

~~~~~~

THE FADEAWAY CARD CHANGE

THERE IS NO MORE BEAUTIFUL and effective sleight in the entire range of card magic than the illusive move to be described in the following paragraphs; it is worthy of the attention of every worshipper at the shrine of Tarot.

In this change this is what the spectators see and what the magician himself will see in his mirror: The conjurer holds a card in his right hand, the six of diamonds for example. Momentarily he holds it face downwards, immediately thereafter its face is turned to the spectators who now perceive that the card they have watched closely has changed to, say, the two of hearts.

The Method. Obviously a change of the two cards is made and, since this is the case, the sleight can be used in any number of tricks in which it is necessary to change one card for another. The method is as simple as the change is good; one card is top changed* for the other. The secret lies, not in the method, but in the application of the principles of the top change in a new manner.

First of all, hold the pack in the left hand, the thumb lying straight across the top of the pack, the first finger slanting upwards at the outer end and the other three fingers at the right side. The position is very similar to that known amongst gamblers as the Mechanics' Grip.

Take the top card, the six of diamonds, for example, in the right hand, holding it by the inner right corner between the thumb at the top, the first finger at the face, with the side of the second finger at its top joint pressing against the inner edge. Holding the pack and the card in this fashion, practice the top change, the two hands performing the following functions:

a. Left Hand. Draw back the thumb, bending it, and drop its tip upon the top card near the left side. Straighten the thumb sharply, sliding the top card off the right side of the pack. At the conclusion of the thrust of

---

* By the oldest and best method. Refer to *More Card Manipulations* by Jean Hugard for a full explanation of this almost forgotten handling.

the left thumb, hold it rigidly straight, pointing towards the right and slightly above the pack.

b. Right Hand. Move the right hand with its card towards the pack, at the same time thrusting outwards sharply with the ball of the thumb, half pushing, half throwing the card upon the pack, Fig. 2. This card

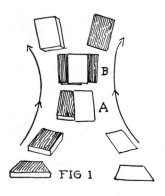

slides under the left thumb which, being raised above the pack a little, does not impede the action. At the same moment the top card of the pack, which the left thumb has thrust to the right, is taken by the right thumb, first and second fingers, in exactly the same grip as that which held the first card.

In practice both actions are made at the same moment, the two cards sliding over one another in a fraction of a second. Once the moves are mastered they will be found to constitute an effortless, frictionless and

FIG 1

very rapid way of making the top change, the two cards being exchanged in the twinkling of an eye. Masked by the usual covering movement of the hands, this is the finest method of making the top change.

To use these moves in the Fadeaway Card Change, proceed thus: Hold the card, the six of diamonds, in the right hand as directed, the left hand holding the pack at the top of which is the two of hearts. Hold both hands easily about waist high and some eight inches apart.

Show the right hand card by turning its face to the spectators, immediately afterwards holding it horizontally.

Move the right hand, with its card still horizontal, to the left and up-

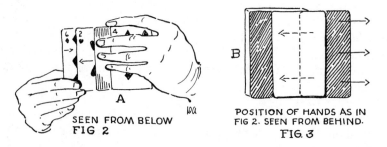

SEEN FROM BELOW
FIG 2

POSITION OF HANDS AS IN
FIG 2. SEEN FROM BEHIND.
FIG. 3

wards in the trajectory of an arc, at the same moment moving the left hand with the pack to the right and upwards, also in an arc, Fig. 1.

The two hands meet and the top change is made as described while both hands continue their upward arcing movement until they are at the level of the chin. The back of the left hand will be towards the audience, while the right holds its card, now the two of hearts, vertically facing outwards. Immediately, with the left hand make a short indicatory gesture, tapping the right hand card with the tips of the fingers which hold the pack, as if to say, "You see?" Figure 1 shows the nature of the preceding action. Figure 2 shows the action at the point marked A in Fig. 1. Figure 3 shows the action at the point marked B in Fig. 1. In the last drawing the hands have been omitted for greater clarity.

The illusiveness of this change comes from two factors. First: Because of the nature of the action and the natural momentum arising from the hands moving towards one another, the top change is made at great speed; moreover, the right hand card shooting onto the pack is masked by the card shooting out from the pack to the right fingers, the pack by that time having turned to a vertical position. Second: To the spectators it seems that the right fingers never relinquish their grasp of the inner corner of its card and it is this single fact, as much as any other, which gives to the sleight its effectiveness. And this effect is so illusive that onlookers, describing it, often claim that they see the card fade away and the second card take its place.

When it is desired secretly to exchange cards by this method, hold both the pack and the right hand card face upwards. With the pack in the Mechanics' Grip as described, stand facing a quarter to the right; thus the back of the pack is towards the spectators and the face card cannot be seen.

Calling attention to the face-up card in the right hand, make the Fadeaway Change as you turn full face to the spectators. At the completion of the action immediately turn the left hand back upwards, so that the face card of the pack (the card originally in the right hand) cannot be seen.

The changed card may now be placed, face downwards, to one side; or it may be handed to the spectator for safe keeping; or it may be blown upon by the spectator or magician to cause a change to occur.

THE SLIDE TOP CHANGE

It is more than passing strange that, with all the thought expended by card manipulators, both amateur and professional, for so many generations, no really practical method of interchanging the top card with the second, without removing it from the pack, has been evolved. The need for such a sleight has been apparent, and yet the only two methods of producing this effect cannot be termed secret sleights since both necessitate an open manipulation, which, if the sleight is to be used as a secret subterfuge in the course of a trick, immediately precludes their use.

The earliest textbooks give the following method: With the pack held as for dealing, the left thumb pushes the top card off the pack an inch to the right where it is supported by the tips of the fingers. The thumb moves back, drops upon the exposed surface of the second card and draws it back an inch towards the left, tipping it up at its right side. The top card is then slid back underneath by the left fingers and the cards are again squared. As stated this method has no practical value except perhaps as a little flourish, Fig. 1.

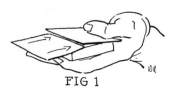

FIG 1

The second method, A New Top Change, was first published in 1935.* It is an excellent sleight, but since the top card must be faced to effect the change, it cannot be used in those tricks in which the exchange must be an entirely secret one, and in which the face of neither card must be seen.

The method given here fulfills these requirements:

1. Hold the pack in the left hand as for dealing, place the right hand over the pack and make a light squaring motion of the ends with the thumb and fingers.

2. Push the top card to the right an inch with the left thumb, immediately gripping it between the first joint of the right little finger and the flesh at the base of the thumb.

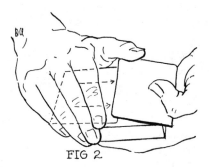

FIG 2

3. Drop the left thumb upon the exposed surface of the second card and draw it to the left until it clears the top card, lifting the right side of the second card a quarter of an inch in the action, Fig. 2.

4. Continue the squaring action by moving the right hand to the left, sliding the left side of the top card under the right side of the second card.

5. Immediately square both cards upon the pack as both hands continue the squaring movements.

The sleight is done in a second under cover of a small and slow motion

---

* *Card Manipulations*, No. 4. Jean Hugard.

of the hands to the left, the top card being concealed at all times by the back of the right hand. The uses to which it can be put are many; one will be cited here. Let us assume that in the Ambitious Card trick, a card has apparently been placed in the center of the pack and magically caused to rise to the top. It is replaced at the top and, by means of this sleight, it is secretly placed under the second card. The operator is now in a position to repeat the double-lifting process. It should be noted that as the top card slides under the second card, the left little finger can be pressed up against its face, making a break at the inner left corner and thus eliminating any further get-set move for the subsequent double lift.

THE THROW TOP CHANGE

The main action in this deceptive change is similar to that of the orthodox top change but the details differ radically. We will suppose that the ace of hearts is to be changed into the ace of clubs and that you have the ace of hearts in your right hand, while the ace of clubs reposes on the top of the pack. The table in use should be to your left and a little to the rear. To execute the change:

1. Hold the ace of hearts between the right thumb and fingers at the lower right corner, and the pack in the left hand in the usual position for dealing. Bend the left arm across the chest to bring the left hand in front of the body.

2. Push the top card, the ace of clubs, about an inch over the side of the pack and hold it between the tips of the left thumb and first and second fingers.

3. Swing the right hand towards the table and, the moment before it reaches the left hand, throw the ace of clubs from the top of the pack onto the table and leave the card in the right hand, the ace of hearts, in its place.

4. At once swing the left hand outwards or upwards in a gesture to the onlookers and continue the motion of the right hand a little way towards the table as if it had actually thrown the card there.

Some practice is necessary to time the action perfectly but this is well worth while since, under cover of a turn to the table or of turning and bending to throw the card onto the floor, the change is invisible to the onlookers.

THE TIP-OVER CHANGE

This sleight is an extremely easy one and it is one of the most surprising changes in the whole range of card conjuring. The method of preparing for the change which we are about to describe is a great improvement upon the method given by Merlin in his book . . . *and a Pack of Cards*, permitting the operator to perform a bewildering series of tip-over changes with the same card without awkward fumbling. The change itself is made by secretly dropping a second card on the first in the act of turning the latter face downwards. Here are the moves:

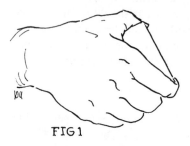

FIG 1

1. Hold the pack in the left hand as for dealing, the little finger maintaining a break above the chosen card.

2. Cut the pack at the break with the right first and second fingers at the outer end, the thumb at the inner end. The two fingers are near the left corners with their top joints curled in against the face card, Fig. 1. In actual practice the first finger curls at the top of the pack and is only moved into the position shown in Fig. 1 for a moment, in order to effect the sleight later to be given in item 4. Thus more of the back of the pack is visible.

3. With the left thumb push the top card of the lower portion, the chosen card, to the left. Turn this card face upwards upon its packet by striking its right edge upwards with the left side of the right hand packet. As the attention of the spectators is concentrated upon this faced card:

4. Press the third phalange of the right second finger flat against the face card of the right packet. Draw this face card outwards an eighth of an inch with this finger and then swing it a quarter of an inch to the right into a diagonal position. Let the inner end of this card drop slightly and place the tip of the right thumb against its inner left corner, the opposite diagonal corner being held against the second joint of the third finger, Fig. 2.

FIG 2

5. Turn the faced card on the left packet face down by pushing it off the deck with the left thumb as before and striking it with the left side of the right packet, which moves over the left packet in the action. When the right hand packet is directly over the left hand packet release the card gripped by the right thumb, thus secretly placing an indifferent card on top of the card just shown.

6. Thumb off the top card of the left packet onto the table. To the spectators it is the card which just before was turned face upwards upon the left hand packet. Actually it is an indifferent card, the chosen card remaining on the top of the packet.

This sleight can be used very effectively as a finale to the trick known as The Ambitious Card. After having shown that the card continually returns to the top of the pack, undercut half the deck retaining the upper half in the left hand. Turn the top card of this packet with the right hand packet as explained above, then execute the tip-over change and thumb off the indifferent card onto the table.

Turn the chosen card face up again and continue the action for as many times as you think desirable, finally spreading the cards on the table and the pack face upwards to prove that no duplicate cards are being used. Smartly done the effect will be found all that one could wish.

THE PUSH-IN CHANGE

This card change, though well known to most conjurers, is still one of the best available when its one weakness is recognized and corrected.

The change is this: The operator makes a double lift and shows the second card, let us say the ten of hearts, above which is the ten of spades. The two cards are taken as one and thrust, face downwards, halfway into the outer end of the deck. With the aid of the left forefinger the ten of hearts is thrust flush into the pack, the upper card remaining projecting from the end. This card is then removed and dropped upon the table.

Since the onlookers believe that only one card is used, and this card apparently always remains in sight, they are willing to concede that the tabled card is the ten of hearts, whereas actually it is the ten of spades.

Using the method generally employed, too many of the spectators see the lower card sliding into the pack, for an overlap of only a fraction of an inch is instantly noticeable. The following method eliminates this flaw in an otherwise excellent sleight.

1. Make a double lift, taking the two cards, perfectly squared, at the outer right corner between the right thumb on the top and the second finger at the face. Rest the tip of the first finger at the edge of the outer end to aid in holding the two cards in alignment.

2. Show the face of the lower card and thrust both cards into the outer end of the pack, which is held in the left hand as for dealing, the left thumb riffling open a break at its side for the convenient entry of the two cards as you shift the pack to the left finger tips.

3. Retaining your grip of the two cards at the right outer corner,

thrust the two cards into the deck until only three-quarters of an inch protrudes from its outer end, Fig. 1.

4. With the right thumb push the top card outward and to the left, at the same moment drawing the lower card a little to the right with the tip of the second finger, both digits acting at the same moment in a sliding motion one against the other. In Fig. 2 the right fingers have been re-

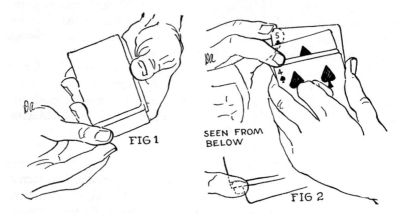

FIG 1

SEEN FROM BELOW

FIG 2

moved, showing the relative position of the cards. The fleshy ball of the right thumb rests on and conceals the outer right corner of the lower card and the edges of the lower card cannot be seen from the end or the left side since it has been drawn inward and to the right.

5. Engage the outer end of the lower card with the tip of the left forefinger, which can be done cleanly since the upper card now projects beyond it, and push the lower card flush into the deck. The card protruding from the pack, the original upper card, can now be employed in any way required for the purpose of the trick.

It is hardly necessary to point out that the sleight can be performed with the cards face upwards or face downwards; with face-up cards and a face-down deck; or face-down cards and a face-up deck.*

THE DROP SWITCH

A subtle and easy method of obtaining possession of a freely selected card is the following:

---

* An interesting use of this sleight, as a secret subterfuge, and not as an exchange, will be found in Dr. Daley's "Reverse Transfer," page 35, Jean Hugard's *More Card Manipulations*, No. 3.

1. Hold the pack in the left hand as for dealing. Have a spectator insert the joker crosswise at any point in the outer end of the deck.

2. Place the right hand over the deck, the thumb at the inner end, and with the second finger at the outer end lift all the cards above the inserted joker. Show the face of the upper packet—say, the ace of diamonds.

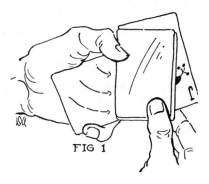

FIG 1

3. Allow this card to drop off the right thumb at the inner end.

4. Move the inner end of the upper packet to the right, the cards pivoting on the right second finger. When this packet extends diagonally over the lower packet as in Fig. 1, remove the right hand. All the cards of the upper packet have thus been moved to the right except the ace of diamonds.

5. Grasp the upper packet and the joker between the right second finger below and the thumb above, carrying them away and placing them to one side on the table. Retain the ace of diamonds at the top of the lower packet by curling the left little finger around the right side of the lower half of the pack.

6. The ace of diamonds, supposedly the face card of the tabled packet, now reposes at the top of the left hand packet, ready to be dealt with as the operator pleases.

Chapter 9
CRIMPS

The Regular Crimp

In this case the crimp is made in the outer right corner of a chosen card when it is returned to the pack by the spectator and the cards have been

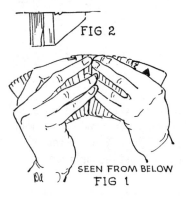

FIG 2

SEEN FROM BELOW
FIG 1

spread between the hands in readiness to receive it.

When the card has been pushed in amongst the others, press the tip of the left second finger upwards against its face at the outer right corner (the top index corner); in the act of closing the spread with the right hand, strike the tip of the right second finger against this index corner and crimp it downwards over the tip of the left second finger, Fig. 1.

Square the pack in the left hand, take it by the outer left corner and hand it to the spectator for shuffling. This action reverses the pack end for end, bringing the crimp to the side away from the spectator and, therefore, it cannot be noticed by him when he makes an overhand shuffle. After the shuffle place the pack in the left hand vertically, back outwards, Fig. 2, and the crimp will be found at the upper inner corner.

The Little Finger Crimp

Hold the card upright by one end, slanting slightly to the right, its face towards you, in the right hand, the thumb pressing against the face, the first, second and third fingers against the back and the middle joint of the little finger resting against the lower left corner, Fig. 1.

Make an upward crimp at this lower left corner by pressing inwards against it with the bony middle knuckle of the little finger.

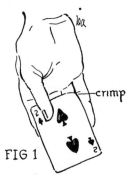

crimp

FIG 1

The crimp can be made in an instant, with perfect safety, merely by picking up a card to note what it is and at once dropping it.

The Gamblers' Crimp

In crimping cards gamblers favor the upward crimp, since it is more difficult to detect the subterfuge when a card so crimped is laid on the table.

The following method of putting an upward crimp in a card is indetectible and easy of execution:

1. Push off the top card with the left thumb and grasp its inner right corner between the right first and second fingers at the face of the card and the thumb at the back, Fig. 1.

2. Turn the card face upwards; in so doing press down upon the face of the card with the second finger and against the back with the thumb, crimping the card against the thumb. This is shown in Fig. 2 with the crimp exaggerated.

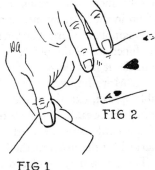

FIG 2

FIG 1

In the simple action of showing the face of a card, you have crimped it for use as a key card for any other purpose. For instance, suppose that in the Merlin Spread trick* a perverse spectator removes a card at too great a distance from your key card; take the card from him under the pretence of showing it to everyone and crimp it as above. Let the spectator indicate a spot for its return to the spread, push it in and invite him to gather the cards and shuffle them. The crimp being in the opposite end to that of the key card there can be no confusion when you come to locate the card.

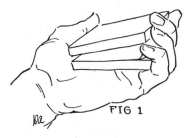

FIG 1

The Peek Crimp

A spectator having peeked at a card in the familiar manner, hold a break under it at the side near the inner right corner with the left little finger.

Cover the pack with the right hand, accepting and holding the break with the thumb at the inner end.

---

* *. . . and a Pack of Cards,* by Jack Merlin, page 87; *Greater Magic,* page 56.

Under cover of the action of squaring the pack, let the spectator's card—the bottom card of the upper packet—slip off the right thumb against the tip of the left little finger. Bend this finger inwards and crimp the corner of the card upwards, Fig. 1.

The card can then be immediately located after honest shuffling and cutting.

CARD MARKING CRIMP

The usual method of crimping a card is to bend a corner up or down. A refinement when using a crimped card as a key card is to place the crimp in the card by means of the method described in connection with the Gamblers' Card Marking system. This type of crimp performs all the functions of the ordinary crimp and yet, no matter how carelessly it is made, it never can be made so heavily that it will be noticeable in the pack. More important, it can be sighted at the top of the pack, or in a table spread, exactly as the crimp is sighted in the marking system—by noting the break in the glaze of the card as the light strikes off the surface of the card—and the card is much more easily found than are cards marked by the usual method.

The crimp may be placed in a single corner, at diagonal corners or at both corners of one end. The last is the best practice since the pack cuts easily to the card and the position of the key card in the pack can be sighted in an instant should this be desirable.

Chapter 10
THE SPECTATOR PEEK

The Spectator Peek Improved

THIS SLEIGHT is very little known although it has been used for decades by the best and almost legendary characters of card conjuring. The original method wherein the break after the peek was held by the tip of the first finger is still prevalent.

1. Hold the pack in the left hand as for dealing, but with the little finger flush with the inner end, the cards being beveled to the right with as much of the face card showing as possible.

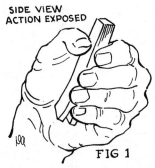

SIDE VIEW
ACTION EXPOSED

FIG 1

2. Holding the pack vertically, invite a spectator to glimpse a card by breaking the pack at the outer right corner and thus sighting an index; as he does this the pack will break open down the length of the right side.

3. Press the left little finger gently against the side at the inner right corner. When the spectator releases the upper packet the left little finger will hold a break which is indetectible at the outer end since you hold it closed tightly by pressure with the left thumb, Fig. 1.

4. Bring the deck before you horizontally and place the right hand over the pack as if to square it. Grasp the ends and tilt the pack to the right and upwards, placing it vertically upon the left fingers with the left thumb at the upper side, and retaining the break with the little finger. This action has a peculiarly narcotic effect upon spectators by lulling their suspicions.

5. Turn the pack down once more upon the left palm, holding it as if for dealing and still retaining the little finger break for further use.

The side slip is generally used after the peek to bring the card to the top. The performer should bide his time before executing this sleight; a minute or so after the glimpse the spectator's perceptions are much less acute. This action is fully explained in The Side Slip, page 31.

The Spectator Peek—The Last Word

The following method of holding a break after a spectator has peeked at a card is the finest and most deceptive yet discovered. The use of the little finger, described above, has been kept a closely guarded secret by first rank card men but, good as that method is, the one now to be described is far superior from every point of view.

During the action the tip of each finger remains fully exposed to view

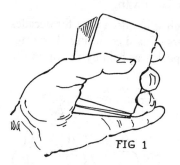

FIG 1

and there does not seem to be any possible way in which the spectator's card can be controlled.

1. Place the pack in the left hand, the middle phalange of the third finger pressing against the side at the inner corner, Fig. 1, the pack being beveled to the right as shown.

2. Offer the pack to a spectator, inviting him to glimpse the index of a card by breaking the pack open at the outer right corner. His action will open a break down the length of the side of the pack; when the spectator releases the cards above his glimpsed card, the break will close automatically, but not before the flesh of the middle phalange of the left third finger has been pressed into, and retains, a break at the inner end.

3. This break is later taken by the right thumb in the act of squaring the pack and the chosen card can then be controlled by the side slip, the the pass, the shuffle or any other means as desired.

After the Spectator Peek

Because of long association, the side slip is generally considered to be the natural complement of the spectator peek, and it is this method which is universally used to bring the spectator's card to the top after such a peek.

Under certain circumstances it is just as satisfactory, however, to shuffle the card to the top, the right fingers grasping the pack at the ends with the thumb retaining the break at the inner end as the pack is turned into position for the overhand shuffle, or the cards are riffled off the right thumb to the break for an end riffle shuffle.

Chapter 11
THE GLIMPSE

A New Glimpse

THIS IS A NEW method of glimpsing a card placed at any number from the top of the pack. Let us say that you wish to sight the fifth card. Here is the method:

1. Remove the four top cards with the right hand and turn them face upwards to show that the chosen card is not amongst them.

2. In replacing these cards upon the pack, insert the left little finger under the fifth card.

3. Transfer the pack from the left hand to the right hand, taking it by the ends; in so doing accept and hold the break with the little finger of the right hand at the outer right corner.

4. Turn the pack face outwards,

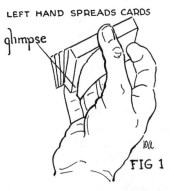

LEFT HAND SPREADS CARDS

glimpse

FIG 1

the right fingers at the lower end, the thumb at the top. With the left hand immediately spread four or five of the bottom cards to the left as in Fig. 1, thus showing that the chosen card is not near the bottom of the pack and at the same time preventing the spectators from detecting the break held by the right little finger. This break enables you to sight the lower index of the fifth card without arousing any suspicion since it is natural for you to look at the cards as you spread them.

Glimpsing a Card

This audacious method of sighting a card can be very useful. Let us assume that a chosen card lies second from the top and that you wish to learn its name. Here is the procedure:

1. Hold the pack in the left hand as for dealing and insert the little finger under the first two cards.

2. Immediately push off the top card with the left thumb, turn it face upwards and square it with the second card.

3. Grasp the two cards, at the ends, between the right thumb and second finger, the first finger resting lightly on the face of the face-up card; the left little finger, having retained the break up to this point, facilitates the action.

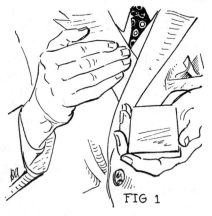

SEEN FROM ABOVE — BUCKLE
EXAGGERATED
FOR CLARITY

FIG 1

4. Lift the two cards into a vertical position as you make any apropos comment concerning the exposed card. Figure 1 shows the action from the conjurer's viewpoint, the five of clubs being the card he will secretly sight. This card should be sighted without focusing the gaze upon it. To acquire this useful knack, take cards one by one and holds them face inwards, focusing the gaze an inch or two to the left of the card. It will be found that a recognizable image of the card will register in the "corner of the eye." This useful dodge prevents the spectators from noting that the operator's gaze has strayed to the card, thus betraying the subterfuge.

5. Replace the two cards squarely upon the pack, then lift the face-up card only into a vertical position, precisely as in the first instance, release the thumb at its end, causing the card to snap outward, face down, and held by the right first and second finger tips.

6. Replace the card, face down, at the top of the pack.

Top Card Glimpse

This extremely useful glimpse of the top card is not nearly as bold as it may seem at first sight, but it calls for perfect execution of the one-hand top palm* and the top card replacement.†

FIG 1

To make the glimpse, palm the top card in the right hand by the one-hand method and place the pack in the left hand; while addressing a spectator make a gesture, away from

---

* See the footnote, page 177.

† *The One Hand Replacement*, page 177.

the body, in which the back of the hand is turned to the spectators; during this gesture sight the card, Fig. 1. Immediately afterwards return the card to the top of the pack.

On his first attempts, the reader, being extremely conscious of the subterfuge, will no doubt feel that the spectators must surely suspect his gesture; but after he has successfully performed the glimpse a dozen times or so, with no one the wiser, the sleight becomes as natural as breathing itself, so much so that often he will hold the card palmed for tens of seconds before he finally glimpses it.

As with all sleights, there is a "feel" to this glimpse which can only be acquired by experience; in this case the knack being that of dropping the eyes to the gesturing hand at the moment made most natural by the operator's speech. This serves to make unnoticeable the telltale focusing of the eyes which betrays so many glimpses.

The Gamblers' Glimpse

This peek is a gamblers' subterfuge and has, to our knowledge, never before been divulged. As with so many moves which come from the gaming table its originator is unknown. At first thought this peek may seem

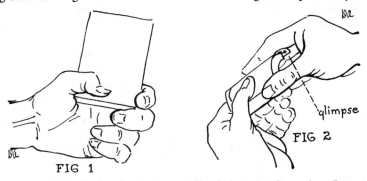

FIG 1
glimpse
FIG 2

to be a dangerous practice but, actually, it is very deceptive. It carries the recommendation of having completely gulled every magician against whom it has been used by Charles Miller, the Western card expert. The feature of the sleight is that, unlike most glimpses, the operator deliberately looks at the pack during the process. It appears to the spectator that he bends the pack merely to straighten an upward bend in it. The moves follow.

1. Take the pack horizontally in the left hand at the inner end, the thumb above and the forefinger below, so that it rests on the side of the forefinger, Fig. 1.

2. Seize the pack by the ends with the right hand, keeping the four

fingers together covering the outer end, and with the left thumb push the top card to the right, just far enough to expose the index at the right upper corner.

3. Retaining the hands in this position, bend the pack downwards at the outer end with the right fingers, as if to remove an upward bend. Look directly at the pack as you do this and you can sight the index of the top card through the arch formed by the right thumb and fingers, Fig. 2.

THE GLIMPSE AFTER THE PEEK

The method usually given for ascertaining the name of the chosen card after a spectator peek is this:

A card having been noted by a spectator by lifting the corners of the cards and looking at the index of one . . . hold a break and turn the left hand over to the right bringing the cards face up. With the tips of the left fingers press the packet now below the break to the right, bringing the lower index into view. The action is covered by the position of the hand.*

The following methods are new and practical:

a. 1. Retain a break with the left little finger after the spectator has sighted his card and place the right hand over the deck, with the thumb, first and second fingers at the ends, and take the break with the right thumb.

2. Allow the face card of the upper packet, the spectator's card, to drop off the right thumb against the tip of the left little finger. Move this finger a quarter of an inch to the left, forcing the inner end of the card diagonally out of the left side of the pack at the inner end, exposing the index. Remove the right thumb, allowing the break to close and simulate the squaring of the ends with the right fingers.

This preparatory action having been completed, the index of the card is sighted in the following manner:

3. Place the left thumb against the face of the deck at the outer left corner and turn the pack face inwards, at the same time moving it into an upright position. The jogged index is now at the lower end.

4. Turn the right hand palm upwards and grasp the pack between the right thumb, at the upper end, and the first and second fingers, at the lower end. Sight the exposed index as you turn the pack face downwards and at once push the jogged card flush with the tip of the right little finger, Fig. 1.

It will be noted that the jogged card is concealed from the spectators,

---

* From *Card Manipulations*, No. 5, Jean Hugard.

first, by the back of the left hand and second, by the back of the right hand as the pack is changed over from hand to hand.

This sleight is also useful for determining the name of a card lying at a given number. In such case you thumb-count to the desired number and transfer the break to the left little finger (page 125). Proceed as above, sighting the index of the card as the pack is transferred from hand to hand.

FIG 1

b. One of the most effective bits of byplay which can be used by the card conjurer is to name the card sighted by a spectator when, apparently, only the spectator can know its name. Audiences derive more genuine amusement from the surprised expression upon the startled spectator's face than from many a more elaborate trick.

1. Holding the pack as for the spectator peek (page 93), ask a spectator to break the pack open and sight the index of any card, specifically requesting that he refrain from selecting the bottom card, which you tap to emphasize your request.

2. After the spectator has sighted a card and the left little finger is holding a break at the inner end of the pack, shift the left thumb flat against the left side of the pack, curl the first finger under it, and square it with the right fingers. The edge of the upper packet rests on the tip of the little finger and can be moved to the left by bending this finger at the outermost joint.

3. Turn the pack face upwards. With the left thumb tip pressed against the side of the deck near the outer corner, the inner index of the selected card is brought into view automatically, the packet above the original break now being jogged a little to the right. The face card of this packet is the chosen card. After turning the pack face upwards the little finger no longer holds the break, the pack being supported by the left second and third fingers and the thumb, Fig. 1, page 117.

4. Tap the face card of the pack with the right fingers, saying, "You didn't think of this bottom card, did you?" at the same time sighting the index of the desired card under the base of the thumb. The misdirection is all that could be asked for: it is impossible for any onlooker to note the condition of the pack, and best of all the jogging of the upper packet is entirely automatic and cannot possibly go wrong at the most important moment.

5. Turn the hand over again, bringing the pack face downwards,

square the cards and move a little away from the assisting spectator. Pause, look over your shoulder at him and say, "You'll be sure and remember that five of diamonds, won't you?" If the timing of the question is correct, and the intonation of the voice makes it an offhand query, in many instances the spectator will nod that he *will* remember the card; then abruptly he will realize that you have named his card and his features will mirror his surprise eloquently.

The reader, upon first using this trick, will find that it is one of those rare feats from which everyone derives pleasure, particularly the operator, who finds his reward in the consternation depicted on the spectator's features.

Max Malini, the diminutive gray master magician, made of this little diversion a high-spot in the extraordinary salon entertainment with which he travelled the world. A dominant, vibrant personality, impeccably clad in the court garments of European royalty, he would request a spectator to "Dink of a cod, one leetle cod." When the internationally famous conjurer turned the pack over, tapped its face, turned away a moment and then in his peculiarly gravel-toned voice growled, "You won't forget dot den off clubs, vill you?" his startled victim's mouth invariably dropped open, his eyes bulged and his eye-brows became two soaring question marks, a sight so irresistibly comic that Malini's audiences rocked and roared with unadulterated joy at the sight.

COVER FOR THE GLIMPSE

a. The Gamblers' Method for a Single Card

We will suppose that you have brought the chosen card second from the top and that you wish to ascertain its suit and denomination.

1. Hold the pack in the left hand as for dealing and remove the top card between the right thumb and forefinger taking it at its lower right corner.

2. Turn this card face upwards, at the same moment moving the pack, with the left hand, from a horizontal to a vertical position, with the back of the card in the right hand resting upon the outer right corner of the pack, concealing it. Direct the spectator's attention to the exposed card proving that his card is not at the top.

3. With the ball of the left thumb at the left outer corner of the pack push the top card down a little and then outwards, holding the other side of the card flush with the pack, Fig. 1. This action will bend the middle of the card upwards and enable you to glimpse the top card easily. The entire action is screened by the card in the right hand and the glimpse can be made in an instant, Fig. 1.

The sleight comes from the gaming table where it is used in black jack.

In blackjack the operator lifts the two cards before him to sight his hole card. The pack goes behind the screening cards and he glimpses the top card.

b. One Card

We will assume that you wish to learn the name of the top card, either to use as a key card, as a force card, or as the spectator's chosen card:

1. Hold the right hand with its palm to the audience on your right side and move your left hand up to it, thus bringing the pack to a vertical position face outwards.

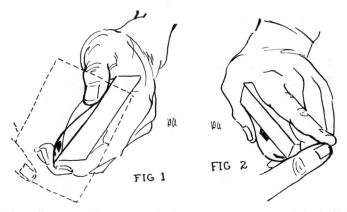

FIG 1   FIG 2

2. Touch the tip of the right forefinger with the tip of the left fore-finger, Fig. 2, making some such remark as, "The tip of my right fore-finger, ladies and gentlemen, has miraculous powers."

3. In the meantime you have buckled the top card with the left thumb, as in "a" above, and have sighted the index.

The action provides a logical excuse for turning your gaze to the pack.

c. Several Cards

In performing a five card routine in which cards peeked at are shifted to the top by the side slip, you wish to learn the name of each card.

1. Holding the pack in position for the glimpse, as given above, turn to the right and place the tip of the left forefinger against the tip of the right little finger, commenting, "That's the first card." The position of the pack in the left hand enables you to buckle the top card and sight the index as you tick off the first spectator, Fig. 2.

2. As each card is brought to the top you count off the spectator's number against the fingers of the right hand. The action is the familiar one of enumerating against the five right fingers and provides a logical reason for looking towards the pack without arousing any suspicions.

Chapter 12
THE JOG

THE SIDE JOG

IT IS USUALLY in the apparently minor details of sleights that the really expert card-man shines, for he has learned from experience that the handling of cards must be natural and, above all, effortless, even the smallest actions being made in the simplest and best possible manner.

In the following sleight, the purpose of which is to jog a card secretly at the right side after its insertion in the end of the deck, ease of accomplishment is matched by absolute control of the card.

1. Riffle the end of the pack for the return of a chosen card, the pack being held in the left hand as for the thumb count, with the thumb flat against the side.

2. With the card inserted three-quarters of its length, place the right second and third fingers at the outer end of the projecting card near the left corner, and the thumb at the inner end of the deck near the left corner. Curl the right forefinger, placing its nail and its entire third joint flat upon the surface of the pack.

3. Push the card flush into the deck, the action automatically jogging the card an eighth of an inch at the inner right side. The jog is picked up by the left little finger at will for further control.

THE JOG AT THE BREAK

It is not necessary, nor indeed desirable, always to hold a break with the left little finger. A jogged card will serve as well, and, with the jog at the inner end, the deck can be handled freely, passed from hand to hand, or laid on the table at will.

We will assume that a spectator has peeked at a card and that you have secured a break under it with your left little finger. After a moment, place the right hand lightly over the deck to square it and jog the card in the following way:

1. Press the right thumb against the inner end of the upper packet, lift it slightly and insert the tip of the left little finger into the break.

2. With the little finger tip push the desired card to the right, jogging

it diagonally about a quarter of an inch at its inner end. Release the thumb so that the break closes, Fig. 1.

3. Move the little finger so that it rests against the side of the projecting card and push it back to the left, causing it to become jogged at the inner end, Fig. 2.

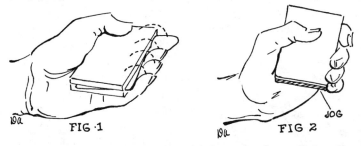

FIG ·1   FIG 2

4. Remove the right hand and with it grasp the pack by the sides near the inner end between the right thumb and second finger. With the left thumb and fingers square the deck by stroking or "milking" its sides near the outer end. This action will place the pack in perfect condition, the grip of the right hand maintaining the jog, which can be so minute that it would escape all but the closest scrutiny even if the inner end should be exposed to view.

In retaking the break, you may lift the jogged card with the right thumb, insert the left little finger and side slip the card to the top of the pack; or, if you wish to use a shuffle or a pass, press downwards on the jogged card making a break above it, insert the left little finger and execute the shuffle or pass as desired.

Alternative Method

After having secured a break with the left little finger, in squaring the pack grip the top packet with the right thumb and second finger, remove the little finger from the break and move the top packet inwards a fraction of an inch. Let the bottom card of the packet slip free from the thumb tip and at once push the packet forward flush with the lower packet.

The action takes but a moment and the squaring movement is continued, the tip of the thumb sliding along the inner end of the upper packet only, above the jogged card. The appearance of squaring both ends of the pack is perfect.

In either case it is a good practice to lay the pack down on the table while you pull back your sleeves or make some other gesture. This will go far towards convincing the spectators that the selected card really is lost in the pack and make its subsequent discovery all the more wonderful.

The Automatic Jog No. I

In the case where you are dealing with two cards, which may have been selected or are being used in a set trick and you have to control them after they have been placed in the middle of the pack, the following method is both simple and indetectible.

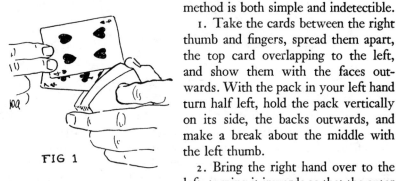

1. Take the cards between the right thumb and fingers, spread them apart, the top card overlapping to the left, and show them with the faces outwards. With the pack in your left hand turn half left, hold the pack vertically on its side, the backs outwards, and make a break about the middle with the left thumb.

FIG 1

2. Bring the right hand over to the left, turning it inwards so that the outer end of the upper card is brought into the break. Let one card slip away from the left thumb tip and insert the face card of the pair below it, the result being that one card has been secretly interleaved between the pair, Fig. 1. Let the two cards protrude about halfway from the top of the pack.

3. Turn to the front, hold the pack face outwards in the left hand and slip the tip of the left little finger under the lower right corner, Fig. 2. Rest the tip of the right thumb on the back of the pack and with the right forefinger push the two cards down slowly. When about a quarter of an inch of their length remains, remove the tip of the left little finger and press on the back of the pack with the right thumb. This action will cause the interleaved card to

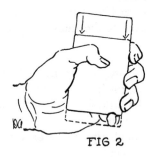

FIG 2

protrude at the inner end of the pack as the two cards are pushed flush with the upper end. The ghost card in Fig. 2 indicates the nature of the jog.

4. Insert the tip of the left little finger below the jogged card, make the pass and you have one of the pair on the top of the pack and the other second from the bottom.

Automatic Jog No. II

A card having been selected, undercut a little more than half the deck and have the card replaced on top of the left hand portion. Slap the right hand packet on top so that its outer end projects over the lower packet by about half an inch, Fig. 1.

At once grasp the whole deck at the inner end by the corners between the thumb and first and second fingers of the right hand. The left hand remains under the deck with the thumb on one side, the second finger at the other and the first finger at the outer end. Retaining the right hand hold, draw the left thumb and fingers outwards in a form of milking movement, making the cards of the lower packet move forward, flush with the upper packet. All the cards will move

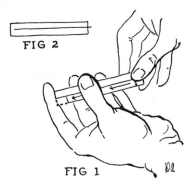

FIG 2

FIG 1

forward except the top card of this lower packet, which remains protruding at the inner end, Fig. 2.

There is no necessity for holding a break, the pack can be passed from hand to hand, or placed casually on the table as in the delayed pass. Again you can go at once into the Hindu shuffle without having to pick up the top card of the lower packet.

FIG 1

Automatic Jog No. III

The action is very similar to that in No. II but, in this case, the upper packet is pushed back flush with the lower packet. We will suppose that you have cut the pack for the return of a chosen card and that you wish to jog this card:

1. Have the card replaced on the packet in the left hand.

2. Place the right hand packet on top so that it overlaps the left hand packet about a quarter of an inch outwards.

3. Press down on the top of the pack with the right forefinger and at the same time push the packets flush with the left forefinger. The top

card of the lower packet (the chosen card) will be jogged at the inner end of the pack, Fig. 1.

4. Make the motions of squaring the ends of the pack with the right fingers and thumb being careful that the thumb does not press against the jogged card.

In all three methods the jog may be so slight that it is not noticeable even if the pack is placed casually on the table.

Chapter 13
THE REVERSE

~~~~~~

FACING THE DECK

WHEN IT IS NECESSARY to have the two halves of the deck face in opposite directions so that there will be a face down card on each side of the deck, the action of the regular pass is generally used to place the pack in this condition. The upper half is drawn off by the left fingers in the usual way, but it is then turned face upwards and drawn under the original lower half. A better method of effecting the same process is as follows:

1. With the right side of your body turned towards the audience, hold the pack in the left hand in position for the Charlier pass, the backs of the cards towards the spectators.

2. Bring the right hand over the pack and grasp it lightly by the ends, keeping the back of the hand towards the front.

3. Allow the lower half of the pack to fall onto the left palm and push that packet upwards against the left thumb with the left forefinger, exactly as in making the Charlier pass, the upper sides of the halves meeting under the ball of the left thumb and forming an inverted V. (See Figs. 1, 2, 3, page 108.)

4. Straighten out the left forefinger and with both hands bring the two packets directly together, thus facing the lower packet, the upper packet remaining with its back to the front throughout.

The move can be made in an instant; it is covered by the right hand and the pack should be squared immediately afterwards with both hands in the usual way.

Exactly the same procedure is followed when, with the two halves of the pack faced, it is desired to restore it to its proper condition. The sleight can be performed without looking at the hands since the pack will automatically break open at the proper place when the left thumb relaxes its pressure at the top side, in the action described in number 3. The principle of the faced deck is one of the oldest subterfuges of the card conjurer. It is fully described by M. Decremps in his book *Testament de Jerome Sharp* (Paris, 1793). He gives interesting tricks depending upon its use. The principle has been sadly neglected by modern performers.

Righting the Faced Deck

New Method

When the principle of the faced deck has been used and it becomes necessary to bring the pack back to its regular condition, i.e. with all the cards facing one way, the following method will be found to be better than the repetition of the half pass.

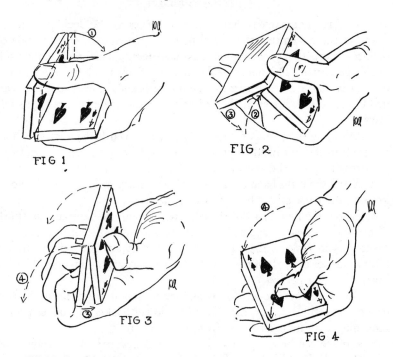

FIG 1

FIG 2

FIG 3

FIG 4

1. Hold the faced deck in the left hand in readiness for the Charlier pass. Relax the pressure of the thumb and the deck will split into two packets, breaking cleanly at the point where the lower face-up cards meet the upper face-down cards, Fig. 1.

2. With the left forefinger push the face-up packet upwards against the thumb exactly as in the Charlier pass. When the upper side of this packet meets the upper side of the other packet, just below the ball of the thumb, the two packets resemble an inverted V, Fig. 2.

3. Straighten out the left forefinger, press firmly on the upper sides of the two packets with the thumb, keeping them together, and bend the left fingers inwards, turning the face-down packet and bringing

it face upwards against and coalescing with the face-up packet, Fig. 3. At the same moment press the left thumb outwards against the original lower packet, thus bringing the whole pack face upwards on the left palm, Fig. 4.

The entire action may be made openly, in which case it appears that the pack, which has been held with its face away from the spectators, has been turned so that its face can be seen. Or, if preferred, the action may be made behind the right hand as it approaches the left hand, ostensibly to square the cards.

Automatic Reverse

The following method of reversing a card in the deck is very easy and effective, being done under cover of showing, apparently, that the chosen card is not at the top nor next to the top.

1. Bring the chosen card second from the top. Hold the pack in the left hand as for dealing, push off the top card, turn it face upwards and square it on the other cards.

2. Secure a break under the top two cards by the method explained on page 4.

3. Grasp these two cards at the ends between the right thumb and second finger, the forefinger pressing lightly on the face of the upper, face-up card. The condition is that this upper face-up card is an indifferent card and under it, face downwards, is the chosen card.

4. Push the next card over the right side of the pack with the left thumb and bring the two cards held by the right hand upward from below sharply, striking the right side of this card and making it flip over, face upwards, upon the deck.

5. Remarking that it also is an indifferent card, place this card under those held in the right hand, turn the packet of three cards face down and place it on the top of the deck, squaring the cards as you do so.

6. The chosen card is now reversed in the second position from the top and can be disposed of in whatever way may be necessary for the trick in hand.

Righting a Reversed Bottom Card

It is sometimes necessary at the conclusion of a trick to right a card secretly which is reversed on the bottom of the deck, particularly in the case in which a reversed card has been used as a locator card. The sleight which follows, being fast and indetectible, is excellent for the purpose.

1. Take the pack, with the bottom card reversed, face down in the right hand between the thumb, at the left side, and the second, third and fourth fingers, at the right side, the forefinger resting on the back.

2. Place the pack across the extended fingers of the left hand so that its left side rests against their roots, Fig. 1, and grasp the pack as shown

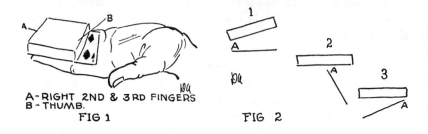

A - RIGHT 2ND & 3RD FINGERS
B - THUMB.
FIG 1   FIG 2

in the figure. Draw all the cards except the reversed bottom card about half an inch towards the tips of the fingers, Fig. 1.

3. Immediately lift all the cards, except the bottom one, with the right hand an inch or two and bend the left fingers inwards, thus turning the bottom card face down onto the left palm, the roots of the fingers forming a hinge.

4. At the same moment that this card turns face down, riffle the remaining cards of the pack off the right thumb onto it and the left palm. Figure 2 shows the nature of this action.

The effect is much the same as in Dr. Elliott's riffle pass in which the transposition of the packets is concealed by, and is apparently part of, the riffling of the pack. In this case, as the reversed card is flipped over by the left fingers, it becomes, to the eyes of the spectators, a part of the larger movement of the cards which are riffled from the right hand onto the left palm.

The same sleight can be used when a number of cards are reversed on the bottom of the pack. A downward bend having been given to the pack prior to facing it, the cards will break at the point where the packets kiss after it is placed on the left fingers. Draw the upper packet to the right and proceed in exactly the same way as with a single card.

FACING THE BOTTOM CARD

A single reversed card in a deck has many uses; as a key card, for example, as cover for a reversed deck, or as a discovery of a chosen card; it is necessary, therefore, to have a perfectly covered method of bringing it about. The following method is the best yet devised for the purpose, the reversal being effected invisibly under cover of beginning an overhand shuffle. These are the moves:

1. With your left side to the front, hold the pack in the right hand

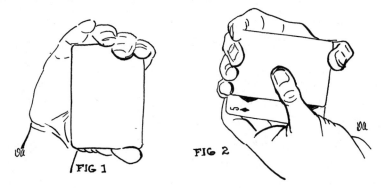

FIG 1   FIG 2

with its palm upwards, between the thumb and first and second fingers at the ends near the left corners, Fig. 1.

2. Bring the hands together, turning the right hand palm downwards so that the tips of the left second and third fingers strike against the middle of the top card; continue the movements of the hands in opposite directions until the card has been pushed off the pack about an inch.

3. At once lift the left side of the pack about two inches and turn it face downwards on the projecting card; the left fingers assist the operation by pressing upwards on the back of the projecting card and the left thumb drops onto the back of the pack which is thus brought into the correct position for the overhand shuffle, Fig. 2.

4. Proceed immediately to an overhand shuffle dropping packets alternately to the front and rear of the first packet and letting the last packet fall to the rear, thus placing the reversed card on the bottom of the pack.

The move must be made with a light touch so that one card only is slid away, and without the least sound.

In those instances when it is desired to reverse a card without shuffling the pack, the reversal may be had in the action of turning the pack face upwards or face downwards, depending upon whether it is desired to reverse a card at the bottom or face a card at the top; the procedure is exactly the same as that given above, but the overhand shuffle is eliminated.

Faced Deck Turnover

The two methods of secretly turning over a faced deck which have been handed down from time immemorial, viz., by placing the pack on the left fingers and then closing the hand, and again by pushing upwards with the left thumb on the left side of the deck, are the only ones which

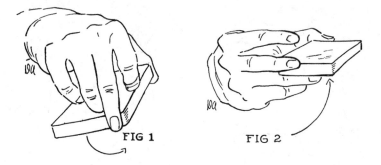

FIG 1   FIG 2

have been explained in the textbooks. The following procedure is cleaner in execution and requires less cover. The mere act of transferring the pack from one hand to the other is sufficient.

1. The pack having been faced, hold it in the right hand by the left corners, between the thumb at the inner corner and the second finger at the outer corner.

2. Curl the third and fourth fingers inward and let the nail of the third finger rest on the back of the top card, Fig. 1.

3. To turn the pack over, extend the third finger forcing the pack to make a semi-revolution, pivoting on the thumb and second fingers; at the end of the move the pack is again in a horizontal plane but with the opposite side uppermost, the thumb and second fingers being at the right side of the pack as it rests on the third finger which remains stretched out, Fig. 2.

With the hand at rest the movement is visible, but, under the cover afforded by the transfer of the pack from the right hand to the left hand, it can be done as quick as a flash and is imperceptible.

Chapter 14

SUNDRY SLEIGHTS

VESTING A CARD

THERE ARE PERHAPS not more than half a dozen card conjurers, if so many, who make use of this useful sleight, the vesting of a card, the ruse having become almost a forgotten art in the last thirty years. To one who

has never tried, nor perhaps even thought of vesting cards, the operation would appear to be difficult, if not impossible; yet a card is one of the easiest of all objects to vest.

It happens at times, when a card has to be secretly disposed of, that it is inadvisable to have recourse to the usual procedure, that of pocketing it. Vesting provides a method, in some ways superior, which can be used to get rid of such a card.

We will suppose that the card is palmed in the right hand which rests naturally at your side. Here is the procedure:

FIG 1

1. Bring both hands towards the edge of the vest on either side. A moment before the heel of the right hand is brought level with the edge of the vest, bend the top joint of the second finger inwards, gripping the end of the card, and release the other end from the palm, Fig. 1.

2. This end will then project from the palm about an inch and you let it strike against the cloth of the trousers just below the edge of the vest. A slight withdrawal or contraction of the abdomen and the upward movement of the hand to grasp the vest will slide the card swiftly and cleanly under the garment.

3. The top joints of the fingers naturally go underneath the vest, giving the card a final push upward and immediately afterwards grip the edge of the vest giving it a little tug downwards. The left hand makes the same action on its side and the result is that the card is disposed of under cover of a perfectly natural action, the straightening or pulling down of the vest.

There should be nothing hasty or furtive about the procedure. A slow movement will pass unquestioned; a swift, darting movement of the hand will immediately draw the spectator's eyes towards that hand.

THE ZINGONE THUMBNAIL GAUGE

Ask any skilled card conjurer to place a pack of cards on the table and instantly, without even looking at the cards, cut off two packets in succession containing the same number of cards and the reply will

FIG 1

be that such a feat is impossible. Here is an infallible solution by Mr. Zingone:

1. Place the pack, perfectly squared, on the table sideways, that is, with its outer side towards the spectators, its inner side towards yourself.

2. Place the fingers of your right hand against the far side of the pack and rest the point of your thumb on the edge of the inner side so that its nail passes over the edge of the top card, Fig. 1.

3. Press the thumb down firmly, compressing the flesh as much as possible, then bend the thumb and dig the nail into the side of the pack.

4. Lift the packet thus separated from the rest of the cards and place it on the table.

5. Repeat the operation with the remainder of the cards, cutting off a second packet. If the position has been rightly taken and the same downward pressure exerted on the tip of the thumb, the two packets will contain exactly the same number of cards.

The following trick will illustrate how this novel idea can be put to work.

A CUTTING DISCOVERY

1. Have the pack shuffled by a spectator, take it back, square it and place it on the table.

2. Using the thumbnail gauge cut off two equal packets placing them to the right of the pack. Call the remainder of the pack A, the first of the two packets B and the second packet C.

3. Invite a spectator to take a card from either of the two packets, B or, C, note it, place it on top of A, and then place the two packets B and C on top of A.

4. Square the pack, place it on the table, repeat the two thumbnail gauge

cuts, have the card named and show it on the bottom of the second cut.

It will readily be seen that a card can be taken from any packet and placed on any other. Suppose, for example, that a card is taken from C and placed on B. You would then have C placed on B and these two packets placed on A and proceed to find the card with one cut only.

Presented as an interlude between more important feats the trick will gain for the operator a rather undeserved reputation for uncanny skill.

Separating the Colors

In this method of separating the red cards from the black, the pack is stacked during the course of a minor flourish without arousing the least suspicion on the part of the onlookers.

1. Take the pack face upwards in the left hand and spread the top cards. Let us assume that the first four cards are red cards. Push them off with the left thumb and take them face upwards in the right hand.

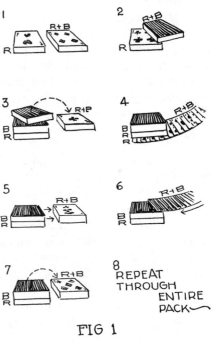

FIG 1

2. Suppose that the next two cards are black cards. Turn the left hand over bringing the pack face downwards and place these two cards face downwards on the face-up red cards in the right hand, Fig. 1.

3. Turn the left hand back downwards, thus bringing the pack face upwards again. Say the next three cards are red cards; place them face upwards at the bottom of the right hand packet, that is to say, under the face-up red cards previously placed in this hand.

4. Suppose the next five cards are black. Again turn the left hand back upwards and put these cards, face downwards, upon the right hand packet, Fig. 1. The small figures 1 to 8 show the course of the action.

5. Continue this series of actions until all the red cards have been

placed face upwards at the bottom of the right hand packet and the black cards face downwards at the top. When the actions are made speedily and rather sloppily, it appears that you are turning, haphazardly, some cards face upwards, some face downwards and that these sequences are scattered throughout the entire deck. Actually the twenty-six face-up cards at the bottom are red cards and the twenty-six face-down cards at the top are black cards.

6. Secretly right the faced deck by means of the sleight explained on page 108. Fan the deck, face inwards, and show that all the cards have mysteriously adjusted themselves so that all the backs face the same way.

This amusing by-play, however, has served to separate the reds and the blacks so that any tricks dependent on this principle can then be performed.

It should be noted here that it is advisable to push one or two cards of the other color prominently amongst those that are face upwards during the action, allowing them to protrude at the outer end so that they are always in sight. This will prevent any spectator from remarking that only cards of one color are turned face upwards. When you fan the pack later on, openly remove these two cards and place them amongst the other cards of the same color.

SETTING A KEY CARD

Time and again it has been proven that a trick simple in principle can be baffling in the extreme, for the straight line in conjuring, as in geometry, remains the shortest distance between the conjurer's two points, method and effect.

The earliest merchants of abracadabra made use of the basic principle of the key card, in which a chosen card is discovered by having it returned to the pack below a card known to the wizard. The principle is still used today in a score of good mysteries, and various machiavellian disguises have been dreamed up to cover the age-old stratagem, some of these camouflages being very gaudy indeed. That which is outlined here has the merit of superlative simplicity.

1. After the spectator has shuffled the cards, take the pack, spread it and allow a free choice to be made.

2. Close the spread immediately and slip the little finger tip into a break in the middle of the pack. The lower edge of the upper packet rests upon the tip of the little finger; thus, by bending the third joint of this finger inwards, the entire upper packet could be moved to the left.

3. Make a gesture towards the spectator with your left hand, turning it over and pointing with the forefinger to the chosen card, making some such remark as this: "Please make a distinct mental picture of that card." The action will jog the top half of the pack towards the right and the index of the bottom card of this packet will be visible to you but concealed from the spectators, Fig. 1. In this gesture the left hand should be brought

FIG 1

presses down

break opens

FIG 2

directly into your line of vision without your gaze moving from the spectator's card; it must be shot flying, so to speak.

4. Bring the left hand back to its former position, retain the little finger break and rest the left thumb against the left side of the pack. Figure 2 shows how the left thumb, by pressing down, enables the little finger to recapture the break.

5. Place the right hand over the pack and gently riffle the outer left corner once or twice, with the left thumb. Riffle again and immediately thereafter cut at the break, lifting the cards above it with the right hand.

6. Extend the lower half, requesting that the card be dropped upon it. Drop the right hand packet upon it and square the pack scrupulously, this latter packet having been handled in such a fashion as to preclude the possibility of your having sighted its bottom card.

7. Place the pack upon the table for a moment, then pick it up and continue the trick. The chosen card is located directly under the sighted key card.

Another method that is easy and straightforward is the following:

1. Hold the pack in the left hand as for the thumb count, faces to the right, with the right fingers lightly covering the deck, Fig. 1.

2. Riffle the pack gently once or twice with the left thumb, without glancing at it, as if toying with the cards.

3. Riffle to the center of the pack, glance down and note the outer left index of the card at which the left thumb holds the break.

4. Press the right thumb, at the inner end, against the break and release the break held by the left thumb, Fig. 2. Square the cards with the right hand as the left holds it in position for dealing, but with its thumb straight against the left side.

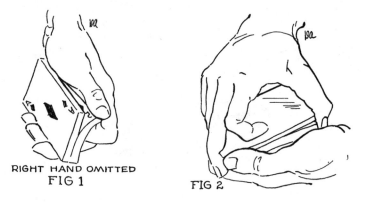

RIGHT HAND OMITTED
FIG 1   FIG 2

5. Insert the left little finger into the break, drop the thumb under the pack and, with an upward pressure of the thumb, turn the pack face down to the right, the little finger still holding its break with the pack now held at the finger tips, the thumb above and the fingers below.

6. Grasp the pack at the ends with the right hand, the thumb at the inner end retaining the break as the left hand shifts into the normal dealing position and its little finger again takes the break.

7. Retaining the little finger break, spread the top cards, requesting that one be chosen.

8. Upon its removal, square the cards once more in the left hand, the left thumb returning to its position flat against the left side and the little finger still holding the break.

From this point proceed exactly as explained in paragraphs 5, 6 and 7 of the preceding method.

THE FIVE CARD QUIBBLE

On occasion the card conjurer finds himself in a position in which he knows that one of five cards is a spectator's chosen card, but he cannot be sure which one of the five he must use to bring his trick to a conclusion. For instance, a spectator may unexpectedly take the pack, cut it, look at a card and then challenge the conjurer to find it; or a spectator peek may go awry; or the magician, being human, may lose control of a card but know its approximate position in the pack, within five cards.

Obviously, the trick which was originally planned cannot be completed; it is up to the conjurer to extricate himself from his dilemma with a minimum loss of prestige.

Let us assume that the spectator has taken the pack in his own hands, cut to a card, reassembled the pack and challenged the conjurer to find the card. Under such circumstances, the procedure is this:

Method. Estimate the position of the card as closely as you can, and make the pass so that it becomes one of the top five cards. For convenience, we will say these five cards are an A, 2, 3, 4 and 5. Then proceed to:

1. Fan the deck and note the five top cards.

2. Whatever the denomination of the third card is, counting the Jack eleven, the Queen twelve and the King thirteen, add one and count that number of cards beyond it (in this case, to the seventh card) and remove these cards with the left hand.

3. Place these cards upon the face of the deck, immediately drawing away the first three cards, the A, 2 and 3, and drop them face downwards to your left. Square the remainder of the pack and place it face downwards to your right. The condition now is this: To your left, the A, 2 and 3, any one of which may be the selected card; three cards from the bottom of the pack is the 5, and below it the 4, either of which again may be the selected card.

4. Pick up the packet of three cards, spread them with the faces towards yourself and ask the spectator to indicate a card. Let us suppose that, as in most cases, he chooses the middle card. Drop this card face upwards on the table and watch his expression; if it is the chosen card, his reaction will inform you of the fact. Apparently, in such case, you have caused him to select the very card he thought of.

5. If it is not his card, ask him to indicate one of the two that remain. Whichever he chooses, drop the right hand card, the 3, face downwards on the tabled card. Turn the remaining card in your hand and again watch his reaction. If it is his card, you have apparently discarded all the cards but the chosen one.

6. If that card is not his, drop it face upwards on the other two cards on the table. Turn the three cards over, placing two face downwards and, for the first time, exposing the face of the third card. Once

more watch his reaction; if it is his card, apparently you have discarded two of the three cards and produced his card face upwards between two face-down cards in a way that you pretend was your intention from the start.

7. If this card was not his card, point to the face-up card and say, "That card is a three spot—mark it well. It proves beyond any reasonable doubt, that your card is three from the bottom of the pack."

8. Take the pack and turn it face upwards. Deal off two cards, exposing the face of the original fifth card. If the spectator's reaction, or lack of it, tells you that this was not his card, remove it as though continuing the deal and display the next card, the fourth of the original set-up. It must be the spectator's card, and you make as much of this fact as you can.

At only one point can the routine go wrong; the third card of the original five must always be placed face down with the other two face upwards. Since the middle card is almost invariably selected, in most cases the routine will progress as described. Should, however, the spectator give the third card as his first choice, immediately shuffle the cards under the pretext that this should have been done first and have the selection repeated, with the percentage all in your favor that another card will be indicated.

It will be noted that as each card of the five is displayed in its turn, the presentation permits the building of a climax, and, if the chosen card does not appear, the climax can be smothered and the trick simply continued.

A certain quick-wittedness and taciturnity are required, together with the ability to make the various extensions of the location seem to be merely a continuation of the effect rather than a search for the desired card.

EMERGENCY CARD STABBING

This is another emergency sleight for use when the performer knows that a chosen card is one of a small number of cards and must conclude the trick he has started as best he can.

Let us assume that, as in the Five Card Quibble, the conjurer knows that a spectator's chosen card is one of five, and must secretly ascertain which is the correct card.

Method. 1. Bring the five cards to the bottom of the pack, fan it and memorize the denominations of these cards as you would memorize a dial system telephone number, viz: 2 - 5 3 J 7. If two cards are of the same denomination, remember the suit of the first card only.

2. Make the pass taking the sequence to the middle of the pack and hold a break under it with the left little finger.

3. Remove the top card and hand it to a spectator, requesting that he insert it wherever he likes in the pack. To facilitate this insertion, place

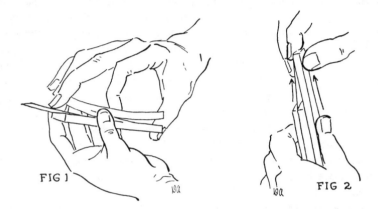

FIG 1   FIG 2

the right hand over the cards, fingers at the outer end and thumb at the inner end, and riffle the outer end. Contrive to have the indicator card inserted below the break, Fig. 1.

4. Take up the break at the inner end with the right thumb and request the spectator to name his card. Knowing the sequence of five cards, allow sufficient cards to drop off the right thumb to place the named card at the top of the lower packet. In the present case, if a Jack were named, you would drop four cards—2 - 5 3 J.

5. Turn the left hand, bringing the pack to a vertical position, and with the right thumb push up the packet of cards above the break level with the top of the indicator card; seize this card and the packet thus brought behind it and draw them away clear of the pack, Fig. 2.

6. Turn the left hand to a horizontal position and hold the remaining packet out to the spectator to take the top card—that is, the chosen card.

THE DROP CONTROL

This method of controlling a card upon its return to the pack has a spurious air of honesty which makes it most effective.

1. As soon as a spectator has chosen a card, square the pack, insert

the tip of the left little finger at about the middle, and from the bottom of the upper half let six cards riffle off the tip of the right thumb. Hold a break between these cards and those above them with the tip of the left third finger, momentarily, while you press the right thumb firmly against the inner end of the pack and hold both breaks with it.

2. Place the left hand four or five inches below the right and invite the spectator to replace his card, "Anywhere in the pack," you say. At the same moment begin dropping little packets of cards from the bottom of the pack onto the left hand. Continue until you reach the first break and have the spectator place his card on top of these cards. Let one or two cards drop as before from the bottom of the upper packet, again one or two cards and then all that remain below the second break held by the thumb; to all appearances, the card is already well lost in the pack. Finally place all the cards remaining in the right hand on top of those in the left hand and hold a break with the tip of the left little finger.

3. When the pass is made or the cards of the upper packet are shuffled off by an overhand shuffle, you have the chosen card seventh from the top and you can deal with it in any way you desire.

Many performers have a habit of showing that a chosen card is not on the top or bottom, inadvisedly overworking the double lift in so doing. By using this method of control, half a dozen of the top cards can be spread and shown face upwards and as many as you like from the bottom.

The Tap

A favorite subterfuge of many of the better card men is to push a selected card into the end of the deck, which is held at the finger tips, until it protrudes but a quarter of an inch. A light tap with the right forefinger will then drive the card through the deck, causing it to protrude minutely from the inner end.

A bad feature of this move is that, with a new pack, a distinct line can be noted at the outer end and this is clearly visible to the first sharp-eyed spectator. Usually this line is concealed by the left forefinger curling round the end of the deck, or by holding the deck so that the end cannot be seen. The method that follows is a novelty.

1. Hold the pack horizontally in the left hand by the ends between the tips of the thumb and the second and third fingers, the backs of the cards towards you and the back of the hand to the audience.

2. Take the card, which has been selected by a spectator, with its back towards you and insert it in the side of the deck. Push it down

until its upper side protrudes about a quarter of an inch only, Fig. 1, then tap it lightly with the right second finger, driving its lower side slightly out of the opposite side of the deck.

3. Take the upper right corner of the deck between the right thumb and fingers at A in Fig. 1, and place it in the left hand in position for dealing. The outer end is quite innocent and the left fingers, curling upwards, conceal the minute jog at the right side. When desired, the left little finger secures a break by pulling down on the protruding edge of the jogged card. The tap must not be an exaggerated one; the jog can be so minute that it is practically unnoticeable even if the side of the deck is exposed.

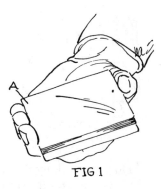

FIG 1

The Single Card Bridge

A single card can be bridged lengthwise instantly and without any possibility of detection in the following manner:

1. Hold the pack in the left hand in position for the overhand shuffle, with the lower side more nearly upon the middle of the left palm than is usual.

2. In this position, the tips of the left fingers rest against the face card near the upper side. As the right fingers undercut the pack to begin the shuffle, press the left fingers downwards, buckling the face card lengthwise, Fig. 1.

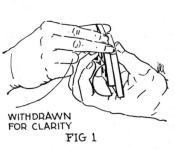

WITHDRAWN
FOR CLARITY
FIG 1

A card bridged in this manner makes an excellent key card which can be used with good effect in many tricks.

The move is by Charles Miller.

A New Glide

The Glide has done yeoman service for card conjurers for over two hundred years and is still a very useful sleight. It has, however, become rather widely known even outside the conjurers' coterie and the following method, equally easy and deceptive, may well be substituted for it.

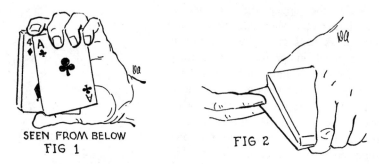

SEEN FROM BELOW
FIG 1

FIG 2

1. Hold the pack by the ends in the left hand between the thumb and fingers, with the third joint of the second finger resting on the face of the bottom card.

2. Raise the left hand to display the bottom card, then drop it to bring the pack parallel with the surface of the table and a few inches above it. Press the ball of the second finger on the bottom card, pull outwards slightly to free its inner end from the ball of the thumb and then press it towards the left, swinging the card diagonally half an inch off the pack, pivoting on the tip of the first finger, Fig. 1.

3. Press the ball of the right second finger against the exposed corner of the second bottom card, draw it out half an inch, drop the first finger on it and draw the card away, gripped thus at the very tips of the two fingers, Fig. 2. Reverse the action of the left second finger and swing the bottom card back, flush with the deck.

Establishing a Break from a Bridge

An excellent way of convincing spectators that a chosen card, returned to the deck, is honestly buried in it, is the familiar action of forming a break with the left little finger above the card, then, by squeezing the packet below the break between the little finger and the base of the thumb, to bridge this lower half at the inner end only, Fig. 1. The pack can then be turned end for end in the hands carelessly, thus tacitly demonstrating that all is fair. Further delay, by placing the pack on the table, with the bridged end innermost, while you talk, is also very convincing.

The chosen card can then be located by cutting, but this is a somewhat obvious procedure. To pick up the break in a guileless fashion, hold the pack in the left hand as for dealing and smooth the ends with the thumb and fingers of the right hand as if merely squaring them. By moving the thumb at the inner end lightly back and forth, the flesh of its ball will be forced into the smallest bridge and, slowly but surely, widen it until it is large enough for the insertion once again of the tip of the left little finger. This, of course, should be done without looking at the cards. The chosen card can then be controlled by the pass or shuffle as desired.

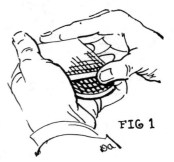

FIG 1

The reader will be surprised to find how tiny a bridge can be found and enlarged in this manner.

Transfer of Thumb-Count Break to the Little Finger

This move is a very valuable one, being especially useful when working at a table. Its purpose is, after the thumb has counted off a number of cards, to enable the left little finger to secure a break under these cards without using the right hand.

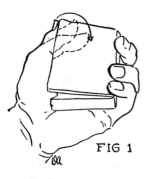

FIG 1

1. Hold the pack in the left hand in position for the thumb count, face outwards and vertically, the left forearm resting on the table, the inner left corner of the pack being pressed firmly against the fleshy mound at the base of the thumb.

2. Thumb count the desired number of cards and press the ball of the thumb against the side of the outer left corner of the lower packet, buckling the cards and forcing the inner left corner to slip free from the rest of the cards. Squeeze the inner end of the pack firmly so that a tiny part of the flesh at the base of the thumb is forced into the break, thus retaining it, Fig. 1.

3. Place the ball of the thumb on the back of the pack at the outer left corner and press downwards, Fig. 1. This action causes the counted

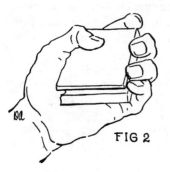

FIG 2

cards to buckle, the heel of the thumb acting as a fulcrum, the lower right corner of the packet moves upwards and the insertion of the left little finger becomes an easy matter, Fig. 2.

The sleight can also be useful as a get-set for double, triple and quadruple lifts. It can be made in seconds and is absolutely imperceptible, being covered by the position of the hand. Needless to say you do not even glance at the pack while making the move.

THE RUFFLE RETURN

This is a very easy and deceptive method of gaining control of a card after its replacement in the pack by a spectator. It is known to but few performers and has never before appeared in print.

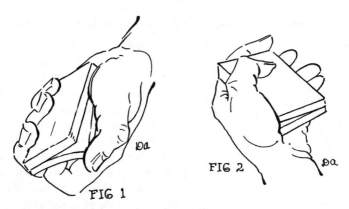

FIG 1   FIG 2

1. Hold the pack in the left hand between the second, third and fourth fingers at the left side, the forefinger curled at the face, the thumb lying along the left side of the pack. In this position the inner left corner presses against the heel of the left thumb.

2. Request the spectator to replace his card, extend the pack and allow the cards to escape from the ball of the thumb at the outer left corner, tacitly inviting the spectator to replace his card wherever he likes, Fig. 1.

3. After the card has been replaced and while the break at the left side, caused by the ruffle, is still open, press the flesh of the base of the thumb into the break at the inner left corner. At the same time fold the left thumb over the top of the pack, pressing downwards and closing the outer end of the deck, although the flesh of the base of the thumb continues to hold a break.

4. Because of the nature of the action, the spectator's card still extends for about half its length beyond the end of the pack. Reach out with the left forefinger and, pressing against the end of the card, force it inward flush with the pack.

5. The chosen card is now the bottom card of the packet above the break held by the small pinch of flesh at the base of the thumb. The deck appears to be perfectly regular and the tips of all the fingers are in sight, apparently precluding the holding of a break, Fig. 2.

Further control may be had by using the overhand or the Hindu shuffles, a pass or any preferred maneuver, the Hindu shuffle being particularly suitable. A notable feature of this method, aside from its use of the flesh-grip, is that the entire action is made by the left hand without any support from the right hand.

THE BRIDGE LOCATION

This method of controlling a spectator's card is so old that, like many another ruse, it may well have been overlooked by the present generation of card conjurers. Charles Bertram, the English entertainer, made great use of it before the turn of the century and has been generally identified with the stratagem. It is a useful weapon against the person who insists upon pushing his card back into the pack wherever he chooses.

Bertram's Method

Make a pressure fan of the cards, exerting enough downward pressure to give a pronounced bend to the cards. The spectator's card will thus have a downward bend. As it is looked at, quietly bend the ends of the pack upwards and immediately spread the pack from hand to hand for the return of the card. Square the pack and give it an overhand shuffle, or request the spectator to mix the cards, indicating by a motion of the hands that an overhand shuffle should be made. By resting the pack upon its side on the left fingers and placing the tip of the left thumb against the face of the bottom card (the pack facing to the left) the selected card is found and controlled, since the downward bend forms a break in the side of the loosely-held pack.

A Variation: Fifty Years Later

Make a pressure fan and have a card removed. Hold the pack at the ends with the right fingers and thumb and riffle half the deck off the thumb onto the left fingers. Make two end riffle shuffles, giving the cards a pronounced upward bend in so doing. Hold the pack by the right fingers at the ends above the flat left palm and again bend the ends upwards; allow the cards to spill from the right hand onto the outstretched left palm, at the same time requesting the spectator to replace his card anywhere he desires. The card is controlled subsequently in the same manner as in the Bertram version.

This deceptive handling is by Charles Miller.

THE MEXICAN TURNOVER

This useful sleight is well known to almost all card conjurers and used by very few of them. An expert can make the turnover upon any kind of surface, smooth or rough; but for the great mass of card conjurers the sleight is worrisome even when made upon green baize.

The sleight is this:

A card lies upon the table, face downwards. The right hand approaches with another card, held face downwards, and in the act of apparently using this card as an aid in flipping the first card face upwards a secret exchange is made of one card for the other.

The technique is this:

1. Grasp the card held by the right hand at the inner right corner between the tips of the right thumb and first finger.

2. Slide the left side of this card under the right side of the table card, the former card extending an inch beyond the outer end of the latter. Tip both cards upwards to a vertical position. Place the tip of the right second finger against the inner right corner of the table card and shift the thumb to this corner, grasping the card. Remove the table card to the left as the right first finger tips the other card face upwards on the table.

The novelty to be offered here, which makes the sleight a sinecure, is this: Before executing the sleight, place the tip of the left second finger upon the inner left corner of the table card, Fig. 1. Perform the sleight exactly as described above, but maintain a firm pressure throughout the action upon the corner of the table card with the left second finger tip. Thus, the table card is prevented from slipping upon a smooth surface. More important, this card is actually snatched from under the left finger; after the right hand card is slid under the table card it is moved upwards very swiftly and during this action the table card is jerked from under the left second finger, making possible an extremely quick action with a minimum of skill.

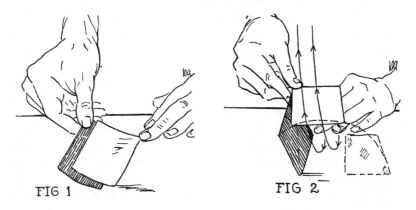

In Fig. 2 the table card is being lifted as the right first finger tip flips the other card over and face upwards. The action is extremely fast but the figure shows its nature as it might be seen if the action were stopped momentarily. The illusion is that the table card has flipped face upwards.

THE SPREAD CULL

In many tricks it is necessary to gather secretly a sequence of cards at the top or bottom of the pack. The following method enables the operator to accomplish this task while apparently running the cards in a casual spread from the left hand to the right.

Let us assume that you wish to gather the four aces at the top of the pack. Here is the procedure:

1. Hold the pack in the left hand as for dealing, but with the faces towards yourself, and with the left thumb push off the first of the face cards into the right hand. Continue moving the cards

from hand to hand with the thumbs resting on their faces, the fingers on their backs.

2. When, presently, an ace appears, place the tip of the left thumb upon it, drawing it back towards the left; at the same moment place the tips of the right fingers, at the back of the pack, upon the card to the left of the ace and draw it to the right, this card serving to screen the withdrawal to the left of the desired ace, Fig. 1.

3. With the left thumb slide the ace to the right over the faces of the spread cards until the tip of the right thumb can drop upon its face and draw it to the face of the deck. Continue this series of actions until the four aces have been brought to the bottom of the pack.

4. Thumb count the desired cards at the bottom and hold a break with the right thumb at the inner end as you turn the pack for an overhand shuffle. Undercut the pack at its center, shuffle off and drop the cards in the packet below the break as the last movement in the shuffle.

It should be noted particularly that the action in the preceding paragraph is far superior to the old method wherein a stock is brought from the bottom to the top by running the last few cards one by one, since it eliminates the necessity of slowing the shuffle and watching the cards.

The Double-Face

In certain card effects it is necessary to reverse both the top and bottom cards. Such a deck, apparently held face downwards, actually has fifty cards face upwards, the top and bottom cards face downwards. The double-face can be made quickly and with a minimum of actions in the following manner:

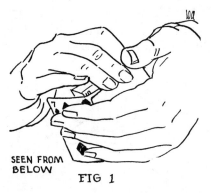

SEEN FROM BELOW

FIG 1

1. Hold the pack face up and reverse a card at the bottom in the act of turning the pack face downwards. (Facing the Bottom Card, page 110.) Omit the overhand shuffle.

2. Hold the pack as for dealing and place the right hand over it, grasping it at the ends. Buckle the bottom card, the card just reversed, with the tips of the left fingers by pressing inwards with them against the right edge of the card.

3. Place the tips of the left fingers upon the next card, the second from the bottom, and push it to the right so that it extends an inch from the pack, Fig. 1.

4. Repeat the actions for Facing the Bottom Card, but retain the projecting card which rests on the tips of the left fingers and place the pack, when it is turned over, upon this card.

There is now a card face downwards at the top, a card face downwards at the bottom. The remainder of the cards are face upwards.

Curiously enough, during the actions in No. 4 an attentive spectator would notice that there is a card face downwards at the top of the pack both before and after the turnover; more curiously still, those few who may penetrate the misdirection which should be used to protect the sleight are confused as to the status quo of the pack and are unable to follow the movements. Since the pack can immediately be handled to show it apparently in good order, these persons attribute the peculiar phenomenon to their own faulty observation.

The sleight, however, should be made when spectator-attention is not centered on the deck.

GAMBLERS' CARD MARKING SYSTEM

On first knowledge this method of marking cards may seem impractical for, without actual experience with the system, those who have been told the modus operandi will examine the cards, one by one, and insist that no eye can be so keen as to distinguish one from the other by the secret markings.

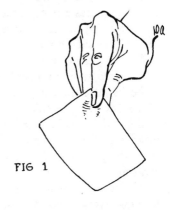

FIG 1

With a minimum of practice, however, the cards can be read as easily from the backs as from the faces. The principle originally was used by card sharps for marking cards during the course of a game—the cards marked being, naturally, those of the highest rank. For conjuring purposes, a few cards or the entire deck may be marked.

The principle is this: 1. Take a card at the inner left corner between the thumb and second finger on its face, the forefinger on the back. By pressing the thumb and second finger upward, the forefinger down, a grooved crimp is formed in the corner of the card, Fig. 1. This indicates an ace.

2. By the same process, place a grooved crimp in the center of the end. This indicates a three.

3. The grooved crimp, at the right inner corner, indicates a five.

4. An inch above this corner, at the right side, place a grooved crimp to indicate a seven.

5. In the middle of the right side, the grooved crimp indicates a nine.

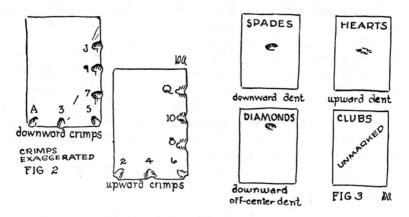

6. An inch from the outer right corner, the grooved crimp indicates a jack.

Turn the cards face up. The grooved crimp placed in the inner left corner indicates a two; in the center of the inner end, a four; at the right corner, a six; an inch above the right corner, an eight; at the middle of the right side, a ten; an inch below the outer right corner, a queen.

The king is not marked.

If desired, the cards may be marked on all four sides, for ease in reading.

To indicate the suits, place the thumbnail at the middle of the back of a spade and press down, making a dent; for a heart, make the dent in the middle of the face; for a diamond, hold the card face down and make the dent off-center; leave the clubs unmarked. Figures 2 and 3 show the placement of the crimps and dents to key the denominations and suits.

The grooved crimp so applied is not a deep crimp; it is applied lightly, forming a very minor depression for odd cards (or protuberance for even cards) in the backs of the cards, which can be clearly noted when the pack is held so that the light shines upon its glazed back. Movement of the pack in the hand no more than a quarter of an inch will shift the glaze thus highlighting the markings.

With the cards marked in this fashion, a close examination will not betray the secret; indeed, as has been noted, even after one is familiar with the system, unless experience with it has been had, it is practically impossible to detect the markings.

When using a strange pack, the cards may be marked one at a time at convenient moments; it is surprising, with eight or ten such marked cards in the pack, what use can be made of them. For impromptu work, if the borrowed pack is taken from the room, the deck may be marked in a matter of minutes.

Chapter 15

THE REAR PALM

For MANY YEARS certain expert card men have realized the advantages which may be had by the palming of cards in such a manner that the fingers of the hand could be spread wide without disclosing the palmed card. In the past, however, it has been used more as a flourish than as a sleight; Max Malini, for instance, whose hands are very small, has used the palm as a means of catching a single card from the air. Larsen and Wright, in their *Notebook*, suggest the idea for use as a color change; P. W. Miller, in 1938, evolved the same idea while working upon a gamblers' move known as "capping the deck"; M. Latapie palmed cards crosswise in the palm, being a man with an unusually large hand; and the same basic principle, that of palming a card at the rear of the palm, is presented in *La Prestidigitateur* for March, 1932, the action of the palm being concealed by placing the hand in a hat.

It is indeed a natural progression for a card man to order his thinking from the natural palm to the rear palm, for the benefits of such a palm are all too obvious. That the palm, however, was regarded as something of a freak and of little practical value is shown by the uses to which it was put.

The first obstacle placed in the path of those who wish to utilize the rear palm is that of placing the card in this palm as secretly and as easily as in placing a card in the regular palm. Once this difficulty is met and overcome, the rear palm becomes one of the most useful sleights, with which feats may be performed not possible by any other means.

The method of rear palming to be described has been used over a period of years and has proved its practicability and value. Its deceptiveness may be illustrated by offering the instance in which one of the six finest American card men, upon being shown feats dependent on the system, was entirely nonplussed and at a loss to explain the method by which the feats were accomplished, although the sleight was used repeatedly and this expert's eyes were upon the operator's hands at all times.

THE NATURE OF THE PALM

The rear palm is exactly what its name implies, the palming of a card at the rear of the palm, so that the fingers may be spread wide and the card remain hidden.

1. Turn your right palm upward and place a card upon it, with the outer end paralleling the roots of the fingers, the inner end paralleling the creases at the wrist.

2. Place the second finger of the left hand upon the center of the card and press downward. Bend the right thumb inward, at the same time flexing the base of the little finger in a movement which simulates the action in palming a billiard ball. The card, creasing, will be retained firmly in the palm, Fig. 1.

FIG 1

3. Invert the right hand and the card will be retained in the rear palm, with the fingers spread wide. With practice, the fingers may be moved independently without dislodging the card.

Control of the card will at first be found difficult, as it will tend to slip or spring from the grip. It actually is retained in the palm by the pressure of the base of the thumb, against which it presses but by which it is not gripped, the flesh at the root of the little finger acting as a check against this pressure. Figure 4 shows another view of the palm and shows how the inner right corner is curled back under the base of the thumb.

REAR PALMING THE TOP CARD

In this action the card is moved from the regular palm to the rear palm and it is this action which makes the rear palm of practical value.

1. Palm a card from the top of the pack by any method, but preferably

FIG 2   FIG 3

by means of the one-hand top palm, explained in the footnote on page 177, and hold the hand palm downwards.

2. Bend the second finger inwards, Fig. 2, and move the second and third fingers inward until the card has been pushed backward to the position shown in Fig. 3. The outer edge of the card presses against the phalange between the third and second joints of the second finger; the tip of the bent second finger, pressing inward upon the face of the card, prevents it from dropping from the hand.

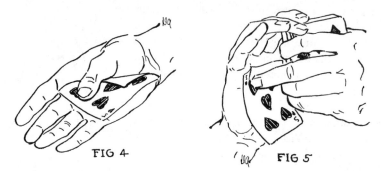

FIG 4   FIG 5

3. Contract the base of the thumb and the flesh at the root of the little finger as the second finger continues to press its tip firmly against the center of the card near the outer end, Fig. 3. This pressure is maintained until the card is gripped between the bases of the thumb and the little finger. The palm is made as the fingers curl naturally into the palm, as in Figs. 1–3.

4. Straighten the fingers and the card will be retained in the rear palm, as in Fig. 4.

On his first attempts to perform the sleight the reader is almost certain to be rewarded with dismal failure; the card will slip and drop from the hand if it is held palm downwards. For this reason it is suggested that, until the knack is acquired, the sleight be practiced with the palm upwards. Facility will come with practice and then the move should be made palm downwards until it can be made noiselessly and with dead certainty. The transfer of the card from the regular to the rear palm should be made in the time it takes normally to curl the fingers inward.

Until the method of gripping the card has been learned, the card may be pressed more firmly into the rear palm, should it begin to slip, with the second finger of the left hand as the right hand squares the ends of the pack, or rests lightly over it, Fig. 5. It is suggested however, that the reader first learn to make the palm without such assistance from the left hand until by practice the muscles of the right hand retain the card without danger of dropping it. If the most difficult action of the various sleights to be described is learned well, the other phases will be more easily mastered.

The Bottom Rear Palm

The purpose of this extremely useful sleight is to take a card from the bottom of the pack into the rear palm. The card moves directly into the palm without any intermediate action; it is quick, certain and indetectible.

1. Hold the pack face downwards in the left hand and square the ends with the right fingers and thumb.

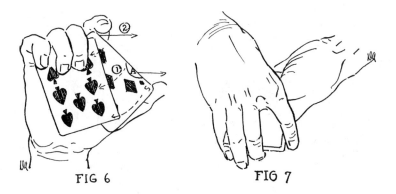

FIG 6   FIG 7

2. Grasp the pack with the right hand, the thumb at the inner left corner and the fingers at the outer end, with the finger tips pressing up against the face of the bottom card. Move the bottom card diagonally to the right by a pressure of these finger tips. Figure 6 shows this action as seen from below, with the card to be palmed directly under the right palm.

3. Grasp the pack at the point marked A in Fig. 6 and remove it to the left, the pressure of the right second and third finger tips retaining the pivoted card under the right hand as in Fig. 3.

4. Take the card into the rear palm by pressing against its face with the second finger tip and by contracting the base of the thumb and the flesh at the root of the little finger.

5. Grip the pack as in Fig. 7 as you square the cards. Press the card more firmly into the rear palm with the tip of the left second finger, if this is necessary, in an action similar to that shown in Fig. 5.

Note that when the pack is gripped as in Fig. 7, the back of the pack can be seen through the widely spread first and second fingers. To those looking at the hand, it is apparently clear that a card could not be palmed. For this reason, this grip is a very good one and is resorted to whenever the right hand covers the deck.

The Rear Palm Side Slip

By this means a card returned to the pack by a spectator is taken into the rear palm and brought to the top.

1. Riffle the pack for the return of the card. Press on the inner end allowing it to be pushed half-way into the deck. Hold the pack in the left hand as for dealing, the thumb extending across towards the second finger.

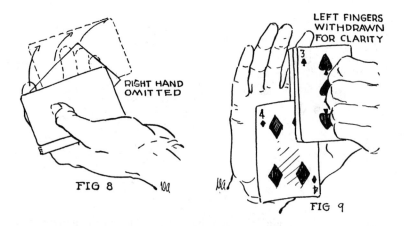

RIGHT HAND OMITTED

FIG 8

LEFT FINGERS WITHDRAWN FOR CLARITY

FIG 9

2. Place the right fingers at the outer end of the card and apparently push it into the deck. Actually push it to the left and diagonally through, the right first finger controlling the movement of the card at the left corner and sliding down the left side of the pack on this corner as the card moves diagonally through the deck, Fig. 8.

3. Place the tips of the left second, third and fourth fingers upon the face of the card and push it to the right and inward in a swinging action which moves the card into the final position shown in Fig. 8, in which the right hand has been omitted for clarity.

4. Remove the right fingers from the pack and press the card upwards against the palm with the left fingers. In Fig. 9 the position of the card is shown from below, the left fingers having been withdrawn to show how a corner of the card remains in the pack at the inner right corner.

5. Move the pack straight forward with the left hand, parallel to the right first finger, the right hand remaining motionless, its fingers curling naturally, taking the card into the rear palm. The right hand should remain motionless during this action, for if it is moved there

will be a sharp tell-tale click as the outer left corner of the card scrapes against the edge of the pack.

6. Square the pack at the ends with the right fingers and grip it as shown in Fig. 7. Replace the card at the top as described under Replacement.

The sleight is best performed under cover of a slow movement of the hands to the left at the end of which the pack is held vertically in the left hand and the card is in the rear palm as shown in Fig. 13. This side slip is so deceptive that it can be used in the Ambitious Card Trick, with attention centered on the hands, and pass undetected.

THE LITTLE FINGER PUSH-OUT

In this method the card above a break held by the left little finger is slipped to the top of the pack by means of the rear palm. This method

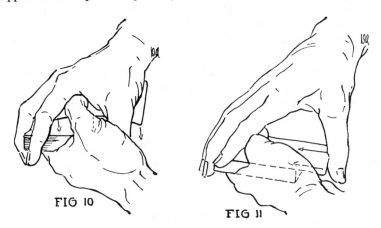

FIG 10 FIG 11

is of greater general utility than the preceding method since it can be used in a wider range of effects.

1. Hold the pack in the left hand as for dealing, the left little finger holding a break under the desired card.

2. Place the right hand over the pack, the fingers at the outer end and the thumb at the inner end near the left corner.

3. Press the tip of the little finger up against the face of the desired card and push it out into the first position shown in Fig. 8. Place the tips of the second, third and fourth fingers upon the face of the card and swing it to the right and inward into the second position shown in Fig. 9, the action being concealed by the back of the right

hand, the right hand being dropped so that its palm is on the same plane as the pack.

4. Perform the actions described in the preceding method, from 4 through 6.

REPLACEMENT

A card is replaced upon the pack after being rear palmed in the right hand in the following manner:

1. Hold the pack in the left hand as for dealing, with the thumb pointing to the second finger. Square the deck with the right hand, which has a card in the rear palm, and finally grip it as in Fig. 7.

2. Slant the pack upwards at the outer end. Lift the left thumb and thrust it into the arch formed by the right thumb and first finger, sliding it between the palm and the rear-palmed card, Fig. 10. Press the card down upon the top of the pack, its inner end protruding an inch and a half beyond the pack. This action is concealed by the back of the hand.

3. Lift the right thumb at the inner end, press it against the end of the card and push it forward onto the pack, Fig. 11.

The replacement is noiseless and is made in a matter of seconds, the hands moving slowly from left to right. On the evidence of his eyes, few spectators would be willing to claim that a card had either been palmed or replaced.

THE REAR PALM EXCHANGE

This makes an excellent addition to the list of good card switches.

1. Remove the two top cards as one and grasp them in the right hand as shown in Fig. 12, which shows the sleight at a later stage but which nevertheless depicts the nature of the grip. One end of the cards rests on the second joint of the second finger, the innermost joint of the little finger. The thumb is at the upper end.

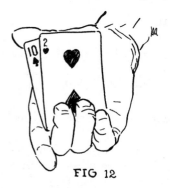

FIG 12

2. Turn the hand palm down, at the same time pressing the face card of the two to the right with the tips of the fingers, Fig. 12, the thumb still at the end of the top card. Continue this action until the position is that shown in Fig. 6, as seen from below.

3. Grasp this card at the point marked A in Fig. 6 and remove it with the left hand, handing it face downwards to a spectator or placing

it on the table to one side. The right hand curls naturally into the position shown in Fig. 13.

4. Pick up the pack with the left hand and grip it with the right hand as in Fig. 7.

5. Continue your trick, at the first opportune moment replacing the palmed card on the pack as described under Replacement.

In Lieu of the Double Lift

Those tricks dependent upon the double lift can be performed with added effect through use of the rear palm.

1. Rear palm a card in the right hand, either from the top or from the bottom, the latter being the better procedure. Face to the left, the hands at the level of the waist, the right hand close to the body.

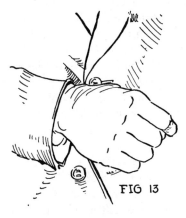

FIG 13

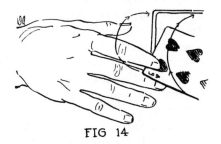

FIG 14

2. Push the top card off the pack with the left thumb and clip it between the right first and second fingers, Fig. 14. Turn it face upwards on the pack. Repeat the procedure, turning it face downwards. Turn the card in this manner several times to impress without so stating that it is a single card.

3. Square the pack as in Fig. 7, at the same time moving it directly in front of the body. During this action replace the palmed card as previously described.

The card which the spectators believe to be at the top is now actually second from the top.

Using the Rear Palm

In most cases where the regular palm is required the action is made when the onlookers have no reason to suspect a palm and the palm and subsequent replacement are made under cover of natural actions. Since the standard palm is perfectly deceptive, when used under these conditions it would be foolish not to make use of it.

The use of the rear palm, however, can and does turn certain other feats into extremely puzzling mysteries. By reserving the rear palm as a secret weapon for use in these tricks the conjurer can get the maximum effect from the sleight. For instance, its use just once in an Ambitious Card routine will serve to upset any spectator who may have thought that he perceived how the trick was being worked.

There are certain contingencies which must be guarded against when using the rear palm. Because of the manner in which the inner corner of the card curls downward under pressure of the base of the thumb, the hand must not be tipped into the horizontal if there are persons on the right whose line of sight is below the level of the hand. After a very little experiment the sight-lines to be guarded against become apparent and, in using the palm, the conjurer keeps these restrictions in mind.

It should also be remembered that the only justification for the rear palm is that, by enabling those present to look between the fingers, it discounts in advance the possibility of palming cards. For this reason when the pack is gripped as in Fig. 7 the position should be held long enough so that those who look at the hands will note the apparent impossibility of palming.

Moreover, because palming apparently *is* impossible, all sleights dependent upon the rear palm should be performed in a leisurely fashion. The tendency to rush should be fought, for in this palm after those present have glanced at the right hand and noted that it could not have a palmed card, they thereafter are not watchful for palming: they see the pack and the empty hand, decide that all is fair and their vigilance relaxes.

Chapter 16
THE PERFECT FARO SHUFFLE

J. N. MASKELYNE, DESCRIBING THE FARO dealer's shuffle, has written: "This shuffle is a very difficult one to learn; but with practice and patience it can be accomplished, and the cards can be made to fly up alternately, without any chance of failure. . . . It must not be thought that this manipulative device is essentially a trick for cheating; on the contrary, it is an exceedingly fair and honest shuffle, provided that there is no previous arrangement of the cards. . . . "

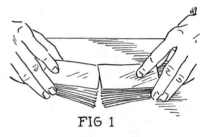

FIG 1

The method described by Maskelyne in *Sharps and Flats* is indeed a difficult one to learn. It is necessary to buckle the cards breadthwise by strongly pressing the ends together, the tension of the cards springing them together.

The method to be described is very easily learned. The cards are not buckled and the element of tension, which makes the control of the cards difficult, is absent.

1. Prior to attempting the shuffle, place the right fingers at one end of the pack, the thumb at the other, and bridge the cards across their width very slightly, making the backs convex. The bridge should not be so strong that it is noticeable.

2. Cut the pack at twenty-six, taking the upper half in the right hand. Hold the packets at the outer ends, near the corners, between the thumbs at the inner sides, the second and third fingers at the outer sides, Fig. 1. Hold the forefingers of both hands above the packets throughout the shuffle and do not allow them to touch the packets at any time.

3. Place the inner ends of the packets together so that they are parallel and touching. Raise the outer ends an inch and a half, Fig. 1. The packets resemble a very shallow V and the inner ends, touching and parallel at the apex of the V, press lightly against one another. They should not be forced together, for the shuffle is made not by

springing the cards by tension but by causing them to mesh in the manner to be described.

4. To make the shuffle: squeeze inward with the second and third fingers and the thumb of each hand, bridging the cards lengthwise. This causes the cards of each packet to straighten and hence move upwards, meshing perfectly. This mesh is made without either hand moving, the squeezing pressure alone causing the cards to weave, and the top card of the right packet should weave above that of the left packet (the twenty-seventh card).

5. Continue to squeeze the packets and at the same time, now that shuffle has been started, lift the inner ends of both packets off the table, the outer ends being moved downwards by the thumb and fingers of each hand. The ball of each thumb rests almost parallel to the side of the packet it grips, and when so held and the pressure is applied to bridge the cards lengthwise, the mesh of the cards, as it progresses from the bottom to the top of the packets, can be felt.

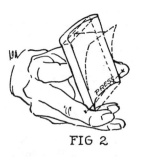

FIG 2

The cards can be made to weave upward with amazing rapidity, or to mesh slowly, at the desire of the operator, this depending upon the degree of pressure applied in squeezing the packets.

To understand the character of the shuffle, hold a pack of cards at the sides near the outer corners between the right thumb and second and third finger. Bend down the bottom card with the left first finger and release it, allowing it to spring back to the face of the pack. It does so without any great force.

Now hold the pack in the hands as in Fig. 2. Crease the top card as shown by the ghost card, so that it curves away from the pack, which is shown in this figure in its normal condition by the ghost outline. Press the inner ends of the pack, forming the concave pack shown in the drawing, and the card will snap back with great force, bridging exactly in conformity with the rest of the pack. This is the principle applied in making the perfect faro shuffle: the pack is bridged across its width, making the pack convex. The pressure of the fingers places a lengthwise convex bridge in the pack which removes the bridge across the width of the pack and straightens the cards, causing the inner ends of the packets to move upwards as little as a sixteenth of an inch, sufficient to cause the cards to weave.

The shuffle may be made with bridge cards but it is much more difficult as these narrower cards require greater strength in the fingers if they are to be bridged lengthwise. The cards used should be new or in good condition.

THE SHUFFLE

The following chart shows the movement of the cards through eight perfect shuffles. In each shuffle the pack must be cut at 26, the right hand holding the cards from 1 to 26, the left the cards from 27 to 52. In making the shuffles, the first card of the pack remains always at the top of the pack, the first card of the left hand packet (27) meshing under the right hand top card into the number 2 position. The 52nd card of the pack, the last of the left hand packet, remains always at the bottom of the pack, meshing under the 26th card of the right hand packet.

After the first shuffle an interval of 26 separates the cards; for instance, the first card remains 1, the second is the original 27. After a second shuffle, the interval is 13; the first card remains 1, the second is the original 14th card. In the third shuffle, the interval is 32; the fourth, 16; the fifth, 8; the sixth, 4; the seventh, 2; and after the eighth shuffle the pack is in its original order.

After each shuffle, a differing number of cards lie between each consecutive card of the original sequence:

After the first shuffle, one card: *1*, 27, *2*, 28, *3*, 29. . . .
After the second shuffle, three cards: *1* 14 37 40; *2* 15 28 41.
After the third shuffle, seven cards: *1* 33 14 46 27 8 40 21; *2*.
After the fourth shuffle, fifteen cards.
After the fifth shuffle, thirty-one cards.
After the sixth shuffle, twelve cards.
After the seventh shuffle, twenty-five cards.

After each shuffle, the cards move double their own number less one. The tenth card moves to twenty, less one: it will be found at nineteen. When this total exceeds fifty-two, fifty-two is deducted from it: for instance, the forty-fourth card doubled totals eighty-eight; deduct fifty-two and the card will be found at twenty-six.

It should be noted that, for convenience, the charts read from left to right, rather than vertically.

It may be well to point out at this time that, although these charts have an academic flavor, the knowledge contained therein will be found to be of great utility, as will be shown later, when the regular shuffle is used; their study will thus prove profitable.

Original Order

1	2	3	4	5	6	7	8
9	10	11	12	13	14	15	16
17	18	19	20	21	22	23	24
25	26	27	28	29	30	31	32
33	34	35	36	37	38	39	40
41	42	43	44	45	46	47	48
49	50	51	52				

1st Shuffle

1	27	2	28	3	29	4	30
5	31	6	32	7	33	8	34
9	35	10	36	11	37	12	38
13	39	14	40	15	41	16	42
17	43	18	44	19	45	20	46
21	47	22	48	23	49	24	50
25	51	26	52				

5th Shuffle

1	9	17	25	33	41	49	6
14	22	30	38	46	3	11	19
27	35	43	51	8	16	24	32
40	48	5	13	21	29	37	45
2	10	18	26	34	42	50	7
15	23	31	39	47	4	12	20
28	36	44	52				

2nd Shuffle

1	14	27	40	2	15	28	41
3	16	29	42	4	17	30	43
5	18	31	44	6	19	32	45
7	20	33	46	8	21	34	47
9	22	35	48	10	23	36	49
11	24	37	50	12	25	38	51
13	26	39	52				

6th Shuffle

1	5	9	13	17	21	25	29
33	37	41	45	49	2	6	10
14	18	22	26	30	34	38	42
46	50	3	7	11	15	19	23
27	31	35	39	43	47	51	4
8	12	16	20	24	28	32	36
40	44	48	52				

3rd Shuffle

1	33	14	46	27	8	40	21
2	34	15	47	28	9	41	22
3	35	16	48	29	10	42	23
4	36	17	49	30	11	43	24
5	37	18	50	31	12	44	25
6	38	19	51	32	13	45	26
7	39	20	52				

7th Shuffle

1	3	5	7	9	11	13	15
17	19	21	23	25	27	29	31
33	35	37	39	41	43	45	47
49	51	2	4	6	8	10	12
14	16	18	20	22	24	26	28
30	32	34	36	38	40	42	44
46	48	50	52				

4th Shuffle

1	17	33	49	14	30	46	11
27	43	8	24	40	5	21	37
2	18	34	50	15	31	47	12
28	44	9	25	41	6	22	38
3	19	35	51	16	32	48	13
29	45	10	26	42	7	23	39
4	20	36	52				

8th Shuffle

1	2	3	4	5	6	7	8
9	10	11	12	13	14	15	16
17	18	19	20	21	22	23	24
25	26	27	28	29	30	31	32
33	34	35	36	37	38	39	40
41	42	43	44	45	46	47	48
49	50	51	52				

The Endless Belts

The following chart shows the nature and movement of the six groups of eight cards each which move through the pack during the eight perfect shuffles required to re-establish a pack in its original order.

The cards which compose each group move like an endless belt. The first group includes the 2nd, 3rd, 5th, 9th, 17th, 33rd, 14th and 27th cards of the pack in its original order. After the first shuffle each card moves one step, into the number formerly held by the card next in the sequence. Thus, the 2nd card becomes the 3rd, the 3rd moves to 5, 5 to 9, 9 to 17, 17 to 33, 33 to 14, 14 to 27. The 27th card, the last of the group, moves into the 2nd position.

It will be noted that, in the course of eight shuffles, the 2nd card is progressively the 3rd, the 5th, the 9th, the 17th, the 33rd, the 14th

The Endless Belts

Shuffle:	1	2	3	4	5	6	7	8
2	3	5	9	17	33	14	27	2
4	7	13	25	49	46	40	28	4
6	11	21	41	30	8	15	29	6
10	19	37	22	43	34	16	31	10
12	23	45	38	24	47	42	32	12
20	39	26	51	50	48	44	36	20
18	35	18	35	18	35	18	35	18
1	1	1	1	1	1	1	1	1
52	52	52	52	52	52	52	52	52

and the 27th card of the pack. After the next, the eighth, shuffle, the 2nd card returns to its original position.

This movement of the endless belts is characteristic of each of the six groups of eight cards each. The remaining four cards move in this manner: The first card, as has been explained, remains always at the top, the 52nd always at the bottom. The 18th and 35th cards move between themselves; after the first shuffle, the 18th card is at 35, the 35th card at 18. After a second shuffle, the 18th card returns to its original position, as does the 35th.

The Chart of Seventeen

Showing how, through eight shuffles, the forty-eight cards are sub-divided into cells of three, each of which is removed by seventeen from its other units; and how, although the order may change, the same three remain always separated by seventeen.

After the first shuffle, the 2nd card is the original 27th card; the 19th is the original 10th card; the 36th is the original 44th card. Each of these cards was originally separated from its fellows by 17 degrees; after a shuffle, each card remains separated by 17. After a second shuffle, the 3rd card is the original 27th card; the 20th card is the original 44th; the 37th card is the original 10th card.

Through continuing shuffles, although the positions of the cards may change, the relation of each of the three cards in a cell remains constantly at 17.

THE CHART OF SEVENTEEN

1st Shuffle

1	27	2	28	3	29	4	30	5	31	6	32	7	33	8	34	9
35	10	36	11	37	12	38	13	39	14	40	15	41	16	42	17	43
18	44	19	45	20	46	21	47	22	48	23	49	24	50	25	51	26
52

2nd Shuffle

1	14	27	40	2	15	28	41	3	16	29	42	4	17	30	43	5
18	31	44	6	19	32	45	7	20	33	46	8	21	34	47	9	22
35	48	10	23	36	49	11	24	37	50	12	25	38	51	13	26	39
52

3rd Shuffle

1	33	14	46	27	8	40	21	2	34	15	47	28	9	41	22	3
35	16	48	29	10	42	23	4	36	17	49	30	11	43	24	5	37
18	50	31	12	44	25	6	38	19	51	32	13	45	26	7	39	20
52

4th Shuffle

1	17	33	49	14	30	46	11	27	43	8	24	40	5	21	37	2
18	34	50	15	31	47	12	28	44	9	25	41	6	22	38	3	19
35	51	16	32	48	13	29	45	10	26	42	7	23	39	4	20	36
52

5th Shuffle

1	9	17	25	33	41	49	6	14	22	30	38	46	3	11	19	27
35	43	51	8	16	24	32	40	48	5	13	21	29	37	45	2	10
18	26	34	42	50	7	15	23	31	39	47	4	12	20	28	36	44
52

6th Shuffle

1	5	9	13	17	21	25	29	33	37	41	45	49	2	6	10	14
18	22	26	30	34	38	42	46	50	3	7	11	15	19	23	27	31
35	39	43	47	51	4	8	12	16	20	24	28	32	36	40	44	48
52																

7th Shuffle

1	3	5	7	9	11	13	15	17	19	21	23	25	27	29	31	33
35	37	39	41	43	45	47	49	51	2	4	6	8	10	12	14	16
18	20	22	24	26	28	30	32	34	36	38	40	42	44	46	48	50
52																

8th Shuffle

1	2	3	4	5	6	7	8	9	10	11	12	13	14	15	16	17
18	19	20	21	22	23	24	25	26	27	28	29	30	31	32	33	34
35	36	37	38	39	40	41	42	43	44	45	46	47	48	49	50	51
52																

PERFECT SHUFFLE STOCK

In certain card tricks it is necessary to place a set-up sequence of cards at the top of the pack with an indifferent card between each card of the sequence. The procedure in the past has been to use the overhand shuffle. Use of the perfect shuffle enables the performer to make the set up easily in one quick shuffle.

Preparation. Let us say that you are performing An Indetectible Stop Trick, *Card Manipulations*, No. 5, and that you wish to place a nine, seven, five, three and ace at four, six, eight, ten and twelve from the top. Place the set-up, the nine being the first card, at the top of the pack, in which the bottom card has had its inner left corner crimped upwards.

Method. 1. Cut the pack at about forty and complete the cut. The crimped card and the set-up below it are placed at about twelve, continuing down to about eighteen.

2. Cut the pack at or near twenty-six (an unbalanced cut is permissible if it is within two or three of twenty-six) and take the upper packet with the right hand, the crimped corner being at the right end of this packet. Make a single perfect shuffle, meshing the cards in the middle but, if you like, riffling the last few cards at the top of each packet irregularly.

3. Square the pack and cut the crimped card to the top. The third, fifth, seventh, ninth and eleventh cards will be the nine, seven, five, three and ace respectively. Place a single card at the top, by means

of the side slip or a quick overhand shuffle, to place these cards at the required four, six, eight, ten and twelve.

When it is desired to place cards at even numbers, the procedure is the same but the extra card is not placed at the top as in 3. The movement of the cards in these shuffles is shown in the charts at the beginning of this section.

THE EIGHTEENTH CARD

Of considerable practical value is the knowledge that, in a perfect shuffle, the eighteenth card moves to the thirty-fifth position after the first shuffle; returns to eighteen after a second shuffle; returns to thirty-five after a third shuffle, and continues shuttling between these numbers with each successive shuffle.

This knowledge can be put to use in this manner: Have the chosen card returned at eighteen by any of the various methods in use. Hand the pack to the spectator immediately and request him to shuffle it. If he is a fairly smooth shuffler and cuts at or very near twenty-six, after two shuffles his card will have returned to eighteen, or be very near it.

This again is a method in which the performer must run the risk of failure but which, successful, can be very impressive. The card is discovered by any of the various emergency methods.

BRAUE POKER DEAL

This exceedingly simple feat makes one of the best demonstrations of skill at gamblers' sleights which it is possible to use. It will be found to make a strong impression upon those who see it performed.

Effect: The four aces are dropped upon the pack, which is shuffled. Four poker hands are dealt and the conjurer shows that he has dealt himself the four aces. If desired, the five cards of a royal flush may be used in place of the aces.

Method: 1. Secretly place a downward crimp in the inner left corner of the bottom card of the pack.

2. Show the four aces and drop them upon the top of the pack; place it upon the table so that the crimped corner is on the side nearest yourself, the crimp being on the right side.

3. Cut the pack near the twenty-sixth card and complete the cut. The crimped key card is now at the middle of the pack. Cut fifteen cards from the top and complete the cut. The crimped card is now at about the eleventh card.

These cuts are made with the apparent purpose of losing the aces in the pack.

4. Make an unbalanced cut, taking approximately the top twenty-

three cards in the right hand. Make a single perfect shuffle by any of the methods and square the pack.

5. Sight the position of the crimped card, which will be somewhere between the twentieth and twenty-fifth card, and cut enough cards from the top to bring the crimped key card back to the tenth or eleventh positions. Complete the cut.

6. Make an unbalanced cut, taking approximately twenty-three cards from the top into the right hand packet. Make another perfect shuffle.

7. Cut to and including the crimped key card and complete the cut. The key is now at the bottom. Make one or two false cuts.

8. Deal four poker hands of five cards each. The four aces will fall to you on the deal.

THE ROYAL FLUSH DEAL

Place the five cards of a royal flush at the top of the pack as you promise to show how gamblers control cards. Follow the procedure exactly as described above and the five cards of the royal flush will fall to you on the deal.

DISHONESTY AT ITS APOGEE

This is another demonstration of skill at gamblers' feats, utilizing the perfect shuffle.

Effect. After a free cut, the conjurer deals any number of stud poker hands. As the deal progresses he names, from time to time, the cards before they are dealt, or the names of concealed hole cards.

Preparation. Secretly secure at the top of the pack ten cards in any set sequence with which you are familiar. For effectiveness, these should be predominantly aces and court cards.

Method. 1. Make a casual overhand shuffle as you state that you will show how gamblers cheat at cards, retaining the stock of ten at the top.

2. Make an unbalanced cut, taking the top twenty-three cards (approximately) in the right hand. Make a single perfect shuffle. The mesh starting at the bottom, three or four of the top cards of the left packet will drop as one at the top of the pack.

3. Make a strip-out false shuffle, page 67, and follow this by genuinely cutting the pack at twenty-six, completing this cut.

The condition is this: The first card of the memorized sequence is a few cards below twenty-six; two cards below it is the second card; two below this is the third card, and so on to the tenth card, which is near fifty-two.

4. As an afterthought, place the pack before a spectator and invite him to cut. If possible, choose a man whom you may have noted cuts at or near twenty-six. When this cut is completed the stocked sequence will be brought near the top of the pack.

5. Ask how many hands of stud poker shall be dealt. Deal this number of face-down hole cards and upon each deal a card face upwards. Look over these cards and note which of the sequence appear. Knowing the original position of these cards in the sequence, it is possible to tell if any of the hole cards are sequence cards, and also to determine the positions and names of sequence cards which remain near the top of the pack. For instance, you have dealt a five-handed game; and the exposed card of the fifth hand dealt is the fifth card of the sequence, the exposed card of the third player is the fourth card of the sequence, and the exposed card of the first player is the third card. You therefore know that the concealed hole card of the fourth player is the second sequence card, the hole card of the second player is the first sequence card.

Further, you know the name of the second card from the top of the pack (the sixth sequence card), the fourth card (the seventh sequence card), the sixth card (the eighth card) and so on.

This knowledge should be revealed in as amusing a manner as possible. For instance, you deal a card face upwards to the first player. Before dealing to the second player say, "This ace of diamonds may help your hand," and deal him the ace of diamonds. "On the other hand," you continue, pointing to the fourth player, whose hole card you know to be the ace of hearts, "I'll wager he'd like to have that diamond ace, particularly since he has the ace of hearts in the hole."

Deal the next card, an indifferent card, without comment. Knowing the name of the next card, you can name this before dealing it. You can also peek at the index of an indifferent card, using the method on page 100, but this should not be overdone; once or twice is more than enough. By gradually revealing the names of the sequence cards as the deal progresses you create the impression that you know the names of all the cards.

When the last of the sequence cards has been dealt, look about you, say, "I don't think you want to play cards with me," gather the cards and continue with other feats.

A BRIDGE DEAL

This feat is an excellent one with which to dazzle the bridge expert who wishes to know what a card expert can do with a pack of cards. It calls for the ability to cut at twenty-six and to make a perfect shuffle in which the top card of the pack always remains at the top, dropping off the right thumb above the first card of the left hand packet (the twenty-seventh card), if the riffle method is used. If the faro method is used, the first card in this case springs up before the twenty-seventh card.

Effect. Four bridge hands are dealt and the players remember as many of their cards as possible, or list these cards. The conjurer assembles the pack, shuffles, and deals to each player the hand he originally held.

Method. 1. Deal four bridge hands and invite the players to remember their cards. Gather the hands in order, clockwise from left to right.

2. Cut the pack exactly at twenty-six, taking the upper half in the right hand. Make a perfect shuffle, the first card of the right packet weaving above the first card of the left packet and, consequently, the bottom card of the right packet weaving above the bottom card of the left packet, the fifty-second, which always remains at the bottom in a perfect shuffle.

3. Cut the pack exactly at twenty-six as before and repeat the shuffle.

4. Make a single strip-out false shuffle, page 67, letting it be seen that the cards are mixed indiscriminately, and make a false cut.

5. Deal the cards into four hands in the usual manner and each player will hold the cards of his original hand.

The pack is now offered for the cut to the spectator at the right. To do this, cut the pack after the two shuffles and bridge the lower half. Place before the player at the right so that he will cut into the bridge.

Cutting at twenty-six is not nearly so difficult as it may seem. In acquiring the knack, blacken the edge of a single card and place it at twenty-six with the darkened side edge away from you, so that it cannot be seen. A glance at this edge tells you if the cut has been accurate without the bother of counting the cards.

The accuracy of the cut can be gauged when the two packets are placed side by side for the shuffle. If the cut has been faulty, use the strip-out shuffle and cut at twenty-six again for the perfect shuffle.

AT THE TOP

This is another extremely useful application of the movement of cards in a perfect shuffle again applied to the spectator shuffle.

Effect. A freely chosen card is replaced in the pack, after which the spectator shuffles. The conjurer discovers the card in a suitable manner.

Method. 1. If possible, choose for this trick one of those present whom you may have noted cuts fairly close to twenty-six and who in shuffling the cards distributes them evenly in the riffle.

Have a card chosen and, as it is shown to those present, thumb count to the fourteenth card and split the pack at this point for the return of the card.

2. Hand the pack, after squaring, to the spectator and invite him to shuffle it. After the first shuffle, the card will have moved from fifteen to or near the twenty-ninth position. After a second shuffle it will be at or near the sixth position from the top. Note the depth at which the spectator cuts on the second shuffle; if it is thirty or more the card will be found near the bottom.

3. Discover the card by using any of the alternative-ending tricks which permit you to discover the one card of four or five amongst which you know a chosen card to be.

It should be noted that, when the conjurer himself makes the shuffles, the method is almost infallible. In such a case have the card replaced at fourteen. With a cut at twenty-six for the first honest shuffle the card will move to or near twenty-seven. On the second shuffle, preceded by a cut at twenty-six, the card will move to the second position in the pack.

This last method is very effective since those present consider the card lost in the pack and cannot have reason to believe that you know it is near the top.

These tricks in which the conjurer must take risks are naturally chancey and should not be attempted unless the conjurer is adept at wiggling out of tight corners; however when they succeed they pay big dividends by the manner in which they impress the onlookers.

When the perfect shuffle is used for this trick, the conjurer of course knows the exact position of the card without possibility of error.

DOUBLE LESS ONE

This is another puzzling discovery based on the principle of the perfect shuffle.

Effect. The location of a chosen card under conditions which make such a discovery seemingly impossible.

Preparation. Upon return of the pack after a spectator shuffle, hold it from below with the left fingers and thumb at the ends. Grasp the sides from above with the right hand. Riffle off the bottom card with the right thumb and crimp its inner right corner downward with the left little finger tip. Do this so that you cannot be suspected of having sighted the bottom card.

Method. 1. Place the pack at your right and spread the cards to the left. Request a spectator to remove any card.

2. Gather the pack and grasp it with the right hand at the sides near the inner end; that is to say, at the end at which the crimp has been placed. Run-cut cards into the left hand as in the Hindu Shuffle and request the return of the chosen card; contrive to have it replaced about eighteen cards from the top and drop the remaining cards in the right hand on top. The crimped key card is above the chosen card. Square the pack.

3. Cut the pack at twenty-six, or within one or two cards (an unbalanced cut is immaterial) and make a single perfect shuffle. Mesh the packets from the bottom of each up to within ten cards of the top; allow these last ten cards to fall off the thumbs in careless small packets. In other words, weave that portion of the pack in which lie the key and the chosen card; shuffle carelessly those cards above this section. A perfect shuffle may be made throughout but a little sloppiness when it is unimportant can be very deceptive.

The key card is now at or near the thirty-fifth position; two cards below it is the chosen card.

4. Square the pack and cut at about eighteen, completing the cut. This returns the key and the chosen card near eighteen from the top. Sighting the crimped corner of the key card aids in making this cut.

5. Cut at or near twenty-six, taking the upper half with the right hand, and make another shuffle as in 3.

6. Cut at and including the crimped card and complete the cut taking the crimped card to the bottom. The chosen card will be fourth from the top.

7. If a third such shuffle is made the procedure is the same, but in this case prior to the shuffle cut to bring the crimped key card, which is sighted in the side of the pack, to or near the fifteenth card. After the shuffle, cut the crimped key to the bottom and the chosen card will be the eighth card from the top.

Note that during the shuffles the crimped key card is kept in the packet cut by the right hand from the top; this prevents interference with the meshing of the cards which would occur if the crimped corner were allowed to move to a position in which, after a cut, the crimp would be at the inner ends.

The system is very easy since unbalanced cuts are permissible and only the middle cards of the packets are meshed. It is very perplexing to the onlookers when used for impromptu work of the "try and catch me" type.

Part 2
FLOURISHES

~~~~~~

IT IS THROUGH THE USE OF THE FLOURISH that the card conjurer imparts to his performances those small touches of wit and sparkle which are expected of those who walk with their feet in the clouds, for the flourish is the spice with which the conjurer seasons his ephemeral diableries; these are the charming and graceful impromptus which do so much to establish the conjurer as a man of adroitness and imagination. The true necromancer is not content merely to seek out the card lost in the pack; he flicks its face and there, from nowhere, is the missing card; or sardonically, he demonstrates that his is an ordinary pack by springing the cards from hand to hand in a smooth ribbon; or with an easy touch of the hand, spreads the pasteboards in an immaculately symmetrical fan; or, passing his hand over the pack, lazily plucks the required card from the air.

On the following pages are listed new flourishes with which the conjurer may garnish his performances. These should be employed, not as proof of the performer's dexterity, but rather as an off-hand demonstration of his amazing powers. Used in this manner, they will go a long way towards creating that atmosphere of informal hocus-pocus so endearing to audiences.

Part 2

FLOURISHES

Interlocked Production

THIS VERY EFFECTIVE FLOURISH was introduced some twenty years ago by Mr. Cliff Green who was at that time one of the leading card specialists in American vaudeville. The sleight, which is really a variation of the back and front palm, has not (like that much abused flourish) been

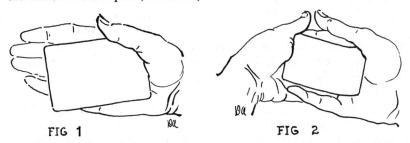

FIG 1   FIG 2

overdone and is, therefore, all the more valuable to those who master it. The moves, which are explained here for the first time, are not difficult but call for perfect timing.

The effect is that, with the fingers of the hands interlocked, the backs and fronts of the hands are alternately shown empty yet single cards make their appearance and drop from the hands to the floor in seemingly endless procession.

It is best to begin to learn the sleight with a single card and master the process of passing it from the back to the front of the hands and vice versa before attempting to deal with a number of cards. Proceed as follows:

1. With a card palmed in the right hand bring the tips of the fingers of both hands, backs outwards, together in front of the body.

2. As the finger tips touch, grip the upper inner corner of the palmed card by pressing the right thumb against the side of the hand and release the hold of the right fingers; the card will project from the thumb crotch as in Fig. 1.

3. Separate the fingers of each hand and interlock them, the right forefinger going between the left first and second fingers. The card will then be held firmly by its upper corners in the thumb crotches of the two hands

with its face towards you, Fig. 2. The edge of the lower side of the card rests on the inner side of the right little finger and its upper side against the side of the left first finger.

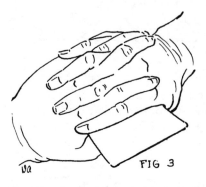

FIG 3

4. With the left thumb press firmly on the upper left corner of the card, tilting it away from the palm, drop the right thumb, press its side against the lower lengthwise edge of the card and push it so that it slides upwards through the crotch of the left thumb; at the same moment turn the hands over upwards bringing the palms squarely to the front. This turning of the hands must be so timed that the movement of the card is hidden by it throughout. At the conclusion of the movement the card projects horizontally from the left thumb crotch, Fig. 3, and is completely concealed from the front.

5. To bring the card and the hands back to their original position, Fig. 2, the movements of the right thumb and the hands are simply reversed. At the moment that the hands begin their downwards turning movement, raise the right thumb, press it on the edge of the upper side of the card and push the card through the left thumb crotch back to its original position.

If the positions of the hands are taken exactly and the instructions followed carefully it will be found that the card can be passed invisibly from the front of the hands to the back and vice versa with the greatest facility.

The Actual Flourish

To execute the production of cards one by one, begin by palming a packet of some six or eight cards in the right hand, then:

1. Interlock the fingers in exactly the same way as has been described for one card, bringing the packet into the position shown in Fig. 2.

2. With the tip of the left first finger press on the outer top corner of the innermost card, buckling it inwards and separating it from the other cards.

3. In exactly the same way as described for one card drop the right thumb to the lower side of the remaining cards and push them through the left thumb crotch as the hands turn over upwards, leaving the sepa-

rated, innermost card behind. At the end of this movement the card will be gripped by its sides between the right thumb and little finger facing the audience, while the packet of cards projects from the left thumb crotch at the back of the hands.

4. Display this single card for a moment or two, then let it fall and at once reverse the hands bringing the packet back to its original position by pushing it down with the right thumb.

5. Repeat the same movements for as many cards as you care to produce.

This flourish will be found to make an effective finish to a series of card manipulations, but it should not be overdone. The production of from ten to twelve cards will be sufficient.

The Color Change

This is supposed to be the original color change invented by Trewey, the famous French magician and shadowgraph artist, many years ago and explanations of it have appeared in many textbooks. Unfortunately, owing to the omission of a very important detail, the mortality rate of the sleight has been terrific, the palmed cards perversely exposing themselves at the bottom of the performer's hand with such inevitability that conjurers employing the method usually deceive themselves only.

The secret of successful performance, here recorded for the first time, is to hold the thumb rigid and pressed against the side of the palm. The necessary moves follow:

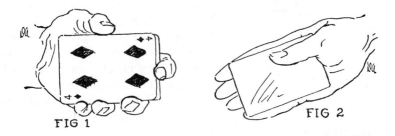

FIG 1   FIG 2

a. The Correct Method of Stealing the Card

1. Hold the pack in the left hand between the thumb and the second, third and fourth fingers at the sides, the first finger at the end, Fig. 1.

2. Place the right fingers, held close together, over the face card, the thumb at the back, and press the inner end of the pack firmly into the

crotch of the thumb. The upper side of the right first finger should be flush with the upper side of the deck.

3. Draw the right hand back over the face card and at the same moment push the rear cards to be palmed about an inch inward with the tip of the left forefinger, replacing it at the end of the pack immediately afterwards. Move the right thumb against the side of the palm, holding it rigid, and clip these cards between its side and the side of the palm, Fig. 2.

4. Immediately press the rigid thumb against the side of the hand, holding the packet flat against the right hand and the moment the packet is drawn clear of the pack, curl the fingers bringing the cards into the orthodox palm.

5. Finally tap the end of the pack with the back of the curled right fingers, squaring it, and again call attention to the face card being unchanged.

b. The Color Change

The mechanics of the grip being understood, there remains only the technique of presenting the sleight in such a manner that it does not, as in so many cases, appear that the cards have been snatched from the deck.

1. Hold the right hand flat, a little below the pack, move it upwards lightly over the face card, repeating this operation once or twice.

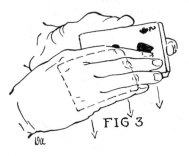

FIG 3

2. Push the rear card inwards an inch or so with the left forefinger, clipping it in the crotch of the right thumb as described above, the right hand moving inwards the same distance. Immediately remove the left third and fourth fingers from the lower side and hold the pack with the left thumb and second finger only near the outer corners. Curl the left forefinger against the back of the pack.

3. Move the right hand directly downwards, Fig. 3, and palm the card. Tap the end of the pack with the back of the curled right fingers and a moment later bring the right hand up over the face card. Deposit the palmed card on it, thus completing the color change.

With this method the card, or cards, to be palmed can be secured with surprising ease and swiftness, with no telltale hesitation in the action.

When the sleight is used for simply palming cards from the back of the pack, the steal is made in the same way under cover of squaring the deck.

The Impossible Color Change.

Smoothly done, there is no move in this color change that can be questioned by the most observant spectator.

1. Stand with your left side to the front and shuffle the cards overhand, with their backs to the onlookers.

2. Take the pack with the right hand between the thumb at the inner end and the four fingers at the outer end, the bottom card facing the palm of the hand.

3. Turn to the front, lift both hands, one on each side of the body, showing the palms, the fingers pointing upwards; turn to the left and, in the act of transferring the pack to the left hand with its face outwards, execute the one-hand top palm with the right hand, palming the bottom card face inwards.

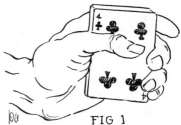

FIG 1

4. Take the pack in the left hand and hold it upright, face outwards, the thumb pressed full length across the middle of the face card, Fig. 1.

5. Point to the face card with the right forefinger, the other fingers curling in naturally towards the palm, and slip the little finger under the outer right corner of the palmed card, clipping it against the side of the third finger. This action cannot be detected since the fingers have curled behind the protecting screen of the back of the hand. Straighten out the fingers, causing the card to bend outwards by the pressure on the diagonal corners, and move the hand, held upright and perfectly flat, a few inches to the left of the deck.

6. Draw the right hand back over the pack, raise the left thumb just enough to allow the passage below it of the bent middle of the palmed card and place this card squarely on the face of the deck. Continue the movement of the right hand towards the left shoulder without any hesitation and so reveal the change. With a casual gesture let it be seen that the right hand is empty.

Owing to the position of the left thumb and the perfect flatness of the right hand, there does not appear to be any possibility of sleight of hand. The change is a surprising one.

The Covinous Color Change

The effect is the same as usual, the face card of the deck being changed, but the method used is, perhaps, the smoothest yet devised for the trick. Here are the moves:

1. Face the front, holding the pack face outwards in the left hand as for dealing, and with the right forefinger point to the face card, holding the right hand so that it is seen to be empty.

2. Take the pack in the right hand at the ends near the right corners between the thumb and the second finger, the tip of the forefinger pressing on the face card and swing around to the right, bringing the right hand palm to the front, the back of the pack outwards, the left forefinger pointing to the right hand with its tip a few inches from the back of the pack.

3. Swing back to the left to transfer the pack to the left hand into its original position face outwards in that hand and, in the action, execute the Face Card Palm (page 51), applied in this case to the top card of the pack, palming the card in the right hand with its face to the palm.

4. Point to the face card with the right forefinger, then straighten out the right fingers, retaining the card by means of the Gamblers' Flat Palm (page 56), that is to say, by a slight contraction of the little finger tip and the base of the thumb.

5. Place the right hand flat against the face card of the deck bringing the palmed card exactly upon it, open the fingers as widely as possible and draw the hand slowly downwards, rendering the change visible to the spectators.

The action of transferring the pack from hand to hand is a natural one, showing the hands empty in turn and the change of the face card comes as a complete surprise.

The Pressure Fan

It is the accepted practice of the modern card conjurer, when displaying the faces of the cards to spectators, to spread them in a wide fan in the left hand. To make a perfect fan, the cards equidistant one from the other, radiating like the spokes of a wheel, requires considerable practice; however, careful attention to the details of the following description will make its accomplishment much easier. Fanning the cards is a legitimate flourish and tends to give the onlookers a high opinion of the performer's dexterity.

1. Hold the pack in the left hand as for dealing and bevel its side well

to the right with the left thumb. The right hand aids by steadying the cards at the ends.

2. Grasp the ends of the pack near the right corners of the bottom cards (which are, of course, farther to the left than the corners of the top cards) between the right thumb at the inner end and the second and third fingers at the outer end. The third joints of these fingers should be bent so that the tips rest upon the ends of the cards flush with the bottom card.

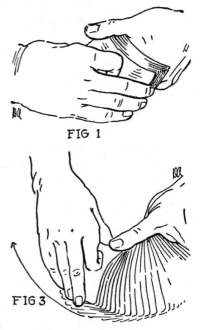

FIG 1

3. Place the pack diagonally in the crotch of the left thumb, the

SAME POSITION AS FIG 1
SEEN FROM BELOW

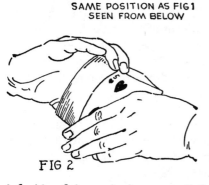

FIG 2

FIG 3

left side of the pack almost paralleling the left thumb as it lies with its tip upon the inner left corner of the pack. The first joint of the left fore-finger rests at the inner right corner, the finger thus lying across the face of the bottom card in a diagonal position, Figs. 1 and 2.

4. Make the fan by pressing lightly inwards with the tips of the right second and third fingers, bending the cards in a small degree, and snap these fingers to the right, this being the only term which will describe the action. The right thumb maintains its position resting lightly at the inner end of the top card as the right fingers at the outer end move around to the right allowing the cards to slip off their extreme tips, Fig. 3.

The flourish is difficult to describe and only practice will give the knack. The two points mentioned above, beveling the pack to the right and placing only the tips of the right second and third fingers upon the outer end of the deck, will go far to aid in mastering the action and to ensure a perfect spoke-like periphery.

The pressure fan has one great advantage over other methods of making the fan: it can be made with a pack in any condition, new or old.

Fan Flourish

A pretty flourish when asking that the choice of a card be made is to fan the pack face down, then place the fan upon the table so that the person drawing the card may be assured of a free choice. Cards fanned in this manner have an attractive appearance upon the tabletop.

Springing the Cards—A New Method

The following method of springing the cards from hand to hand will be found to give greater and easier control of the flourish. It makes practical a slower and hence more effective action, and the cards can be sprung with the hands farther apart.

1. Hold the deck in the right hand between the thumb at the inner end and the fingers at the outer end as in the orthodox method, but place the

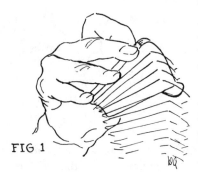

thumb at the left inner corner and the right little finger at the right outer corner, diagonally opposite, the other three fingers taking no part in the action.

2. Press the thumb and little finger inwards causing the cards to buckle from the right inner corner to the left outer corner.

FIG 1

3. Place the left hand at a little distance from the right hand and, continuing the pressure on the corners of the cards, allow them to slip off the ball of the thumb and spring into the left hand, increasing or decreasing the speed of their flight by increasing or decreasing the pressure of the thumb and little finger, Fig. 1.

The Top and Bottom Changes

Apart from their use as sleights in the course of a set trick these changes can be used independently with good effect.

Suppose, for example, you have just finished a card trick which has not turned out quite as well as you intended and the termination needs a little warming up. You are left with a red card in your hand and on the top of the pack you have a black card followed by a red one.

"The fact is," you say, "these things are done in the simplest possible way. Here is a red card, I rub it on my sleeve so . . . and you see it changes to a black card."

Suiting the action to the words, you turn half right to display the face of the red card, then turn to the left executing the bottom change, the hands meeting and separating as you face front, then completing the turn to the left you extend the left arm to full length and, holding the card face down, brush it along the sleeve from the wrist to the elbow.

Again display the face of the card, now a black one.

Facing to the front, you continue, "If I should want a red card I rub it on my hair so . . . and the card changes back to red." This time you make the top change as you lift both hands in front of the body and, after the change, continue the motion of the right hand up to your head and rub the face of the card on your hair, afterwards showing the change.

Make use of the classic change as given in *More Card Manipulations*, No. 1. It will be found that the upward motion of the hands renders the change invisible. If you are not so fortunate as to be blessed with the

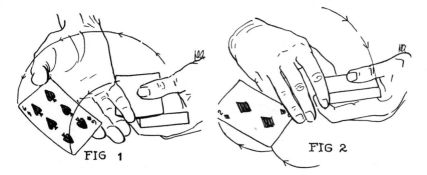

FIG 1   FIG 2

comeliness of red or auburn hair, you can get the same effect by lifting the card to your lips and blowing on it.

Executed in this manner these two changes fit in excellently with a series of manipulations such as a medley of fans, color changes, palms and recoveries and so on.

THERE IT IS!

This is one of those amusing novelties which spring up out of nowhere and which for that reason cannot be ascribed to any originator. Apparently it is little known. It makes an amusing bit of by-play to enliven a routine of card work.

Effect. The conjurer fails to locate the chosen card and, failing, locates it in a novel manner.

Method. 1. Bring the chosen card second from the top. Grasp the top card at the ends between the right first finger and the thumb. Turn the hand palm upwards to the right, showing the face of the card.

2. Push the next card, which is the chosen card, off the pack with the left thumb. Clip it at the right outer corner between the right third and little fingers, Fig. 1.

3. Replace the first card face downwards at the top of the pack when advised that it is not the chosen card. This action automatically brings the desired card face upwards, extending from between the right third and little fingers of the hand, which is now palm down, Fig. 2.

Part 3
TECHNIQUE

~~~~~~

TECHNIQUE HAS BEEN DEFINED as the method of performance or manipulation in any art, or that peculiar to any artist or school. It concerns itself not with the means, but the manner in which the means are employed.

Technique plays a part in every sleight the conjurer performs, no matter how simple; but there are certain sleights in which the method of performance is of far greater importance than the mechanical actions involved. For the most part, these comprise the so-called "dangerous" sleights, such as the palms, replacements, additions and forces, which are anathema to the neophyte and are often nervously regarded by the professional. These have been grouped in the following section, where special emphasis can be placed upon them and the little-known techniques which have been developed to make possible their undetected use.

Part 3
TECHNIQUE

~~~~~~

SECRET ADDITION OF CARDS TO THE PACK

BEFORE DESCRIBING IN DETAIL the various methods of replacing cards palmed off the pack itself it is necessary to explain how to obtain possession secretly of cards hidden on your person for addition to the deck. There are several methods which are well known and of which mention only need be made. For example, the cards are in a pocket or clip under the coat, they are palmed and added to the deck; or they lie on the table underneath a silk handkerchief, as this is removed the pack is dropped on the cards; or again the cards are held underneath an envelope which is dropped casually onto the pack.

To these we add the following easy and indetectible methods:

a. Place the cards in your right upper vest pocket beforehand. To obtain them, turn your back for any plausible reason while the deck is being shuffled, draw the packet from the pocket and thrust it, face downwards, up the right sleeve between the cloth and the shirt cuff, holding the arm naturally and horizontally. Turn around, take the shuffled deck, holding it at the second joints of the right second and third fingers at the end, the first and fourth fingers, at their second joints, pressing against the opposite sides. Drop the hand, its back to the onlookers, and the sleeved cards drop invisibly and noiselessly upon the pack.

This move is very useful when demonstrating, while standing, your mastery of gamblers' sleights. For example, having sleeved the cards you require, have the deck shuffled and cut. Deal the desired number of hands, have the spectators look at their cards, but do not look at your own hand. Give each player as many cards as he calls for to replace his discards. Then for the first time look at your hand, this action distracting attention from your right hand, which drops to your side thus adding the sleeved cards to the deck. By discarding four cards, you can then deal yourself the four aces, if they were the cards you sleeved, or of course any other hand you arranged.

b. A card or cards are clipped horizontally under a bobby pin which has been thrust over the lip of the upper left vest pocket, Fig. 1, and your watch rests in this pocket. You say, "What time is it?" and answer your own question by removing the watch and glancing at it. Replace the timepiece, and in removing your hand, do so with a downward movement, palming the cards and then adding them to the pack.

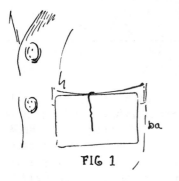

FIG 1

The action of glancing at the watch is such an everyday, plausible action that not one person in a hundred will suspect that it has acted as cover for stealing the cards. Use of this method makes possible the following simple direct trick which has an extraordinary effect:

Place a duplicate card, say a four of spades, under the bobby pin. Force the four of spades, have it returned to the deck and allow a spectator to shuffle the cards. "I'll show you a ten second trick," you say. Then, as an afterthought, address a spectator, asking him, "Do you believe you can estimate the passage of ten seconds?" Remove your watch, tell the spectator when the second hand is on 60 and have him call when he thinks ten seconds have elapsed. In most cases he will call when seven or even fewer seconds have passed, the resultant amusement making the experiment seem mere by-play.

When you return the watch to the pocket—an action so natural and, as a matter of fact, imperative, that afterwards few will remember it— you steal the duplicate card. You add the card to the deck and, after a spectator names a number, you find this duplicate card at that number by any one of the count down methods you care to employ. Using this means you will be given credit for amazing skill in controlling cards. Many other uses for it will suggest themselves.

c. The required cards are concealed by thrusting them under a paper clip of the trombone variety, sewn near the bottom of the coat at the back. These cards are added to the pack when, under some suitable pretext, you put the pack behind your back.

The principle is a bold one which can be used effectively to prove that you can duplicate gamblers' feats while holding the cards behind your back. To do this, hand the pack to be shuffled. Turn your back, put your hands behind you and receive the pack thus. Deal cards to the required number of persons, handing each player his card in rotation with your back still turned, then have the players make their discards and deal them the necessary cards to fill their hands again.

Turn to look at the cards you dealt to yourself, pull down and add the hidden cards to the pack. Make your discard, according to the hand you have arranged, turn around again and deal yourself, say, the four aces. Finish with a flourish.

The awkwardness of dealing cards behind the back creates an amusing background and can be built into a plot concerning a gambler so crooked that, when playing with fellow gamblers, they forced him to deal the cards behind his back to prevent manipulation.

This same principle is also useful as a convincing force. Place the required card in the clip beforehand. After a spectator has shuffled the deck, turn your back and hold your hands to receive it in that position. Invite him to cut the cards and, as he does this, turn and ask him if he is satisfied. At once pull the card from the clip onto the remainder of the deck. Turn away again and have him remove the top card, presumably the card he cut to, really the force card. Naturally several cards can be thus forced at the same time.

REPLACEMENT OF PALMED CARDS

The secret replacement of palmed cards onto the pack is a more difficult operation than their secret abstraction by palming. Writers on magic have devoted much space to explaining many ways of palming cards but the replacement principle has been almost entirely ignored. Several methods are given by Robert-Houdin in *Les Secrets* (translated by Professor Hoffmann) and some more modern methods are explained in *Card Manipulations*, No. 4 by Jean Hugard, but apart from these we do not know of any explanations of the principle in the textbooks.

Any performer who takes pride in handling cards cleanly and neatly and is not satisfied with "getting away with it," as is too often heard from careless operators, will do well to study the following methods.

We will assume that you have a card, or a small packet of cards, palmed in the right hand, that a spectator has shuffled the pack and has placed it on the table before you, and that you wish to add the palmed card to the pack in picking it up; there are several methods of procedure.

a. *Replacement by Laying the Hand Flat on the Pack and Drawing It Towards You*

This is the general practice but a moment's reflection will prove that it is wrong and suggests to the onlooker the very fact which you wish to conceal. The natural action in drawing the pack away, or picking it up, is to place the tips of the thumb and fingers on the ends of the pack, keeping the hand arched. Placing the hand flat on the pack suggests that you have added something and, considering the widespread knowledge of the possibility of palming, this is fatal.

There is one way in which this action can be done naturally and without arousing suspicion. Place the hand flat on the pack, adding the palmed cards, and instantly spread all the cards ribbonwise towards the left. Accompany the action with the remark, "You see there is no preparation on this side," slip the forefinger under the bottom card and turn it over, Fig. 1, taking care that the finger follows in the same direction, as you continue, "nor on this." All the cards are thus caused to turn face upwards. Repeat the turnover from the opposite end, turning the cards face downwards again. Then slip the tips of the right fingers under the bottom cards and gather the whole pack with a sweep to the left.

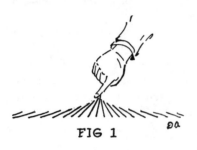

FIG 1

This pleasing little flourish intrigues the spectators and effectually diverts any suspicion from their minds.

b. Buckling the Palmed Cards

Pick up the pack from the table by its ends between the tips of the thumb and fingers, keeping the hand arched. Turn half left and take the pack in the left hand by its sides at the tips of the thumb and second, third and fourth fingers, bending the first finger below.

Release the right thumb at the inner end and, without changing the position of the right little finger, press inwards with it against the right outer corner of the palmed packet, forcing the cards to buckle outwards from the palm, Fig. 2. Grip

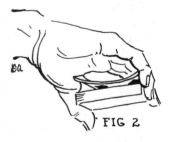

FIG 2

the sides of the packet with the left thumb and fingers and relax the grip of the right little finger and the base of the thumb at the diagonal corners of the packet, drawing the cards squarely on top of the pack. Run the top joints of the right fingers along the outer end of the pack squaring it.

In this way the cards have been replaced with the palm of the right hand well away from the pack and the only contact has been with the top joints of the fingers in the natural action of squaring the outer end.

c. Using the Front Finger Palm

As the spectator is finishing his shuffle and at the moment the pack is placed upon the table, the right hand, holding the palmed cards naturally at the side, transfers them to the front finger palm; that is, it grips the outer corners between the first and second fingers and the third and fourth fingers, Fig. 3. To do this you have merely to move the first and fourth fingers a little outwards and downwards, then close them again gripping the corners of the cards and taking care that these corners do not protrude.

FIG 3

Pick up the pack with the tips of the thumb and fingers and, in the act of placing it in the left hand, release the corner between the third and fourth fingers, bend the fourth finger and press its tip against the middle of the back of the packet. This action brings the cards squarely onto the top of the pack, the right hand remaining arched and immediately proceeding to square the pack in a perfectly natural way.

d. Using the Riffle Flourish

After picking up the pack between the tips of the thumb and fingers, place it in the left hand, making a half turn to the left at the same time. Ruffle the ends of the deck with the right fingers and thumb, moving the hands a little apart at the end of the flourish.

Press on the diagonal corners of the palmed packet with the outermost joint of the little finger and the root of the thumb, buckling the cards outwards, Fig. 2. Bring the hands together to repeat the ruffle and slip the left thumb above the bulging middle of the palmed packet, pressing it onto the top of the pack as the ruffle is completed.

When the right hand is removed, the left thumb is seen to be pressing down on the back of the pack apparently precluding the possibility of the addition of any cards.

e. The Deck Placed Sideways

It sometimes happens that, after having shuffled the deck, a spectator will place it before you with its side and not its end nearest to you. This is an awkward position if you use the sliding-back pick-up. In such cases strike the right inner corner of the pack with the tip of the right second finger, Fig. 4, pushing it so that the cards will turn and fan slightly. Apparently this is accidental but it enables you to add the palmed cards in drawing the pack towards you.

Or, you can pick up the pack by the sides, place it in the left hand and

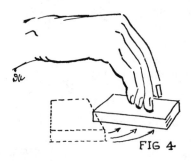

add the palmed cards to it by the ruffling method explained in the preceding section.

f. Dropping the Packet

An audacious method is to place the tips of the right hand fingers just in front of the outer end of the deck bringing the palmed cards squarely over it; drop the packet onto the pack and instantly flick the second finger outwards as if to dislodge a particle of dust a couple of inches in front of the pack. Pick up the pack by the ends, bend forward and blow on the spot to complete the misdirection.

FIG 4

g. Replacing a Card at the Bottom of the Pack

We will suppose that you have a card palmed in the right hand and that you desire to place it at the bottom of a packet which lies on the table. As you move the hand towards the packet from the left, release the hold of the fingers on the palmed card and retain it by the left inner corner in a fold of the flesh at the crotch of the thumb. (The grip is the same as that used in the Flat Table Palm, page 56.) Slide the card under the packet from left to right and tip the cards up vertically, the faces to the left, and square the packet by tapping its side upon the table, Fig. 5.

If the sides of the table packet are crimped upwards a little, the insertion of the palmed card is made very easy.

h. In Turning the Top Card

In cases where a table is not at hand, the spectator shuffles the pack and you have a card, or cards, palmed in your right hand; at the moment when he is ready to hand the pack back, take your handkerchief in your right hand, wipe your forehead and at the same time take the pack back with your left hand. Replace the handkerchief in your pocket, push the top card over the side of the pack with the left thumb and turn it face upwards by striking it with the side of your right hand. Repeat the action, turning the card face downwards, adding the palmed cards to the top of the pack and immediately draw the right fingers along the ends of the pack, squaring it.

i. One Hand Replacement

This replacement may be made with one or a number of cards. It is, in effect, the one-hand top palm* worked backward and, like this palm, it is an extremely deceptive and valuable sleight.

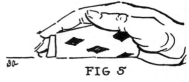

FIG 5

1. Bring the right hand with the palmed cards over the pack, which is held in the left hand. Place the fingers over the outer end, the thumb at the inner end near the left corner. The outer left corner of the palmed cards rests flush with the top of the pack but the outer right corner slants diagonally over the end. In Fig. 6 the little finger has been lifted to show how this corner slants down over the end of the pack. If the right hand is placed over the pack,

---

* The One-Hand Top Palm, an invaluable sleight first described in *Card Manipulations*, Nos. 1 and 2, is graphically illustrated by these figures if they are looked at in the order Fig. 8, Fig. 7 and Fig. 6.

Fig. 8 shows the right hand holding the pack. Note particularly that the side of the right first finger parallels the left side of the pack, the back of the hand being thrown into the somewhat concave position depicted. Note also the accented outline of the little finger, which extends straight forward with the fleshy ball of its third phalange pressing downward upon the upper surface of the card at the outer right corner. The smaller figure shows how the left side of the first finger must parallel the left side of the pack.

Fig. 7 shows the second step in the palm. The rigid fourth finger has pushed the outer right corner of the card forward over the outer end of the pack and, by pressing downward, is in the process of levering this card up into the right palm.

Fig. 6 shows the last step of the palm, with the card levered up against the right palm. The little finger has been lifted in this illustration to show how the outer right corner of the top card moves down over the outer end of the pack. At this point the back of the right hand arches naturally over the pack.

When the sleight is performed these actions are made in less than a second and the strained position of the hand in the first phases of the palm cannot be noted. In studying the illustrations, note particularly those parts of the hand which have been more heavily outlined, for they make more emphatic the position of the hand which must be taken if the palm is to be made with the greatest efficiency and speed.

The card conjurer who takes the trouble to master this sleight will never regret the effort expended.

with the outer left corner of the palmed packet flush with the top of the pack at its outer left corner, as described, the correct position is taken automatically.

2. Straighten the right little finger and, holding it rigidly straight, move it inward, pressing down on the surface of the corner of the card. Note the emphasized line of the little finger in Fig. 7, which shows the palmed cards swinging inward and downward onto the top of the pack under the pressure of the little finger.

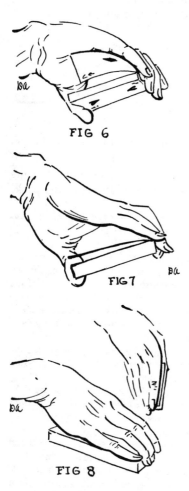

FIG 6

FIG 7

FIG 8

3. The action in the preceding section moves the back of the hand into the position shown in Fig. 8. The cards have swung squarely upon the top of the pack. Note the emphasized line of the little finger, paralleling the right side of the pack and perfectly straight; note also the emphasized line of the side of the first finger, as depicted in the supplementary figure, showing how it parallels the left side of the pack. Note further that the action has made the back of the hand slightly concave; this is due to the fact that the right first, second and third fingers and the thumb remain stationary as the little finger is moved inward, thus forcing the hand into the curious position shown.

In practice the replacement is effected by the action of the right little finger and lasts but a fraction of a second. It is made in the act of picking up the pack from the left hand and in moving the pack to place it upon the table or to hand it to a spectator. It is practically indetectible even to those who may look for it.

The replacement may also be made in the act of lightly squaring the cards as they are held in the left hand. In this case the right hand is placed over the pack and the little finger swings the palmed packet inward and downward onto the top. The left hand immediately shifts its position and grasps the pack with the fingers at the face, the thumb at the middle of the back. The cards are lightly squared at the ends with the right fingers and thumb.

THE PALM IN ACTION

This is another action to which very little attention is paid by the present-day conjurer: With a card palmed in the right hand, how should the pack be handed to a spectator for shuffling?

Methods in general use today include offering the pack to the spectator with the right hand, the fingers and thumb of which grasp it at the ends from above; and offering the cards upon the palm of the left hand. The former method has two faults: The back of the right hand obscures the pack and makes the entire action abnormal in appearance, and secondly, not infrequently the spectator, forced to grip the pack at the sides from underneath, accidentally touches the palmed cards with the tips of his fingers. The latter method can be perfectly deceptive but it is nonetheless not entirely natural, the hand action being somewhat awkward.

It is always interesting to note that the old-time conjurers met and mastered these problems, and that their methods in many cases are as good today as they were sixty, eighty and a hundred years ago. It should never be forgotten that, while times may change, human nature does not; the conjurer who fails to profit by the hard-won knowledge of his predecessors is indeed a foolish man, for while in a good many instances methods have improved, the basic psychology of deception which they learned by experience still remains the same.

Thus it is profitable to recall that Charles Bertram counseled that when cards are palmed and it is desired to hand the pack to a spectator, this action should *not* be made with the left hand, but by extending the pack held between the right thumb and fingers, at the inner end. "This action does not in any way interfere with the palmed cards, yet without ostensibly appearing to do so, it disarms any suspicion as to cards being concealed there."

The modern method of performing the sleight differs as to technique but retains the same deceptive psychology:

1. Square the pack with the right fingers and thumb at the ends, the left fingers and thumb at the sides.

2. Palm the top card or cards, using the one-hand top palm or diagonal tip-up palm respectively, grip the pack from below with the left hand at the sides and, retaining the right thumb resting lightly at the inner end, draw the right fingers directly backward until these rigid fingers rest

upon the back of the pack at the inner end. The right thumb grasps the pack at its face and the pack is extended to the spectator, Fig. 1.

The action is entirely natural, is made in an instant and the position of the right fingers at the inner end of the pack is such that the palming of a card seems improbable.

Another method is this: The action remains exactly the same except that, with the card or cards palmed in the right hand, the pack is grasped at the right inner corner with the fingers at the face and the thumb at the back of the pack, Fig. 2.

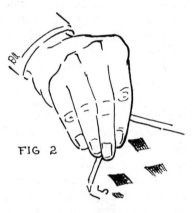

FIG 2

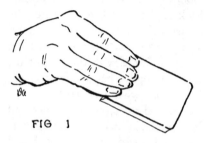

FIG 1

Either of these methods will be found easy and deceptive.

Covering a Palm

The most difficult task confronting a beginner when he first attempts to palm a card is to convince himself that he will not be detected in performing the sleight. He becomes self-conscious, he knows he has a card palmed and he thinks everyone else must realize it, his wrist and elbow become semi-paralyzed, his thumb sticks up at a right angle and he even glances furtively at his hand. Is it any wonder that the spectators detect the maneuver and that the small boy, having no adult inhibitions of politeness, screams, "You've got it in your hand!" After a few experiences of this kind, the neophyte decides that his hand is too small, the universal excuse, and gives up the attempt. We have known card conjurers, expert in all the other sleights, who have never overcome this initial difficulty and therefore shunned all tricks requiring the use of the palm, thereby cutting themselves off from some of the most startling feats of card magic.

The difficulty is a mental one. In most sleights the action is swift, it is over in a second or two; but in retaining a card or cards in the palm while a spectator shuffles the pack, for instance, the sleight is, so to speak, a continuous one. The card is there in your hand, liable to challenge at any moment, and it seems an eternity elapses before you can get it safely back onto the pack.

There is only one way to overcome this consciousness of palming and it is to become so accustomed to holding cards in your hand that you can practically forget that they are there at all. This is not difficult and requires merely a little perseverance. Take a card or a small packet of cards in the right hand in the correct position for palming and keep them there while you practice cutting and shuffling the pack, picking it up and laying it down, taking and lighting a cigarette, holding a cigar or cigarette between the tips of the first and second fingers and so on.

Soon the dreadful card-consciousness will wear off, the wrist and elbow become relaxed and supple, you forget you have a card palmed and you can devote your whole attention to the proper presentation of your patter. It should not be necessary to insist that the hand when palming cards should be held in a natural, half-closed position. Study the condition of your own hand when it is at rest and copy that.

Naturally the routine of a trick should be so arranged that palmed cards remain in the hand for as short a time as possible. There are, however, some most effective tricks in which there has to be an appreciable interval between palming and releasing the cards and, to cover these dangerous interludes, various subterfuges have been devised to conceal the fact. We detail some of these but each performer should study and arrange gestures which are natural and appropriate to his own style of delivery.

I. Top Palm—Right Hand

After you have palmed cards in your right hand, it should retain the pack for a few moments. Then place the pack in the left hand, on the table, or hand it to a spectator, letting the right hand drop easily and naturally to the side. One or other of the following subterfuges may then be used:

1. You may grasp a spectator's arm to draw him to one side, or nearer to you, and hold the hand there, naturally concealing the palmed cards, while he counts cards onto the table or does any other action required of him. This cover is extremely useful in platform work in such tricks as The Three Cards Across.

2. If a chair is in a convenient position, you can drop the right hand onto the upper rail in a natural grip and let it rest there, or remove the chair to another position. This cover is useful in platform work and can be used for close work also.

3. When seated at a table, you can extend the right hand with the

cards (or the left hand, for that matter) along the edge of the table, the thumb resting on the surface and the fingers dropping over the side, Fig. 1.

4. You may fold your arms, cover being thus given to cards palmed in either hand. The Napoleonic stance involved, however may make one appear rather self-important and should be used sparingly.

5. A less imposing gesture is to grasp the left upper arm with the right

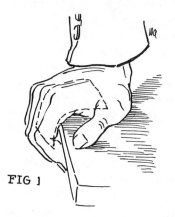

hand and with the left hand stroke your chin, assuming a rather quizzical expression as you watch the operations of your volunteer assistant.

6. Again you may place your arms akimbo, that is to say, put your hands on your hips with the elbows outwards. This gesture should be accompanied by some appropriate remark, such as, "Well, what do you think of that?"

7. When seated at a card table, you can drop either hand upon the thigh and rest it there quite naturally as you lean forward to address a person. Again you can leave the cards resting above the knee, bring the hands upon the table in some necessary gesture and regain possession of the cards later by dropping the hand upon the thigh.

FIG 1

8. With either hand you can straighten the cravat or the side of your coat. This is a short cover only and might possibly create the impression that the performer is nervous or poorly groomed.

9. Another short cover is to move the hand back from the wrist, keeping it open and almost flat, in gesturing to illustrate some remark concerning yourself; for instance, you might exclaim, "I wouldn't deceive you, not for the world."

10. When standing, with a table nearby, you can place your hands upon your knees as you lean forward, watching with interest a spectator handle the cards.

II. Bottom Palm—Left Hand

Immediately after you have palmed cards in your left hand, give the pack an end ruffle with the right hand and take the pack in that hand, moving it towards the right. At once take hold of the right sleeve, high up, with the left hand and tug at it lightly as if to pull the cuff back from the right wrist. With the right hand place the pack on the table, hand it to a spectator, or make whatever action is appropriate at the moment.

This gesture, which gives the left hand a natural and plausible action, centers attention on the extended right hand and obviates any awkwardness sometimes noticeable in turning the left hand down after making the palm.

It should be noted that when the cards are palmed in the left hand and the pack is held as for dealing, the palmed cards are so perfectly concealed that they could be seen only by a person looking directly over your left shoulder.

III. Either Hand

On occasions when smoking is permissible, the handling of a lighted cigar or cigarette affords perfect cover for a palmed card. In fact a lighted cigar is a potent weapon in the hands of gamblers, not only in covering a palmed card or cards, but in making the action of putting it aside with one hand cover the making of the pass with the other hand.

A glass of water and a handkerchief are very useful things to have on your table. Nothing can be more natural than to take a drink or use the handkerchief, and the actions tend to divert suspicion of the possibility of your having palmed a card.

THE SECRET COUNT

I. The Side Count

The method of buckling cards, described under The Double Lift, page 4, can be used as a means of counting a small number of cards, up to, say, six or seven, with ease and certainty. The second finger allows each card to slip off its tip in turn; when the desired number is reached, a break is secured by that finger and this break is then transferred to the little finger. The operation is completely covered by the right hand.

The greater the bevel towards the left which is given to the pack, the larger the number of cards which can be counted with accuracy but the method is not recommended for more than a few cards. Naturally, however, as with all sleights, the more practice that is given to the move, the greater the facility which will be attained.

II. The Top Thumb Count

This familiar sleight has been inaccurately described in most cases; the correct method is as follows:

1. Hold the pack face downwards in the left hand between the thumb, held rigidly straight against the left side, and the second, third and fourth

fingers at the right side, the first finger being doubled under the deck, which should be beveled to the right at the upper right corner and the left inner corner pressed firmly into the flesh at the base of the thumb, Fig. 1.

2. Press the outer left corners of the cards downwards with the thumb against the left forefinger and let the cards spring off the flesh of the ball of the thumb. The slight beveling of the cards provides for an accurate count being made.

3. By turning the hand, bringing the back of the hand towards the body, the sleight is completely covered. Again, it can be made under cover of the right hand which is brought over the pack, the fingers being held close together at the outer end.

The transfer to the little finger of the break between the counted cards and the remainder of the pack is described on page 125.

FIG 1

III. The Bottom Thumb Count

a. 1. Hold the pack in the left hand as for dealing but with the thumb lying straight across its back, its tip touching the tip of the forefinger.

2. Bring the right hand over the pack, its fingers, held close together, at the outer end and the thumb at the inner end. Push forwards with the ball of the thumb and pull backwards with the third joints of the second and third fingers, slightly beveling the ends of the pack, Fig. 1.

3. Bend the inner end of the pack upwards with the right thumb and allow the cards to slip off its tip progressively, beginning with the bottom card. Beveling the cards ensures the release of the cards one by one.

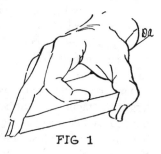

FIG 1

4. When the desired number of cards has been dropped, insert the tip of the left little finger above them and, with the thumb, ruffle the ends of the cards sharply upwards; repeat the ruffle immediately to give the impression that to make this little flourish was the only reason for placing the right hand over the deck.

The best way to make a quick and accurate count is to form the habit of counting by threes; thus, let three cards fall rapidly, make an infinitesimal pause, then let three more fall and so on until the next multiple of three is reached and, finally, drop one or two cards as may be necessary. For instance, you want ten cards, the count would run—1 2 3-1 2 3-1 2 3-1. With a little practice the method becomes as easy as habit and the count is much quicker than by the straight ahead system. The same thing applies to the top thumb count.

b. Another method is to hold the pack face upwards in the left hand and thumb count by the first method, with the right hand covering the pack. Transfer the break under the counted packet to the little finger (see page 125) and insert it firmly.

Place the left thumb under the pack at the left side and by pressing upwards and to the right, turn the pack face downwards, retaining the little finger in the break which is now on the left side.

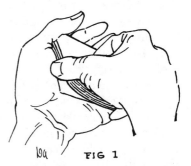

FIG 1

Pick up the break at the inner end with the right thumb, move the left little finger to the left side of the pack and secure the break in the orthodox fashion.

For many operators this method will prove faster than the preceding action and it can be used in many effects.

c. This method is a variation using the right thumb count at the inner end of the deck.

1. Hold the deck by the inner end between the right thumb at the left corner and the second and third fingers at the right corner, the thumb parallel with the side of the deck and the forefinger pressing down on the middle of the back of the top card. Hold the left hand loosely around the outer end of the deck, Fig. 1.

2. Bend the inner corners of the pack upwards by pressing down with the right forefinger, at the same time slightly beveling the cards. Allow the cards to escape from the ball of the right thumb, one at a time, in rhythmical progression as already described, and at the same time tilt the deck with the left hand to hide the maneuver.

3. When the desired number of cards have escaped from the thumb, grasp the pack more firmly with the left fingers at the outer end and slide the right thumb to the left inner corner, retaining the break. Transfer the right fingers to the outer end of the pack and place it in the left

hand in position for dealing. Slide the right thumb across the inner end of the deck towards the right, carrying the break with it, and insert the tip of the left little finger, securing the break in the orthodox manner.

IV. The Overhand Count

The card conjurer, expected to perform his miracles with any deck handed to him, often finds that the thumb count is inaccurate with a proffered pack of well worn and sticky cards.

The top count may, in such instances, be made by means of the overhand shuffle. For instance, to make a break under the twelfth card, proceed as follows:

1. Undercut half the pack, injog the first card, run eleven and outjog the twelfth card, shuffling off the remainder.
2. Undercut at the outjog, forming a break at the injog.
3. Throw all the cards below the break, retaining the packet of twelve cards in the right hand.
4. Injog the first card of this packet and shuffle off the remainder.
5. Form a break under the injog.

The shuffle should be made unobtrusively under the protection of a brisk covering conversation. Because of the long run of twelve cards, it is a good practice to run six cards, pause, glancing at your spectators as though absorbed in the topic of conversation; then continue the run.

Forcing

The Classic Force

The classic force has been described so well and so often that there is no need to review the action here. It is an instinct that can be developed mainly by practice, which brings confidence; after the first hundred forces the operator loses his fear of failure and acquires the knack of placing the force card before the spectator's reaching hand at precisely the right psychological moment. A successful force is almost entirely a matter of convincing the spectator that you do not care which card he takes; he then will take the card most convenient to his hand.

In all tricks where such a course is practical it is good psychology, after the force by this method, to have the card returned to the pack, shuffle it lightly yourself and immediately thereafter offer the deck to be shuffled by the spectator. By their willingness to let the spectator shuffle immediately after the return of a card to a pack, cardworkers too often betray the fact that a force has been made. For some reason the shuffle by the performer befogs the issue and makes the subsequent discovery all the more remarkable.

On the other hand, if the force fails, be careful not to show the slightest perturbation. Smile amiably, thank the spectator, leave the card he has drawn in his hands and proceed to some more accommodating person. Later you return to him and use his card in some other trick.

The classic force should never be used with any obviously mechanical trick, such as a prediction trick in which the name of the card is written down beforehand; in such a case it may be all too clear that the choice of the card was forced. Use a mechanical force which will not reveal that you can control the choice of a card by timing.

The Fan Force

This force is rarely seen, although it dates back almost as far as the classic force itself and is exceedingly useful for all purposes.

Here is the procedure: Sight the top card of the pack and shuffle it to the middle or make the pass. Cant the upper half of the pack an eighth of an inch to the right, forming a minute step between the transposed halves of the deck. The card to be forced is the top card of the lower packet.

Take the pack in the right hand, between the thumb above and the fingers below and, with the fingers of the left hand, spread the cards in a fan, pushing them off with the thumb as the hand moves to the left. Watch the top card of the lower packet and, as the left thumb pushes it while forming the fan, leave exposed about a quarter of

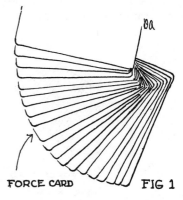

FORCE CARD   FIG 1

an inch more of its surface than in the case of the other cards, Fig. 1.

Present the fanned deck to the spectator with the right hand only. As his hand approaches the fan, it will in most cases move towards its center. The smallest motion of the right hand, timing the movement to the motion of the spectator's hand, will bring the force card into such a position that it is the most convenient card for the spectator to choose. At the same time, both in this and the classic force, all the cards except the force card should be held firmly by pressure of the thumb on the back of the fan. If the spectator at first tries to draw another card, he finds it hard to remove and, not having any reason to suspect design on the part of the operator, he relinquishes it and takes the force card which draws away easily.

Charles Bertram, the famous English conjurer, was an adept at this force. He used a run-down and, for his rising cards and other tricks, would simply fan the deck, lean down and force the cards one-handed. He could, and did, force as many as eight or nine cards in a row by this method.

There are, however, rare instances in which a spectator, perversely, will refuse to accept the proper card. He may take the third, fourth or fifth card to the right or left of the force card. In such a case you request him merely to peek at the index of the card and you use the force card as a key card, noting how many cards his card is distant from it. If he chooses a card ten to fifteen cards away, have him remove it and as he replaces it in the spread, contrive to have him place it near the key card, a very easy matter in practice.

The Table Spread Force

The influence of the slightly greater exposure of the back of a certain card is so great that if the cards are so spread on the table that one

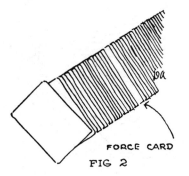

FORCE CARD

FIG 2

card is a shade more exposed than the others, that card will almost inevitably be chosen. The spread must be made in an apparently casual manner and the best way to do this is to pass or shuffle the card to the middle and hold a break above it with the left little finger. Square the pack with the right hand and press the ends downwards, as if taking out a bend, then pull the ends of the top packet upwards. A reversed bridge is thus formed at the force card and if the pack is thrown on the table with a sliding motion the cards of the upper packet will glide a little further than the others, leaving the force card a little more exposed, Fig. 2. A little practice is required to gauge the extent of the bridge and the force of the throw necessary to expose the card in the most tempting way.

The Perfect Score Card Force

This force can be made in such a deliberately open and aboveboard manner that it is impossible for the spectator to suspect that his choice of a card has been influenced.

With the card to be forced on the top of the pack, begin by:

1. Undercutting three-fourths of the pack, injog the first card and shuffle off. Undercut at the injog, injog the first card (the chosen card) and shuffle off.

2. Grasp the pack at the outer right corner with the right fingers and

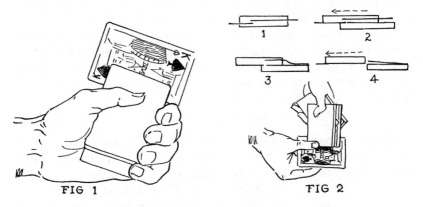

FIG 1   FIG 2

place it in the left hand much as for dealing, but with the left third finger even with the right inner corner, the left little finger pressing against the side of the jogged force card just below the inner right corner. Hold the pack diagonally upwards.

3. Have the spectator insert a score card at will in the outer end of the pack, contriving, however, that it shall enter below the force card. Fig. 1.*

4. Deliberately insert the right second finger under the score card at the outer end and draw all the cards above it outwards in such a way that manipulation is plainly impossible. Slide these cards forward until the inner end of the jogged card is flush with the inner end of the lower packet.

5. Tighten the left third and fourth fingers against the side of the lower packet, thus securely grasping the inner end of the force card and retaining it flush with the inner end of the lower packet as the right hand removes the score card and the packet above it, Fig. 2.

6. Place the score card and the cards above it to one side and offer the top card of the lower packet to the spectator. The small figures 1 to 4 show side views of the removal of the upper packet and the retention of the force card.

---

* The figure shows KS. Wherever possible a score card should be used to avoid any suspicion.

Using a Force

For all practical purposes, a card conjurer needs only a half a dozen good methods of forcing a card or cards, in addition to the classical force. Many clever ruses will be found in Theodore Annemann's excellent reference book, *Two Hundred Methods of Forcing*, from amongst which the performer can select those few he will need.

It is a very good practice to decide which type of force should be used for any given trick, and, thereafter, use that method only for that particular trick; this prevents the abuse of a "pet" force and aids in creating the impression amongst the spectators that the operator does not care how a card is chosen.

THE MULTIPLE FORCE

When it is necessary to force several cards, say three, four or five, the following method will be found quick, easy and satisfactory. Place the required cards on the bottom of the deck with an indifferent card below them. Make a false shuffle and a blind cut, retaining them in this position. We will suppose that five cards are to be forced. Proceed thus:

SEEN FROM BELOW
FIG 1

1. Turn the deck face upwards in the left hand and form a break at the inner end with the right thumb as it apparently squares the cards; this break should be at the sixth card, but if it is made at a few more (but not less) no harm is done. Hold the cards as for dealing and press the tip of the left little finger against the sides of the six cards to retain a break between them and the remainder of the pack.

2. Display the bottom card by holding the pack upright in the left hand, then drop the hand turning it back upwards and bringing the back of the pack uppermost.

3. Grasp the outer end with the right hand and draw it outwards an inch, at the same time pressing the face packet of six cards firmly between the tip of the left little finger and the flesh at the heel of the thumb, retaining it in its original position. The packet will now project at the inner end of the pack, the jog being concealed by the back of the left hand, while the left fingers prevent the set-back condition from being noticed at the side, Fig. 1.

4. Reach under the pack with the right second finger and draw away the face card of the jogged packet of six. Display it and deal it face upwards on the table.

5. Draw cards from the pack proper, exactly as when performing the glide and request a spectator to stop the deal whenever he desires.

6. When the request is made, push the jogged packet flush with the deck by pressing inwards with the second joint of the left little finger at the inner end of the five jogged cards.

7. Draw out the five cards one by one, placing them face downwards on the spectator's hands.

Thus, apparently, a free choice of five cards has been made; actually a quick force has been accomplished with a minimum of action and wasted time.

Four Card Force

This force can be put to many uses where it is desired to force a number of cards quickly and easily. Its weakness is that it calls for pre-arrangement of the pack; yet there are many feats in which this is not intolerable, and the deceptiveness of the force more than compensates for the inconvenience of introducing a set-up pack.

Place the cards to be forced tenth, twentieth, thirtieth and fortieth from the top of the pack. Request spectator A to choose a number between ten and twenty. Deal this number of cards on the table, face down, one on the other. Add the two digits together, pick up the packet of dealt cards and from it deal that many cards, placing the last card to one side. (Thus, if thirteen is named, deal thirteen cards. Add one and three, totaling four. Deal three cards from the packet of thirteen cards and place the fourth card to one side; this card is the one which was originally in the tenth position.) Gather the remaining cards and replace them on the pack, that is to say, replace all twelve of the cards on the top of the pack.

Request spectator B to name a number between twenty and thirty. Follow exactly the same procedure as with spectator A, using B's number. Ask C to name a number between thirty and forty and, finally, D to name a number between forty and fifty. Follow exactly the same procedure with both of these numbers. The four cards thus apparently selected at random will be the cards originally placed tenth, twentieth, thirtieth and fortieth from the top of the pack.

This method is very useful for forcing the page and word numbers in a so-called "book test"; the first two cards dealt denoting the page to be used and the second two indicating which word on that page shall be chosen.

To arrange the cards for this force, that is to place the required cards tenth, twentieth, thirtieth and fortieth in the pack, proceed as follows:

1. Place the four cards in order on the bottom of the pack.

2. Begin an overhand shuffle by running twelve cards from the top into the left hand.

3. Pull off the bottom card onto these twelve cards with the tips of the left second and third fingers.

4. Run nine cards from the right hand and then pull off the second of the force cards on top of them.

5. Run nine cards, pull off the third force card; run nine more and pull off the fourth force card.

6. Finally throw the nine cards remaining in the right hand on top. The force cards will be in the required positions.

THE LOST CARD

Even to the most skilful card conjurer there comes a time when, through no fault of his own, he loses control of a chosen card, or when he wishes to control a card whose position in the deck he does not know. In the past, the two methods generally used were: (a) To riffle the pack as for the thumb count until the index of the desired card was sighted and then to slip it to the top of the pack,* (b) To shuffle the cards, with their faces to the left, until the chosen card appears.†

Both methods are, at best, leisurely, with the operator holding his gaze on the pack for too long an interval. The methods offered here provide a logical reason for glancing at the pack, eliminate the furtive element and control the desired card in a minimum of time.

I. The Fan and Riffle

1. Fan the cards in the left hand and hold them face outwards, well to the left as though simply displaying the fan of cards to the onlookers.

2. If the desired card is within thirteen of the top or bottom, make a rapid count to the card before closing the fan. Table the pack for a moment, then secure the card by means of an overhand shuffle or the thumb count and side slip.

3. If, on the other hand, the card is well towards the middle, note its approximate position before closing the fan. Place the pack, face to the

---

* *Card Manipulations*, No. 5, Hugard, page 147; *The Expert at the Card Table*, Erdnase, page 60 ff.

† *More Card Manipulations*, No. 2, Hugard, page 23.

right, in the left hand in position for the thumb count. Knowing the approximate position of the card, the left thumb can break the pack very close to the card and quickly riffle to it, thus eliminating the slow process of riffling the entire pack in a search for the card. With a little practice it is surprising with what certainty the pack can be broken at, or extremely near, the desired card.

4. When the desired card has been found, press the right thumb into the break at the inner end as the left thumb releases its break at the side.

5. Immediately transfer the break to the left little finger, squaring the pack on the left hand, which holds it as for dealing but with its thumb flat against the left side.

6. Make the Invisible Turn-Over Pass (page 37) in turning the pack face down, thus bringing the card to the bottom of the deck. If it is desired to bring it to the top, allow the card to slip off the left thumb before forming the break.

II. The Fan

Fan the pack face inwards as in the previous method and ascertain if the desired card is amongst the top or bottom cards. If not, utilize the following procedure:

a. 1. Support the fan with both hands, the thumbs at the face and the fingers, overlapping, at the backs.

2. Place the left thumb upon that small strip of the left side of the desired card which is visible and, with the right hand, draw the cards to its right a quarter of an inch to the right, Fig. 1.

3. Move that part of the fan in the right hand in a small counter-clockwise

FIG 1

arc, and that part of the fan in the left hand in a small clockwise arc, the left hand moving against the right hand. This action causes the inner left corner of the right hand portion to extend below the left hand segment, as in Fig. 1.

4. Close the fan by moving the hands towards one another. It will be found easy to make a break with the right thumb as the pack is squared by lifting upwards on the projecting corner at the inner end.

Further control is as in the previous method.

b. 1. After spotting the desired card somewhere about the middle, press the left little finger at that point at the back of the fan and push it towards the right. A break will form near the card; note the number of cards between it and the break, either above or below.

2. Close the fan with the right hand from left to right, bringing the cards to a vertical position at the tips of the left fingers, with the tip of the left little finger inserted in the break at the lower side of the pack by pressing downwards with the little finger.

3. Close the pack down on the left palm thus bringing the little finger break to the orthodox position on the right side of the pack.

4. Make the pass or a simple cut and you know the exact position of the required card from the top or bottom according to whether the break was above or below it.

Second Method

Again supposing that you have lost track of a chosen card and that you are unable to produce it in the manner you intended, an easy way to save face is the following:

1. Offer the pack to a spectator to be shuffled. Take it back and have a second spectator freely select a card.

2. Have it replaced and control it to the top, then by means of an overhand shuffle place it second from the bottom, that is to say, you begin the shuffle by pulling out all the cards except the top and bottom cards and shuffle off onto these.

3. Addressing the first spectator assert that you have sent the second card in search of his card and that the two cards are now together in the pack. Have him name his card.

4. Show the bottom card by holding the pack upright in your left hand in readiness for the glide. Drop the hand and deal the bottom card face upwards, glide the next card (the second spectator's card) and continue the deal face upwards until the first spectator's card (the lost card) appears. Lay this card face upwards apart from the other cards, draw out the second spectator's card and place it face downwards beside the first man's card.

5. Have the second spectator name his card, turn it face upwards and so prove that you have carried out your undertaking.

The Prearranged Pack

There is a tendency amongst card conjurers to be sniffish towards that very useful expedient, the prearranged pack, an attitude induced no doubt by the subconscious feeling that using such a pack is, like cheating at cards, unfair and dishonorable. This conviction, coming from men who are adepts at the side slip, the pass, the top change and other variegated trickeries is, to say the least, ironic. And yet many a magician, learning that a trick which has utterly and hopelessly bewildered him is made possible by prearrangement, looks pityingly down his nose and exclaims, "Oh, a prearranged pack!" and forthwith loses all interest in the deception.

Others, having no artistic standards which prohibit such plebian strategies, lack the ability to make the false shuffles and cuts which are essential if the onlookers are to be convinced that an ordinary pack is being used.

The method of handling the prearranged pack which is to be described is addressed to the true expert, who will use any ruse, no matter how old or barefaced, which will enable him to deceive his audiences. This is the man who, with skill to spare at his finger tips, is not so enamoured of his ability that he has lost his sense of proportion. It is also addressed, paradoxically, to the tyro who has five thumbs on each hand; for him it will be a boon until that time when one by one his thumbs become fingers, trained and trustworthy.

That the Nikola system of card prearrangement is to the ancient Si Stebbins and Eight Kings systems what the modern racing car is to the horse-drawn hansom cab is generally conceded by those who have used the different systems. It is suggested that the reader interested in feats dependent upon the set-up pack devote the extra time necessary to master this system; he will be well repaid for the effort. Since it is not our purpose, nor our province, to give the system in this volume, we refer the reader to the brochure published by the author, Nikola; or to the printed *Encyclopedia of Card Tricks*.

Arranging the Set-Up Pack

This method of arranging the cards of a set-up pack is used by French experts who seem to make a specialty of the prearranged pack. It is interesting to note that the mnemonic system of memory aid is apparently little used, or known, by them; their method is to take a shuffled deck and learn the cards by rote, always retaining the same order until each card and its particular number is so familiar that the name of any card instantly recalls its number, and vice versa.

To arrange a pack in a prearranged order quickly, take it in the left hand face upwards and, starting with the face card, push off the cards into the spaces between the fingers, the cards between one and thirteen going between the thumb and first finger, those from fourteen to twenty-six between the first and second fingers, those from twenty-seven to thirty-nine between the second and third fingers, and those from forty to fifty-two between the third and fourth fingers.

This done, each packet of thirteen cards is arranged in the proper sequence and finally the whole pack is counted face upwards, reversing their order and so bringing the cards in the set-up from one to fifty-two. This arrangement is made under cover of a brisk conversation and as if merely counting the cards to see if the pack is in order.

M. Ceillier, the French writer, claims that an expert can arrange a piquet pack of thirty-two cards in forty seconds.

When applied to the arrangement of twenty-six cards only, two sets of thirteen go between the right thumb and first finger and the first and second fingers, the unwanted cards being placed between the second and third fingers.

Assembling the Pack

No matter which system is used, prepare the pack by setting up the first twenty-six cards of the prearrangement in their proper order. The twenty-sixth card is a narrow card. Place the remaining twenty-six cards above this arranged stock, in any order.

Shuffling the Cards

1. Hold the pack as for an overhand shuffle and shuffle off the first twenty cards, letting it be seen that the order of the cards is being changed. Injog the next card and throw. The exact number of cards shuffled is immaterial so long as the bottom twenty-six remain undisturbed.

2. Undercut at the injog and shuffle off slowly. Repeat this shuffle as many times as may be advisable. Since it is a genuine shuffle, so far as it goes, its fairness must be noted by the onlookers.

3. With the cards held in the hands, cut the pack several times, on the last cut riffling to the narrow card and cutting the stocked prearrangement to the bottom.

The Spectator Shuffle

a. 1. Hold the pack as for the thumb count and allow approximately twenty cards to spring off the left thumb. Cut the pack at this point, placing the lower half with the prearranged stock to one side. A glance at the bottom card of the upper packet will insure against the inclusion of any of the prearranged cards should the cut have been too deep.

2. Shuffle the cards remaining in the hands; drop one or two cards in the shuffle, if this can be done naturally, to impress the onlookers that the cards are handled carelessly.

3. Perform any trick which can be done with a small number of cards and preface this trick by having the spectator shuffle the packet.

4. At the conclusion of this trick, gather the cards and replace them upon the discarded packet. The assembled pack still has twenty-six cards in prearranged order at its bottom, yet the handling of the cards will have convinced even the confirmed dissenter that the entire pack is well mixed.

The following will serve to show the type of trick which may be used to convince the spectators that the pack is well mixed.

1. Cut the narrow card to the bottom and place the pack on the table. Have a spectator cut it into three packets, C, B and A. The cards in C will be the lowest part of the prearrangement; the lower cards of B will be the remainder of the stock; the cards in A will be indifferent cards exclusively.

2. Request a spectator to shuffle A and make a note of the top card after the shuffle. Have him place B upon A and cut these two packets freely. Do not specifically mention that the use of a key card is impossible; the original free cuts preclude this and most spectators will realize it.

3. Take the combined packets A and B and fan them face inwards. A number of the first cards of the prearranged sequence will be noted somewhere in the fan, still in their proper order. Cut the last card of the sequence to the bottom and the chosen card will be at the top.

4. Note this card and drop A and B upon C, cut the entire pack and then produce the chosen card as effectively as you can.

Cutting to the narrow card will place the prearranged twenty-six cards at the bottom, in their proper order.

Any other quick trick will serve as well.

Using the Pack

It will be clear that this pack can be used for any of the feats dependent upon prearrangement. The twenty-six card stock can be brought to the top, placed at the middle or retained at the bottom, as the conjurer desires.

Locating the Cards

Let us say that the prearrangement makes use of the first twenty-six cards in the Nikola system, and that you have these at the top. If any number from one to twenty-six is named you call its position instantly; If the number is between twenty-seven and fifty-two, make the pass at the narrow card, or indeed casually cut at this point, subtract twenty-six from the number and name the card. For instance, forty is called. Make the pass, subtract twenty-six from forty, leaving fourteen, and call the jack of diamonds.

With the twenty-six cards at the bottom, the narrow card being the face card, the position of any card of the prearrangement is determined by adding twenty-six. Thus, using the Nikola system, the tenth card (the ten of clubs) will be the thirty-sixth card.

When, however, the second half of the prearrangement is used, cutting the narrow card to the bottom will place each card at its proper number; viz, the fortieth card in the prearrangement will be fortieth from the top.

Part 4
TRICKS WITH CARDS

~~~~~~

A CARD TRICK to be entertaining, and that is its sole excuse for being performed for an audience, must embody the following principles: First, it must have a definite plot, however fanciful; Second, it must reveal some amusing incidents; Third, it must have a definite climax, the more startling the better. It is not sufficient merely to have a card drawn, noted and replaced, and then to produce it with the comment, "That's your card." Except in the case of the performer who delights in fooling another magician with some clever move or location, such tricks are useless to the magician who wishes to entertain his audience.

The tricks that follow embody the lifetime experience, not of one magician alone but that of many of the leading exponents of the art of entertaining by conjuring with cards.

Chapter 1
THE RISING CARDS

~~~~~~

The Hugard Rising Cards

THE RISING CARDS, the most truly magical of all effects with playing cards, has for nearly two centuries been a source of delight and amazement to countless thousands and in its latest dress is as intriguing as ever. What recollections the very name recalls! A little boy, crouched under a large dining table, whose cover, reaching almost to the floor, hid him from sight. Above, the great magician (an elder brother) performing his "latest invention," the cards that rise at command. The youngster below, thread in hand, waiting tensely for his cues and thrilled with the knowledge that he is the *deus ex machina*, that he is the real master of the situation. Small wonder that his soul was lost to magic and that the rising cards became, and remains, his favorite trick.

Robert-Houdin writing in 1868 says of the rising cards that it dates back to the latter part of the previous century and was, therefore, even then an ancient amongst card tricks. This is confirmed by Decremps in his book *Magie Blanche Devoilee*. After describing a makeshift method of causing a card to rise by means of a thread and a bent pin, he says:

There is a method of doing this trick in a more subtle manner, which can baffle the greatest connoisseurs since one can ask people to come close to show them that there is neither thread nor hook; but as we have not divined this method for ourselves and since it has been confided to us by its inventor, under seal of secrecy, we would be unfaithful trustees and we would surely be recreant to the laws of honor if we should give it publicity here.

Ponsin, writing in 1853, claims that the secret had never been published but he says:

. . . as I have bought it and paid well for it, I have not the same motive as M. Decremps for keeping it from my readers to whom in my turn I am about to give it in confidence.

The secret he gives is the original and still the best method, a black silk thread passed alternately above and below single cards so that a pull on it will cause the alternate cards to rise and, at the finish, the thread is pulled clear away leaving no trace of the mysterious agency responsible for the movement.

A volume could be written describing the cumbrous and involved mechanical arrangements which have been devised to bring about this simple effect, the rising of a card out of a pack. However, the use of a thread remains the best as will, I think, be seen from the following arrangement devised by myself. It must not be thought that this method sprang into being full-fledged, on the contrary, it was the growth of quite a number of years. When the youngster aforesaid first tackled the trick for himself, the only method known was the exchange of the ordinary pack for the threaded pack behind an object on the table. Later he found the improved method of hiding the threaded packet under a handkerchief on the table, and adding the pack to it, in picking up the handkerchief to wipe and polish the glass.

This was satisfactory for a time but still called for the use of an assistant to pull the thread. After much cogitation the plan of putting the threaded packet in a vest pocket and using a short thread hooked under the bottom of the vest by means of a bent black pin was evolved, the cards being made to rise by bending over to fan them. The packet was palmed under cover of turning away while the chosen cards were shown to everyone and then secretly added to the pack. This proved satisfactory nearly always, but because of the packet having to be carried in the pocket for some time, the thread became disarranged occasionally with disastrous effect. This difficulty was finally overcome by punching holes in the fulcrum cards and passing the thread through them with the result that the packet could be carried safely for any length of time.

It was at a much later date that the idea of stowing the slack of the thread into an envelope card was obtained from Hofzinser's method and the final step of fastening the thread to the rubber band itself and making the necessary attachment by placing the band in a vest pocket was a natural evolution. The actual working of this final method is very simple and straightforward as will be seen from the following explanation:

Effect. Three cards are selected from a shuffled pack, they are replaced and the pack is shuffled by the spectators. Two rubber bands are placed around the pack and it is held by one of the audience while two glasses are examined. These are set on the table. The magician takes the pack, very openly removes the bands and drops it into one of the glasses, neither adding anything nor taking anything away. The glass can be placed at any spot on the table, a book or a plate can be placed under it and the performer can riffle, fan or spring the cards before putting them into the glass.

Under these conditions, on the first chosen card being named, it rises at command. A second glass is placed mouth downwards over the first so that the pack is completely isolated and yet the second card rises. In the same way the last card ascends, then it is pushed back into the pack and at command it jumps high into the air. Before the rising of each card, the pack can be taken from the glass and the cards riffled, fanned and sprung from hand to hand.

Preparation. The thread method with alternate cards as fulcrums is used but it is applied in a very ingenious way. Duplicates of the cards to rise are required, we will suppose these to be the two of diamonds, queen of spades and ten of hearts. Three other cards have holes punched in them near the top edges, Fig. 1, and an envelope card must be made by glueing two cards together at one end and two sides, Fig. 2. Make a pen-

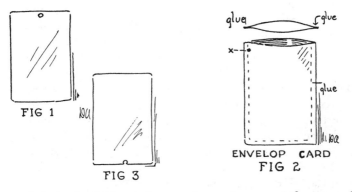

FIG 1

FIG 3

ENVELOP CARD
FIG 2

cil dot on the back of this envelope card near the upper left corner. (X in Fig. 2.) A length of fine black silk, a small rubber band, two large bands and two glasses make up the list of articles required. The glasses must not be the tapering kind; their sides must be parallel and they must be large enough to take the pack easily without any friction.

To prepare the cards that are to rise: First, tie a knot in one end of the thread, place the three punched cards together and pass the knotted end through the holes from the back of the packet to the face. Second, in the middle of the end of the card which is to rise last of all cut a tiny slit with a razor blade. Slip the end of the thread into this slit so that the knot comes on the face of the card and put this card, face outwards, on the packet of punched cards with the knot at the opposite end to the holes; pull the thread taut.

Third, take the other two cards that are to rise and punch a tiny semi-circle out of one end of each, Fig. 3. Push the one which is to rise second down between the first two punched cards so that the thread is engaged in the cut and is carried down by the card. Take the third card, which will be the first to rise, and push it down in the same way between the two rear punched cards. Leave about fifteen inches of free thread and tie a small thin rubber band to the end. Fourth, place the envelope card at the back of the third punched card, with its mouth at the same end as the holes, push the slack of the thread into it until the attached rubber band is drawn close to the top. Stretch the band round the packet lengthwise and all is set. Fig. 4 shows the arrangement.

Place this packet face inwards in your right trousers pocket, the

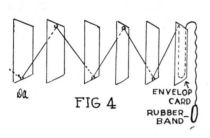

FIG 4

dotted end downwards. Place the two large rubber bands, the larger of which should be half an inch in width, in your left trousers pocket. With the two glasses and the pack with the three duplicate cards on the top in readiness on the table, you are prepared to show the mystery.

Working. The first step is to force the three cards and the following force was devised for the trick. False shuffle, retaining the cards on the top; ask for the loan of a handkerchief and, while getting it, secretly reverse the bottom card. Spread the handkerchief before your left hand and, as soon as the pack is hidden by it, deftly reverse the pack. Let the handkerchief fall over the left hand so that its middle covers the pack.

Invite a spectator to cut the cards through the fabric, but as soon as the cut is made and lifted a couple of inches, grip the person's hand and hold it in that position while you offer to let him take more or fewer cards. When he is satisfied and while the pack is still covered, Fig 5, deftly turn over the portion on your left hand. Thus the three force cards

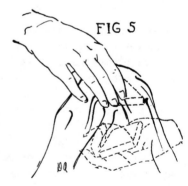

FIG 5

are brought to the top of this packet, apparently by a free cut by a spectator. Invite him to take the top card and hand the next two to two other persons.

Reassemble the pack by placing the packet in your left hand face upwards under the handkerchief and turn the whole pack over before uncovering it. The bottom card being still reversed, you right it while the selected cards are being noted. Hand the pack to each person for the return of the chosen cards and for shuffling. This done, take the pack, note if by chance any one of the three cards is at its face and, if so, cut or shuffle to bring an indifferent card to that position.

"As a guarantee of good faith," you say, "to prevent any manipulation of the cards, I will use two rubber bands." Holding the pack in your left hand, thrust your right hand into your right trousers pocket and palm the prepared packet. "Not there," you say, bringing out your hand and at once taking the pack from the left hand, adding the palmed packet to the top; dive your left hand into the left pocket, bring out the two bands and say, "Ah, here they are." Drop them on the table.

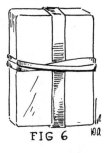

FIG 6

Take the pack in the left hand, holding it upright, facing outwards, and stretch the broad band around it lengthwise so that it covers the thin rubber band at the back of the prepared packet. Slip the other band around the middle of the pack, doubled, Fig. 6, and toss the pack to a spectator to hold.

Bring forward the two glasses, show them, have the pack dropped into one and go back to your table, being careful to hold the pack and the glasses in full view. Stand behind the table, pull back your cuffs, casually showing your hands, and invite everyone to watch very closely. Take out your handkerchief and carefully polish the glasses, then drop the handkerchief on the table. Take the pack, remove the side band and put it in your lower right vest pocket. Hold the pack upright, slip your first and second right fingers under the broad band *and the thin one* which is around the special packet, lift them off *as one* with an upward motion and place them also in your right vest pocket. The thread attached to the band will pull out and allow this to be done if the left hand is held not more than a foot from the body. Push the bands well down in the left corner of the pocket.

Now you can riffle the pack, spread it fanwise and spring the cards a distance of four or five inches from the right hand into the left. Thanks to the holes and the notches in the prepared cards the arrangement of the thread will not be interfered with in any way. Take a glass in your left hand and drop the pack into it.

Invite the first person to name the card he chose. "The two of diamonds? Very well. Merely by the mesmeric power of my fingers I will make your card rise out of the pack. Two of diamonds, Rise!" Twiddle your right fingers over the pack and with the left hand move the glass very slowly straight forwards. The card rises. Take it low down to conceal the little notch in its lower end and put it face upwards on the table.

It will be noted that throughout the rising of the cards the thread runs straight back from the top of the glass to the vest pocket and even at close quarters it is invisible from the front, while your arms on each side of it conceal it from any who may have a side view.

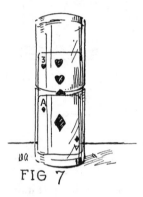

FIG 7

Put the glass on the table, remove the pack, fan it and spring the cards as before, then drop it into the glass again. Have the second card named: "The queen of diamonds? To prove to you that there is absolutely no force at work except my marvelous mesmeric power, I will place this other glass over the pack, so." Invert the second glass and put it over the first, mouth to mouth, Fig. 7. In doing this set the glasses so that the thread is taut and the slightest movement of your body as you very naturally bend a little forward, will bring up the second card. At first thought it would seem that the pull on the thread would upset the second glass; but this is not so, the silk slides quite freely and there is not the least movement of the upper glass.

Lift the inverted glass and remove this second card, again hiding the notch. Replace the top glass and push both a little farther forward to take up the slack caused by the rising of the second card. Make the third card rise in exactly the same way as the second card, remove the glass and put it aside but do not lift this third card, push it down in exactly the same place. Take the pack out of the glass and again fan it and spring the cards as you say, "I will give you an even more striking demonstration of this peculiar power. At the word three your card will jump out of the pack into the air." Count one, two, three, waving your hand, or wand if you use one, and at the third downward stroke engage the thread, the card flies up and the thread is pulled clear away. A startling finish to a mysterious trick.

Pick up this card, place it face upwards on the other two cards, take the pack out of the glass and lay it face upwards on all three. The envelope card, the three punched cards and the three cards that rose, seven cards in all, will thus be at the top of the pack. Move the glasses to one side, pick up the pack, palm off the seven cards in the action of squaring it and drop the pack into one of the glasses. Pick up your handkerchief off the table. Place it in your pocket and leave the palmed cards in the pocket.

This version of the rising cards has been used for many years by its originator, by those to whom he has confided the secret and, more recently, by those who have purchased it at magical depots throughout the world. It is a source of satisfaction to the inventor to know that onlookers, immediately suspecting the employment of a thread in a trick of this kind, find the use of such a thread logically impossible under the imposed conditions of performance as, one by one, any theories they may evolve to explain the phenomenon are destroyed by the extremely honest presentation.

To the spectators, the cards slowly, very slowly, rise at the performers behest in an uncanny defiance of the laws of nature, these cards floating upwards from an unprepared deck to which it was clearly impossible to attach a thread. Their sense of the rightness of things shattered, spectators gaze upon the rising cards with an unbelieving delight in the knowledge that at last the greatest mystery in the never-never land of magic has been shown them. . . . There are not many tricks with which such a perfect sense of the truly magical can be created.

THE MESMERISED CARDS

This version of a trick which has long been a favorite with all kinds of audiences is notable for its clean and natural handling; there is not a single wasted or unnecessary action. The routine is based on the one described by Robert-Houdin in *Les Secrets*, page 241, invented by Professor Alberti; the handling explained hereunder is by Charles Miller.

Preparation. Attach a black silk thread or a hair to the top button of your trousers and fasten a minute piece of a playing card to its free end, then mould a small quantity of magicians' wax around the fragment. The best method of doing this is to tie a knot in the end of the thread and slip it into a tiny slit in the morsel of a card. Wind the thread around the piece several times and then mould the wax over both sides.

Drop the wax pellet into the right coat pocket, out of the way, until it is needed, then press it against the nail of the right thumb, near the tip, Fig. 1. With the wax so placed, and a goblet of suitable size near at hand, you are prepared to present the trick. Mr. Miller's procedure follows:

1. Take the pack in the right hand, the fingers at the outer end, the thumb at the inner end. Place it in the left hand and make a wide fan, inviting three spectators each to remove a card.

WAX

FIG 1

2. Close the fan, cut the pack and have each spectator place his card upon the lower packet. Replace the upper packet, secretly securing a break, and bring the three cards to the top by means of an overhand shuffle in the regular way.

3. Take the deck horizontally, with the right hand, the thumb always being at the inner end and thus keeping the wax pellet on its nail out of view, and place it on a spectator's palm, face downwards.

4. Pick up the goblet with the right hand, transfer it to the left hand, showing it to everyone, take the pack from the spectator with the right hand, the thumb at the inner end, and give the spectator the goblet with the left hand for examination.

5. Using both hands, grasp the pack with the right hand, the thumb on the back, the fingers on the face. In this action the thumb is parallel with the end of the deck, Fig. 2.

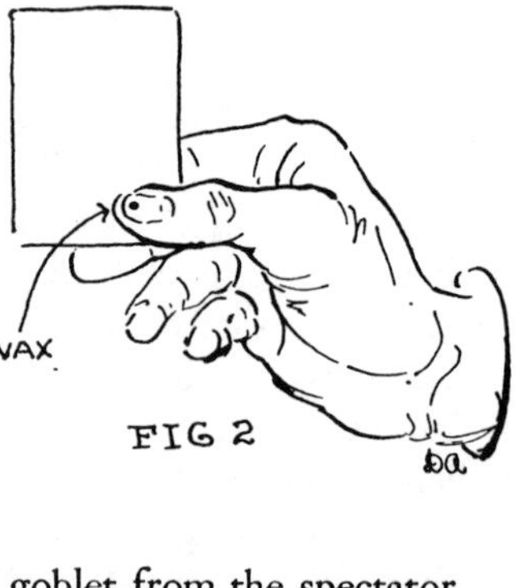

6. Place the left thumb over the right thumb and, with a rubbing motion, draw the wax pellet from the right thumbnail and press it upon the top card. This should be made a part of the natural action of transferring the pack from the right hand to the left so that the right hand can take the goblet from the spectator.

WAX

FIG 2

7. Drop the pack into the goblet with the left hand, the wax pellet being at the lower end, and put the goblet on the table.

8. Hold the right hand a little above the pack and move the fingers as if mesmerising the card, at the same time bend forward a little thus moving the body backwards slightly and causing the first chosen card to rise slowly out of the pack.

9. When this card has risen almost to its full length, take it from

the goblet and transfer it to the right hand, which grasps it by its lower end, the fingers on its face, the thumb at the back next to the wax pellet as in Fig. 2. This action is made apparently to show the card to the spectator who acknowledges it.

10. Scrape the wax off the card onto the right thumbnail, as in Fig. 3, at the same moment snapping the card with the left forefinger apparently to emphasize the fact that it is the first chosen card, but actually to cover any sound which might be made by the sticky wax. Drop this first card on the table as you snap it.

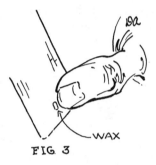

FIG. 3

11. Take the pack from the goblet with the right hand by its upper end, the thumb at the back and the fingers at the face.

12. Place the deck flat upon the left palm, in the position for dealing and, during this action, transfer the waxed pellet from the right thumbnail to the back of the top card, the second chosen card, near its outer end by pressure of the ball of the left thumb.

13. Grasp the pack with the right hand by the ends, the thumb being at the inner end. With this right thumb riffle off half the cards onto the extended left finger tips and make an end riffle shuffle, retaining the two chosen cards at the top. The shuffle, and the subsequent squaring, reverses the pack so that the wax pellet is again at the lower end and the pack is then placed in the goblet in the proper position to effect the rising of the second card.

14. Repeat the series of moves from 8 to 13 for the third card. By way of variation this last card can be made to spring from the goblet by throwing a balled handkerchief down behind the goblet against the taut thread.

It should be noted particularly that every move in this extraordinarily fine routine is demanded by necessity and therefore appears perfectly natural to the spectators.

THE ONE-HAND PLUNGER RISING CARDS

Effect. A spectator chooses a card; it is shuffled into the pack, which is then held in the right hand. After a mystic pass or two, the card rises from the deck.

Presentation. Invite a spectator to choose a card freely, note it and return it to the pack. Then proceed as follows:

1. Bring the chosen card second from the top by means of an overhand shuffle. Then continue the shuffle by undercutting half the deck, injogging the first card and shuffling off. Undercut at the injog, injog the first card, run the second card (the chosen card), injog the third card and shuffle off. The chosen card is thus placed between two jogged cards but is itself flush with the end of the deck.

2. Grasp the pack at its outer right corners with the right fingers and turn it face downwards upon the left palm, much as for dealing but with the pack extending well beyond the side of the hand, the inner corners being gripped between the left third finger and the thumbcrotch. The two jogged cards are concealed during this action by the back of the left hand.

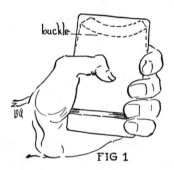

buckle

FIG 1

3. Hold the pack face outwards and vertically in the left hand, the back of the hand to the audience concealing the jogged cards, and grasp these two protruding cards between the tip of the left little finger and the flesh of the palm, Fig. 1.

4. Grasp the upper end of the pack with the right fingers and buckle it outwards and lengthwise, as shown in the ghost pack in Fig. 1, at the same time moving the left hand downwards, taking the two jogged cards with it, until they extend from the lower end of the pack a good two inches. The buckling of the upper end of the pack prevents the chosen card from moving downwards with the two jogged cards. During this action both hands move to the right, this larger movement serving to conceal the smaller action of drawing the plunger cards downwards.

5. Take the pack in the right hand and, in so doing, slide the jogged cards between the right second and third fingers until their lower right corners press well into the crotch of the two fingers. Hold the pack, still face outwards, between the right first and second fingers on the right side and the thumb at the middle of the left side, the third and and fourth fingers being at the bottom, so that the jogged cards are bent at right angles to the pack itself, Fig. 2.

6. Cause the card to rise by pressing inwards with the right third and fourth fingers, the pack pivoting at the middle of the sides on the

thumb and first finger. Moving the lower end of the pack inwards forces the jogged cards upwards, pushing the chosen card up in the familiar Jack McMillen plunger action.

The pack must be held low down, apparently to show the spectator the top of the pack, but actually to pre-
vent him from noting the condition of the bottom of the pack and to make the most of the lines of sight. These are im-portant and experiment alone can de-termine the proper method of holding the cards to prevent a spectator from noticing the jogged cards. The trick is best used when shown to but one or two spectators, hence its uses are lim-ited. It will be a boon, however, to those

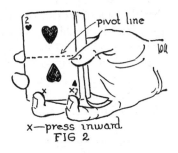

FIG 2

who delight in fooling another magician for he will have no explanation to offer as to what caused the card to rise.

Finally, for the best results, only cards in good condition should be used; sticky cards make the plunger uplift difficult.

THE TWO-HAND PLUNGER RISING CARDS

This method of performing the plunger rising cards can be performed without consideration of sight angles, since the secret action is concealed from sight from all positions, and is thus of more general utility than the one-hand method.

Effect. A chosen card rises from an un-prepared pack, which is held by both hands directly under the onlookers' gaze.

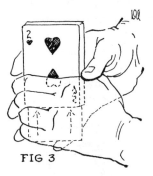

FIG 3

Method. 1. Perform the actions described in the One-Hand Plunger Rising Cards from No. 1 through No. 4.

2. Grasp the pack as shown in Fig. 3, the right thumb and first fingers resting against the sides of the pack, the second and third fingers upon the left fingers, and the concealed little finger pressing up against the lower end of the jogged cards. The left hand, grasping the pack as pictured at the lower end, masks the jogged cards and the right little finger.

3. Press upwards upon the plunger cards with the right little finger,

forcing them up into the pack and thus causing the chosen card to rise from the pack. There should not be the slightest movement of the fingers of either the right or left hands; the right little finger alone moves, and its action cannot be seen.

In performing the trick by this method, the pack should be held so that the onlookers can see the card rise directly from the center of the pack, and it should rise slowly, as though struggling upwards, and not swiftly as though propelled by some hidden mechanism.

In both this method and the One-Hand method the shuffle which is made to jog the plunger cards should be made slowly as you converse with the spectators, the pack being held with its outer end pointing upwards and thus concealing the nature of the shuffle. Although on a casual perusal it would seem that this procedure is dangerous, it has been performed many hundreds of times without detection.

The Witchcraft Card Rise

This is a pure sleight of hand card rise which may be performed on a moment's notice with a borrowed deck. The trick can be done in slow motion as all the moves are covered.

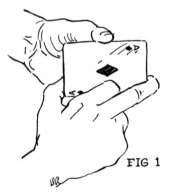

FIG 1

1. Bring the selected card to the top of the pack, then transfer the pack to the left hand in position for dealing, but with the face upwards.

2. Seize the decks by the ends near the right corners with the right thumb and second finger, Fig. 1.

3. Release one card, exactly as in the thumb count. The lower right corner of this card should spring into the crotch of the second and third fingers. The

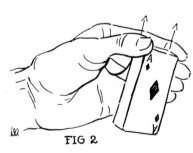

FIG 2

FIG 3

entire action up to this point is screened by the right hand, as in Fig. 1.

4. Slide the left fingers to the top of the deck, immediately bringing the pack into an upright position, Fig. 2.

5. Relax the grip on the cards and allow the selected card to rise, apparently from the middle of the deck, the tension caused by buckling it providing the motive power, Fig. 3.

The feature of this card rise is that it is done with the tips of the fingers and the thumb in full view, thus forestalling any assumption on the part of the spectators that the card may have been pushed up out of the pack.

Mr. Jack McMillen is the originator of this excellent impromptu method.

Chapter 2
SELECTED TRICKS

~~~~~~

THE ZINGONE SPREAD

THIS IS A FEAT of pure skill which, on the face of it, appears to be absolutely impossible. The effect will puzzle the advanced magician as completely as the veriest layman. We feel tempted to apply some of those greatly overworked adjectives (so dear to the magical dealers) but we will content ourselves with saying that the trick is the acme of skill.

Effect. Any pack of cards having been thoroughly shuffled by a spectator is spread face down on the table. Three spectators each draw a card halfway out of the spread, note it and push it back into line. One of them gathers up the pack, squares it carefully and hands it to the magician. He shuffles the cards and again spreads them ribbonwise. Instantly he takes three cards from his trousers pocket and lays them face downwards before the ribbon of cards. The spectators name their cards, the three cards just laid down are turned over and shown to be the selected cards.

While the effect is similar to the Merlin Spread, the method is vastly superior since no key cards or crimps are used.

Method. After having had the pack shuffled by a spectator, take it and spread the cards face downwards in an arc on the table. In doing this handle the cards in such a way that even the person with that dangerous little knowledge must notice that you do not glimpse any card and, in making the spread, see to it that each card is separated from its neighbor. Then:

1. Invite a spectator to step forward, touch any card and draw it halfway out of the line. Have two other persons do the same. It is advisable to have the first card touched as near the left end of the line as possible and the others at intervals of not more than a dozen cards. To ensure this, as you invite the first spectator to touch a card, wave your right hand over the spread from the right end towards the left and stop the gesture at a point some ten or twelve cards from the left end. Quite naturally the spectator will draw out one of these cards since he is convinced you cannot know any of the cards and therefore

it can make no difference which card he touches. Repeat the operation with the two other spectators, using the same gesture to ensure that the cards will not be very far apart. Let us suppose that the eighth, fourteenth and twenty-third cards have been touched, Fig. 1.

2. When the first spectator puts his finger on a card, count rapidly to it from the top card, that is to say, the card at the left end of the spread. We will suppose that the first card touched is the eighth card. As soon as the second spectator touches his card count the number of cards between it and the first card. Let us say that it is the sixth card. Do the same with the third spectator whose card, we will suppose, lies nine cards from the second card. Remember the three numbers eight, six, nine, only; take no notice of the number at which the cards lie in the spread.

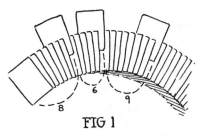

FIG 1

3. Invite each spectator in turn to turn up the left outer index corner of his card, note what it is and then push the card back into line.

4. Have one of the spectators gather up the cards, carefully square the pack and hand it to you.

Up to this point it must be admitted that nothing could be fairer. Even an advanced card man would be baffled by the conditions thus set.

5. To control the cards and bring them to the bottom of the pack, you have recourse to what is known as the *cull* shuffle. First, mentally subtract one from your first number, add one to the second and subtract one from the third number. Thus, in this case, you arrive at seven, seven, eight. Begin an overhand shuffle by undercutting about half the deck, injog the first card and shuffle off. This first action has no bearing on the result to be achieved but it lulls any possible suspicion at the start of the shuffle and carries the required cards well down in the deck. Then:

a. Undercut to injog, run seven cards and injog the next (the first chosen card).

b. Run seven cards, counting the injog card as one, and outjog the seventh (the second desired card).

c. Run eight cards and throw on top thus bringing the third chosen card to the top of the pack. Two of the required cards are now at the top and bottom of the packet in the middle marked by the jogged cards and the third is on the top.

d. Injog the top card by pulling it inwards with the left thumb, undercut to the outjog forming a break at the injog, run one card (a desired card), throw to the break and shuffle off. (The three cards are now together in proper order at the injog.)

e. Undercut below the injog and shuffle off with the result that the three desired cards are at the bottom of the deck.*

6. Execute a couple of riffle shuffles retaining the three cards at the bottom. Square the pack, palm the three bottom cards in the left hand and instantly ribbon spread the cards on the table as at the start. To do this you naturally turn your left side away from the table and take advantage of this to slide the palmed cards deftly into your left trousers pocket. Since it makes no difference if you palm a card or two more than the three which are necessary, do not take time to count them, simply make sure that you have three cards or more.

7. The trick is now finished really although to the onlookers you have done nothing but casually shuffle the cards. Recapitulate what has been done and call attention to the fact that the only way in which the chosen cards can be found is to have them named, turn the pack face upwards and pick them out. "But," you say, "magic affords me a very much simpler way to discover your cards. I merely put my hand in my pocket and bring them out one by one, so," and you do this, laying the cards face downwards in front of the spread at about the same positions from which they were taken. The outer card of the palmed packet will be the one chosen by the third spectator, the next that of the second

---

* Another method of making this cull shuffle is this: With the cards at 8 - 6 - 9, deduct 1 - 0 - 2 from this number. The resultant figure of 7 - 6 - 7 is easily arrived at without confusing addition and subtraction. Use this figure, 7 - 6 - 7, as your formula number in making this shuffle:

1. Undercut less than half the pack, injog the first card and shuffle off.
2. Undercut at the injog.
3. Run seven, the first number, *and injog the next card.*
4. Run six, the second number, *and outjog the next card.*
5. Run seven, the third number, *and throw on top.*
6. Undercut to the outjog, holding a break at the injog.
7. As you do this, injog the top card of the left hand packet by drawing it inwards with the left thumb.
8. Run the first card and throw to the break. Shuffle off.
9. Undercut at the injog and shuffle off. The three cards are at the bottom.

No matter how many cards separate those to be culled, the figure 1 - 0 - 2 is in every case deducted before making the shuffle. When the cards to be culled are separated by more than nine cards, the formula is used in the same manner. For instance, 9 - 15 - 7 would resolve to 8 - 15 - 5; 6 - 3 - 12 would be 5 - 3 - 10.

spectator and the third card will be that chosen by the first. Finally have the cards named and turn them over.

The student should not be deterred by the apparent intricacy of the *cull* shuffle. Once the system is understood the action is very simple and the whole action can be completed in a few seconds. The best way to learn it is to take, say, three aces, place them face upwards in the pack at the positions given above and then perform each action with the cards exactly as described. The changes in the positions of the desired cards can then be followed and the reasons for them will become clear.

THE GAMBLERS OUTWITTED

There is an interesting story to be told in connection with the extraordinarily effective trick which will presently be described—a story which once again points out the moral that all good deceptions are straightforward in conception and execution.

Since the days of the gold rush San Francisco has been known as a city which will not tolerate mediocrity in its actors, but which, conversely, extends a heart-warming reception to any artist of front rank.

Not often does a personality so swiftly become the talk of the town as did Mr. Paul Rosini during his recent phenomenally successful engagement at the western city's smartest café. San Francisco took to its heart this dapper, amusing young man with a twinkle in his eye and a shrug on his shoulders who jubilantly challenged it to match wits with him. In a fortnight the necromantic comedian's "It's a dazzler!" became a city-wide catch-phrase, drama critics were writing column-long reviews of earnest praise, columnists were terming him "the greatest sleight-of-hand performer in America today." Nob Hill society was bestowing its accolade by overflowing the night club in which he appeared.

Fabulous stories of Rosini's skill with a pack of cards began to penetrate the gambling houses of the city. Toward the end of the fourth month of the conjurer's engagement a number of operators in the city's most elaborate gambling house at last decided that it might be interesting to investigate the talents of this young man. No one, they felt, could be quite so good as all that.

Impressed by what they saw, they invited the magician to be their guest at their established place of business, a modernistic triumph of streamlined chromium and scarlet leather. Presumably they felt that there they would have him at their mercy.

But here again, surrounded by men to whom artifice with cards was second nature, Rosini performed his feats with sure skill, particularly perplexing the gamblers by unerringly locating, with unfailing sangfroid, cards of which they had merely thought.

At length one of those present, a nationally-known character who shall here go nameless, demanded test conditions. "I will open a new pack of cards and shuffle it," said he curtly. "I'll cut, note a card and again shuffle. You, Rosini, will attempt to find that card—and you'll fail."

Rosini demurred only long enough to build suspense; then, under the stipulated conditions, surrounded by cold-eyed spectators, he took the shuffled deck from the gambler, after a card had been noted, removed a single card, pushed it face down across the table, flipped it face up, and—it was the gambler's card.

To the knights of the green table in the city by the Golden Gate, "It's a dazzler!" now has a special meaning, recalling as it does the amiable young man with the quick wit and the skilful fingers whose final tour-de-force still puzzles those who were present.

This true story has been told to point a moral once again: It is not what you do, but the manner in which you do it. Rosini on this occasion used against the gamblers a subterfuge as well known to them as their own names, but which, because of his psychologically shrewd handling, not one of those present recognized.

The trick, which Mr. Rosini has given for this book, is simplicity itself: While the new pack was being opened and shuffled, and all

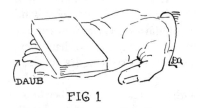

DAUB

FIG 1

attention was centered upon it, Rosini secured daub upon the tip of his second left finger, near the nail. The pack was placed by the gambler upon the magician's extended left hand, its left side at the roots of the fingers, Fig. 1.

The gambler cut, noted the bottom card, and replaced the cut. During this last action Rosini contrived to have the packet replaced from the right; then, bending the third joint of his left second finger upward so that the face card of the packet brushed upon it, he thus transferred a tiny spot of daub to the face of the gambler's card.

The pack, after being shuffled by the gambler, was handed to Rosini. He fanned it, located the daubed card and removed the daub by pressure of the right thumb in removing it from the fan.

Dropping the card face down upon the green baize, Rosini placed his second finger against the side of the card and pushed it slowly towards the gambler. This action not only built up the dénouement, but served the admirable hidden purpose of rubbing the daubed surface against the cloth, removing any final trace of the marking substance which might have remained.

The shout which went up when the card was flipped face upwards, that welcome shout which rewards any magician who has outwitted a challenger, was a tribute, not only to a cleverly conceived handling of a familiar stratagem, but to the showmanly presentation of the trick.

The test of a good trick is always its effect upon a spectator. Here is a trick the handling of which deceived men thoroughly familiar with the principle used. Performed with an air, it will do for the reader what it has done for Paul Rosini.

A Rosi-Crucian Mystery

Presented with artistic enthusiasm, with the air of a man presenting a masterpiece of mystery, this trick will gain for the operator a response out of all proportion to the ease of its execution. Mr. Rosini, with his extraordinarily amusing presentation, makes of it a chicanery which lay onlookers long remember. The routine has been credited in a recent book to another quarter; we are pleased to be able to place the credit correctly.

Effect. Using any pack, the magician hands it to a spectator with the request that it be thoroughly shuffled. This done, he places it on the table and freely cuts it into two fairly equal piles. He is then invited to cut either packet and remove a card from the middle of that packet, which we will call A; cut the other packet, B, and bury the card in it. Packet B is then shuffled by the spectator, after which he is asked to cut A, place B upon the lower half and replace the upper half of A upon all.

The assembled pack is cut several times, after which the magician discovers the chosen card, impressively, and repeats the trick ad libitum.

Preparation. Sew a small button under the left flap of the vest and cover it with daub. Choose a button which has a raised rim around its edges to prevent the daub rubbing off on the trousers.

Working. First phase. The procedure is exactly as outlined above but, as the spectator shuffles the entire pack, the operator's right second finger steals under the flap of the vest and removes a little of the daub upon its tip. After the spectator has noted the card he removed from packet A, the magician courteously explains what is to be done by taking the card for a moment while he indicates how it is to be placed into the packet B. In the interval in which the card is in his right hand he applies the daub to its face with his second finger.

The procedure explained is followed to its conclusion, after which the operator takes the assembled deck and, requesting that the spectator brood upon the name of his card, runs through the deck in an apparently aimless fashion. Actually he sorts the red cards to one end, the black cards to the other, as he carries on a lively conversation, scrutinizing the cards, occasionally removing a card and placing it face downwards on the table, later changing his mind, replacing it in the pack and laying down another card, and so on.

When he has separated the colors, the operator finally picks out the daubed card, first carefully removing the daub by brushing it with the ball of his thumb, places it face downwards on the table and requests the spectator to name his card. As a final precaution, to remove all traces of the daub, he pushes the card towards the spectator, pressing its face on the cloth, and flips it face upwards. This discovery is so startling that the preliminary manipulation in sorting the cards is entirely overlooked.

Second phase: Hold the pack in the left hand, the left little finger holding a break between the red cards and the black. Place the card just located amongst the cards of the same color. Then:

1. Cut the cards at the break, apparently without calculation, and table the packet of red cards beside the packet of black cards.

2. Request the spectator to remove any card from the center of either packet. Since the packets rest upon the table, he must cut a packet with one hand and remove a card with the other hand, thus he is prevented from noting the faces of the other cards. Suppose he takes a card from packet A.

3. Have him replace the card in the other packet B and then shuffle that packet.

4. Invite him to cut packet A, place B on the lower half and top all with the upper half of A.

5. Take the pack, fan it face inwards and pretend to search for the chosen card. Actually, however, you cut the pack bringing all the reds and all the blacks together.

6. Remove the chosen card, the only strange card in one of the packets, and display it as impressively as possible. It is best to first

draw out several cards tentatively and replace them, as in the first phase, before producing the chosen card.

7. Repeat the trick, if desired, and finally shuffle the pack before turning over the last card you discover, thus covering your tracks and leaving the trick an insolvable mystery.

This most ingenious trick again affords proof that the old principles, cleverly routined and effectively presented, can be made into stunning mysteries. In the present case, the genuine shuffle of the first phase, in which the card is marked with daub, convinces the spectators that the cards are thoroughly mixed and that the operator cannot be using key cards or similar subterfuges. Moreover, the first phase establishes the procedure to be followed in subsequent attempts when it is important that it be followed correctly.

Two—Six—Four

Although this trick gives an astonishing result, its working, which calls for a set-up of three cards only and an elementary shuffle, has that simplicity which is found in all good tricks. It is Dai Vernon at his best.

Effect. A spectator thinks of one card from amongst a number spread face upwards on the table. The cards are replaced in the pack and the pack is shuffled and cut into two packets. By a calculation based on the values of the two top cards of these two packets the conjurer divines the exact position of the mentally selected card.

Working. 1. Spread the pack fanwise with the faces towards you; take out a two of any suit and lay it on the table face upwards as you say, "If I place one card on the table and ask you to think of it and I name it—that is not a trick."

2. Take out a six of any suit and lay it face upwards on the two overlapping it to the right, saying, "If I ask you to think of one of two cards and then name the card, you will still be unimpressed since I have one chance in two of guessing the card."

3. Remove any four from the pack and place it on the six spot, overlapping it to the right, and continue, "If I place three cards on the table and name the card you select mentally you will probably say, 'That is rather interesting' but you will still feel that I merely guessed the correct card."

4. "But if I lay out a number of cards [take off six cards and spread them to the left of the three already on the table so that they overlap one another to the right and the right side of the sixth card is under the left side of the two spot] and you think of one and I tell

you the card you are thinking of, you will admit that would be astonishing."

5. "But if I lay out a great number of cards [take off six more cards
and spread them, also face upwards, overlapping one another from the
side of the four spot, Fig. 1] and I find the card you are thinking of, then
you'll call that a miracle."

6. Invite a spectator to think of any card in the row and to remember its position in the row counting
from the left.

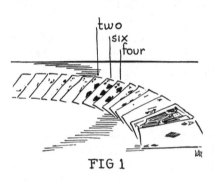

two
six
four

FIG 1

7. This done, gather the cards in
order and place them on the top of
the pack. Undercut about half the
pack, injog the first card and shuffle
off. Undercut at the injog, run
seven cards, injog the next card and
throw the remainder on top. Make
a break at the injog, cut at the break
and put the cards above it to the
right, the lower packet to the left.

8. The first card of the left hand packet is the two which was the
seventh card in the original spread and under it lie the first six cards but
in reversed order; the top card of the right hand packet is the four,
the original ninth card of the spread, and the bottom card is the six, the
original eighth card. Under the four lie the remaining six cards, the tenth
to the fifteenth, in their original order.

9. Ask the spectator to name the number at which his card lay and
by a pretended calculation arrive at the card of which he is thinking.
For example, suppose he thought of the seventh card, the two. Turn
over the top card of the right hand packet showing the four, then turn
that packet over displaying the six on the bottom. Subtract four from
six and announce that the required card is a two. Take the top card of
the left hand packet, have the spectator name the suit of his card, turn
the card and show you have found the card he thought of. In similar
fashion you make a calculation arriving at the eighth and ninth cards,
the six and the four.

The cards in the two sets of six can be revealed by the same procedure. Suppose the spectator says he thought of the fifth card. You
know that this card now lies third in the left hand packet. Turn the top
card of that packet, the two, and lay it down alongside, face upwards.

Then, by way of checking up, turn the top card of the right hand packet, the four; turn the packet over displaying the six on the bottom; subtract four from six, again arriving at two. "That proves I'm right," you say. Deal off the first card in the left hand packet and lay the second card face downwards. Have the spectator name the card he thought of and turn it face upwards.

In like fashion you can arrive at any of the other cards. For instance, to show the fifteenth card of the original set-up: Show the bottom card of the right packet, a six. Remove the top cards of both packets, a four and a two, add these and again arrive at six. Deal six cards from the top of the right packet and show the card originally at fifteen. Naturally the trick will not bear repetition since the reappearance of the two, six and four in the same positions would betray the fact that a set-up is used.

THE MIND MIRROR

This is one of the few really good tricks depending upon a set-up. Its one drawback is paradoxically that it is too good; to the spectators the location of the chosen card seems so impossible that they at once demand a repetition. To make the original set-up again under such circumstances is out of the question and, even if that could be done, there would be the danger that an over-curious spectator might examine the pack and discover the prearrangement. We give a method whereby the trick can be repeated safely.

Effect. While the performer's back is turned, a spectator deals any small number of cards from the top of the pack, notes and replaces the next card, and then places on it the cards he dealt on the table. Finally he riffle shuffles the pack twice. To all appearance the noted card is hopelessly lost amongst the others; however, the performer infallibly locates it and that without asking any questions and without any apparent clue whatever.

Preparation. Any pack can be used but all the cards of one suit must be set on the top, in any order of values, and the top card must be noted and used as key card. The pack can be so arranged beforehand and the trick used as an opener, for which purpose, however, it is almost too good; or the greater part of the required cards can be gotten together in the course of the various preceding tricks. The final arrangement should be made quite openly while apparently playing with the cards and carrying on a brisk conversation. Any furtive procedure will be sure to arouse suspicion. To bring the cards to the top you can use the

Barnyard shuffle, *More Card Manipulations*, No. 2, page 23, or the Erdnase method, page 61, *The Expert at the Card Table*.

Working. Having brought the thirteen cards of one suit, say hearts, to the top of the pack and having noted the top card, the ace for example, execute a false shuffle running a few cards, say five, on top of the set-up and make several blind cuts.

Instruct the spectator that, when your back is turned, he is to deal any small number of cards face down onto the table, look at the card which will then be on the top of the remaining cards, note and remember it and then replace the cards he dealt on top of it. Finally he is to riffle shuffle the pack twice, thus thoroughly mixing the cards. Illustrate what he is to do by dealing off five cards (the indifferent cards you shuffled onto the top of the set-up) and lifting the top card of the remainder (your key card), but do not look at it. Replace this card on the top, put the five cards just dealt back on the pack, get rid of them by a quick overhand shuffle and give the whole pack to the spectator. Caution him to deal noiselessly so that there can be no suspicion that you can hear the number dealt, then turn away.

Now, when the spectator carries out your instructions, at the conclusion of the second riffle shuffle his card will be the first card of the stacked suit to the right of the key card when you spread the deck face up before you. In this case it will be the first heart to the right of the ace of hearts. You can reveal the card by simply picking it out, laying it face downwards on the table, have it named and turn it over. That is surprising enough, or you may reveal it in any startling manner you may desire.

Repetition. As we have already said, the trick is so surprising that a repetition will usually be demanded. To cull immediately the thirteen cards of one suit and put them at the top is quite out of the question, and, even if that were done, you would run the risk that this time the spectator might turn the pack face upwards and note the assembly of the one suit.

To overcome this difficulty, a new set-up must be made in the course of the first discovery, in this manner: When you receive the pack from the spectator, fan the cards, the faces towards yourself, and, with an air of indecision and talking all the time about the impossibility of finding the card, tentatively remove various cards, study them and replace them. What you really do is this: You take out all the clubs, hearts and spades with an odd pip, that is to say the threes, fives, sevens and nines and put them at the back of the fan, that is, on top of the pack.

When you have this new set-up complete, close the fan of cards, as if in desperation, but first note the top card and remember it as your key card for the repetition. Say that you will make a final attempt and ask the spectator to think intently of his card. Fan the deck once more, remove the card, place it face down on the table and have it named. Turn it face upwards and show that you have succeeded.

You are now in a position to repeat the trick immediately without again touching the cards and even if the spectator should turn the pack to run over the faces of the cards, there will be no glaring set-up staring him in the face. The trick is one of the most puzzling and effective discoveries it is possible to do, Jack McMillen's most brilliant conception.

Predestined Choice

One of the popular tricks of recent years has been that in which an unknown red backed card, placed in a blue backed deck, is named by a spectator when the deck is fanned before him, face upwards. This result is achieved by means of a prepared pack which will not stand examination.

This feat is duplicated in the following trick by Mr. Charles Miller in which any two packs may be used, there being no preparation.

Effect. Two packs, one red backed and one blue backed, are used and one of the two is chosen by a spectator. Suppose that the red backed pack is chosen; the magician takes a card from the blue backed pack, places it in the red backed pack and thoroughly shuffles the cards. A spectator is then invited to make a free selection from these cards as they are held face upwards before him. He may change his mind as often as he pleases, yet, infallibly, the card he chooses is found to be the lone blue backed card in that pack.

Method. At the first opportunity palm off seven cards from the blue pack and smuggle them, backs inwards, into your right trousers pocket. In the same way place seven red cards secretly in your left pocket. Prefacing the real feat, allow a spectator to choose a card from the red pack. Upon its return to the pack, control it to the bottom and place the pack in your right trousers pocket, backs inwards, thus adding the seven blue cards to the top.

Invite another spectator to select a card from the blue pack, control it to the bottom and place that pack in your left trousers pocket so that the seven red cards there will be at the top.

As effectively as possible, with the right hand produce the red chosen card from the right pocket and the blue card from the left pocket with the left hand. Despite the simplicity of this effect, it can be made amusing and it serves the necessary purpose of adding the seven strange cards to each pack.

Take the packs from the pockets, one in each hand, faces outwards. Transfer the right hand pack to the left hand, the left hand pack to the right hand, and put both packs on the table, the faces upwards. All this serves to make uncertain the actual position of the blue and the red packs in the unlikely chance that a spectator has tried to follow them.

Square both packs and place them backs upwards. The red pack has seven blue cards at its top, therefore, in the spectators' eyes, it is the blue pack. In the same way, the blue pack is to the spectators a red pack. Now ask a spectator to choose one of the packs. Whichever one he names, pick it up and execute the feat with that deck.

Let us say that he chooses the supposed blue deck, therefore, you take in your hands the red deck with seven blue cards at its top. As you explain what you propose to do, idly turn up the top card, a blue one, glance at it and insert it in the middle of the deck amongst the red cards. Thrust the card in diagonally and, with the left little finger, hold a break above it.

Announce that you are about to place an unknown red card in the blue pack, cut the pack in your hands at the break and place the upper half on the table. Remove the top red card of the other pack on the table, drop it on the cards in the left hand (the top card of which is a blue card), pick up the tabled half pack and apparently place it squarely on the lower half, actually make and hold a break, with the left little finger, beneath the red card just placed in the pack, thus adding it to the red cards of the top half.

Grasp the pack with the right hand, holding the break with the right thumb at the inner end, and turn it upwards for an overhand shuffle, the backs of the cards towards the spectators. For the first movement in the shuffle, draw the top half of the pack, above the break, upwards with the right hand, allowing the lower half, with a single blue card at its top, to remain in the left hand. Now execute the Hunter false shuffle thus: Run five blue cards from the right hand packet onto the packet in the left hand, then drop the right hand packet onto the left, outjogging it a quarter of an inch.

Undercut at the outjog, taking the lower packet with the six blue cards at its top in the right hand. Again run five blue cards onto the left hand packet and repeat the process twice more. Apparently the pack is being well shuffled and many blue backed cards are exposed to the spectators' view; actually, however, only the same seven cards are seen by them in each shuffle.

At the end of the third shuffle the condition is this: The upper half of the deck, with the lone blue card on the top, is outjogged a quarter of an inch on the lower half, which is topped by six blue cards.

Apparently square the pack, actually with the right thumb make and hold a break between the packets at the inner end. Turn the whole pack face upwards, transferring the break from the thumb to the left little finger and invite the spectator to think of any card that he sees, telling him that he may change his mind as often as he pleases as you pass the cards before him, but that infallibly he will pick out the lone red card. Spread the cards from left to right, timing the action so that a selection is sure to be made before reaching the blue backed cards.

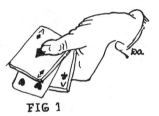

FIG 1

When a card is named, remove it and drop it face upwards on the table, square the pack and immediately cut at the break, place the upper half diagonally to the right, forming a V. Insert the spectator's card into the V, face upwards and extending from the pack, Fig. 1.

Make a short résumé of what has been done, the blue pack chosen freely, one red card placed in it face downwards, the deck shuffled and, finally one card selected by the spectator. Grip the pack at its inner end and turn it over, revealing a red card inserted between the halves of what is apparently a blue deck. This climax is a startling one, make the most of it.

It will be remembered that directly below the spectator's card are the six blue cards and at the top of the pack there is a single blue card. Remove the red card and drop it face downwards on top of the six red cards at the top of the supposed red backed pack on the table.

It now remains to prepare the pack in hand for a repetition or to remove the evidence of the preparation. To do the former, square the pack, face upwards, again securing a break with the left little finger. Hold the pack ready for an overhand shuffle, the right thumb now holding the break and the left fingers resting on the single blue card on the top of the pack, the faces of the cards to the left. Begin the shuffle by holding back the single blue card with the left fingers as the right hand lifts the cards to the right of the break and shuffles them, face upwards, onto the lower half of the pack.

When this shuffle is completed, square the pack and the seven blue cards are again at the top. The trick can now be repeated, again offering the spectator a choice of packs. If no repetition is required, drop the pack in hand on the tabled pack and casually cut the resulting pile once, thus destroying all evidence of the modus operandi of the trick.

The feat, which is not nearly so complicated as it may seem, calls for smooth, easy performance and a confident knowledge of the routine. It is not always necessary to add the seven strange cards to each pack by the subterfuge that is given above, that is to say, by placing the packs in the pocket. Often the preparation can be made under the noses of the spectators while casually moving the packs.

It is most important that the spectator should understand the nature of the trick thoroughly and that he has a free choice of any card in the face-up spread of cards. The operator must make the most of the startling fact that despite every effort on the part of the spectator to outwit him, the only red card in the blue pack is named infallibly.

READING THE CARDS OF ANY DECK

That the effect of this trick is mystifying and entertaining is proved by the fact that it is still in vogue. Two methods are well known to magicians; the first, wherein the operator sights the reversed top card as he holds the pack upright and names the bottom card, was dismissed by Ponsin in 1853 as being known to "tout le monde" (all the world); the second, explained for the first time by the same writer, in which a card is palmed in the hand that brings a named card forward and thus is glimpsed, to be brought forward in its turn while another card is palmed, is also too familiar to be used outside the family circle. The method now to be explained, however, is so subtle that even an expert in card conjuring will be puzzled by it.

Effect. The cards of any pack, which has been shuffled by a spectator, are read one by one by the magician who finally succeeds in reading a card at a number from the top chosen by a spectator.

Working. 1. After the pack has been shuffled by a spectator, take it in the left hand and execute the Gamblers' Glimpse (page 97), sighting the top card.

2. Announce what you are about to do, namely to read the cards with your finger tips, and put the pack behind your back. With the right hand cut off about half the pack and with the left hand turn the

lower half face upwards. Thus the pack is faced but the sighted card is still uppermost.

3. Hold the pack as for dealing with the left thumb flat against the left side and with it press the pack to the right but retain the bottom faced card against the palm, just enough to expose the index of this card. Press the left first finger along the outer end of the pack, its first joint bent against the outer right corner and the tip of the bent thumb against the outer left corner, Fig. 1.

4. Name the card you sighted and bring the pack forward. Take off the top card and show it. As you do this, it is quite natural for you to look at the pack and you note the index of the lowermost card in the bend of the left thumb; the slight displacement of this card is hidden by the thumb and forefinger.

FIG 1

5. Throw the named card face upwards on the table and, without even glancing at the pack again, place it behind your back. Turn the pack over, bringing the newly sighted card uppermost, and push off the lowermost card as before. Name the card just sighted, bring the pack forward and repeat the whole procedure as often as you think desirable.

The correct naming of six cards should be enough to convince the onlookers that you are able to name every card, so you proceed to the climax.

6. As you pretend to read the last card sighted, with the pack still behind your back, take it in the left hand as for the Charlier pass, relax the pressure of the thumb and the pack will split at the bridge formed between the two packets, the bend given to the cards in making the Gamblers' Peek ensuring this. Press the lower portion upwards against the left thumb and let the upper packet fall on it; in other words make a half Charlier pass.

7. The pack will now be in regular order again with the card last sighted on the top. Name this card, bring the pack forward and turn the card face upwards. Hand the pack to be shuffled as you say you will give a further exhibition of the sensitiveness of your fingers.

8. Take the pack in your left hand and hold it in position for the Top Thumb Count (page 183). Ask someone to name a number, "Two, three, four," you say, holding the left hand back upwards and rather close to

your body. We will suppose that three is called. Instantly riffle off three cards with the left thumb and place its tip against the left corner of the packet. At the same time lift your right hand, forefinger extended, the other fingers bent into the palm, and look at it intently.

9. "This finger," you say, "is the cleverest of them all." Bring the left hand up, its forefinger extended, and with it tap the right forefinger as if merely to accentuate your statement, but at the same moment press the tip of the left thumb downwards, buckling the packet of three cards and enabling you to glimpse the index of the third card (see page 101).

10. Release the left thumb, bring it back to its normal position on the back of the pack and drop the left hand, still keeping your attention fixed on the right forefinger.

11. "It has never failed me yet," you continue as you begin to rub it over the back of the pack. Pretend to decipher first the number of spots, or the complicated pattern of a court card, as the case may be, then the color and finally the suit. Deal off two cards slowly and openly, then name the card again and slowly turn it face upwards.

Taking into consideration the ease of the handling and its apparent impossibility, there are not many card tricks more effective than this one for a small audience.

Dexterous Fingers

Some years ago Mr. Billy O'Connor introduced a subtle method of rapid card counting which depended, apparently, upon both dexterity and sensitivity of the fingers. Actually, a short card was employed. Using this trick as a basis, Mr. Charles Miller has devised the following effective feat:

Effect. The conjurer instantly states the number of cards handed to him by a spectator, and as quickly picks off the pack any requested number of cards.

Method. 1. Take any pack of cards and while demonstrating how cards are usually counted—that is, one upon another—deal off ten cards. Replace these cards at the top of the pack and hold a break under them with the left little finger.

2. Request a spectator to call any number between five and ten. If he does not give seven, the usual response, drop as many cards as may be necessary off the right thumb at the inner end. Thus, if five were called, release five cards with the thumb at the inner end, but continue to hold the little finger break under the remaining cards.

3. Drop the packet of five cards, requested in this instance, and as the spectator verifies the count secretly thumb count eight more cards at the outer left corner and transfer a break under these cards to the inner right corner, the left little finger accepting and holding this break. When the cards now being counted by the spectator are returned to the top of the pack there will be eighteen cards above the little finger tip.

4. Request that a number be called from ten to twenty. If less than eighteen, again drop cards off the right thumb at the inner end; if more than eighteen, pick up the required cards with the tip of the thumb. Drop the cards on the table with a flourish and request that your accuracy be verified. (This phase of the routine may be repeated ad libitum.)

5. As the cards are counted secretly edge-mark, or crimp, the inner right corner of the top card of the pack. Thumb count seven cards and back slip this marked key card to the seventh position from the top in gesturing.

6. Replace the cards just counted by the spectator at the bottom of the pack, square it meticulously and hand it to the assisting spectator. You have shown how you can cut any required number of cards from the pack; now you prove how you can estimate, by weight, the number of cards cut by another. Request the spectator to cut any small number of cards from the top and hand them to you. Take these cards and as you apparently weigh them, bevel the sides, sight the key card and count the cards below it. With a minimum of practice, a small number of cards can be estimated at a glance. Name the number of cards you hold and hand the packet to the spectator for verification.

7. As he does this the position of the key card may or may not be altered in the counting, depending upon the manner of the count used. If the cards are dealt one upon the other you know the new position of the key card by a simple calculation.

8. Replace the packet of counted cards at the top and, in making an overhand shuffle, run seven to eleven cards upon the packet; at the end of the shuffle another simple calculation tells you the new position of the key card in the pack.

9. Request another spectator to cut off a larger number of cards and determine the number in the same manner as previously, by sighting the key card and adding to its number in the packet the number of cards below it. Announce this number and again have your accuracy proved by a spectator count.

By increasing the number of cards cut from the pack in each repetition the trick apparently becomes progressively more difficult, and this fact aids in sustaining the interest and curiosity of the onlookers, who have a natural hope that the conjurer will fail in his estimate and usually look forward to this failure with some pleasure—such is the perversity of humans. The feat may naturally be continued just so long as audience interest merits repetition.

The trick itself depends more upon the ability of the performer to convince the onlookers of his rare skill, and to his ability to force the selection of a number within a limited range which will bring it near the key card, than upon any actual manipulation. Not a trick in the accepted sense, it is a pleasant diversion which causes the spectators to attribute to the conjurer a skill he does not possess but which he gracefully admits, since it enhances his prestige and gives his other feats an added plausibility.

Chapter 3
BIRDS OF A FEATHER

~~~~~~

MERLIN'S "LOST" ACE TRICK

THIS TRICK IS SO TITLED because Merlin regarded it so highly that he suppressed it when writing his book . . . *and a Pack of Cards*. It affords an excellent example of the effect which can be had when audacity and skill are component parts of a trick.

Effect. Four aces and twelve indifferent cards are counted onto the table. The aces are placed face downwards, the remaining cards being dealt face upwards, showing that the aces are no longer amongst them. Three cards are dealt on each tabled ace; a packet is chosen and the four aces assemble in this packet.

Method. 1. Remove the four aces and twelve indifferent cards from any pack which is in good condition and place the balance of the pack aside.

2. Show the aces and drop them face downwards upon the twelve cards which are also face downwards.

3. Bottom deal twice, placing an indifferent card at A and B; deal an ace at C and bottom deal again, placing an indifferent card at D.

4. Turn the remaining cards face upwards and hold them in the left hand in position for the bottom deal.

5. Push off the face card of the packet and deal it upon the table; deal a second card upon it; double deal (page 27) the face and bottom cards (an ace) as one. Deal two more cards and double deal again; deal two more cards and deal the last two as one. The deal is made to show, apparently the faces of the twelve indifferent cards once more but the cards are not counted and the fact that only nine cards are shown is never noticed.

6. Place the packet face downwards in the left hand and deal the cards, from left to right, upon A, B, C and D, supposedly the four aces. The four aces will be in packet C.

7. Force this packet; gather the other piles, spread them face upwards; turn packet C and show that the four aces have assembled in the one pile.

The trick calls for less skill than may be imagined since the deals are made with only sixteen cards. Nevertheless, it is not for those who are unwilling to master the sleights required or who lack the audacity which the working demands.

ACE AFFINITY

Of all the tricks with playing cards, as much thought has been expended on the Four Ace trick as on any other, and some extremely effective methods of causing the four aces to gather mysteriously in one packet have been devised. The method to be given here has one feature which no other method can boast: each ace is shown immediately before it is placed upon the table in such a manner as to dispel any belief in the spectators' minds that another card is substituted in its place. For this reason, it is a very strong version of the trick.

Effect. The same as that of the usual four ace trick.

Method. 1. Fan the pack in the left hand, remove the four aces and drop them face downwards on the table. Place the pack at your left and pick up the four aces in this order: clubs, hearts, spades and diamonds. "The ace of clubs, of hearts, of spades and of diamonds," you comment. Pass them from hand to hand, showing that they are undeniably the four aces.

2. Pick up the pack with the left hand and place the four aces on top one at a time. "Clubs, hearts, spades and diamonds," you reiterate. "Ladies and gentlemen, birds of a feather are known to flock together. Let me show you what strange birds these four aces are. Strange as it may seem, the aces are very much like human beings; they feel an affinity for one another precisely as, for instance, stamp collectors yearn for the company of other philatelists, or aviators just can't wait to compare notes with other aviators about zooms and barrel-rolls and things like that; or, to take a particularly virulent case, as opera singers seek out others of their profession, even the ones they don't like—and opera singers, I can assure you, *never* like one another. The point is, the aces are like that—they want to flock together." Insert the left little finger tip in the middle of the deck as you talk and make the pass, holding a break between the two packets and immediately thereafter making a fumbling cut which brings the aces back to the top. Slowly deal the aces in a row on the table. "Watch the aces closely," you urge your spectators, "for the hocus-pocus is about to start."

Point to each card and say, "But no hocus-pocus as yet . . . the four aces—club, heart, spade and diamond—were placed on the table as honestly as you could desire." Someone is sure to challenge this statement; but if the challenge is not made pretend to hear someone claim that the aces are not the tabled cards.

3. "For the benefit of skeptics, we'll start again," you remark amiably. Pick up the four aces and replace them at the top of the pack, showing each ace with great fairness and emphasizing the fact that, from right to left, they are club, heart, spade and diamond. Hold the pack for the Charlier pass and, while protesting that you wouldn't think of cheating so early in a trick, gesture to the left with the right hand, the arm crossing the body, and for a moment half concealing the pack. During this instant let half the deck drop off the left thumb onto the palm, then drop the upper half. Although the aces remain at the top, the spectators will have observed a furtive movement of the packets and will decide that some sleight has been made.

4. "I deal the four aces, club, heart, spade and diamond, honestly and fairly on the table," you continue. Deal three cards; as the third ace is pushed off the pack with the left thumb the fourth ace and the indifferent card below it are also pushed to the left. As the right hand deals the third ace the left fingers square the deck, the little finger tip being inserted under the two top cards in readiness for the double lift.

5. "And the fourth ace is placed at the right of the row," you conclude, beaming. Push off the two top cards as one and grasp them at the ends between the right second finger and thumb; gesture with the right hand, exposing the face of the indifferent card as you speak. Bring the hands together, drop the face card off the right thumb onto the pack, remove the ace remaining in the hand to the right and drop it on the table. "Surely you do not now suspect me of duplicity," you remark. "The four aces are on the table, and the trick will now proceed."

The spectators, however, feeling certain that at least one card is not an ace, will demand that the right hand card be shown. With an air of injured innocence, slowly turn up the four aces calling the suits as you do so—clubs, hearts, spades and diamonds. (This continued reiteration of the order of the suits is to establish this sequence of suits in the minds of the onlookers.) Gather the aces, show that they remain in the proper suit order and place them openly and cleanly at the top of the pack.

6. "I have never before been confronted by such a suspicious audience," you remark in a tone of pained wonderment. "How do you expect me to fool you if you watch me like a hawk every moment?" As you say this palm two cards from the bottom of the pack by means of the bottom palm on page 60, and replace them at the top by means of the one-hand replacement; or, if you prefer, side slip two cards from the center to the top, separately, under cover of turning about to gaze at the various persons watching you.

7. "I'll deal the aces in the fairest possible manner," you announce, "under conditions which absolutely preclude sleight of hand and such nonsense." You have already secretly prepared for a triple lift, using the methods described on page 7, et seq, so that now the left little finger tip holds a break under the three top cards. Push these three cards off the pack with the left thumb, as one, and turn them face upwards squarely upon the pack. "The first ace, the ace of clubs," you observe. Turn the three cards face downwards and push off the top indifferent card, using the same technique used in triple lifting, and place this card on the table.

8. "The next ace was the . . . let me see, the ace of hearts," you remark. Having previously established the sequence of the suits there can be no doubt in the onlookers' minds that each ace is being shown, one after another, an important psychological point. Make the lift get-ready and, as in the preceding action, turn three cards face upwards exposing the face of the ace of hearts, thus tacitly "proving" that the ace of clubs actually was placed on the table. Turn the three cards face downwards, remove the top indifferent card and place it to the right of the first tabled card.

9. Make the lift get-ready as you say, "The club ace, and the heart ace are on the table; the third ace is the ace of spades." Triple lift, show the ace of spades, turn the three cards face down and remove the top card, the ace of clubs, and place this on the table. Follow the same procedure once again, showing the fourth ace, the ace of diamonds, by triple lifting; turn the three cards face down and remove the top card, the heart ace, and place it on the table.

The condition is now this: four cards lie face downwards on the table. From left to right they are

$$\frac{A}{X} \qquad \frac{B}{X} \qquad \frac{C}{AC} \qquad \frac{D}{AH}$$

The spade and diamond aces remain at the top of the pack. From the viewpoint of the spectator, four aces have been shown, each of which has been placed on the table.

10. Make the lift get-ready and turn the three top cards face upwards on the pack, exposing the face of an indifferent card, thus finally and conclusively demonstrating that the aces have been tabled. This action may well be made without comment, as if done idly; it will be noted by the onlookers and it is not a good policy at this point to insist too vehemently that the aces actually are on the table lest it be decided that the performer, as Shakespeare phrased it, "doth protest too much."

11. Run nine cards above the spade and diamond aces in an overhand shuffle. Request a spectator to think of a number from one to four; whatever his number, force one of the aces at C or D. Push this ace, which we will say is the club ace at C, a little forward.

12. Count off three cards from the pack and drop them on A; count off three more and drop them on B; count off three more and drop them on D; simulate exactly the previous actions but make a false count and remove two cards as three, placing these on C, the ace of clubs, the card selected by the onlooker.

13. Pause now and recapitulate what has been done. "Three cards have been placed upon each of the four aces," you state. "What I now purpose to do, in defiance of the law of optics, is to cause the aces to fly together in one pile, as like seeks like, as birds of a feather flock together." Pick up packet A and place it in the left hand; pick up B and drop this also in the left hand. Lift packet D and, instead of dropping it on the packets in the left hand, place it under this group of cards, placing the ace of diamonds at the face of the packet. Undercut this packet of twelve cards for an overhand shuffle, retaining the diamond ace at its face, and shuffle off. A moment later turn the packet up for another shuffle and allow the diamond ace to be seen by the spectators. Run two or three cards and throw the packet, retaining a break under the diamond ace with the tip of the left little finger.

14. Pause, gaze at your spectators benevolently, and announce: "The hocus-pocus will now start in earnest, and I suggest that you watch my every move. If you watch closely enough, you'll see how the trick is done; keep your eye on the cards on the table, but be watchful: if you so much as wink, you'll not see the cards, like the man on the trapeze, fly through the air with the greatest of ease." As you say this side-slip the diamond ace above the left little finger into the palm of the right hand. Abruptly and unexpectedly cry: "*Go!*"

15. "Look!" you exclaim, immediately spreading the cards in the left hand faces upwards on the table. "The aces have vanished!" During the moment in which the spectators are gazing at the cards spread by the left hand, reach out with the right hand and, in drawing the three aces towards yourself, add to them the palmed ace.

16. Hold the four aces, back outwards, in the right hand as with the left hand you scatter the face upwards indifferent cards. "Not an ace!" you marvel. "I'm afraid that all of you winked at precisely the wrong moment, because during that brief eye-wink the aces flew across the table and . . . here they are!"

Slowly turn the cards in the right hand, spreading them, and show that the four aces have indeed congregated in one packet.

There is no other four ace trick in which the aces are apparently placed on the table with such extreme fairness. Using the technique of the triple lift as explained on page 7, and provided that the operator remains at a distance of six or seven feet from his audience, it will be found that the triple lift is not nearly so difficult a sleight as it has been believed to be in the past. Indeed, the triple lift can be made under close-up conditions without detection; consequently, under the conditions outlined above, its use is wholly indetectible, and this version of the four ace trick will be found surprisingly easy and deceptive.

Although the trick, for convenience, has been explained for performance at a table, it is especially well suited for use as a platform trick or, at the other extreme, for use as an intimate trick. In the latter case, the deal is made while kneeling, the cards being dealt onto the floor.

ACE ASSEMBLY

The following is a new method of performing a trick which enjoyed a great popularity a number of years ago. The old method is briefly recapitulated here since it amply demonstrates how different minds, approaching an identical problem, solve it by differing means.

Effect. Four cards are shuffled into a pack, which is handed the spectator to cut into four packets. An adjustment of the top cards is made by the assistant. When the top card of each packet is turned face upwards, each is one of the four original cards.

The Old Method

1. Fan the pack, have a spectator remove four cards of the same denomination—we will say that they are aces—and have them replaced separately as you shuffle the pack. Bring these cards to the top by any means, the Hindu shuffle providing as good a method as any, since it is quick and deceptive. A trick of this type, which depends for its success upon confusing the minds of the onlookers, should always be performed briskly, without wasted time.

2. Make a false shuffle and a false cut, retaining the aces at the top.

3. Place it on the table and request a spectator to cut a quarter of the cards from the top and place them on the table; then cut a quarter more, placing these to the right of the first two packets; then a quarter more. Considering the packets as A, B, C and D, the four aces will be at the top of packet B.

4. Request the spectator to take one card from the top of A and place it upon D; one card from the top of C and place it on A; one from B to D (an ace); one from A to C; one from B to A (an ace); one from D to C (an ace); and one from B to D (an ace).

This movement of the cards is confusing to the onlookers, who are unable to follow the pattern if instructions are given without pause. The card at the top of each packet is turned face upwards, each proving to be an ace.

The New Method

The following method, recently introduced, achieves the same result but by a different means:

1. Spread the cards in a ribbon on the table, face downwards, and invite a spectator to remove any card. Gather the deck, make a pressure fan and remove the three other cards of the same denomination as the chosen card. Let us assume that the four aces are used.

2. Show the aces and have them replaced in the pack, controlling them to the top. Make a series of false shuffles and cuts.

3. Place the pack before a spectator and request him to cut it into four packets, A, B, C and D, of which the first four cards of packet D will be the four aces.

4. Request the spectator to take A in his hands, place three cards from top to bottom, and to place the next card upon B, the next upon C, and a third card upon D.

5. Have him take B, place three cards from top to bottom, and to place the next card upon A, the next upon C, and a third upon D.

6 Repeat the same procedure with C, placing three from top to bottom and one card upon A, B and D.

7. Finally, have him perform the same action with D, placing three cards from top to bottom and one at the top of A, B and C. The top card of each of the four packets is now an ace.

It will be noted that although in both methods the trick has been described as a variation of the four ace trick, it also makes a very acceptable method of revealing four cards chosen by as many spectators.

Both methods are easy and effective, and can be given a variety of presentations. In the first method, the reason for moving the top cards can be given as a desire to mix these cards thoroughly; it will be so construed by the onlookers.

ANENT THE BERTRAM ACES

As every card conjurer knows, a little twist in the presentation of a trick often will transform it from a trick received apathetically by an audience into one which arouses their appreciative interest.

One of the most effective tricks in the repertoire of Charles Bertram, the great English sleight of hand artist, was the Four Ace Trick. His method has been given in *The Modern Conjurer*, but in this description Bertram withheld the twist which he used at the climax of the trick, and which gave the trick much of its brilliance.

A brief recapitulation of the trick as performed by Bertram is this:

1. Palm four indifferent cards in the right hand before handing the pack to an assisting spectator for the removal of the four aces.

2. As the spectator finds and removes the aces, thrust your hand into his inner breast pocket, leaving three cards there and removing one. Exchange good-natured banter with the assistant as you show this card, deploring his duplicity in stealing cards from the pack.

3. Place the four aces at the top of the pack and, by handling it suspiciously, arouse a belief that you have manipulated the deck. Ask, "Where are the four aces?" and if the response is that they are at the top, secretly make the pass taking them to the middle and show them there; but if the response is, "In the middle," show the cards at the top.

4. Replace the aces face down on the pack, make a loud riffling noise by running the thumb sharply against the side of the deck, and deal the four aces face downwards on the table. Ask if the spectator is satisfied that the tabled cards are the aces; he will usually reply that he does not believe that they are.

5. Show the four aces, palm off three cards from the top of the pack and place it upon the table, requesting the assistant to replace the four aces at the top. When he has done this pick up the pack and secretly replace the three palmed cards. Make a gesture as of being about to deal the aces, then as an afterthought say, "Here, you satisfy yourself by dealing the aces," and place the pack in the spectator's left hand. Continue by saying, "Deal the aces in a row, like this," and, under the guise of instruction as to the nature of the deal, grasp the person's wrist with your left hand and guide it to the spots at which you wish the four cards to be dealt, when the three indifferent cards (supposedly the aces) will be in a row upon the table, and the fourth card, the ace, will be at the right end of this row.

6. Turn up the fourth card, the ace, allowing the spectators to glimpse its face, and say, "Place three cards upon this ace." Guide the assistant's arm throughout until the three aces (supposedly indifferent cards) have been dealt upon the tabled ace, and one or two indifferent cards have been

placed on the second supposed ace of the row on the table. Release the spectator's wrist and tell him to look at the cards now being dealt to prove that they are indifferent cards, giving him the option of removing these dealt cards from any part of the pack he may desire, this action continuing until there are four packets of four cards upon the table, the packet to the right being composed of the four aces.

It is at this point that the trick strikes off at a tangent from the printed description of the feat and the little "twist" makes its appearance.

7. Request the spectator to choose one of the four packets and by means of the usual conjurers' equivoque force the choice of the packet at the right end. When this packet is finally selected, or forced, request the spectator to place both hands over it, hiding it completely.

Pick up the rejected packets and palm three cards from these twelve cards as you say, "My trick is this: I am going to take away from you your three indifferent cards, thus . . ." Run your hand rapidly up the spectator's arm and produce the three palmed cards in a fan from his armpit, showing the backs only, " . . . and now I shall send you the three aces. *Go!*" Riffle the packet in your left hand, spread the cards showing their faces to prove that the aces have vanished, and have the spectator turn his packet face upwards and show the four aces to the audience.

8. Accept your applause and say, "Did you see how that was done? Let me show you. Here are the three cards I took from you." Take three cards from the packet of twelve, which you have openly counted, and fan them, showing the backs only. "I'll send them into one of your pockets." Replace the three cards on the packet, riffle it sharply, showing the right hand casually, and then palm the three cards from the packet and spread the remaining nine cards on the table. Count them one by one. "Nine cards only. Three have vanished. Now if you will search your pockets, sir, you will find the three cards."

The spectator ultimately finds the three missing cards in his inner breast pocket and the trick is finished with eclat. "Now, sir, I thank you for your assistance, and I would ask of you one favor," Bertram would conclude. "Do not tell anyone how it is done."

Such was Charles Bertram's ace trick. It will be noted that the change in the routine is apparently only a minor one, and yet it serves to enhance the effect of the trick a thousandfold. It is the final *proof* that three cards have vanished from amongst the twelve held in the hands which makes the final discovery of these cards in the assistant's pocket so puzzling and which lends credibility to the theory that the magician actually has a secret method of making the cards fly invisibly from place to place.

STREAMLINING THE SYMPATHETIC ACES

The principle of the Sympathetic Coins, first described by Hilliard in *The Art of Magic* and credited by him to Yank Hoe, has already been applied to cards. In general, the aces are used, but with cards there is the difficulty which arises from their varied suits. In the method which follows this difficulty is eliminated in a very ingenious manner and the trick will be found even more effective and popular than that with coins.

Effect. The four aces are placed at the corners of a newspaper which is spread on the table or the carpet; one ace is covered with a pad of paper and the other three join it invisibly, one after the other.

Requisites. Any pack of cards, a newspaper, a black crayon and two pads made by folding half sheets of newspaper. Failing a crayon, a pencil, the blacker and softer the better, will serve the purpose.

Working. Spread a full sheet of newspaper on the table and fold two half sheets in half, again and again, to make two pads about nine inches by seven. Remove the four aces from the pack and lay the remaining cards aside. Arrange the aces in this order: clubs, hearts, spades, diamonds, the ace of clubs being the top card of the packet. Call particular attention to this order and deal the four cards in a row, face downwards, on the newspaper, but showing the face of each one and naming it as you deal it.

Check yourself at this point, remarking, "No, I'll do it differently." Pick up the aces one by one, beginning with the ace of clubs, and put them fanwise in the left hand in the same order, clubs, hearts, spades, diamonds, with the faces towards the spectators. With the crayon write a bold capital C at the upper left corner of the newspaper, H at the upper right corner, S at the lower left corner and D at the lower right corner, Fig. 1. Square the packet and deal the first card, the ace of clubs, just below the letter C, giving the spectators a flash of its face as you do so. Second deal the next and put the ace of spades face down under the letter H. Second deal again and lay down the ace of diamonds below the letter S. Finally place the remaining card, the ace of Hearts, below the letter D, Fig. 2. The deal should be made at the same tempo as before, without haste, then proceed immediately with the next action.

Take the two folded paper pads, one in each hand, thumbs above, fingers below, and with them cover the two aces at the top of the paper, the ace of clubs and the ace of hearts (in reality the ace of spades) naming them and calling attention to the fact that the other two aces (supposedly) the ace of spades and the ace of diamonds remain visible (these two are really the ace of diamonds and the ace of hearts). Next, move the pads to cover the lower two aces, leaving the upper two visible, always calling the cards according to the letters on the paper. Cover the two cards on the left side, then the two on the right side, the pad in the left hand covering the supposed ace of hearts and that in the right hand the supposed ace of diamonds. Look straight at the spectators and ask them if they understand the situation perfectly, namely that with two aces covered, the other two are always in full view. At the same time pick up the ace of hearts with the right fingers under the pad and hold it against the lower side. This is best done by making a little forward movement of the hand and pad as the card is covered. This same movement should be made every time you cover a card, so that it becomes inconspicuous.

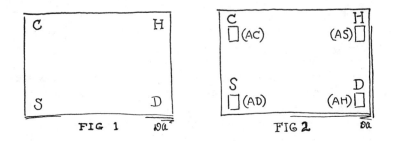

The critical moment has now arrived. Lift the pad in the right hand, keeping its front edge pointing downwards and immediately put the left hand pad over the spot just uncovered, doing it in such a way that there is no possibility of the spectators discovering that the card has been removed. Move the right hand pad to cover the supposed ace of spades at the lower left corner, asking if the aces at the other two corners are still visible. Finally move the right hand pad up to the ace of clubs and leave it there, dropping the ace of hearts secretly and, with the left hand, release its pad which is supposed to cover the ace of diamonds.

Take hold of the lower left corner of the newspaper with the left hand, thumb above, fingers below, and lift it a couple of inches. With the right hand pick up the ace of spades, calling it the ace of hearts, thrust it under the paper at the corner raised by the left hand and push the hand under the paper up to the point above which the ace of clubs is covered by the pad but, as the right hand passes the left hand, leave the ace of spades between the left first and second fingers, allowing not the least hesitation in the passage of the right hand. Retain your hold of the left corner of the paper with your left hand.

Order the ace of hearts to pass upwards through the paper to join the ace of clubs. With the right hand lift the pad covering the ace of clubs and show two cards lying there. Pass the pad back to the left hand, which takes it with the thumb above and the fingers below, thus bringing the ace of spades below it secretly. Turn the ace of hearts face upwards with the right hand to prove that it has obeyed orders. Also turn the ace of clubs face upwards.

Place the pad in the left hand over these two aces, leaving them face upwards, and secretly drop the ace of spades with the pad. Again lift the left corner of the newspaper with the left hand, pick up the supposed ace of spades with the right hand and repeat exactly the same operations to pass it, apparently, through the newspaper to join the ace of clubs and the ace of hearts. When you lift the pad to show its arrival, pass the pad back to the left hand to bring the ace of diamonds secretly under it. Turn the ace of spades face upwards. When you replace the pad over the three aces and secretly drop the ace of diamonds, the tally becomes complete, unknown, of course, to the spectators.

To complete the illusion all that is required is the apparent passage of the ace of diamonds which is supposed to be under the pad at the right lower corner of the newspaper. You say that you will pass this one downwards and, taking the pad by the sides between your hands, thumbs on top and fingers underneath, make a pretence of lifting the card under the pad and of placing both on top of the pad covering the three aces. Order the ace of diamonds to pass downwards to join the other three aces, lift the top pad to show that it has gone and then raise the second pad revealing a fourth card. Turn this card face up, thus showing that the assembly is complete.

The trick should be worked rather deliberately at the beginning to impress the order of the suits on the minds of the spectator, and then proceed briskly to the finish.

In place of the second deal which, however, is very easy with only three cards in hand, the glide can be used. In such case the order of the suits must be reversed. The bottom card of the packet, the ace of clubs, is shown and dealt first, a glimpse of its face being given; then the ace of hearts is drawn back, the other two aces are dealt to their positions and the ace of hearts is dealt last of all. The rest of the routine proceeds as explained above.

THE "SLAP" ACES

This is one of the few feats with cards suitable for small or large audiences. Devised by the late lamented Nate Leipzig, it was one of his tours-de-force and remained in the great magician's program to the end, a gem of a trick which has mystified and delighted countless hundreds of thousands of persons. Technically the trick is not difficult but its effect depends upon showmanship without which it becomes just another four ace trick. Several explanations have appeared in print; these were neither correct nor complete. Some modifications have been made in this handling to bring the trick within the reach of the average card conjurer but the effect remains unchanged.

Effect. The performer invites two (or more) spectators to come forward to assist him. He places one on each side of him and to each he hands two of the four aces. One man places his aces, one on the top and one on the bottom of the pack. The other places his two in the middle. The performer slaps the pack and the aces vanish, this being proved by his showing every card in the deck. Then, holding the pack face outwards and showing his right hand empty, he slaps the face card and it is instantly transformed into an ace. He repeats the operation with two more aces and finally the last ace appears when one of the helpers himself taps the face of the pack.

Working. Having induced two spectators to come forward to help you, stand one on each side of, and close to, you, then proceed as follows:

1. Run through the pack and take out the four aces, incidentally showing that the pack is an ordinary one and that there are four aces only. Hand two aces to each of the assistants; we will call them A and B.

2. Turn to the man on your right, A, hold the pack by the ends in your right hand and have him place an ace on the bottom; put the pack on your left hand, face down, and have his second ace placed on the top. Lift the pack and show the bottom ace, replace the pack on your left hand and again show the top ace. Replace it.

3. Turn to the man on the left, B, telling him to hold up his two aces and show them to everybody. As he does so, make the pass, bringing the first two aces to the middle, hold the break between the two packets, lift the inner end of the ace on top of the lower packet with the right thumb and slip the left little finger tip under it. Take the pack by the ends with the right hand, the thumb securing the break at the inner end. Invite B to place his two aces in the middle of the pack, at the same time hold your left hand below it and let the cards of the lower packet fall, a few at a time, until the break is reached. Have him place his two aces on top of these cards, replace the right hand packet on top, allow the ace at the bottom of this latter packet to slip off the tip of the right thumb and put the tip of the left little finger on it. Square the pack, retaining the break.

4. Turn to A, making the pass as you do so. The position now is this: The first two aces are again on the top and bottom, but the other two lie

directly under the ace at the top. As before, show the bottom ace and the top ace deliberately. Turn to B and, casually spreading the deck, say to him, "And your two aces are here in the middle," at once squaring the pack again. Since everyone has seen the first two aces are still in position, it is taken for granted that the other two remain in the middle. In any case you allow no time for discussion.

5. Turn to A saying, "Do you believe I can make all four aces vanish from the pack instantly?" At the same moment palm the two bottom cards in the right hand by means of the palm explained on page 60, retaining the pack in that hand and making a casual gesture with the left

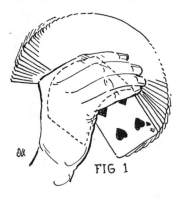

FIG 1

hand. "You don't believe it?" you continue. "Watch! I simply slap the pack so and away they go." Put the pack in the left hand, face downwards, and slap the right hand down on it depositing the two palmed cards there, thus placing the fourth ace with the other three and an indifferent card on the top. Show the top card, saying, "You see one ace has gone," then casually push it into the middle of the deck. Lift the deck upright, showing the bottom card, and continue, "The other ace has vanished also."

6. Take advantage of this surprise, as you turn to B, to palm five or six cards off the top of the pack. Do not wait to count them, simply make sure you get at least five, two or three more will make no difference. Hold the pack face outwards near its lower end in the crotch of the right thumb and spread the cards with the left fingers, fanning them vertically, as you say to B, "And you see your two aces are gone." The palmed aces are perfectly concealed as you hold the fanned cards towards B who scans their faces and agrees that there are no aces amongst them, Fig. 1.

7. Close the fan with the left hand from right to left, the action bringing the right hand over the pack naturally, and deposit the palmed cards on top in squaring the pack. Thus you have the four aces again at the top.

8. Hold the pack face outwards in the left hand and say, "So far a complete success; the aces have vanished. That is the simple part of the experiment, the hard part is to bring them back. I shall merely slap the face of the pack with my empty hand, so . . . " you slap your right hand on the face card, "and at each slap one ace will appear right there," and you tap the bottom card. Face front and take the pack by the extreme right

corners between the right thumb and forefinger. Turn your hands over outwards to show the palms and the back of the pack. Turn towards B and, in placing the pack face outwards in the left hand, with the left second and third fingers side slip the top ace into the right palm. At the end of the movement the left hand holds the pack face outwards and the right forefinger points to the face card.

"Are you ready?" you exclaim. Face front, holding the pack in the left hand a little below the waistline, the right hand about a foot above it, the forefinger still pointing. Suddenly slap the right hand onto the face of the deck, depositing the palmed ace and lifting the hand sharply afterwards. There must be no dwelling on the pack; at the slap straighten the right hand flat and retain the card by slightly curling the left fingers inwards.

9. After a slight pause to enable all to realise what has happened, take the pack with the right hand as before. Turn to A and with the left hand pull up the right sleeve, saying to him, "Here's where you must watch." Turn to B, transferring the pack to the left hand and, as before, side slipping the top ace into the right hand. With this hand at once pull up the left sleeve, saying to B, "And you watch this one. Are you both ready?" Turn front, holding the hands as before, make another slap and the second ace appears.

10. Turn to A asking him if he saw where that ace came from and seize the opportunity to whisper to him to grasp your hand the next time. Assume the position for slapping the pack, hold the right hand half closed and glance furtively at it. Raise the hand as if about to slap it down and A seizes your wrist. Pretend reluctance to turn your hand over, then show it empty. Take the pack by the right corners as before, make the delayed side slip with the third ace (page 34) and show the left hand empty. "They don't come from my sleeves or my pockets, just from the empty air," you say, and you take the pack in the left hand, slap it with the right and there is the third ace.

11. Two courses are open for the production of the fourth ace:

a. You assure A that the process is quite easy and that he can do it himself, he has only to tap the pack so, and, holding the pack face down, you tap it with your right fingers, but in making this explanation you have side slipped the last ace into the right hand and left it on the face of the pack in tapping it. Hold the pack towards him in your left hand, keeping it face down; have him tap the bottom card, at once lifting the pack upright to show the fourth ace.

b. Secretly reverse the last ace, have A hold out his left hand, place the pack upon it face upwards and make him grasp it firmly. The reversed ace is thus against his palm and perfectly concealed. Tell him to slap the pack with his right hand and *will* the ace to appear. He slaps and nothing happens. Let him try several times, then decide you will have to do it yourself. Lift the pack and disclose the missing ace reversed. "Why," you exclaim, "you slapped too hard! You drove the ace right through the pack."

Much depends upon the way in which you manage your helpers. There is an art in this which some performers never master. On no account should they be placed in a ridiculous position to excite a laugh at their expense. Have all the goodnatured fun with them that you can but be sure that they laugh with you. It is a good plan when welcoming a man to the stage and shaking his hand, to say, sotto voce, "Let's have some fun with them." The great majority will help you all they can, but if the exceptional, contrary fellow arrives, as he will occasionally, there is one set rule to be followed . . . keep your temper, keep smiling and keep your wits about you. If you do this and exercise a little ingenuity you are sure to win, for then the audience will be with you; but if you allow yourself to be ruffled and show your annoyance, nothing can save you.

Le Temps Four Aces

This version of the perennial has been devised for use when seated at a table and for that purpose it is perhaps the best that has been worked out. The principle used is that of switching three aces for three indifferent cards, the name being taken from the French technical term for the favorable moment at which the sleight is executed. The misdirection used is so strong that even well informed magicians are taken in by it.

Effect: This is the same as usual and any deck can be used.

Presentation. Take the four aces in the right hand and hold the pack in the left hand as for dealing. Under cover of showing the aces fanned in the right hand, thumb count three cards with the left thumb and insert the tip of the thumb under them at the outer side, covering the action by turning the pack back towards the table and near the body. Square the four aces and bend them lengthwise, quite openly, by squeezing the sides downwards between the right thumb and second finger. At the same time bend the three thumb-counted cards on the top of the pack in exactly the same way by squeezing them between the left thumb and fingers. This action is covered by the left arm being rested on the table, the right arm practically concealing the left hand and the pack.

Lay the aces on the table, faces downwards, and push them around, mixing them thoroughly. Point out that the position of any particular ace can only be guessed at, with the odds of four to one against the guess being correct. As you say this, insert the left little finger tip under the three bridged cards on the top of the pack. Invite a spectator to choose one of the four aces by touching it. Gather the remaining three, taking them by the ends between the tips of the right thumb and second finger. Ask the spectator to hazard a guess as to the name of the ace he has chosen.

Tap the three aces on the table to square them, thus exposing the ace at the bottom, so you change the odds from four to one to three to one, "Because," as you say, smiling, "you cheated a little. You looked at this bottom ace." In this way you plant the conviction that the three aces are

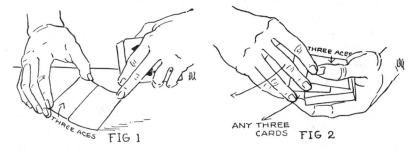

still in the right hand. The spectator attempts to name the face-down ace; you turn it face upwards and here is the move upon which the success of the trick depends.

Place the tip of the left second finger on the inner left corner of the tabled ace, as if merely to aid in turning it over. This action brings the left hand packet face upwards with the break held by the little finger concealed. Still holding the three aces between the right thumb and second finger, slide the left edge of the packet under the right side of the tabled ace, Fig. 1, and flip it face upwards, as in executing the Mexican turnover. Irresistibily the spectators watch that ace to learn its identity. At this instant continue the motion of the right hand towards the left, while the left also moves in the same direction and turns the pack face downwards. At the end of this casual action (and it must be a slow movement, not a hasty one), the packet held by the right hand will be brought directly above the cards in the left hand.

Grip the ends of the three crimped indifferent cards, which are separated on the top of the pack by the left little finger, between the tips of the right thumb and third finger, at the same moment releasing the three aces, leaving them on the top of the pack; then move the right hand forward naturally, Fig. 2, and with the second finger push the faced ace forward as you comment on the success or failure of the spectator's guess. Abolish the bend in the three aces on the top of the pack by riffling the cards.

Spread the three supposed aces in the right hand face downwards on the table and turn the chosen ace down in line with them. Finish the trick in the usual way by dealing the three aces on the chosen ace, three indifferent cards on each of the other cards and finally showing all four aces assembled in one packet.

The strong feature of the trick is the conviction of the spectators that the hands do not approach one another and that the four aces really are placed on the table.

Passe-Passe Aces

This supposed demonstration of skill with gamblers' sleights not only enables the conjurer to show how he can control cards, but concludes with a welcome surprise twist which makes this a very satisfactory trick, since it gives the exhibition a plot form not usually found in this type of work.

Effect. The conjurer offers to show that, despite shuffles and cuts, he can bring the four aces to the top of the pack at will. After the first shuffle, he turns the top card: it is a red ace. The second red ace is turned after a second shuffle. These cards are placed to the left, face downwards. The performer's skill fails him after a third shuffle, however; he turns an indifferent card; and he similarly fails after a fourth attempt. The two indifferent cards are placed face downwards to the right.

The two supposed indifferent cards are flipped face upwards: they are the red aces. The two cards at the left, supposedly red aces, are turned face upwards: they are the missing black aces.

Preparation. The four aces are secretly brought to the top of the pack, the black aces at positions one and two, the red aces at positions three and four.

Method. 1. False shuffle and false cut the cards as you make a short background talk explaining that you purpose to show how gamblers can reserve the good cards for themselves and bring them to the top whenever needed. The ace stock is retained at the top.

2. Make a triple lift, showing the ace of hearts. Turn the three cards face downwards and drop the top card, a black ace, to the left face downwards.

3. Undercut half the pack, injog the first card and shuffle off. Form a break at the injog, shuffle off to the break and drop the remaining cards on top. The stock of three aces is again at the top.

4. Triple lift, showing the ace of diamonds, look pleased with yourself, turn the three cards face downwards, take off the top card, the second black ace, and drop it face downwards on the first card dealt. The two black aces are upon the table, although the onlookers believe them to be the red aces.

5. "Gamblers generally agree that it is extremely easy to control two aces," you explain. "They claim, however, that the third and fourth aces are, for various technical reasons, more difficult to control. During the first two shuffles the third and fourth aces are usually lost in the pack, and it's quite a trick to find them. Curiously enough, I never experience any trouble in finding them." Look blandly pleased with yourself, smiling to take any trace of conceit out of your words.

6. Repeat the false shuffle as in No. 3, bringing the two black aces back to the top. Triple lift once more and, beaming somewhat fatuously, turn these cards face up, showing an indifferent card. "I've never known it to fail!" you exclaim morosely. "The moment I start to brag, something goes wrong!" Turn the three cards face downwards, take the red ace at the top of the pack and toss it to the right, face downwards.

7. Repeat the false shuffle, bringing the last red ace back to the top. Hold the pack to your left, riffle its side with your left thumb and listen attentively to the sound of the riffle, the head cocked on one side. "That's more like it," you explain, your confidence returning. "I never fail twice in a row." During these last words you have prepared for another triple lift. Pause for a moment and, without comment, reach out and knock wood with the knuckles of the right hand.

8. Triple lift, showing another indifferent card. "I should have said, a moment ago, that I never fail—often." Turn the three cards face downwards, take the top card, the last red ace, and place it face downwards to the right on the tabled red ace.

9. With a perfectly serious mien, explain that although you succeeded in controlling only two of the aces, the red aces—here you tap the pile to your left, supposedly the red aces but actually the black aces—the gambler who showed you the method had warned you that you must expect a certain number of failures, particularly with the black aces, which are often incorrigible and irresponsible. "Gamblers are surprisingly superstitious about the black aces," you continue. "Particularly the ace of spades. Do you know, one gambler claimed that—." Break off abruptly, allow a look of comprehension to appear upon your features, lean over the tap the left hand pile, supposedly of red aces. Address a spectator: "I know exactly what went wrong!" you exclaim, laughing.

"These are the two red aces, aren't they?" He acknowledges that they are. "That's what *I* thought," you continue. "But that gambler warned me . . . *look!*" Turn the two cards face upwards, and show that they are the black aces.

10. "Do you know, I never thought it would happen to me!" you murmur in awe. "But seeing is believing. Here are the red aces!" Turn the two cards to the right, supposedly the indifferent cards, faces upwards, showing that they are the red aces.

The trick gives the impression of great skill and is an example of the results to be had with the triple lift.

The Migratory Aces

The routine to be described, while simple of execution, will be found to give the impression of difficult sleight of hand. A shuffled deck is cut four times, the top card of the lower packet in each instance being placed to the right. When turned face upwards, they prove to be the four aces. They are shuffled back into the pack, from which they disappear to be brought forth from the magician's pockets, one by one. The moves follow:

1. Secretly place the four aces at the top of the pack and false shuffle, retaining the top stock. Holding the pack in the left hand as for dealing, with the left thumb riffle off six cards and insert the tip of the little finger under them, using the sleight explained on page 125.

2. Riffle the ends of the pack with the right fingers, stop the riffle near the top, and with the right fingers open the pack bookwise. Remove those cards grasped by the right fingers but retain the top packet, with the aces, by pressure of the third and fourth fingers, keeping the little finger break.

3. Discard the packet held by the right hand, remove the top card of the left packet, an ace, and toss it face downwards on the table, the left little finger still holding the break.

4. Repeat the actions in 2 and 3, throwing the second ace down.

5. For the third ace, invite a spectator to stop the riffle at any point; again make the slip and, discarding the right hand packet, place the third ace face downwards on the table.

6. With but one ace left on the top of the few remaining cards, invite a spectator to stop you during the riffle and slip the top card in the usual manner.

7. Put the top card out with the others, then slowly turn the four cards face upwards, one by one, revealing the aces.

Having produced the aces in a surprising manner, continue as follows:

1. Fan the cards in the left hand and insert the aces at different points from left to right, placing the fourth ace about twelfth from the top. (This is to prevent the subsequent shuffle from being short in duration.) Close the fan, leaving the aces projecting at the outer end. Square the lower end of the pack by tapping it with the back of the right fingers, place it flat upon the left palm with the thumb lying along the left side, and with the right fingers push the aces into the pack, actually jogging them at the right side, Fig. 1.

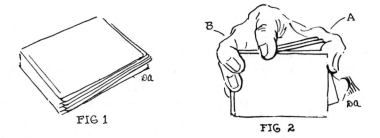

FIG 1   FIG 2

2. Grasp the jogged aces at the upper side, in their diagonally jogged position, between the ball of the right thumb at A, and the second finger at B, Fig. 2. Run a few cards in an overhand shuffle and then, in an upward movement, with the right hand draw the aces from the pack and shuffle them one after the other onto the top. Run three aces to the bottom by way of finishing the shuffle.

3. Palm two aces in the left hand by means of the Erdnase bottom palm and hold the pack in the same hand, covering the palmed cards and thus concealing them.

4. Riffle rather suspiciously as you announce that the aces will fly to your pockets. Thrust the right hand into the right trousers pocket and show confusion as you remove your hand empty.

5. Place the left hand in the left pocket and withdraw it with one of the two palmed aces, leaving the other behind.

6. During this last action palm the ace at the top of the pack by means of the one-hand top palm; then change the pack to the left hand and thrust the right hand into the right pocket bringing out the ace.

7. Change the pack to the right hand, show the left hand empty and bring out the ace previously left in this pocket.

8. Take the pack in the left hand, palming the bottom ace by means of

the Erdnase bottom palm as the right hand riffles the outer end. Place the right hand into the pocket and withdraw it empty. The card has failed to arrive.

9. Take the pack in the right hand and produce the last ace from the right armhole of the vest with the left hand.

10. Spread the pack face upwards with a flourish and show that the aces have actually vanished.

Performed with dash, this routine will be found both effective and amusing.

Solo Flight Aces

This effect in its first phase utilizes the ace trick generally ascribed to Stanley Collins; its dénouement is a new and interesting assembly of the aces suggested for another trick by Dai Vernon.

Effect. Four aces vanish before the spectator's eyes. Four indifferent cards are shown; these turn into the aces in a mysterious manner.

Method. 1. Make a pressure fan and remove the four aces, placing them in any order face upwards upon the table. Profess to deal three indifferent cards, but actually deal four cards, face upwards upon each ace. Place the remainder of the pack face upwards to your right.

2. Pick up one packet, turn it face downwards, bringing the ace to the top. Hold the packet as for the glide and remove, with the right fingers, the face card, placing this face upwards upon the table. Deal the next card in the same manner. Glide back the next card with the left fingers and, with the right fingers at the outer end, remove the next two cards as one and place them face upwards upon the cards previously dealt. The ace is concealed underneath this card, the spectators logically believing that the remaining face-down card held in the left hand is the ace. This in turn is dealt face upwards, and shown to be an indifferent card.

3. Repeat this procedure with the remaining three packets of cards, dealing them into one face-upwards pile.

4. Pick up, with the left hand, the packet of sixteen cards just dealt and place it upon the remainder of the pack, which is face upwards to your right, inserting the tip of the left little finger in doing this. Turn the left hand with its back downwards, bringing the pack face downwards, with the little finger holding its break at the right side. Grasp the pack at the ends, near the right corners, between the right second finger and thumb, holding the break with the thumb, and turn the cards for an overhand shuffle. Shuffle to the break and throw the remainder of the cards on top. The sixteen cards are at the top.

5. Deal five packets of four cards each, from left to right. The aces will be assembled in the third pile. Have a spectator choose any pile and push this packet forward. It must not be the ace pile; if this is chosen, force one of the other packets by the process of elimination.

6. Holding the pack face downwards in the left hand, which is back upwards, gather the four rejected packets one by one by gathering them to the face of the pack with the left fingers. Last of all gather the third pile, the four aces, in the same manner but insert the left little finger between the four cards and the pack.

7. Pick up the chosen pile with the right hand and place it at the face of the deck, above the four aces; immediately turn the pack face upwards and spread these four cards and show that they are indifferent, the left little finger still retaining the break under the four aces. Remove the four cards and the aces below them and place the eight cards in the left hand, dropping the remainder of the pack face upwards on the table.

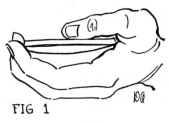

FIG 1

8. Hold the packet of eight cards with their right edges pressing against the tips of the four left fingers, the tips of which are flush with the top of the packet. Push off three cards with the left thumb, fanning them; the remaining five cards remain under perfect control of the tips of the left fingers, the faces of the cards being buckled slightly concave.

9. Square the packet and, holding the cards as described in No. 8, place the right hand over the cards to square them lightly at the ends; under cover of this action press the tips of the four left fingers against the surface of the bottom card at the right side, buckling this card downwards, and replace the finger tips at the right side of the packet but with the right edge of the bottom card now resting against the first phalanges of the four fingers a quarter of an inch below the packet, Fig. 1.

10. Push the first indifferent card off the packet with the thumb; push off the second indifferent card; taking it under the first with the right hand; place the left thumb flat against the left side of the packet and, as the right hand approaches with its two cards, move the left fingers inwards, buckling the bottom card heavily, and remove all the cards above it at the bottom of the right hand cards, as one card. Immediately show the card remaining in the left hand, an ace, and place it at the top of the cards in the right hand.

The left fingers at the right side keep the cards under control, preventing any overlap of the edges, as the first two cards are taken away; the left thumb at the left side prevents a similar overlap as the right hand removes the five cards as one.

11. Replace the cards in the left hand and repeat the procedure in No. 10 three times, which will cause an indifferent card to vanish and an ace to appear on each operation. Apparently you have caused the aces to materialize as mysteriously as they vanished.

12. Drop the entire packet face upwards upon the pack, previously placed face up on the table. The four indifferent cards are thus added to the pack and got rid of.

The student should particularly note the economy of movement in the routining of this trick; there is hardly a waste or an unnecessary action in the entire trick.

The Nomad Aces

This ingenious version of the four ace classic is the invention of Charles Miller, the brilliant California magician. In his hands it is genuinely mystifying to magicians and laymen alike.

Effect. The four aces are laid out in a row and three indifferent cards are dealt on each of them. One pile is selected by the spectators and the aces assemble in this packet. Any deck can be used.

Working. Begin by displaying the four aces, then drop them on the top of the pack. Make the pass bringing the aces to the middle and hold a break between the two packets. Then glancing covertly at your hands, make the pass rather awkwardly, so that the action will be noticed by the spectators. Deal three aces face down on the table in a row, and, in apparently dealing the fourth ace, deal a second and put down an indifferent card. The four cards lie face down on the table thus: A A A X (X being the indifferent card); the fourth ace is on the top of the pack.

In lieu of the orthodox second deal, Mr. Miller often follows this procedure: In dealing the aces he pushes them off the pack with the left thumb, which rests on the middle of the cards at the left side, and takes them between the tips of the right thumb and first and second fingers at the inner right corner. Coming to the fourth ace, he pushes it, and the indifferent card below it, to the right and draws out the indifferent card with the tip of the right first finger as the left thumb draws back the ace flush with the pack. This false deal exactly simulates the previous honest deals.

Whichever procedure is used, continue by making a riffle shuffle, dropping one card on top of the ace at the top of the pack, and prepare to go on with the trick. The spectators, having seen an obvious manipulation, generally hasten to state that the aces are not on the table. If they are too polite to make any remark, a leading statement, such as: "Now, you are convinced the aces are on the table," will bring the denial you require. With a good-natured grimace, you show that they are actually there, thus: Pick up the indifferent card on the right by the ends with the right hand and place it upon its neighbor to the left so that its left side overlaps this card to the left by half its width. Place these two on the third card, letting it overlap to the left, and all three on the fourth card in the same way, Fig. 1. Turn the cards face upwards with the right hand and the indifferent card is concealed behind the aces, the latter only being visible.

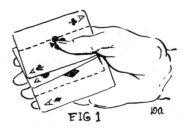

FIG 1

"You mustn't watch me so closely," you protest. "How am I to do tricks when you stare at me like that?" You seem to enjoy your little joke thoroughly. The spectators, seeing three aces, accept them as four, jumping to the conclusion that, with your barefaced manipulation, you laid a trap for them. The psychological reaction here is excellent.

Drop the four cards, with the indifferent card at the top, neatly and precisely on the pack, making any subterfuge impossible. Deal the top indifferent card on the table and then two aces. At the fourth card you second-deal again, placing another indifferent card on the right and retaining the ace on the top of the pack. The position then is this: On the table X A A X; on the top of the pack, two aces.

Invite a spectator to indicate an ace and force one of the two middle cards, an ace, which you turn face up. Make an overhand shuffle, running four cards on top of the two aces, so that at the conclusion of the shuffle these four indifferent cards are on the top of the pack, followed by the two aces. Count off three cards into the right hand, reversing their order, turn them face up and square them, then drop the packet face downwards on the supposed ace at the extreme left of the row of four cards.

Again count off three cards into the right hand, reversing their order to bring an indifferent card to the face of the packet, covering the two aces. Square the packet and turn it face upwards, showing the indifferent card. Make a motion of being about to drop the packet, then notice that the chosen ace is face upwards. Drop the packet on the pack to free your right hand and turn the ace face downwards. Once again count off three cards, really making a false count and taking the two aces only. Drop them on the chosen ace. Repeat the real count of three cards from the pack for each of the two single cards remaining on the table, dropping the packets on them.

The condition of affairs now is this: On the table you have three packets of four cards and one packet of three cards, as under:

1	2	3	4
X	A	A	X
X	X	A	X
X	X	A	X
X	X		X

Pick up packet No. 1, make a break with the left thumb near the top of the pack and insert the packet. Thrust packet No. 2 into the middle of the pack in the same way, allowing the spectators to sight the ace on the bottom. Immediately side slip this ace into the right hand, with this hand reach out and push packet No. 3 towards the spectator, adding the palmed ace in the action. Have the spectator place his hand on the packet. Drop the pack on the table, cut it, put packet No. 4 on the lower portion and complete the cut.

Spread the pack in long ribbon and command the aces to gather in the spectator's packet. Flip the ribbon spread face upwards, show that the aces have vanished and have the spectator turn his cards face upwards showing that they have arrived.

The unusual effectiveness of this method lies in the certainty of the spectators that the four aces are on the table when the packets of three cards are dealt. In Mr. Miller's gifted hands the trick deceives, not only well-posted magicians, but—best of all—entertains and amuses ordinary mortals.

THE CHARLES MILLER ACES

The following method of performing the Four Ace trick is used by Mr. Miller as an alternative to the previous method. There is nothing difficult, technically, in the routine, but it must be done with an air, with bounce and zest. Done in this manner it will confound and exasperate those who may have discovered the secret of more pedestrian methods.

Effect. This is the same as usual, three aces vanishing from their respective packets and assembling in the one chosen.

Working. The principle of the faced deck is used; the necessary moves follow:

1. Remove the four aces throwing them face upwards on the table, then secretly face the deck (page 107), and retain it in the left hand throughout the trick. Turn the aces face downwards in a row, the red aces to the left, the black aces to the right.

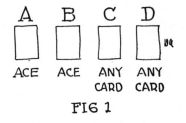

FIG 1

2. Pick up the red aces, show their faces and drop them on the pack. Reach for the two black aces, pause for a moment and talk easily of what you propose to do. Then, as you turn the two black aces face upwards and at the moment when attention is fixed upon them, quietly turn the left hand over, reversing the pack and bringing the two red aces to the bottom of the faced deck. Drop the two black aces onto the pack, apparently on top of the two red aces, but actually above indifferent cards.

3. Deal the four top cards in a row face down so that the two cards on the left are the black aces and the two to the right are indifferent cards; for convenience we will call the cards A B C D, Fig. 1. Supposedly the four cards are all aces. In dealing the aces a flash of the first two can be given but the action must be natural. Hold the pack rather high for the first ace, a little lower for the second and for the third and fourth so low that the faces cannot be seen.

4. Invite a spectator to indicate an ace and contrive to force A or B. If, for instance, he chooses A, push this card forward out of line. Here again you pause to explain that you will place three indifferent cards upon each ace, and, suiting the action to the word, push the three top cards to the right with the left thumb. With the right hand turn these three cards face upwards, square them with the left thumb, first and second fingers, and slide them, still face upwards, under the face-down card D. Repeat the action with three more cards, placing them under C, and finally with three more which you slide under B.

5. Pause again and, pointing to A, ask a spectator if he can name that ace. He hazards a guess and, as you turn this card face upwards with your right hand and all attention is directed to it, turn your left hand over quietly, again reversing the deck. The two red aces will now be uppermost. Drop A face upwards on the table and with the left thumb push the three top cards to the right; two of these are aces, the third an

indifferent card, so you square them before turning them face upwards to show the indifferent card, then hold them, face down, between the left thumb, first and second fingers.

6. Move the right hand to the mouth and moisten the forefinger in a gesture which, Mr. Miller has proved many times, goes completely unnoticed. Grasp the three cards with the right thumb and second finger, turning them face upwards. Place them thus in the left hand for an instant and then take them by the sides between the right thumb and second finger, at the same time drawing the wet forefinger lengthwise down the face of the top indifferent card.

7. Drop the packet on the table, face upwards, and put the chosen ace, A, on it also face upwards but slightly diagonally so that the presence of the indifferent card must be noted. After a moment or two, square the packet and press the tip of the forefinger down on the top ace, causing the indifferent card to adhere to it.

The position now is this: Packets B, C and D are composed of three cards, face upwards, in each, with a face-down card on top, the card on B being an ace; packet A consists of three aces with an indifferent card concealed under the top ace.

8. Place packet D on C, pick them up, square the cards and put them face down on the table, reversing them so that there will be six cards face down and two face up. Pick up B, turn the packet over bringing the ace face up and the three cards face down and drop it on the table in such a way that the face-up ace can be seen. Place the combined packets C and D on B and square the cards, doing all this casually as though merely to clear the table of the cards. Place the twelve cards into the upper half of the deck, amongst the face-down cards, pushing the packet in slightly diagonally so that the left little finger can secure a break under the lowest card, a face-up ace.

(An easier method of handling is to cut off a packet of the face-down cards from the top of the pack, drop it on top of the combined packets B, C, D, slide the lot off the table and place the packet on top of the pack, securing a break with the left little finger tip.)

9. Immediately side slip the face-up ace into the right palm, move the hand to packet A and, in spreading the cards of this packet to the right, slide the palmed card under the bottom card, as shown in Fig. 5, see page 177. The indifferent card, which the spectators previously noted, has disappeared; actually it clings to the back of the top ace and, spread on the table, the four aces only are visible.

10. Finally, and under cover of this unexpected development, quietly

right the faced deck and, after a moment or two, pick up the four aces and drop them on the top of the deck. The two reversed cards which remain in the deck must be righted at the first opportunity.

As has been noted already, the application of the principle of the faced deck is the earliest recorded method of performing this trick. Combining it with another principle, equally old, that of moistening a card to secure adhesion, Mr. Miller has developed a routine which is as surprising to those well versed in card artifice as it is to less sophisticated audiences.

COPS AND ROBBERS—A VARIATION

This variation upon a familiar theme is based on the principle of the faced deck. It makes an excellent impromptu trick since it can be done with any deck, the execution is easy and the climax startling. Here is the procedure:

1. Fan through the face-up deck and jog the kings upwards as you do so. Square the deck, leaving the four kings projecting from the outer end.

2. Turn the deck face down on the left palm and, holding its inner end between the right thumb and second and third fingers, riffle off the four bottom cards (see page 185) and let them drop against the palm of the left hand. Cover the slight pause required for this action by remarking that you will use the four kings as super-detectives. Move the left hand outwards, carrying the four bottom cards with it and strip the four kings from the pack, the four indifferent cards lying concealed below them. Immediately drop the pack upon the supposed four—actually eight—cards. Supposedly, the four kings are now at the bottom of the deck.

3. Pleading forgetfulness, draw the four indifferent cards one by one from the bottom, holding the pack as for the glide, and drop them face downwards on the table, calling them kings. Explain that they will be used later.

4. Riffle off the four kings at the bottom of the pack with the right thumb and hold a break above them with the left little finger. Run the cards from the left hand into the right for the choice of a card. As the selected card is looked at, face the four kings by closing the spread of cards onto the left palm (see page 110, Facing the Bottom Card).

5. Riffle off the lowest king, then riffle off the next, letting it fall on the tip of the left little finger. Crimp the inner right corner downwards with the right thumb. Openly cut the pack, bringing the kings to the middle, reversed.

6. Hold the pack vertically in the left hand, then take the chosen card and, without looking at it, insert it above the crimp at the outer end, thus placing it in the middle of the four faced kings. Square the pack and drop it face down on top of the four supposed kings.

7. Order them, as your detectives, to go in search of the criminal, the chosen card. Make a sweeping spread with the pack on the table and the four kings show up instantly, face upwards, with a face-down card in their midst. Have the card named, push it forward and slowly turn it face upwards.

Chapter 4
ROUTINES

~~~~~~

FIVE STAR FINALE

THE FOLLOWING five card routine is so contrived as to gain for the performer a reputation for uncanny skill, whereas the sleights used are the simplest in the conjurer's repertoire, a subtle use of the double lift taking the place of manipulative skill.

Effect. Five cards are noted by spectators and the pack is shuffled. Spectator A names a number, say seven, and his card is found seven down in the pack. These cards are placed aside. Spectator B names a number and, without shuffling the pack or performing any sleight, his card is found at the number named. Again the cards dealt are discarded. This procedure is repeated with the remaining spectators.

The effectiveness of the routine lies in the discard of the cards which are counted off in each discovery. The pack gradually becomes smaller, there are no shuffles or suspicious moves which would enable the operator to place a spectator's card at the desired number, and yet five cards are so located. Apparently you have succeeded, in the original shuffle, in placing each of the five cards at a number which later is freely called for by the spectators.

Working. Have three cards freely selected by three spectators and bring them to the top by means of the Hindu shuffle in one round in the usual way. Then decide to have two more cards chosen and have two cards peeked at, each time requesting the spectator to think of a card; later the action of peeking will be forgotten and these spectators will maintain that they merely thought of their cards. Bring these two cards above the other three by the side slip. Using the ace, two, three, four and five of hearts for the purpose of illustration, the five of hearts will be at the top of the pack, the others following in order and the ace of hearts, representing the first spectator's card, will be the fifth card.

Shuffle overhand as follows: Draw out all the cards except the top and bottom cards, retaining them by pressure of the thumb and fingers and so bring the five of hearts on the back of the bottom card; bring the pack down on top of these two cards, release a packet of eight or ten cards into the left hand, bring up all the rest, including the original bottom card and the five of hearts, with the right hand, run seven cards, tilt the cards in the left hand and drop a packet at the back, tilt the left hand cards back again and feign to draw off a packet on top of them with the left thumb, finally drop all the remaining cards at the back. The five of hearts remains second from the bottom and the four, three, two and ace of hearts are the eighth, ninth, tenth and eleventh cards from the top.

An alternative method for so placing the five cards is this: Draw out all the cards except the top and bottom cards, retaining them by pressure of the thumb and fingers and so bringing the five of hearts on the back of the bottom card; bring the pack down on top of these cards, release a packet of fifteen or twenty cards into the left hand, bring up all the rest with the right hand, run seven cards, injog the next card and shuffle off.

Take the pack at the right outer corner with the right hand and place it upon the left palm, forming a break with the right thumb under the injogged card which is immediately transferred to the left little finger. With the right fingers draw out fifteen or twenty cards directly below the little finger break, as if making a cut, and drop them on top of the pack.

Having placed the five cards in position by one means or the other, begin by locating the fourth card. Invite the fourth spectator to name a number between one and ten; in the meantime you have slipped your left little finger below the second card in order to be prepared for the call of five, six, seven or eight. If four or less is named, under pretence of eliminating any possible suspicion of confederacy, invite someone else to name a number between one and four, add the two numbers together and proceed accordingly.

If five is chosen, deal the first two cards as one, then single cards for two, three, four and five. Point to the top card of the deck, have the spectator name his card, make a double lift and show the four of hearts. Place the two cards down as one card on the others and push the pile aside.

If the number called is six, deal the first two cards as one, then five more single cards, have the card named and turn the top card. If it is seven, deal seven cards and turn the next; if eight, deal seven cards and turn the eighth; finally for nine, side slip an indifferent card from the center to the top of the pack, deal eight cards and turn the next, the ninth.

Next locate the third card. The position is that the third, second and first cards are on the top of the pack in that order and the fifth card is still second from the bottom. Invite the third spectator to name a number as you secretly secure a break with the left little finger under the third card. Whatever number he names, ask him if he has a magic breath and say that if he has, then by blowing on the pack he will cause his card to appear at the number chosen. Get him to blow on the cards and, as he does so, make a slight grimace and express some doubt about the success of his attempt. Push off the top three cards as one at the count of one, taking them in the right hand. Then take single cards on top of this supposed single card up to and including the chosen number. Put the packet on the table and have the spectator name his card. Turn the top card, a wrong card, of course, for which you blame the spectator's wrong kind of breath. Bury this wrong card in the packet and replace the packet on the pack. Blow on the cards yourself, deal to the required number and turn up the chosen card, in this case the three of hearts. Push the dealt cards to one side as before.

Now proceed to locate the first card. Request that a third number be given and prepare for it by inserting the left little finger under the top two cards. Suppose fourteen is called. Take the first two cards as one in the right hand at the count of one, then single cards until you reach the count of thirteen. Pause and say, "The next card, the fourteenth, should be your card. I think though that I miscounted." Replace the right hand packet on the pack and count off thirteen cards slowly and fairly into the right hand. Push off the fourteenth card with the left thumb face down onto the table and invite the spectator to name his card and turn it himself. Place the pack to your left and, under cover of the surprise caused by the appearance of this card, palm the top card of the packet held in the right hand, the second chosen card; take the remaining cards with the left hand and drop them upon the discard pile; add the palmed card to the pack in drawing it towards yourself.

Turn now to the fifth spectator and invite him to name a number. Continue: "The cards can just as easily be dealt from the bottom as the top," and suit the action to the words. Draw off the bottom card, glide the next, the fifth chosen card, and continue drawing cards to the required number, producing it and turning it face up as it is named. Push the cards dealt to one side.

The second card only remains to be located, and for this you use a very bold method which, though old, is still comparatively little known. The card chosen second is now on the top of the cards remaining in your left hand. When a number has been called, begin the count by taking off the top card with your right hand, face down, and count the other cards one by one on top of it until the number is reached so that the chosen card is the face card of the packet. Look at the spectator and say, "That was the number you asked for, wasn't it?" On receiving an acknowledgment in the affirmative, slap the right hand packet face up on the remaining cards in the left hand saying, "Then the two of hearts [in this case] is the card you chose!"

The very boldness of the maneuver ensures its success; however, you take care to insert the tip of the left little finger between the two packets and, after showing the card, you turn the whole packet face downwards on the other cards. Thus if the cards are examined by any skeptic afterwards the chosen card will be at the number named.

During the locations a spectator may try to trap you by asking for one or fifty-two. Should the first card be asked for, simply turn the top card over and have it identified. If fifty-two is requested have the fifth card named, glide back the bottom card and draw out the desired card.

In the case of the cards peeked at—that is, the fourth and fifth—when asking those spectators to name a number, lay stress on their having *thought* of a card. During the action you may secretly glimpse some of the cards, thus enabling you to name them before turning them face upwards and heightening the effect.

The Razzle Dazzler

One of the fundamental axioms of advertising is that repetition makes reputation. A sound principle, of late years conjurers have applied it to their craft in a manner not intended by the unknown creator of the truism. The card expert has learned that three or four tricks of the same type, upon being combined into one routine with one variation of the basic plot following hard on the heels of the other, creates a vastly greater impression amongst spectators than the same tricks would if performed as separate feats. In this case, repetition makes, for the conjurer, greater illusion.

Each of the feats in this routine is in itself a good trick; since they have been described in detail elsewhere in this book only the salient operations of the routine will be treated.

Requirements. Any borrowed pack of cards; a stranger card, say the four of spades, which has been cut narrow; a small coin purse, opened, which rests in the right coat pocket.

Preparation. Secretly remove the four of spades from the borrowed pack, place the deck to one side and leave the room under any pretext.

Place this card in the right shoe. Later, prior to performance, secretly introduce the stranger four of spades into the borrowed pack. This may be done by any of the familiar methods, such as placing the pack in the pocket in which the stranger card reposes while performing a get-set trick; by palming the card from the right trousers pocket onto the face of the pack; by placing the stranger behind any object on a convenient table, then dropping the pack upon it while drawing back the coat cuffs.

Working. 1. Shuffle the pack idly, faces outwards, as you make your introductory remarks; turn the pack face down and riffle with the left thumb to the narrow stranger card, allow the card below it to drop off the thumb, and cut the pack. The stranger is thus brought second from the bottom. Advance to a spectator and slowly riffle the pack with the left thumb, requesting that he stop you at any point; when he has done so, lift the upper half of the pack, show the card at its face to the company, Fig. 1, then extend this packet to the spec-

FIG 1

tator and request him to remove the card. "If the owner of this pack of cards doesn't object, I'd like to have you mark that card in some distinctive manner. Then hold the card between the flat palms of your hands, to permeate it with your personality. Thank you, sir; I'll be back in a moment."

2. Reassemble the pack and repeat the preceding action with a second spectator, showing the card at which he stops the riffle in the same manner. "Will you also mark your card?" you ask. "You can write your name, or make a geometric figure, or you can draw a pretty girl. Anything that will irretrievably damage the card." Look at the owner of the pack and say drily, "I know you don't mind."

3. Have a third card chosen in the same manner but, after showing it to the spectators, remark as the spectator removes his card, "You can mark that card if you like, but between the two of us, it's a little silly, don't you think? I mean, grown people marking cards. Confidentially, I asked the other two gentlemen to mark their cards in case they get lost in the pack. It's the easiest way to find them when you haven't the foggiest notion what card which spectator took, and there you are right in the middle of an embarrassing moment."

4. As you address the third spectator, cut the pack idly bringing the narrow stranger four of spades to the middle. Insert the left little finger under this card. Turn to a fourth spectator, riffle the pack with the left thumb as before but, when he stops the riffle, break the pack at the inner end with the right thumb and lift those cards above the little finger break, the face card of this packet being the stranger four of spaces. Show this card to the entire company in the same manner, look at the fourth spectator and say, "You'll be sure and remember this card?" and drop the right hand packet onto the lower half, carefully squaring the assembled pack. Cut the pack, taking the stranger four of spades to within two or three of the bottom.

5. For convenience, let us call the first spectator's card A, the second card B, the third C. Return to the first spectator and, holding the pack in readiness for the Hindu shuffle, lift all the cards with the right second finger and thumb except a half-dozen at the face of the pack, one of which is the short stranger card. This is done to prevent an accidental exposure of the back of the stranger card during the subsequent shuffle.

Begin the shuffle, drawing off a few cards with the left fingers as you request the spectator to return his card, A. Stop the shuffle when he advances his hand with the card, have the card replaced at the top of the left hand packet. Continue the shuffle as you turn to the second spectator by picking up a few cards at the top of the left hand packet between the right thumb and second fingers in the first stroking movement of the shuffle, the left thumb holding a break above A. Request the second spectator to replace his card; as his hand advances drop the cards below the thumb break upon the left hand packet. Card B is thus replaced upon card A.

Repeat this sequence of actions with the third spectator. At the conclusion of the shuffle bring the three chosen cards to the top of the pack in the familiar action. These cards now lie, from the top down, C, B and A; A and B have been marked.

An Expert at Figures

1. Card C is at the top of the pack. Press the left fingers upon it, cut the pack at about the tenth card and slip C to the top of the lower packet. Place the upper packet to the right.

2. Again cut the pack, this time at more than twenty cards, and place the upper packet with C at its top on the table. Pick up the packet first discarded, place it upon the cards remaining in the left hand,

thus retaining the stranger card at the bottom of this assembled packet, cards B and A at the top. As you do this, observe that you will use cards from the heart of the pack to obviate the possibility of sleight of hand.

3. Place the packet you now hold to one side, pick up the tabled packet with C at the top. Make a quick overhand shuffle, running nine cards upon C. Make a pressure fan, close the fan and hand it to the proper spectator.

4. Request him to name a number between ten and nineteen, and to deal that many cards onto the table.

As he begins the deal, pick up the remainder of the pack and palm off the top card, B. Fold this card as described under Mercury's Card, place it in the coin purse, close the purse, and immediately withdraw the hand from the coat pocket with the purse palmed. Reach into the right trousers pocket and remove the palmed coin purse at the finger tips. Place it on the table beside the spectator's dealt packet.

"Not only my reputation, but my fortune as well is at stake, sir," you say glibly, "and if I should fail in this delicately morbid problem which confronts us, all that I have in my purse—it isn't much!—is yours."

5. Let us assume that the spectator's number is fifteen, and that he deals off this number of cards. Request him to add the two digits, in this case totaling six, and count down to, and place to one side, the card at that number, in the dealt packet of fifteen.

"Will you, sir, kindly place your hand upon that card and breathe a little incantation? That's admirable. Now name your card . . . there it is!"

Flip the card face upwards; it is the chosen card.

As spectator attention focuses upon the tabled card, palm the top card of the pack with the right hand. Vest this card, A, at the right side of the waistcoat.

Mercury's Card

Assemble the entire pack, fan the cards faces outwards, close the fan, place the pack upon the table and tap it three times.

"There is more to magic than you think," you state, turning to the spectator who drew B. "If you will name any number between one and ten, your card will be at that number."

When the number is named, hand the spectator the pack and request that he himself count down to his card. He does so, turning up an indifferent card. "Every cloud has a silver lining," you ruminate. "This is your silver lining; the contents of my purse belong to you."

Hand the spectator the purse. He opens it, withdraws the folded card, smooths it, and finds that it is his chosen card.

A Card for Pegasus

Pick up the pack, make a pressure fan, close the fan and gaze at the first spectator. "The name of your card, sir?" When he names it smile broadly and say mockingly, "There is more to magic than you think!", thrust the empty left hand under the vest and as effectively as possible withdraw the named card A, as described elsewhere (A Card for Pegasus, page 307).

The Card in the Shoe

Pick up the pack, make a pressure fan, close the fan and cut the stranger narrow card second from the top. Palm the top two cards in the right hand, immediately throwing the pack into the left hand, face downwards. "I will command the last card to leave the pack, shoot up the arm, richochet off the collarbone, spin across the chest, drop down the right side and burrow its way into the outer right coat pocket, all this happening in less time than it takes to wink an eye. *Watch!*"

Ruffle the pack sharply with the left thumb, pause for a moment, then dip the right hand with its palmed cards into the pocket. Drop the stranger card and withdraw the indifferent top card at the finger tips, face inwards.

Hold it before the first spectator, request him to breathe gently upon the card, then slowly turn it face upwards. Beam upon your audience as though you had triumphantly found the card. When, presently, you are told that you have produced the wrong card, affect a momentary surprise, then enquire as to the name of the chosen card. When it is named, repeat the name of the card musingly; then without further comment seat yourself, gesture with the hands to show them empty, quickly remove the shoe and show that the missing card rests in it.

Briskly performed, this admirable trick builds to one of the most effective climaxes in all card conjuring. Use of the stranger card, plus the psychological preparation of finding other chosen cards in out-of-the-ordinary places, convinces onlookers that somehow you contrived to place the four of spades in the shoe, and they will spend many a futile moment pondering on exactly when this action took place.

The action during the location of the last three cards should be at a constantly accelerating tempo, each location following quickly after that preceding it. In handing the various cards to the assisting spectators the identifying markings should not be commented upon; the spectators will observe them of their own volition, and by ignoring the markings on these cards the fact that only two cards are so marked is not emphasized. Later many of the onlookers will insist that all the cards, including the one taken from the shoe, were marked by those drawing them. Of such stuff are real miracles all compact.

FIVE CARD ROUTINE

There are many good tricks in which the card expert finds the one card of which a person has thought from amongst five, but these feats, used singly, have the drawback that the onlooker may decide that, with one chance in five of being successful, the odds were not too greatly against the magician to prevent him from having found the card by sheer luck.

When, however, the magician finds the mentally selected card time after time, without a failure, the feats take on an entirely different aspect: The onlooker is forced to believe that the operator is a man of extraordinary perceptions. The cumulative effect of three or four successful five card locations is simply enormous.

The following five card tricks are standard feats; in each of them the conjurer discovers which of five cards is thought of. Combined into one smooth-running routine, they make an impressive demonstration of pseudo-mindreading.

I. Dai Vernon's Mental Force

Remove the KH, 7C, AD, 4H, and 9D from the pack and place them in a row on the table. Say, "I have chosen five cards at random and I want you to mentally select just one of them. You have an unrestricted choice and you must not think that I am trying to influence you in any way. Here is an ace, occupying the central position; you may think of it, and again you may not. Perhaps you think I had a motive in placing just one black card amongst the five. This might influence your choice, or again it might not. At any rate, look over the five cards carefully, as long as you wish, but rest assured that whatever card you definitely decide upon I shall presently place face down upon your hand and, when you yourself are holding the card, I shall ask you to name your card. Even when the card is on your hand you have the privilege of changing your mind; still the card will be the one you have mentally selected."

When the spectator has thought of a card, pick up the five cards, mix them, draw out the four of hearts and put it on the spectator's hand, face downwards. The card is named; it is almost invariably the 4H.

The trick is purely psychological. The spectator rejects the ace and king as being too conspicuous; the seven of clubs is the only black card; the nine of diamonds is never chosen being widely considered an unlucky card; and this reasoning leaves but one card, the four of hearts.

Your instructions must be directed towards making the spectator consider each card and form a reason for rejecting or choosing it; if you allow a snap choice the trick is almost certain to fail.

II. The Princess Card Trick

During the previous trick you have secretly removed four cards from the pack and placed them in the right trousers pocket. Now, continuing the routine, add the five cards just used to the pack, shuffle it and, fanning the pack face downwards, remove five cards at intervals and hand them to a spectator. As you turn away, request him to think of any one of the five cards and then to shuffle them.

This done, take the five cards from him and, while apparently studying them, move them about and place them in numerical order from left to right, for example, 3H, 5S, 9C, 9S, KD. Remember 3, 5, 9, 9, K; remember also club, spade, so that if later one of the nines is needed, its suit position can be recalled.

"Very well," you say. "Touch the tips of your right fingers to my arm. Concentrate upon your card."

Thrust the five cards into your right trousers pocket, appear to fumble about, then remove the four indifferent cards previously placed there. Place these upon the pack, one at a time and face downwards; then casually cut the deck. Apparently but one card remains in the pocket.

"The problem is progressing nicely," you affirm pleasantly. "For the benefit of these other skeptics, please name your card." Indicate the others in the assemblage, thus bringing them into the trick, and pay little apparent heed as the spectator names his card. In the meantime you have inserted your hand into the pocket and placed your fingers between each of the five cards.

Thus as soon as the card is named, thanks to the memorized numerical order, you can grip the required card and bring it out instantly, just as you would if there were only one card in the pocket. Hold it before you face downwards and ask, "The name of your card?" as though it had not been named before. "The king of diamonds? I knew you would choose that card, sir; for clearly the best is none too good for you; naturally you would select that card."

III. Five Card Royale

Drop the chosen card upon the pack, shuffle it, have a spectator cut it and remove the first five cards. "To prove that I have not at any time resorted to sleight of hand, please note that I shall not even so much as touch the cards," you say, turning your back. "Nor shall I watch the procedure."

Request the party to shuffle the five cards, face downwards. Ask him to look at and remember the top card, replacing it face downwards at the top. Direct the spectator to think of any number, from one to fifty-two, and to transfer that number one at a time and individually from top to bottom. There is no need to request that a small number be thought of: The trick will work with any number and few spectators will transfer more than a small number of cards.

When this transfer has been completed, turn about and take the cards. Holding them face inwards, transfer them from the left hand to the right as you apparently study them, reversing their order in the process.

Hand the packet back to the spectator and, remaining thereafter facing him, ask that he again transfer from top to bottom as many cards as he transferred in the original action, plus one.

When this is done the chosen card is the fourth from the top. Have the spectator place the top card at the bottom and then another card the same way, and place the next card on the table. Have him repeat these actions until one card only remains in his hand, the action being made in the last case with two cards only.

The chosen card is named and the spectator is directed to turn the card he holds face upwards. It is his card!

IV. Phantaso

Gather the cards, shuffle them, fan them and remove any four of the following cards: ace, three, five, six, seven or nine of hearts, clubs or spades. Each of these cards has an odd number of pips which, when they are arranged with the odd pips pointing in the same direction, permit them to be used for tricks of the one-way pack type. Remove also any court card making five cards in all.

Arrange the four spot cards with their pips pointing alike and add the court card to them. Let us assume that the cards are the 3C, 5S, 9S, 9C and KD. Arrange the spot cards with the pips pointing outwards. This can be done in dealing the cards to show them to the onlookers by turning them either sidewise or endwise, as the need may be, in placing them on the table.

Hand the cards to a spectator and request that, when you have turned your back, he give them an overhand shuffle. Ask him then to remove the top card and place it face upwards on the table, to look at it intently and form a picture of it in his mind, "For that is the image, sir, which you must project to me," you aver. Request that the remaining four cards be shuffled overhand and that they then be dropped face upwards on the face-up table card. Lastly, ask that the cards be given another overhand shuffle.

Turn around and, taking the five cards, fan them before you. After a suitable period of concentration, remove the card whose odd pips point in the reverse direction to those of the other cards; this will be the chosen card since, if the instructions are followed, the chosen card automatically is reversed. However, should all the odd indicator pips point together, then the chosen card was the court card.

The tricks which comprise the routine are self-working; no skill is required but as with all other card tricks the presentation must be effective. The use of the various methods of achieving the same result serves to confuse the onlookers and make them uncertain later on as to exactly what was done, the net result being that they leave with the thought that cards were merely thought of and that you found them without touching the cards.

The tricks may be routined in any order, but the last given is an excellent climax trick since it is perplexing in itself and may be repeated several times with perfect safety if an encore is requested.

Chapter 5
ONE HAND CARD MAGIC

~~~~~~

SOONER OR LATER, and generally sooner rather than later, the ardent student of card conjuring will encounter that almost ubiquitous person who proclaims loudly that the quickness of the hand deceives the eye. The best way to meet this situation is to be prepared to do some tricks using one hand only, in which case you remark amiably; "Using two hands, that may be so. Let me show you an experiment in which the hands are *not* swift; in which, as a matter of fact, one hand only is used." Then you proceed with one or another of the tricks which follow.

AN AUTOMATIC REVERSE

Effect. After a spectator has shuffled the cards, the performer puts his right hand in his trousers pocket, and, turning around, holds out his left hand behind his back to receive the pack. In this position the spectator peeks at a card in the usual manner. The performer turns, holds the pack on his left hand, the spectator cuts the cards and reveals his card face upwards on the lower portion.

Working. After having placed your right hand in your trousers pocket, turned your back and received the pack in your left hand:

1. Invite the spectator to lift the corner of the pack near the tip of your left forefinger and peek at the index of a card. The moment he releases the corners he has raised, turn to face him, making a quick remark, such as: "You are sure you'll remember your card?"

2. In the meantime secure the break in the usual way for the side slip, keep the pack behind your back and, as you face the spectator, insert the tips of the second and third fingers into the break and push the card just sighted out of the pack towards the right. When it is almost free, close the fingers and turn the card, face upwards on top of the pack, Fig. 1.

3. With the hand still behind the back, push the pack to the finger tips and make the Charlier pass or, better, the Erdnase One Hand Shift,* thus bringing the faced chosen card to the middle of the pack. Drop the left thumb under the deck, turn it face upwards, Fig. 2, and immediately bring it forward. The whole operation takes a second or two.

---

* *The Expert at the Card Table*, S. W. Erdnase, page 99 ff.

4. Square the face-up pack with your left fingers and thumb, and invite ·
the spectator to make a quick cut. He does so and in nine cases out of
ten he will cut directly into the reversed card, which lies face down on
top of the face-up lower packet. Push this card off the right side of the
pack with the left thumb. Grasp it between the left first finger at its face,

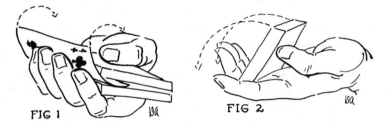

FIG 1   FIG 2

the second finger at the back; extend these fingers outwards and turn
the card face upwards. It is the chosen card.

5. When, as will happen, the spectator fails to cut to the reversed
card, have him replace his packet and turn the pack face downwards, using the left thumb as before, and say that the mistake was yours, that the
cut should have been made face downwards. Square the cards and again
invite the spectator to make a quick cut. He does so and, by all the laws
of averages, this time he should cut to the reversed card, which lies face
upwards at the top of the lower packet.

6. If, however, the spectator is one of those canny folk who insist upon
cutting the deck at a deliberately estimated depth, continue the trick by
reassembling the pack as you admit that, using one hand alone, the trick
will not work. "But," you add, "see what happens when I do use two
hands!" Remove your right hand from the pocket, hold it at least a foot
away from the pack, make a mystic pass with the right fingers and immediately thereafter plunge the hand into the trousers pocket once more.
"That," you confide, "will certainly turn the trick."

Have the card named and ribbon spread the pack on the table with a
sweep of the hand. The chosen card shows up reversed.

A Rapid Reverse

Effect. A card freely chosen from a shuffled pack is found reversed,
the pack being held in the left hand only.

Working. The pack having been shuffled by a spectator, take it in your
left hand, fan it, or ribbon spread the cards on the table, and allow a card
to be freely selected. Then:

1. Explain that you will turn your back, holding the pack behind you, and that the spectator is to thrust his card into the middle himself. As you say this, put the pack behind you, turn it face upwards, push the top face card over the side with the left thumb and turn it over, face downwards, by closing the top joints of the left fingers on it. This takes but a moment.

2. Turn your back and invite the spectator to push his card into the pack. Hold it well squared and rather tightly to avoid any exposure of the faces as he does this. In all reverse tricks, remember, only cards with white margins should be used.

3. This done, turn to the front, keeping the pack behind you for a moment while you turn the top card face upwards and turn the whole pack face downwards.

4. Hand the pack to the spectator, have him name his card and then spread the pack face upwards on the table. One card is seen to be face downwards. Let him name his card again, then turn the reversed card: It is his card.

The trick is an excellent one for the discovery of the first card in a series of five card discoveries, the four remaining cards, presumably on the top of the pack, not being disturbed.

THE IMPROMPTU MAGICIAN

Effect. The spectator himself finds his card which has been buried in the pack.

Working. Invite a spectator to shuffle the pack and then place it on your left hand. Proceed as follows:

1. Tell him to take about half the pack, place the packet behind his back, remove any card from the middle, bring it forward, look at it and remember it, then place it on top of his packet and bring the packet forward.

2. As you give these instructions, place your packet behind your back, as if merely showing him what he is to do, and rapidly make the following moves: Push off the two top cards with the left thumb onto the finger tips, turn them face upwards on the top, push the top one off and turn it face downwards on the other face-up card, turn the pack over, push off the bottom card and reverse it, finally, turn the whole packet over once more. The position is that the top card of your packet is face down, the second card and the bottom card are face upwards. The whole operation can be done easily while the spectator is choosing and noting his card. Bring your packet forward as soon as you have set the cards.

3. Place your packet on top of the spectator's, pointing out that his card is thus buried in the middle of the deck. Have the spectator square the cards and place them behind his back.

4. Instruct him to take the top card and push it into the middle of the deck. When he has done this suddenly recall that the card should have been reversed and then pushed in; so you tell him to take the next card, reverse it and thrust it into the deck and then square the cards.

5. Have the spectator bring the pack forward, name his card and let him discover that it lies next to the reversed card which he, himself, thrust into the pack.

SECOND METHOD

Working. Begin operations in exactly the same way as in An Automatic Reverse, page 275, following the instructions in paragraphs 1 and 2, that is to say, with the pack behind your back a spectator peeks at a card which is then brought secretly to the top of the pack; this done, proceed thus:

3. With the pack still behind your back, turn the selected card face downwards, push out the bottom card with the tips of the left fingers, turn it face upwards on the top of the deck and at once turn it face downwards. These maneuvers are very easy; they can be done rapidly and, if the wrist is pressed firmly against the back, there will be no movement of the arm to arouse suspicion. The chosen card has thus been placed second from the top with an indifferent card face down upon it.

4. Bring the pack forward, stand the spectator on your left, facing the spectators with you. "Now," you say, "have you ever performed a feat of magic? No? Well, you're about to get the thrill of a lifetime. You shall do the whole feat yourself. The card you are thinking of is somewhere in the deck; to find it by ordinary, everyday procedure you would have to run over the faces of the cards until you came to it. That would be very prosaic, so for the moment I shall invest you with magic powers— so," and you make mesmeric passes over his face. "Now this is all you have to do. You see this card," you turn the top card face upwards, "the two of hearts [or whatever the card may be]. You must thrust this card into the deck, at the same time thinking intently of your card, and you will find your card by magic."

5. "To prove that this really is magic, you shall do it without looking at the cards. Please place your hands behind your back." As he does this, put your left hand behind him, make the Charlier pass and put the pack

in his hands. (Some magicians prefer the Erdnase One Hand Shift since the pack lies flat on the palm prior to the sleight.) The spectator takes the top card, now a face-down indifferent card, and pushes it into the pack, where, of course, it is lost amongst the others.

6. Have him square the cards and bring the pack forward. It only remains for him to name his card, find the reversed card and turn over the card next to it. Congratulate him on his success and beg him to keep the method strictly a secret between yourselves.

THREE IN ONE

This one hand card trick, although it employs one of the oldest devices in card magic, becomes almost a new feat because of the novelty inherent in manipulating the cards with but one hand.

Effect. Three cards are discovered, one by the sense of touch; one by the sense of hearing; and the last rises from the pack of its own volition.

Requirements. A card cut narrow at diagonally opposite corners, making the ends about 1/16" narrower.

Working. 1. After a spectator has shuffled the pack, thrust the right hand into the trousers pocket and hold the pack in the left hand, the thumb flat against the left side, the first finger curled at the face of the bottom card, the second, third and little fingers at the right side. Riffle the pack lightly with the thumb to determine if the narrow card is near the middle; if it is not, cut the pack at the middle by means of the Erdnase One Hand Shift and again riffle the sides to determine if the narrow card is now at or near the middle.

2. Extend the hand towards spectator A, requesting him to remove a card as you riffle the sides. When he has done so, have spectator B similarly choose a card, and do the same with spectator C.

3. Riffle with the thumb to the narrow card, allowing it to slip to the bottom of the upper packet, forming a break. Have A replace his card under the narrow card. Square the pack with the fingers and make two one hand shifts, both shifts being made near the middle, thus bringing the narrow card (and A's card under it) back to the center of the deck.

4. Again riffle to the narrow card, and have B's card replaced below it; repeat exactly the same procedure with C.

5. Make a series of one hand cuts; since in each cut the pack is broken near the middle, at the end of an even number of cuts the narrow card and the stock below it is returned to the middle of the deck.

6. State that you will find the first card by means of the sense of hearing alone. Hold the pack to the left ear, riffle to the narrow card and allow the card directly under it, C's card, to spring off to the face of the upper packet. Thrust the thumb into the break and draw out C's card, turning it face up on top of the pack, and have the card acknowledged by him.

7. Make a number of one hand cuts as you state that you will find B's card by the sense of touch. Place the pack behind the back and riffle down to the narrow card, allow the next card, B's card, to spring off the thumb to the face of the upper packet. Insert the thumb, draw out B's card with its tip and turn it face up upon the top of the pack. Push it off the side with the left thumb, slipping the tip of the first finger under it and placing the tip of the second finger upon it. Straighten these fingers outwards and the card will be grasped, face downwards, between their tips, Fig. 1. Bring the hand forward, showing the face-down card. Have B name his card and turn the hand over so that the spectator can see that you hold his card.

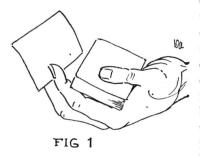

FIG 1

8. Riffle the left side of the pack to the narrow card and make the Charlier pass with the cards above the break, the action being the same as that employed when this pass is made with the pack lying flat upon the palm before the action is started. When the packets have been transposed A's card is the top card of the pack.

9. The third card, you say, will rise of its own accord. Turn the pack face outwards in the hand, the thumb lying flat on the upper side, the first finger at the middle of the outer end and the other three fingers supporting the lower side. Press inwards with the thumb and second fingers at the sides, buckling the cards nearest the palm of the hand, and with the tip of the left first finger at the middle of the outer end separate the top card a little from the others. Push on this card, first inwards and then upwards, making it turn between the base of the thumb and the deck, until it arrives at a position at right angles to the deck and above it.

You See?

The following extremely effective trick by Mr. Harold Lloyd, the famous movie star, is reprinted in this series by the kind permission of

Mr. Theodore Annemann, editor, proprietor and publisher of the unique magical weekly *The Jinx*. The feat forms a fitting climax to other one hand tricks in which sleight of hand has played its part and will leave the onlookers without any clue to the methods employed.

Effect. Three cards are selected under conditions which appear to make it absolutely impossible for the magician to locate them, yet he succeeds in doing this, apparently by purely mental processes.

Requirement. A one-way deck.

Working. You have three cards selected in the following way:

First card. Hand the pack to a spectator and request him to shuffle it thoroughly, indicating in pantomime an overhand shuffle. Request him to think of a card, fan the deck, take out the card thought of, lay it face downwards on the table, again shuffle the deck, then lay it face downwards on the chosen card, pick up the whole pack, shuffle it once more and, finally, place the pack face downwards on the palm of your left hand.

In appearance nothing could be fairer, yet, if the procedure is carried through exactly as given, the chosen card lies reversed in the pack awaiting location at your pleasure.

Second card. As the pack is placed on your left hand, glimpse the bottom card and remember it. Extend the hand to a second spectator as you invite him to make a free cut and look at the card on the face of the cut making sure that you cannot see it. Turn your head away to the right, then, as if to make it still more certain that you cannot get a glimpse of the card, turn to the right and swing your left hand with the remainder of the pack around so that it is held behind your back.

When the spectator, having noted his card, replaces the cut on the cards in your left hand, that entire section is reversed. The location of this card, therefore, also becomes a certainty since it will be the last card of the reversed section that is nowhere near the card that was secretly glimpsed.

Third card. With the pack still held behind your back, invite a third spectator to remove a card from the middle, look at it, remember it, place it on the top of the pack and bury it by making a free cut. Let him then take the pack, place it on the table face down and make several more free cuts. His first cut has placed the original bottom card, which you glimpsed, above this third selected card and the subsequent complete cuts do not disturb this condition of the two cards. This third card, therefore, also awaits your pleasure.

Request a fourth spectator to take the pack and deal the cards face upwards on the table; you locate the three cards, at the same time indicating which of the three spectators selected each card. As each one appears stop the deal, pick up the card, saying that you feel that some person is thinking of it and then, after a moment or two of pretended intense mental concentration, hand the card to the spectator who chose it.

Throughout stress should be laid on the fact that the whole effect is a mental phenomenon, the use of the left hand only precluding the employment of any manipulation.

The One Hand Fan

In all one hand work it is necessary to be able to make a fan of cards with the left hand only. To do this the pack should be held between the tips of the thumb and the first and second fingers at the lower right hand corner. The thumb is then twisted to the left and the fingers to the right. With a little practice the cards can be fanned very smartly.

Chapter 6
THE AMBITIOUS CARD

The First Phase

HERE IS ANOTHER plot which has stood the test of time, the trick having been invented by the Parisian prestidigitateur, Alberti, in the early part of the last century. Since the introduction of the double lift the feat has become, more than ever, a favorite with card conjurers and there are few indeed who do not include it in their repertoire.

The following method of working the first return of the card to the top of the pack is so convincing that the maneuvers which follow are accepted without suspicion. The trick should be introduced somewhat after this fashion. "It is a curious fact," you remark, "that cards, like men, are consumed with the passion of ambition. For them the place of honor is the top of the pack and when a card has been chosen by a spectator it instantly mounts to the first rank, the top, from whence it looks down upon its less fortunate brethren. Let us try the experiment." Then proceed in this manner:

a. 1. Holding the pack face down, turn it face upwards on the left fingers, reversing a card at the top of the deck. For a full explanation of this move, see Facing the Bottom Card, page 110. The pack is now face upwards with single face-down card next to the fingers.

2. Spread a few of the cards, inviting a choice of one. Remove this card, say the ace of hearts, and place it to one side.

3. With the right hand grasp the pack at the inner end and lift it to a vertical position against the left palm, Fig. 1, thus concealing the faced card from the spectators.

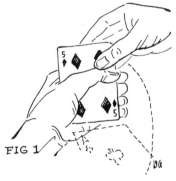

FIG 1

4. Pick up the ace of hearts and place it face upwards at the top of the pack, turning the pack to a horizontal position as soon as the secretly faced card is concealed; at the same time lift the inner end of this latter

card with the right thumb tip and hold the break in readiness for the double lift. Apparently there is a lone faced card at the top, the spectator's ace of hearts; actually there are two.

5. Make the double lift with the two face-up cards, using Method *b* (see page 9). Note that in this case the final snap move will again bring the cards face upwards. Rest their right sides on the right edge of the pack and allow the two cards to fall on top of the pack as in closing a book.

6. Take the indifferent card now on the top and, without showing its face, insert it in the middle of the pack. Tap the top of the pack with the right forefinger as you say: "Your card instantly rises to the coveted position," and you turn the top card face upwards showing that it has arrived.

From this point proceed with whatever routine you prefer for this intriguing effect.

Using Double Lift Turnup, *a*

Stand with your right side turned to the spectators and hold the pack in the left hand in regular dealing position, then:

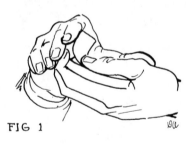

FIG 1

1. Square the cards with the right hand and in the action palm the top card. Move the hand toward the right and, as it clears the right side of the deck, push the next card to the right over the tips of the left second and third fingers which push its right side upwards.

2. Bring the right hand back over the deck, catch the bent up side of the second card against the side of the first finger, Fig. 1, and turn it face up under the palmed card as you replace this squarely on the pack.

3. Turn to the front, hold the pack vertically and with the right hand take off the top card and show it. Replace the card on the top face upwards, and drop the left hand to the dealing position.

4. Make the double lift with the two face-up cards, using method *b*. Note that in this case the final snap move will bring the cards back outwards. Rest the left sides on the right edge of the pack and allow the two cards to fall on top of the pack as in closing a book.

5. Take the indifferent card now on the top and without showing its face insert it in the middle of the pack. Order the card to return to the top, riffle the ends of the cards, turn the top card and show it. .

THE POP-UP CARD

For intimate work, this pretty little feat will enhance **any** Ambitious Card routine.

Effect. A card is shown and marked distinctively. It is placed in the center of the pack and, upon command, rises visibly to the top.

Method. 1. Lift two cards as one from the pack, holding them at the ends between the right thumb and second fingers, face outwards.

2. State that you will mark the card so that it will be easily recognizable. Bend the cards smartly bringing the tips of the thumb and fingers almost together, placing a strong bend in the cards.

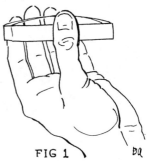

3. Hold the pack with the ball of the left thumb at the left side, the tip of the first finger at the outer end, the tips of the remaining fingers at the right side, Fig. 1. Place the two cards upon the pack as with your right hand you gesture for a spectator to step a little closer, and press the tips of the fingers and thumb inwards to hold the cards flat upon the pack.

FIG 1

4. Apparently turning your attention to the trick once more, draw the top indifferent card off the inner end, the bend being noticeable in the card. Thrust this into the middle of the deck from the inner end.

5. Command the card to rise to the top of the pack. As you say, "See, there it comes!" relax pressure on the sides of the top card, allowing it visibly to spring upwards as if it had just risen to the top of the pack, Fig. 1.

The effect is all that could be asked for.

THE AMBITIOUS TWINS

The following trick is not only effective in its own right, making a worthwhile addition to the Ambitious Card trick, but affords excellent exercise in the triple lift.

Effect. The top two cards of the pack are shown and thrust into the center of the pack. These cards mysteriously fly back to the top.

Method. 1. Triple lift, showing the third card. Turn the three cards down, remove the top card and place it face downwards on the table.

2. Repeat the actions in No. 1.

3. Thrust the tabled cards into the center of the pack.

4. Tap the top of the pack and order the two cards to rise to the top.

Turn the top cards face upwards and show that they are the cards originally shown and presumably thrust into the deck.

AMBITIOUS CARD MOVE

This sleight is very useful in an Ambitious Card routine; it is a new method of secretly placing an indifferent card above the card supposedly at the top of the pack.

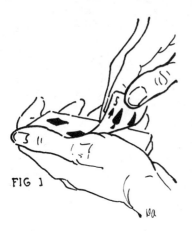

FIG 1

1. Secretly insert the left little finger under the first two cards by means of the Lift Get-Ready, page 4.

2. Remove the top card of the pack, turn it face upwards squarely upon the pack. Let us say that this is the ace of diamonds.

3. Grasp the ace and the card below it at the inner end between the right thumb below and the first and second fingers above, Fig. 1.

4. Lift these two cards at the inner end, as one, upward and outwards. The outer ends of the cards move inwards the length of the pack, much as in the paint-brush color change. This action places the ace face outwards, in a vertical position, with the card below it face inwards.

5. During the preceding action the left hand has turned the pack from a horizontal to a vertical position; it is now in the same plane as the cards held in the right hand, which are directly behind it.

6. Place the cards held by the right hand flat against the vertical pack and press inwards against the two cards with the left third and fourth fingers at one side, the fleshy base of the thumb on the other.

7. Draw the right hand, with the ace, directly upwards and away from the pack, as if

FIG 2

to further show the card, Fig. 2. Retain the indifferent card, now face upwards on top of the pack, gripped between the base of the thumb and the left fingers.

8. Place the ace, face upwards, horizontally upon the upper end of the

pack. Move the pack, with the left hand, from a vertical to a horizontal position, pressing the ace squarely upon the faced card at the top of the pack. This series of actions is the work of five seconds and at the end of the sequence the ace is face upwards on top of the pack and under it, unbeknownst to the spectators, is a second face upwards card.

9. Turn the two cards face downwards as one. Remove the top card, ostensibly the ace, and push it into the middle of the pack. Flip the top card, turn it face upwards and show that it is the ace.

Cover for the Ambitious Card Double Lift

After making the double lift turnup, place the two cards upon the pack, then place the deck, with the left hand, upon the table. State that the pack was placed upon the table to obviate sleight of hand. Remove the top card, an indifferent one, and slide it into the pack at the middle. The handling gives a tacit reason for replacing the two cards upon the pack's top; a small point but a convincing one.

The Omnipresent Eight

The following routine serves to introduce the Omnipresent Eight, a card notorious for its derring-do and reputedly a first cousin of that other gad-about, the Ambitious Card.

Effect. The eight of spades, at the command of the conjurer, jumps hither, thither and yon, in a series of astonishing adventures.

Preparation. Place the eight of spades third from the top; under it place the seven of spades, with its odd pip at the outer end.

Method. By way of introduction, some such statement as this may be made: "All of us are acquainted with the person who seems to be ubiquitous—you meet him wherever you go; he is constantly in the most unlikely places doing the queerest things. He may just be returning from Africa, where he has been shooting at lions; or he may just have enjoyed his first parachute jump; or he may be the pugnacious center of a street brawl. He is unpredictable, volatile, and you are never surprised to learn that he has been engaged in some fantastic venture.

"There is one card in the pack which has the same extraordinary characteristics; I call it the Omnipresent Eight. Let me show you exactly what I mean."

1. Secretly prepare for a triple lift. Turn the three cards and show the eight of spades. Turn the cards face downwards but retain a little finger break under them. Remove the top card, calling it the eight, and thrust it into the middle of the pack.

2. Command the eight to rise to the top. Double lift, showing the eight again at the top. Turn the two cards face downwards, remove the top indifferent card, calling it the eight; thrust it into the middle of the pack.

3. Command the eight to rise to the top once more. Show that the top card is the eight by means of the flourish count described on page 280, paragraph 7, Three in One. With the card held face upwards between the left first and second fingers, remove the pack by grasping it at the ends with the right hand as you extend the eight as if to better display it. Palm the top card of the pack, the seven of spades, with the right hand, using the one-hand top palm. Replace the pack upon the left palm and fold the eight onto its top by closing the left first and second fingers. Look up sharply, say, "I see a skeptical look in that gentleman's eye: he thinks that the eight is no longer on top of the pack." Face the eight at the top by pushing it off the pack with the left thumb and tipping it over by striking it with the side of the right palm. In turning the card face downwards in the same manner, allow the palmed seven to fall upon it.

4. Remove the seven by grasping it with the right fingers at the outer right corner, the second finger covering the index of the card at the face. Thrust this card half-way into the middle of the pack at the end, pause, glance at the man in whose eyes you detected the "skeptical" gleam; bend the seven of spades upwards so that the onlookers can see the pips but not the index. "You see, it *is* the eight," you affirm, a statement the truth of which the onlookers mistakenly accept. Push the card cleanly into the pack, command the eight to rise to the top, snap the pack and show that it has done so by cleanly turning the top card, the eight, face upwards.

5. Announce that you will lose the card in the pack. Undercut half the pack, injog the first card and shuffle off. Form a break at the injog, shuffle off to the break and throw, bringing the eight back to the top. Turn so that the backs of the cards are to the spectators; undercut half the pack, injog the top card of the left hand packet (the eight) and shuffle off. Undercut at the injog and shuffle off. The eight is now at the bottom. Perform the Impossible Color Change, page 163, thus changing an indifferent face card to the ubiquitous eight.

6. Overhand shuffle, retaining the eight at the bottom by pressing on it with the left finger tips. Form a break with the right thumb above the last two cards and undercut half the pack; shuffle to the break and drop the last two cards on top, a procedure made easy by the break. The eight is now the second card from the top.

7. Perform the Invisible Transit, page 290, thus demonstrating that the eight also flies through the air with the greatest of ease.

8. Replace the eight on the top of the pack, undercut half the pack, run one card, injog and shuffle off. Form a break at the injog, shuffle to the break and throw the remainder of the cards on top. The eight is second from the top. Perform the Two-Hand Plunger Rising Cards, page 211, causing the omnipresent eight to rise from the pack on command, directly under the noses of the onlookers, thus providing a suitable and perplexing finish to the routine.

This short routine comprises a welcome departure from the plot of the better-known Ambitious Card trick. Obviously it can be elaborated by the addition of other standard tricks and sleights, or it can be curtailed by the elimination of some of those given above, at the option of the reader.

Chapter 7
USING DOUBLE AND TRIPLE LIFTS

THE INVISIBLE TRANSIT

THE PLOT OF THIS TRICK, the simple one of two cards changing places, is one of the oldest in card conjuring. It was first explained by Guyot in 1749 and was probably an old trick in his time for he does not claim any originality but simply explained the tricks then in vogue. Ponsin reprinted the trick in 1853 and Hoffmann in 1876 (*Modern Magic*). All three authorities give exactly the same method, namely the use of a duplicate card and the glide. That the plot is a good one is proved by the survival of the trick for more than two centuries, but the use of duplicate cards, which prevented its execution with a borrowed deck, remained a decided drawback. It was not until 1934 that a method was revealed eliminating this inconvenience and allowing the trick to be done as an impromptu effect with any deck at any time without any preparation.*

If those who may have overlooked this trick, or to whom it may be unknown, will master the simple routine that follows they will add to their repertoire a trick which, performed hundreds of times, has never yet failed to cause the kind of uproar which is manna to any card conjurer.

a. 1. First have the deck shuffled by a spectator, take it back and insert the left little finger under the two top cards, preparatory to the double lift. Address spectator A, saying: "Do you think, sir, that you can remember the name of one card for as long as two minutes? You do? Then let's try an experiment." Double lift the two top cards, placing them squarely face up on the top of the pack. "The ace of diamonds," you continue. "Banish every other thought from your mind, sir, and concentrate on the ace of diamonds."

2. Turn the two cards face downwards on the pack, push off the top indifferent card and place it face downwards on the table to your left.

---

* *Card Manipulations*, Nos. 1 and 2, Jean Hugard.

Look at A and, tapping the card, repeat. "Remember that card—the ace of diamonds."

3. You have secretly got set for another double lift. Turn the two top cards face upwards squarely on the pack, retaining the tip of the left little finger under the two cards. Say the faced card is the ace of clubs. Turn to the spectator B and say, "Do you feel at all like that strange person who used to run around remembering Mr. Addison Simms of Seattle, Washington? Then remember this ace of clubs for me, if you will." Turn the two cards face downwards, retaining the tip of the left little finger under the two cards, push off the top card, the ace of diamonds, and place it to your right. Tap it and say, "Remember, the ace of clubs."

4. Turn back to A, tap his card and say, "The ace of diamonds." Pick up the card and, as you state that B's card is the ace of clubs, drop the card upon the pack. The left little finger has remained under the top card and you are now ready for another double lift without any further get-set. "The ace of diamonds," you continue, "at the top of the deck and the ace of clubs on the table before you. That's right, isn't it? Well, then, do you know that there's something very strange going on around here, because this card on the top of the pack is the ace of clubs [double lift the two top cards, placing them squarely upon the pack showing the club ace], and *this* card, on the table, is really the ace of diamonds." Turn it face upwards on the table.

5. Quietly turn the faced cards at the top of the pack face downwards and idly cut the pack.

The trick must be performed briskly and should last no longer than about thirty seconds. It should not be presented as a set trick but more or less as an off-hand demonstration of a curious phenomenon and the more casual the operator can be the better.

b. 1. Double lift, showing (say) the ten of spades; turn the two cards face downwards on the pack and place the top card, an indifferent one, to the left.

2. Triple lift, showing the four of hearts; turn the three cards face downwards and place the top card, the ten of spades, to the right.

3. Holding a break with the left little finger tip, idly remove the top card, an indifferent card; show it, and bury it in the middle of the pack, or drop it back on top, as you desire.

4. Pick up the tabled card to the left and place it on top of the pack. Triple lift (or double lift, if you have buried the indifferent card) and show that the four of hearts is at the top of the pack, the ten of spades is on the table, the two cards thus having changed places.

Transposition Extraordinary

Here again the plot of two cards changing places is used but the method employed is entirely different and the dénouement equally startling, one of the cards being chosen by a spectator and its position in the pack known only to himself.

Effect. A spectator takes the shuffled deck and, having mentally selected a number, secretly ascertains which card lies in that position. The deck is returned to the operator, who removes a card from the middle, shows it to everyone and places it face downwards on the table. The two cards are commanded to change places. The spectator, on counting down to the number he thought of, finds the card just shown by the performer, while the card on the table proves to be the very card he chose.

Working. Hand the pack to a spectator to be thoroughly shuffled. Take it back and:

1. Square the pack and, under cover of the action, crimp the inner right corner of the top card upwards by pressing it against the tip of the left little finger with the ball of the right thumb.

2. Explain to the spectator that he is to think of any number between, say, ten and twenty, take the pack, and deal off cards to that number in·a pile on the table. He is then to look at the top card of the pile, note what it is, replace it, drop the rest of the cards on top and square the deck.

Illustrate exactly what he is to do by counting off a small number of cards, look at the top card of the packet and then drop the rest of the pack on top. In this way you have not only made it quite plain to the spectator what he is to do but you have also placed the crimped card on the bottom of the pack in the most natural way possible.

3. Turn away while the spectator does his part, first cautioning him to deal silently to avoid any suspicion that you might be able to count the cards by hearing them fall.

4. When the spectator indicates that he is ready, turn and take the pack. Casually riffle the inner end of the deck with the right thumb as you say, "I will take a card myself from the middle of the deck." Riffle again, this time at the right inner corner, stop at the crimped card and insert the right forefinger under it; the card below the forefinger is the spectator's card.

5. Remove this card and, without showing it, drop it at the top of the pack. "Now there is one chance in fifty-two that I have picked out your card." You have prepared for a double lift as you made this statement and now you turn the two top cards face up on the pack. "Is this king of

spades [or whatever the indifferent card may be] your card? It is not your card. Very well . . . I will put it here on the table." Turn the two cards face down on top of the pack and push the top card, the spectator's card, off onto the table with the left thumb.

6. Riffle to, but not including, the crimped card and make the pass at this point; or, if you prefer, openly cut the pack several times, on the last cut taking the crimped key card to the bottom of the deck. Lay the deck on the table.

7. The trick is done; you have only to bring it to a dramatic conclusion. Point out that the spectator's card lies in the pack at a number that you cannot possibly know, while on the table there is a card which has been freely shown to everyone—in this case, the king of spades. "You must admit," you say, "that what I propose to try is an utter impossibility. I shall make this card on the table fly to the very position in the pack now occupied by your card, while your card shall leave the pack and take the place of my card. Pass! What was the number you thought of? Sixteen? Please take the pack yourself and deal to that number." The spectator does this and turns your card, the king of spades, very much to his surprise. "What was your card?" you ask. "The ace of hearts? Here it is." And you triumphantly flip the card on the table face upwards.

The Telepathic Card

A goodly number of years ago Mr. Theo Annemann produced a card trick which created a considerable stir amongst card experts but did not achieve the popularity which its ingenious construction deserved.

The trick was titled, "Initialed Card Telepathy." It had two serious flaws; one was that it called for a double-back card, thus limiting the trick to those occasions when the performer could use his own pack; secondly, it called for continuous triple lifts and, the technique of the triple lift having been up to the present time almost completely unexplored, it quickly became all too apparent to audiences that some furtive arrangement was being made before each of a number of cards was turned face upwards upon the pack.

These two faults have been eliminated in the present version of the trick, making of it an extraordinarily effective trick of the pseudo-telepathic type. Although the technique of the present version differs in all respects from that of the original Annemann trick, the brilliant editor and performer may rightly lay claim to having conceived the ingenious basic principle which makes possible the version to be given here.

Effect. A spectator glances at a card in the pack, which is then held on the palm of the conjurer's extended hand. A second and third spectator each think of a number, and cards are removed from the pack in such a manner as apparently to make subterfuge impossible, until the spectators' combined number is arrived at. The conjurer cannot know what this total will be until, a second before the top card of the pack is faced, the assistants state that their number has been arrived at. Nonetheless, when this card is shown, it proves to be the card selected by the original spectator.

Preparation. Prior to performance, secretly reverse the second card of the pack by means of the sleight given on page 109, or by any other method. Thus, the top card will be face downwards, the second card face upwards, the remainder of the pack face downwards.

Method. 1. Advance to a spectator, extend the pack at arms length and have this party peek at any card, using the method given on page 93.

2. Hold the pack upon the flat left palm, well away from the body, as you address the company: "Ladies and gentlemen, I am going to attempt a really remarkable experiment in psychic coincidence. A card has been thought of by a member of the audience; under conditions absolutely precluding the possibility of sleight of hand, I shall attempt to place the card at a number in the pack to be named in a manner over which I could not possibly have control." Quietly side slip the peeked card to the top.

"To do this, it is only necessary to move the left hand, upon which the pack rests, in a small arc, like this." Move the hand in a small arc from left to right. "The card being thought of has now moved from its original position to a position which even I do not know."

Pause for a moment and continue: "This experiment is so unbelievable that often those who witness it suspect collusion on the part of the spectator whom presently I shall ask to name a number. To obviate this possibility in your minds, I shall have the number at which the card is to be found in the pack determined, not by any one person alone, but by two persons, in the fairest possible manner."

Turn to a nearby spectator and address him thus: "Will you, sir, think of any small even number? Think of two, or four, or six, or eight, being certain in your own mind that the number you finally select could not have been influenced by anything I may have said."

Turn to another party and to him say, "Will you, sir, think of any odd number, say between one and nine. Choose, uninfluenced by anything I may have said, either one or three or five or seven or nine."

Address the audience as an entity: "I believe that you will agree that

I cannot conceivably know what number is being thought of by either of these parties; nor do I want to know."

You have achieved two purposes by means of the procedure outlined: you have convinced the audience that confederacy is highly improbable, since while one spectator might conceivably act in collusion with you, the audience will admit the unlikelihood of two such confederates; and, more important, by the phrasing of the request you have ensured that the total of the two numbers will be an odd number.

3. Place the right hand over the deck and insert the tip of the left little finger under the top four cards, using the method outlined on page 4. From the top down, these cards are the face downwards chosen card; a face down indifferent card; a face upwards indifferent card; and lastly a face downwards indifferent card.

Hold the pack in readiness for a quadruple lift, in an almost vertical position, the hands a little below the level of the waist, the pack before the body and squarely facing the company. This position is ostensibly taken to show the pack more clearly and preclude sleight of hand, and all the subsequent actions should expose as much of the surface of the pack as possible, since it is your intent to demonstrate the apparent impossibility of manipulation.

Address either spectator: "I am not going to ask you to name your number at this time. When, however, I call out your number, please call out 'stop!'."

4. Call out "One!" and if stop is not called, push the top four cards off the pack with the left thumb, as described on page 5, grasp them with the right hand and turn these four cards over, placing them squarely upon the pack, in so doing retaining a break at the inner corner with the left little finger preparatory to another quadruple lift.

Apparently you have turned but a single card, which now is faced at the top of the pack.

5. Place the right thumb and second fingers at the ends at the extreme right corners and lift the card directly under the left little finger tip with the ball of the right thumb, insert the little finger tip under it, and immediately allow three cards to drop off the ball of the right thumb as the right hand removes the faced top card between its thumb and second finger. The impression must be given the onlookers that you are meticulously avoiding the merest semblance of sleight of hand in removing the card in this manner; thus you have prepared for another quadruple lift in the most innocent manner, without fumbling or suspicious moves, in the commonplace action of removing the faced card.

Drop the faced card just removed to the floor. There is now a card face downwards at the top of the pack and below it two cards face upwards, the second of which is the chosen card; and lastly, resting on the left little finger tip, is a fourth face-down card.

6. Call out "Two!" and, if the spectator fails to call stop, continue quadruple lifting and dropping the faced cards thus placed at the top of the pack until the spectator does call stop. Let us say that he stops you before you turn the sixth card. Make the quadruple lift showing the face of this sixth card, remove it and drop it on the floor. Address the company: "As you can see, ladies and gentlemen, I could not possibly have known what number would be chosen until 'Stop!' was called." Turn to the second spectator and add: "Nor can I know what number you may be thinking of at this moment. When, however, I call out your number, please call 'Stop!'."

7. Continue calling numbers and removing cards as in the previous action until the spectator calls stop. Since he has chosen an odd number, there must be at the top of the pack two face downwards cards, then a card face upwards, and then the remainder of the face down pack. The top card of the pack is the chosen card. Remove this single card exactly as before, between the thumb and second finger, as cleanly as possible, and hold it face inwards well away from the body.

Recapitulate what has transpired, pointing out the utter impossibility of your having foreknowledge that this card would be the one selected by the two spectators; turn to the spectator who originally chose the card and request that he name it.

Turn the card you hold in your hand, very slowly, and show its face to the company. It is the chosen card.

TRANSPOSITION

This feat again demonstrates the perplexing problems which are possible when the double and triple lifts are used.

Effect. Two cards change places under seemingly impossible conditions.

Requirements. A duplicate card with matching back for the pack you use; say the eight of hearts.

Preparation. Place the nine of spades, eight of hearts, nine of clubs, jack of diamonds and the duplicate eight of hearts at the top of the pack in that order, the nine of spades being the top card.

Method. 1. Insert the left little finger tip under the fourth card, using the lift get-ready.

2. Turn the top card, the nine of spades, face upwards on the pack, using the regular lift actions. Turn it face down, remove it and place it face downwards on the table. As an afterthought, turn it face upwards.

3. Triple lift, showing the jack of diamonds. Turn the three cards face downwards, deal off the top card, the eight of hearts, and place it face downwards overlapping the tabled nine of spades.

4. Push off the top card in an action exactly simulating the lift, showing the nine of clubs. Turn this card face downwards, deal it face down and again, as an afterthought, turn it face upwards. Three cards are fanned on the table: The two nines, which are faced upwards, and between them a face-down card, ostensibly the jack of diamonds but actually the eight of hearts.

5. Prepare for a double lift as you recapitulate what has been done, emphasizing that the jack of diamonds is face downwards between the two nines.

6. Double lift, showing the eight of hearts. Turn the two cards face downwards and remove the top card, the jack of diamonds. Place it to one side, calling it the eight of hearts.

7. Command the eight and the jack to change places. Palm off the duplicate eight at the top and vest it as, with the left hand, you turn the cards showing that the transposition has taken place.

Boy Meets Girl

This amusing interlude makes excellent use of the triple lift and will be found to lend itself readily to any number of patter stories.

Effect. The king of spades is placed upon the table; the top card of the pack, the queen of hearts, is placed face downwards upon the king. The next card, the jack of hearts, is moved over the couple, whereupon when the queen is turned face upwards she is found to have magically become the queen of spades.

Preparation. Secretly place the following cards at the top of the pack: The king of spades, queen of spades, jack of hearts, queen of hearts. The king is the top card.

Method. 1. Push the top card, the king of spades, off the pack exactly as if making a triple lift and turn it face upwards squarely upon the pack. Turn it face downwards in the same manner, push it off the pack with the left thumb, remove it with the right hand and drop it face upwards on the table.

2. Prepare for a triple lift. Turn the three cards face upwards squarely upon the deck, showing the queen of hearts. Turn the three cards face

downwards and remove the top card, the queen of spades; drop it face downwards upon the king.

3. Push the top card of the pack, the jack of hearts, off the pack as when making a lift and turn it face upwards on the deck. Turn it face downwards, push it off with the left thumb and remove it with the right hand. This action convinces the onlookers that the queen of hearts was actually placed on the table. The action in showing the three cards must be uniform.

4. Move the jack, face upwards, in a circle above the tabled cards and replace it, face upwards, on the pack.

5. Turn the face downwards card, supposedly the queen of hearts, face upwards. It is now the queen of spades.

The trick lends itself admirably to any number of illustrative stories, such as the following:

The king of spades, a gay young blade, met the queen of hearts, a charming maid.

She was merry, and pretty, and thoughtful and sweet; and she swept the king straight off his feet.

With the world's great lovers he quickly concurred. "Be mine!" he cried; but the queen demurred.

For she was a heart, and he was a spade, and love 'twixt the two had never been made; and besides she preferred to remain a young maid.

As you may have surmised, the king was dismayed.

Now enter, upon this idyllic scene
Cupid, to win over the coquettish queen.

Presto, Chango—the trick is done; a dart is flung and love's battle is won. Two hearts, the king's and queen's, now beat as one.

And true to all convention, due to Cupid's intervention, I am very glad to mention

The queen of hearts is his, all his
And in connubial bliss is

The Mrs.

The king is placed face upwards on the table before the story is started. The triple lift is made on the words "queen of hearts" and the cards remain face upwards until the words "the king was dismayed," at which time the three cards are turned face downwards and the queen of spades is dropped on the table. The jack is shown on the word "Cupid"; it is moved over the tabled cards and replaced on the pack on the words "now beat as one."

The queen of spades is flipped over face upwards, to show the effect of matrimony, on the words "The Mrs."

This particular story becomes more effective if the conjurer can give the impression that he is improvising parts of it as he goes along.

Chapter 8
DISCOVERIES

THE CARD IN THE SHOE

As an impromptu, intimate trick this surprising effect compares favorably with such other well known tricks as the card in the wallet, card in the coin purse and card in the orange. In this instance the marked chosen card vanishes from the pack and is found in the conjurer's shoe.

The trick is most effective following other really striking card tricks which have placed the onlookers in a mood to believe that the mystery-

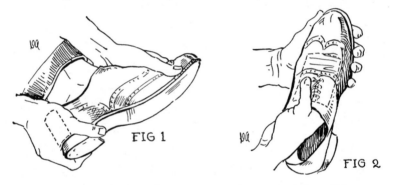

FIG 1

FIG 2

worker can accomplish any feat, no matter how miraculous. The moves follow:

1. After a signed card has been returned to the pack, control it and palm it off with the right hand.

2. Walk to a chair a little apart from the company, the right side of the body towards the spectators. Reaching the chair, sit down; as you do so, place the right hand upon the right thigh and as you lower yourself into the chair slide your right hand down the thigh to the knee in a perfectly natural action; at the same moment turn your left side towards the audience.

3. Cross your legs, placing the left ankle upon the right knee; with the right palm still lightly pressed against the right thigh, reach down with the left hand and loosen the laces of the left shoe.

4. Amply covered by the calf of the left leg, move the right hand with the palmed card to the shoe, cupping the hand around the curved rear of

the shoe at the heel, thus completely concealing the palmed card, Fig. 1.

5. Place the left hand at the instep of the shoe and remove it using both hands, the right hand applying pressure at the heel exactly as in ordinarily removing a shoe.

6. Retaining the position of the two hands, swing to the left, bringing the right side of the body to the front, as though to show the inside of the shoe.

7. Place the left hand, at the instep, on the sole side of the shoe and grasp it. Remove the right hand, the palmed card now being concealed by the back of the hand, and thrust its fingers up into the shoe, the card resting against its tongue. With the fingers work the card well upward as you peer into the shoe, apparently to see what is inside, Fig. 2. Then withdraw the right hand.

8. Hold the shoe in a horizontal position for a moment, as you look into it, then slowly tip it into a vertical position so that the spectators can see into it. Tap the rounded heel with the right hand and the card will slide down into view, face outwards.

The routine of actions is so arranged that cover for the palmed card is always afforded; moreover, the novelty to an audience of the conjurer removing his shoe affords a perfect opportunity for him to indulge in repartee which amply covers the necessarily secret introduction of the card. The trick will be found very easy and decidedly effective.

Rub-A-Dub-Dub

This is an amusing quick trick with a surprise finish.

Effect. The conjurer fails to find a chosen card, but when the indifferent card shown is rubbed on the table, it changes to the required card. When it again is rubbed on the table, it vanishes into thin air.

Method. 1. Control the chosen card to the top of the pack.

2. Double lift, showing an indifferent card, and replace the cards face downwards upon the pack.

3. Push the top card, the chosen card, off the deck as far as the thumb will extend. Place the right edge of the card on the table and, holding the right hand vertically, place the right side of this hand upon the right edge of the card, Fig. 1.

4. Pivoting the right hand upon its right side, move it downward to the left until it presses against the left thumb. Remove the left hand with the pack and press the right hand flat upon the tabled card, which is wholly concealed by the hand. Rub it energetically upon the table top, remove the hand, turn the card over and show that it is the chosen card.

5. Place the card face upwards on the pack. Turn it face downwards. Repeat the actions in No. 3 and 4, up to that point at which the palm of the right hand presses against the left thumb.

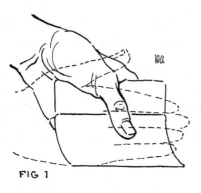

FIG 1

6. Remove the left hand with the pack, at the same time drawing the chosen card swiftly onto the pack by drawing back the thumb. Immediately place the right hand flat upon the table, exactly as in the first instance.

7. Make the same rubbing motion made in the first case. Lift the right hand and show that the card has vanished.

Neatly performed, the trick is a good one.

The Card Through the Magazine

This is another of those fine impromptu tricks which audiences of every type seem to enjoy; a quick and perplexing method of producing a chosen card.

Effect. A chosen card is returned to the pack, which is placed face downwards upon a magazine which, in turn, has been deposited on the bare floor. The operator slaps the pack and removes it; then removes the magazine; and, there, face up on the floor, lies the chosen card, apparently having passed through the magazine and, for good measure, turned face upwards in the process.

Method. The feat is simplicity itself but it calls for assurance and good timing. After the selection of a card, have it returned to the deck, control it to the bottom, and there reverse it. Then:

1. Holding the pack in the right hand between the fingers and thumb at the ends, pick up a magazine of the format of the *New Yorker*, the *Sphinx* or the *Genii*. Hold the periodical with the left hand at the cut edges with the stapled edge towards the right.

2. Briskly sweep the magazine to and fro over the floor, as though to dust it, thus establishing in the onlookers' minds that the floor is bare and the magazine unprepared.

3. Press the tips of the right second and third fingers upon the back of the reversed card at the bottom of the pack pivoting it to the right and swinging it an inch or so below the bottom of the pack, Fig. 1.

4. Hold the magazine an inch above the floor and horizontal, that is to say in the same plane with it. Move the magazine to the right as the right hand, with the pack, moves to the left. Turn the right hand to bring the inner end of the pack outwards to the left, and slide the chosen card under the bound edge of the magazine, Fig. 2, releasing it, the pack itself passing above the magazine.

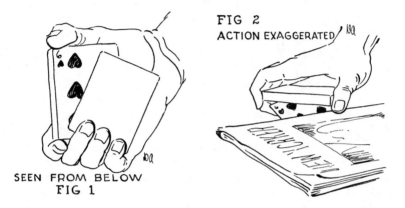

FIG 2
ACTION EXAGGERATED

SEEN FROM BELOW
FIG 1

5. Move the magazine to the right until the card just placed under it is centered; then drop the magazine and put the pack upon its center.

All that remains to be done is to slap the pack, lift it and drawing away the magazine, reveal the chosen card face upwards on the floor.

The trick is a good one if smartly performed; in other words, if the card is swung under the magazine without the slightest hesitation or pause in the sequence of actions. In secretly sliding the card underneath, the right hand holding the pack should appear to have approached the magazine only to aid in placing it neatly on the floor; the chosen card is slipped underneath and immediately the right hand moves to the left and places the pack on the middle of the magazine as the left hand places this last above the hidden card. To all intents and purposes, it should seem that the conjurer has placed a magazine on the floor and a pack of cards on the magazine.

MERCURY'S CARD

This feat has been a favorite of many an expert cardworker since it provides the type of mystification which audiences prefer.

Effect. A card is chosen and, if desired, marked; it is returned to the pack which is then shuffled and placed to one side. A second spectator is requested to think of a number, the conjurer promising that the chosen card will be found at this number. "If I fail," promises the conjurer, "all my earthly wealth is yours." So saying, he places a small coin purse upon the table.

The card is not found at the desired number; nor, indeed, is it in the pack. Claiming his reward, the spectator opens the purse and finds there, neatly folded, his marked chosen card.

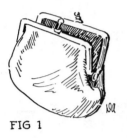

FIG 1

Requirements. Two small coin purses of the type shown in Fig. 1, these being identical in appearance. One is placed in the left coat pocket, the other in the left trousers pocket. Each contains a dime, three pennies and a one cent stamp.

Presentation. 1. Spread the pack in a long ribbon on the table and request a spectator to select a card. Ask him to mark it for later identification and, off-handedly, remove the coin purse from the trousers pocket, open it and drop its contents upon the table. Pick up the stamp and say, "Before 1929,—and *do* you remember 1929, gentlemen?—I always asked the spectators to stick a stamp, like this, on the card. Since 1929—and that's twelve years, so you can imagine the postage I've saved—I just have the spectator sign his name on the card. Will you do that, sir?" Replace the coins and the stamp in the purse and replace it in your left trousers pocket.

2. Gather the pack, have the signed card replaced and control it to the bottom.

3. As you talk—and this is one of those tricks in which it pays to be loquacious—hold the pack face down between the right fingers and the thumb at the ends.

4. Place the outer end of the pack upon the upper side of the left forefinger, the pack extending from the top to the root of the finger, Fig. 2. Drop the right thumb so that it engages the inner end of the pack near the crotch, thus placing the length of the thumb below the deck.

5. Move the left hand inwards, pressing up against the face of the bottom card (the chosen card) with the side of the left forefinger. As the hand moves inwards, the chosen card buckles downwards between the forefinger and the thumb at the inner end, until the finger and thumb, meeting at the inner end, fold the card in half, Fig. 2. The card is held against the left fingers by the right thumb which presses firmly against it.

6. Close the left fingers, thus folding the card into quarters, aided by a continuing outward pressure of the left thumb, Fig. 3.

7. Hold the pack as in Fig. 2 for a moment, then take it with the right hand and place it to one side.

8. Reach into the left coat pocket, drop the folded card in the coin purse, silently lock the purse by snapping the nubs and palm it, then withdraw the left hand from the pocket.

9. Request a spectator to name a number, promising that the chosen card will appear at this number. "Unbelievable as it may seem to you, I am so certain, so completely confident that this trick will terminate in an absolutely revolting success, that I am

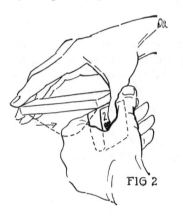

FIG 2

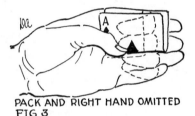

PACK AND RIGHT HAND OMITTED
FIG 3

willing to give my entire private fortune (which I *had* been saving for a rainy day) to you, sir, should the experiment fail. Here it is, sir, one dime, three pennies and a slightly shopworn one cent stamp." As you say this, dip your left hand into the trousers pocket and withdraw it with the palmed coin purse at the tips of the fingers. (Later on, the spectators will argue that you couldn't have put the card in the purse; you didn't have time.)

10. Place the purse to one side, take up the pack and find, to your apparent consternation, that the card has failed to move to the number requested by the spectator and, further, in frantically searching for it, show that it has completely vanished from the pack. Crestfallen, you tell the spectator to take his reward from your purse; he finds there the signed card.

The trick is a good one.

FOLDING A CARD

The following method of folding a card for Mercury's Card or similar tricks is preferred by some performers.

1. Control the card to the top of the pack and palm it by means of the one-hand top palm.

2. Fold the right fingers into the palm at the middle knuckle, folding a third of the card upon itself, Fig. 1.

3. Press the thumb against the card, folding the third of the card nearest the wrist back onto the fingernails, Fig. 2.

FIG 1

4. Open the fingers, place their tips upon the third of the card folded by the thumb and press the card flat. It is now folded in thirds, Fig. 3.

5. Remove the first and second fingers, pressing the card against the palm with the third and fourth fingers, Fig. 4.

6. Place the thumb upon the edge of the folded card and bend the card down upon the folded third and fourth fingers, thus reducing the card to a sixth of its original size. Remove the fingers and, with the thumb, press the card flat upon the palm, Fig. 5.

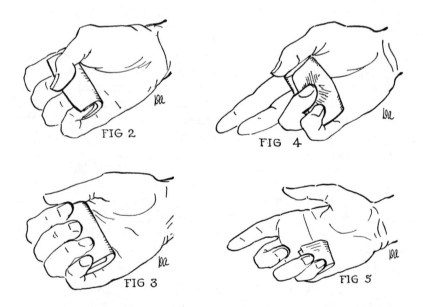

FIG 2

FIG 4

FIG 3

FIG 5

This method has the advantage of folding the card face inwards, with the back showing; of being an exceedingly fast method and of making a smaller and more compact bundle, which is especially suitable for Max Malini's famous trick of finding a lost card in the mouth.

A Card for Pegasus

This discovery of a chosen card, which can be made very amusing, employs the principle of vesting a card.

1. With the chosen card at the top of the pack, palm it in the right hand and vest it as described under Vesting a Card, pushing the card well up under the vest.

2. Hand the pack to be shuffled, take it back and state that by means of your magic powers you will cause the chosen card to rise to the top of the pack. Gingerly remove the top card, holding it at the tips of the right first and second fingers well away from the body, and request that the card be named. In all seriousness, turn the card slowly and triumphantly face upwards. It is a wrong card.

3. Profess a certain dismay at the ignominious failure of your trick. Repeat, thoughtfully, the name of the chosen card: "The five of clubs. Do you know, *that's* the card that's always misbehaving."

4. Unostentatiously show the hands empty, then thrust the left hand into the vest from above, grip the vested card by the tips of the first and second fingers and slowly slide it from under the vest near the shoulder, but not before you have seemingly had great difficulty in finding the card. Remove it at last, slowly turning it face outwards and show that it is the spectator's card.

The trick makes an amusing climax for a series of five card discoveries, the card being vested at the start of the locations and the four other cards being successfully found. Failing with the fifth card you find it under the vest.

The Danbury Deviler

The following trick, utilizing two old principles, combines them to make a new location effect which comes close to being an unfathomable mystery. Its originator is the nimble fingered Charles Miller.

The effect is that a spectator peeks at the outer right index of any card in the pack, the magician holding the deck gingerly by its inner left corner in such a manner as to preclude any of the usual artifices. The pack is shuffled and, apparently, the card is hopelessly lost; and yet the conjurer produces it in any effective manner he may desire.

Card connoisseurs who have seen Mr. Miller present this feat have thought that it might be an instance of estimating the depth of the spectator's peek, a theory which they were forced to abandon upon completion of the subsequent extremely careless mixing of the cards. Repeated many times by the bland Westerner, the trick has nonplussed those who pride themselves upon their knowledge of card artifice.

The secret is very simple. With your thumbnail bruise the edge of a card near the upper left corner. Bruise another card nearer its middle, a third just below the middle and a fourth near the lower left corner. A vigorous shuffle serves to distribute these cards throughout the pack at fairly equidistant intervals.

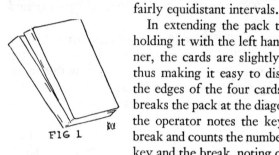

FIG 1

In extending the pack towards the spectator, holding it with the left hand at the inner left corner, the cards are slightly beveled to the right, thus making it easy to discern the markings on the edges of the four cards. When the spectator breaks the pack at the diagonally opposite corner, the operator notes the key card nearest to this break and counts the number of cards between the key and the break, noting of course, which of the four keys is being used, Fig. 1. With a little practice the intervening number of cards can be estimated at one quick glance, for it rarely is more than five or six.

Allow the pack to close after the spectator has ascertained his card and carefully square the pack, turning it about in the hands and showing, without commenting upon the fact, that crimps, breaks and similar subterfuges are not being utilized.

Turn the pack in the hands for an overhand shuffle and mix only those cards which are remote from the group containing the chosen card and the noted key card. Next mix the cards by means of the Charlier shuffle (page 412), a particularly useful shuffle in this case since it can be made very sloppily and thus enhances the belief that the cards are thoroughly mixed.

To place the spectator's card under control, it is only necessary to sight the proper key card, thumb count to the selected card, bring it to the top and produce it in any effective manner.

It is hardly necessary to state that, in place of thumb scratching the key cards, daub can be used. The first method, however, is good practice since it is an ever-ready expedient not dependent upon any accessory.

Double Discovery

Two cards having been freely chosen, insert them in the pack, use the Automatic Jog, No. 1 (page 104) and make the pass, bringing one card to the top, the other second from the bottom. Show the bottom card, turn the pack, make a double lift and apparently show the top card. Replace the cards at the top.

Turn half left, holding the pack in the left hand vertically on its side, with the right hand pull out the bottom card from the outer end and show its face again. With the tip of the left forefinger pull back the outer end of the card now on the bottom (one of the chosen cards) and then insert the card in the right hand between it and the deck, apparently replacing it on the bottom of the pack.

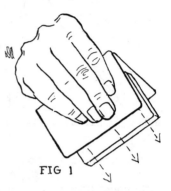

FIG 1

Square the pack and at once seize it with the right hand, the thumb below and the fingers above. Press firmly with the thumb and fingers and, with a rapid jerk of the right hand, throw the pack into the left hand, Fig. 1. The top and bottom cards remain in the right hand and you throw them instantly face downwards on the table.

Have these two cards named, show that they have left the pack and then turn the two cards on the table face upwards. The effect is that the two cards have been pulled from the middle of the deck.

EVERYWHERE AND NOWHERE

Any card trick which can be used either as a spectacular platform feature, or as a brain-teasing intimate magical feat, is not lightly to be dismissed. A favorite of many experts, Everywhere and Nowhere is such a trick, possessing all the virtues which a good trick must have—a plot easy for the spectators to follow, surprise, amusement and a striking climax.

The trick, a specialty of the fabulous Dr. Johann Neponuk Hofzinser, enjoyed renewed popularity following the publication of a new method in 1935,* for the original method was little known in this country and had the disadvantage, from the American point of view, of being cumbrous and unnecessarily difficult.

Effect. The magician promises to cause a spectator's chosen card, shuffled into the pack, to rise to the top. On the first attempt he fails and places the wrong card to one side; again he fails on the second and third attempts, in each case putting aside these wrong cards. One of these being chosen, the conjurer waves his hand over it and turns it face upwards: It is the chosen card. This card is replaced face downwards and one of the remaining two cards is selected and this, too, is magically

---

* *Card Manipulations*, No. 4; Jean Hugard, page 112.

transformed into the chosen card. Finally, the remaining card is conjured into the chosen card; and yet, the spell broken, all three cards are turned face upwards and shown to be the original three cards.

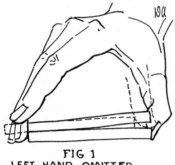

FIG 1
LEFT HAND OMITTED

Requirements. A pack of cards with two extra nines of spades with matching backs and a rabbit's foot which has been placed in the right coat pocket. Secretly and prior to performance, the following six cards, 9S, AH, 9S, AC, 9S, AD, are placed in that order on the top of the deck.

Method. Advancing towards a spectator, undercut the deck, shuffle overhand injogging the first card and shuffle off. Insert the the tip of the left little finger below the jogged card, and, spreading the cards, force the first nine of spades and request the spectator to show it to those near him.

1. Square the pack, holding a little finger break above the remaining stocked cards. Hold the pack in the right hand, fingers at the outer end, thumb at the inner end and now holding the break, allow a few cards to drop from the bottom of the pack onto the left palm, Fig. 1, then a few more, finally letting all the cards drop below the break and extend the left hand for the replacement of the chosen card. Thus the nine of spades is returned to its original position at the top of the six cards.

2. Drop the packet held by the right hand upon the other packet a quarter of an inch beyond its outer end. Place the ball of the right thumb upon the inner end of the lower packet and square both packets with the right fingers at the outer end, this action enabling you to make and hold a break at the inner corner with the right thumb, Fig. 1. Shuffle overhand to the break and throw on top, again bringing the six cards to the top.

3. Look at your audience and recapitulate what has been done. Take the rabbit's foot from your pocket and say: "The magic qualities of this emblem will cause the chosen card to pass through all the intervening cards until it has risen to the top of the pack." Touch the rabbit's foot to the pack and drop it back into the pocket as you caution the spectator not to betray in any way the name of his card.

4. Double lift the first two cards, turning them face upwards on the pack, exposing the ace of hearts. "The chosen card!" you exclaim triumphantly. The spectator disclaiming this card, you amend the sentence

to, "The chosen card always appears upon the *second* attempt." Turn the two cards face downwards, remove the top card—a nine of spades—and place it face downwards on the table.

5. The five card stock remaining at the top of the pack is now—AH, 9S, AC, 9S, AD. Make another overhand shuffle thus: Undercut half the deck, injog the first card and shuffle off. Undercut at the injog and run the first five cards, which are the stocked cards, reversing their order. Injog the next card and shuffle off; undercut at the injog and throw on top. The five cards will now be on the top in this order, AD, 9S, AC, 9S, AH.

6. "I never—or hardly ever—fail," you say, as you remove and show the top card, the ace of diamonds. Informed that this is not the chosen card, you say: "Of course, I failed to rub the pack with the rabbit's foot. Naturally I couldn't hope to succeed." Look at a spectator on your left and say plaintively, "Could I?," at the same moment, in the turn towards the spectator, top-changing the ace of diamonds for the nine of spades. Drop this card beside the first tabled nine of spades and state firmly: "The third time the charm *always* works."

7. Shuffle overhand again by undercutting half the deck, injog the first card and shuffle off. Undercut at the injog, run the first three cards of the set-up, the AD, AC and 9S and injog the next card, the AH, and shuffle off. Undercut at the injog and throw on top. The cards at the top are now the 9S, AC and AD in that order and the AH is at the bottom.

8. Gravely remove the rabbit's foot from your pocket, touch it to the pack and return it to the pocket. Double lift and turn the two top cards face upwards on the deck, exposing the ace of clubs. "Perseverance is always rewarded," you state brightly; but again the spectator refuses the card. "But," you protest worriedly, "I know for a certainty that you took an ace. Since it's none of these, it must be the ace of spades." As you say this turn the two cards face downwards and drop the nine of spades beside the other two nines.

The spectator, who by this time, with the audience, should be thoroughly enjoying the conjurer's predicament, now for the first time names his card, the nine of spades. In the face of this new setback, after some hesitation you offer to find the chosen card.

9. Shuffle again; undercut half the deck, injog the first card and shuffle off to the last card, the ace of hearts, thus bringing it to the top. Directly below the injogged card in the middle of the pack are the ace of clubs and the ace of diamonds. Undercut at the injog, run these two

cards, injog and shuffle off. Undercut at the injog and throw on top. The AD, AC, and AH have been returned to the top in that order.

At the conclusion of the shuffle, lift up the inner end of the top card and glance furtively at it, as if you have tried to locate the nine of spades as you previously located the various aces. Pause dubiously, glance at the three face-down nines which the spectators believe to be the three aces, glance back at the pack and say hopefully, "You're positive you didn't take an ace? You're sure none of these is your card?"

Square your shoulders as if about to take a plunge into cold water and continue: "Very well. You claim you took the nine of spades. Do you think it possible for me, with the aid of my gifted rabbit's foot, to make you see any one of these cards as the nine of spades? You don't? Then by all means, let us try. Which one shall I take? The middle card?"

Take the rabbit's foot and gravely trace an imaginary triangle over the card, and replace the charm in your pocket. Use the foot as you would a wand and hold it in such a way that your hand is seen to be otherwise empty. "Of course," you remark confidentially, "we know that it isn't the nine of spades, but let's see what this ace looks like now."

10. Lift the card gingerly and show its face to the spectators. It is the nine of spades and, if you have played your part well, your audience will assume that the trick has been brought to its conclusion and will reward you with applause. Continue to hold the care face outwards until the spectators realize that the trick is not concluded; then in turning to address a spectator to your left make the top change as you say: "You must realize that you are under a hypnotic spell. How do you feel, sir? Now, of the two remaining cards, which would you like to see as the nine of spades? This one? Very well."

Drop the ace of diamonds, which you are now holding with its face well concealed, in its original place in the middle.

11. Using the one-hand top palm, palm the top nine of spades as you request a second spectator to indicate one of the two remaining aces. Reach into your pocket, drop the palmed card and remove the rabbit's foot, and again go through the cabalistic tracery above the selected card; then replace the charm in your pocket.

12. Show the second nine of spades. "You see? A hypnotic spell. A perfect demonstration of mass suggestion." Top change the nine of spades for the ace of clubs on the top of the pack, dropping it in its place beside the other cards.

13. Palm the nine of spades as before and leave it in your pocket in

bringing out the charm, which you use again to demonstrate its powers on the third card. Drop it in your pocket, pick up the last nine of spades and display it to the onlookers.

14. Hold this last nine at the ends be-
tween the fingers and the thumb of the right hand and change it for the ace at the top of the pack in moving the right hand to the left to rub the card on the left sleeve, a very easy top change which is indetectible. In Fig. 2 as both hands move to the left, the right first finger and thumb place the card on the pack as the thumb and second finger remove the sec-ond card, which the left thumb has

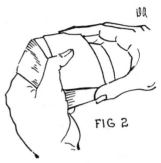

FIG 2

pushed off the pack. The left hand with the pack continues outwards to the left while the right hand with the changed card moves inwards to rub the card lightly against the coat sleeve. "To break the spell," you an-nounced gravely, "I have only to blow on the card." Do this, turn the card around and show that it is the ace. Similarly, show the other two cards to be aces and not nines. Finally, for intimate work, secretly slip the nine of spades from the top to the middle of the pack, spread the cards on the table and show that there is but one nine of spades.

This version of the trick has several strong features. Use of the three aces leads the onlookers to believe that the conjurer genuinely thinks that an ace has been selected and that he is trying to find that particular ace; the subsequent display of the three nines is therefore a psychological change of pace which catches the onlookers unprepared. Moreover, the production of the three aces is in itself surprising if the shuffles are made convincingly.

Finally, the aces are easy cards to remember, and this fact strengthens the dénouement when, after showing the three nines, these apparently self-same cards are once more turned face upwards and prove to be the original three aces. Use of the rabbit's foot is optional and will be ac-cepted or rejected by the individual performer according to the style of his performance.

Lazy Man's Card to Pocket

The late C. O. Williams' Card to Pocket trick remains a perfect gem in its class. Many attempts have been made to improve upon it but these have succeeded only in adding complications and decreasing the effect. However, it is always advisable to have an alternative method of producing an effect in order to throw the onlookers off the scent. The following variation will, no doubt, at first sight seem too barefaced to succeed, yet in practice it has been found to be not only completely deceptive but very effective.

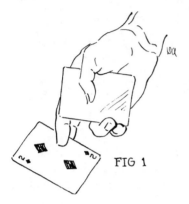

FIG 1

Effect. This is the same as in the Williams' trick: A spectator notes a card and the number at which it stands in the deck, the choice preferably to range from five to twenty-five. Without asking any questions the magician withdraws a card and puts it in his pocket. The card having been named, he shows that it is no longer in the pack and brings it out of his pocket.

Method. A spectator having secretly noted a card and the number at which it lies, proceed as follows:

1. Take the pack and hold it vertically in the left hand. Riffle the inner end with the right thumb as though making a choice of a card, at the same time scrutinizing the spectator's countenance as if to determine from it the card he chose.

2. Remove the top card without allowing the spectators to observe which card is taken, and openly place this card in your right trousers pocket.

3. Ask the spectator to name the number at which his card lay, then count off cards one upon the other onto the right hand until the number is reached. Let us assume that the eleventh card was thought of. Count off ten cards, reversing their order, and put the eleventh face down upon the table, the chosen card will then be the top card of the packet in the right hand.

4. Turn the tabled card face upwards, showing that it is not the chosen card. Retaining the packet of cards in the right hand, reach into the trousers pocket, push off the top card (the chosen card) with the thumb, grip it between the tips of the right first and second fingers and, as you begin to withdraw it, turn it over so that it is face outwards while the remainder of the packet is face downwards.

5. Have the spectator name his card and, in as showmanlike a manner as possible, display the chosen card, Fig. 1, thus proving by conjurer's logic that you have read his mind.

When the supposed correct card is placed in the pocket, it should be turned face outwards. Then when the right hand goes to the pocket to bring it out, this card is gathered onto the face of the packet as the first and second fingers grip the top card. Thus the pocket is left empty after the operation.

As with all tricks whose motif is audacity, on first reading this one may appear unconvincing. Yet Mr. Jack McMillen, the originator, and Mr. Charles Miller, using it, have proved that it is a strong audience trick.

THE VANISHING PACK

It would be hard to find a more suitable finale to an impromptu exhibition of card feats than this eye-popping trick. The routine that follows is the best that has been devised for the trick, the misdirection being perfect.

Effect. Two spectators choose cards freely, and these are shuffled back into the pack. Covering the latter with a pocket handkerchief, the operator locates the two cards by "sensitivity of touch alone." "As for the rest of the cards," he announces, "they're gone!" Snapping the linen from the hand previously holding the pack, he shows that the rest of the cards have vanished.

Preparation. Place a linen handkerchief in your right hip pocket, after having folded it so that one corner projects from the pocket. By grasping this corner and pulling sharply, the handkerchief will unfold fully without any fumbling. See that your left coat pocket is well open; if it has a lapel push this inside.

Presentation. 1. Have two cards chosen, shown to the other spectators and replaced in the pack. Control these cards to the bottom.

2. Hold the pack in the left hand, square the ends with the right hand and allow the two chosen cards to drop off the right thumb, so that you can hold a break above them with the left little finger.

3. Move the left hand with the pack to about the level of your waist; you say: "Ladies and gentlemen, I have a surprise for you!" Turn your right side towards the audience and, pushing back your coat with the right hand, grasp the projecting corner of the handkerchief and flip the fabric as you draw it from the hip pocket with a flourish. As the spectators gaze at the handkerchief, quietly drop all the cards in your left hand above the little finger break into your left coat pocket, retaining the two chosen cards in the palm of the hand. The action is concealed by the side of the body and, moreover, the operation is fully covered by the interest of the audience in the "surprise" and the subsequent introduction of the handkerchief. "At last, a magician

who uses his own handkerchief!" you exclaim, by way of explaining the "surprise."

4. Hold the left hand with the cards in a vertical position, well back towards the body; the spectators, naturally enough, take the two cards to be the whole deck. Cover the left hand and the two cards with the handkerchief and extend the covered hand well away from the body, so that later the audience will believe that the hand never approached the body.

5. Reach under the handkerchief with the right hand and, apparently with some difficulty, remove a card. In controlling the cards you know which card belongs to each spectator, therefore you now ask the proper person to name his card and then turn the card you hold to show that you have found it. "Truly a remarkable feat, discovering a lone card amongst fifty-two by the aid of my talented, and very sensitive, finger tips alone," you smilingly remark. "Watch closely and you'll see how I do it."

6. Again reach under the handkerchief and remove the second card after an interval of apparent exploratory fumbling. Hold the tips of the left thumb and finger apart just the width of a card; the fabric stretched between them makes it appear that the pack is still in your left hand. Address the man who selected this second card, have him name it and slowly turn it around. It is the correct card.

7. Continue to hold the covered hand well away from your body during the applause which follows the location of the second card and say: "As for the rest of the cards . . . *look!*" Snap the handkerchief away sharply with the right hand, showing the left hand empty and making a slight upward movement with it, the fingers wide apart. Follow with your gaze the supposed flight of the cards into the circumambient atmosphere.

The feat is particularly good as a climax trick since it ends the exhibition on an amusing note.

Second Method. In this version the effect is the same but the pack is vanished in a different manner. Three cards are chosen and are controlled to the bottom of the pack where, as in the preceding version, the left little finger holds a break above the two bottom cards.

The hand is covered with the handkerchief and the right hand is then placed under it to locate the first card. Instead it palms the pack above the little finger break, with one of the chosen cards at its face. Removing the hand, it sweeps directly across the body and is placed in the right trousers pocket. The face card is grasped and brought out, the remainder of the pack being left in the pocket. The audience may, and often does, suspect that the magician has palmed a card into the pocket; but it does not suspect the wholesale palming of the rest of the deck.

The second and third cards are then produced from under the handkerchief; the hand is then shown empty. The palming of the pack is made much easier if ten or twelve cards are first removed from it.

The first method is the better, but the second can be used to good effect when, amongst the same group at a later date, you are asked to repeat the trick.

THE DOUBLE LEAPER

This is an excellent illustration of how sleights and two swindles may be combined to make a puzzling effect.

Effect. The conjurer and a spectator each take half the pack and each remembers a card at a freely chosen number from the top of his packet. These cards are subsequently placed on the table, whereupon they are mysteriously transposed: The spectator's card changes to the conjurer's card, and vice versa.

Method. 1. Secretly sight the top card of the pack and make a series of false shuffles and false cuts, retaining the card at the top. Cut the pack and give a spectator the upper half, at the top of which is the sighted card, which we will call the four of hearts.

2. Request the spectator to take his packet in his hands and to name any small number. Assuming that he names eight, request him to do exactly as you do. Slowly deal seven cards onto the table face downwards one upon the other. Tap the top card of your pack and comment that it is the eighth card; ask the spectator if he is satisfied with the number he named, or if he wishes to select a new number. If he wishes to change, deal to one less than this new number; if he is satisfied, proceed at once with the effect.

3. Request the spectator to lift his eighth card and remember it, without allowing anyone near him to see the card. Let us say that his card is the ace of clubs. Tell him that you will remember the eighth card in your pack. Lift this card and apparently make a note of it; actually disregard this card.

4. Have him replace the dealt packet of cards, in this case seven, upon the pack exactly as you do; illustrate by picking up your dealt packet and placing it squarely on top of your pack. Immediately and secretly palm off the top card by means of the one-hand top palm. Place your assembled pack upon the table and request the spectator to do likewise.

5. Pick up the spectator's pack and add the palmed card to it. Slowly and fairly deal (in this case) seven cards upon the table, remove the next card, the eighth card, and place it before the spectator. This card

is the four of hearts which you previously sighted at the top of the complete pack.

6. Drop the cards remaining in your hands upon the dealt cards and, in squaring the assembled packet, palm off the top card, the spectator's ace of clubs. Place the cards to one side and immediately pick up your pack, adding the palmed card.

7. Second deal seven cards and deal the top card, the spectator's ace of clubs, to one side, well away from other cards.

8. Recapitulate what has been done. "You freely chose the number eight and counted down to and noted the eighth card in your pack. I also counted down eight cards in my pack and noted the card at that number. Neither of us could know beforehand which card would lie at your freely chosen number; I cannot possibly know the name of your card, nor can you know the name of my card. My card was the four of hearts." Tap the card before you and always name as your card the card which you first sighted at the top of the pack, which will be the card tabled before the spectator. "What was the name of your card, sir?" Reach over and tap his card as you make this enquiry. Whatever the name of his card, it will be the card which lies before you.

9. Command the two cards to change places. Turn your card face upwards and show that it is the spectator's ace of clubs. He turns his card face upwards and finds that it is your card, the four of hearts. Apparently the two cards have changed places under impossible conditions.

With two palms and the second deal employed, the trick may appear to be a difficult one. The palms are made, however, when they cannot be anticipated since the onlookers have not been told what you purpose to do and cannot be on their guard; moreover, the cards are palmed only long enough to transfer them from the one packet to the other and are not difficult if made smoothly without hesitation or pause as the conjurer discourses upon the trick.

The second deal, however, is another matter: It is not the easiest sleight and it is one which should not be attempted unless it can be done well. For those who have not added it to their repertoire, the spectator's card may be found in the conjurer's packet (the action in No. 7) by counting the required number of cards one upon the other into the right hand, which will retain the top card at the face of the right hand packet, and immediately slap this small packet face upwards onto the remainder of the pack, thus exposing the face of the card which the spectator believes to be on the table before him. This is an old and shameless swindle but it is very effective.

THE DUNBURY DELUSION

Those tricks in which the conjurer has apparently made a mistake which will bring the feat to an ignominious failure, much to the manifest joy of the spectators, but which he finally brings to a triumphant success, are keenly sought after by performers. This superb trick, by Charles Miller, is one of the best of this kind that has ever been devised and will make a strong addition to the repertoire of any card conjurer. The greatest care, however, must be taken that the sell is carried through in the most innocent manner, apparently; there must not be the slightest suggestion of the smart Alec, "sold you that time," style.

Effect. A card, having been freely selected, noted by the spectator and shown to everyone but the magician, is returned to the pack. After thoroughly shuffling the cards, the performer announces that by a haphazard cut he will locate three cards which will indicate the suit, the value and the location of the card in the pack. We will suppose, for instance, that the chosen card is the five of diamonds. He cuts the pack and turns the five of diamonds face upwards. Apparently quite unaware that this is the chosen card, he announces the suit as being diamonds. He turns the card face down and lays it on the table.

The next card, the four of clubs for example, is turned face upwards and this, he says, proves that the value of the card was four, therefore it is the four of diamonds. He puts this card also face down on the table.

He turns up the third card, a ten of spades we will say, and counts off nine cards, taking the tenth card face down in his right hand. He asks the name of the chosen card and the spectators gleefully tell him that it is the five of diamonds which is already on the table. He slowly turns the card in his hand—it *is* the five of diamonds and the card first dealt proves to be an indifferent one. The effect is astonishing.

Presentation. Allow a card to be freely selected and turn away while it is shown to everyone, as it is very important that all present shall know the card. Riffle the pack for the return of the card and control it during a false shuffle and cut. Run the card to the middle of the deck and insert the left little finger above it, forming a break.

With the right thumb, at the inner end of the deck, let three cards slip off the bottom of the upper half onto the left little finger. Hold a break with the thumb between this packet of three cards and the remainder of the top half, Fig. 1. Riffle the pack at the outer end and break it, apparently by mere chance, really by design, at the little finger break. Let your patter run to the effect that you never fail in this particular trick, that you have an infallible system and beg that no one give you the slightest hint as to the identity of the card.

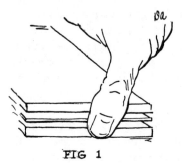

Remove the upper half to the right, retaining the break between it and the

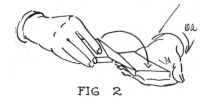

FIG 1   FIG 2

packet of three cards with the right thumb. The selected card is now on the top of the left hand portion of the pack; push it over the side of the packet with the left thumb and flip it over, face upwards, with the left side of the right hand packet, Fig. 2.

Blissfully unconscious that this five of diamonds is the chosen card, you announce that the suit is a diamond. Push it over the side of the packet again and flip it over with the right hand packet as before, but this time, as the card falls face downwards and the right hand packet is directly over it, release the three cards held by the thumb at the bottom of the right hand packet. By this simple and indetectible sleight three cards are placed on top of the selected card.

Thumb off the top card of the left hand packet onto the table face downwards. The spectators think it is the chosen card, a belief which becomes a certainty when you turn the next card face upwards, using the same action as with the first card. We have supposed this card to be the four of clubs and you say that the value of the chosen card is the same. Flip it over, face downwards, with the right hand packet and thumb it off beside the first card.

Announce that the next card will determine the position of the selected card in the pack—if it is a ten, the card will be found ten cards down—if it is a five, five cards down, and so on. Flip this third card over as before. We have supposed it is a ten, turn it face downwards and thumb it off beside the other two cards. The state of affairs now is this: There are three cards face downwards on the table, one of which the spectators *know* is the chosen card, but really this card is the top card of the left hand packet.

Place the right hand packet under that in the left hand and deal nine seconds to bring the chosen card to the required number. Have the spectator name his card and when he says: "The five of diamonds," hesitate and look rather anxiously at the card first dealt on the table. Then slowly turn over the five of diamonds and show that you have made good in your undertaking. Someone will undoubtedly rush to turn over the supposed five of diamonds on the table, only to find that it is an indifferent card. The resulting commotion will be very gratifying to the operator.

Here is an alternative method for setting the break above the three cards to be dropped secretly on the chosen card.

Bring the chosen card to the top of the deck. Undercut about half the cards, injog the first, second and third cards and shuffle off.

Grasp the pack at the outer right corner and place it upon the left palm as for dealing. Square the pack above the three jogged cards, lift the packet and insert the left third finger holding a break. Press upwards with the right thumb on the ends of the three jogged cards, insert the left little finger under them and push the three cards flush with the rest. The cut can now be made without any hesitation, the right thumb retaining the break between the three cards and the upper packet.

For those who cannot deal seconds the following procedure will be found satisfactory: When the third card is turned face upwards do not immediately mention its significance, simply lay it down face upwards. Cut the pack, bringing the chosen card to the top and quietly run the required number of cards on it as you remark: "Let's see—the first card was a diamond; that means your card was a diamond. The second a four; your card was therefore a four. The third card—oh, yes—a six [or whatever its value may be]. That card tells where the chosen card will be found in the deck."

In this way you have the cards set before you tell why the third card was placed on the table. It is a fact that after the chosen card has apparently been placed on the table, the audience is so satisfied the trick will fail that the shuffle passes quite unnoticed.

Mr. Miller, whose skill with cards is of the very highest order, performs this trick with glib zest and unfailingly makes of it a notable feature of his impromptu work.

The Obliging Card

The element of surprise is to the card trick precisely what it is to the familiar short-short story in which the plot is given an ingenious twist producing a climax for which the reader is not prepared.

This little feat is a surprise trick and a great deal of its effectiveness depends upon how well the conjurer can convince his onlookers that, first, the trick has gone awry and that he is in distress; second, that being a magician he has extricated himself from his dilemma by means of quick-witted sorcery.

1. Have a selected card, say the ace of hearts, shown to the others present and then replaced in the pack. Control it to the position of second from the top.

2. Caution the onlookers that under no circumstances are they to indicate to you, by so much as "an unrestrainable gasp of amazement," the name of the chosen card.

3. Request the spectator to give the pack a little shake; proclaim magniloquently that he has thus caused the chosen card to rise to the top of the pack.

4. Double lift the top two cards, exposing the face of the chosen ace of hearts. Prevent any acknowledgement of your success by immediately professing to believe that you have failed in your attempt. Look defeated, embittered and harassed; ask the company's pardon for your ignominious failure and turn the two cards face down, remove the top indifferent card and thrust it into the center of the pack. Unknown to the spectators, the chosen ace of hearts remains at the top.

5. Ask, for the first time, the name of the chosen card. "The ace of hearts," you are informed gleefully. "The card you just placed in the middle of the deck!" Glance at the speaker, raising your eyebrows in consternation; then gather yourself together after the terrific blow which your prestige has apparently suffered; look slyly pleased with yourself, give the pack a little shake, flip over the top card and show that it is the ace of hearts.

A trick such as this, done with good humor and mock seriousness, will often be remembered when more pretentious efforts have been forgotten, for it affords an audience the opportunity of doing that which they most desire to do—have a good laugh, first at the magician and then at themselves for having been outwitted.

Impromptu Location

This trick has been performed previously with the aid of the filings from the point of a pencil or by using a tiny pellet of wax. The method to be described makes the trick entirely impromptu.

Effect. A spectator shuffles the pack, cuts it, notes a card, and completes the cut, after which the conjurer immediately locates the card. During the process of selection the magician does not touch the pack.

Method. 1. Invite a spectator to shuffle the pack well and place it upon any smooth hard surface. (The trick will not work on a surface covered with fabric.) Secretly moisten the right forefinger at the mouth, wetting the finger copiously.

2. Request the spectator to cut the pack and place the upper half to the left of, and by the side of, the lower half. In giving your instructions touch the table top with the forefinger, wetting it, Fig. 1. When your instructions are carried out some of the moisture will be transferred to the face of the bottom card of the upper packet.

FIG 1

3. Have the top card of the other half noted and have the upper half replaced. The moistened card will be directly above the selected card. Any number of cuts may be made without altering this relationship.

4. Take the pack and run through it, faces towards yourself. If sufficient moisture has been retained, the two cards will adhere and the selected card will be the upper card; if the cards do not adhere, moisture can be seen on the face of the card on which it was originally placed. The card to the right of this card will be the chosen card.

It is not advisable to repeat the trick.

Chapter 9
MENTAL DISCOVERIES

Think of a Card

In this effective trick, which Paul Rosini uses with surprising results, a spectator merely thinks of a card and the operator at once names it.

Method. This is an improvement upon the familiar trick in which the cards are sprung from hand to hand, faces upward, as a spectator is invited to think of a card, Fig. 1. In the old method, a momentary hesitation in the springing of the cards allowed the spectator to sight one card only. In most instances, however, the "momentary" hesitation was of such pronounced duration that even the least canny of the spectators followed the procedure.

FIG 1

In this new method, the spectator is invited to think of a card freely, emphasis being laid upon this freedom of choice, the magician explaining that he does not use any such subterfuge as that explained in the preceding paragraph. It is important that the spectator should be convinced that the operator does not care which card is chosen, and that he also be convinced that so complete is the magician's indifference that he does not even so much as glance at the cards.

To achieve this end the cards are first sprung faces downward from hand to hand so swiftly that it is impossible for the spectator to see anything but a blur of flying cards. The operator, whose gaze has been elsewhere, squares the cards and innocently asks if one of them has been thought of. Upon receiving a negative response he again springs the cards faces downward, this time not so quickly as in the first instance. The spectator thinks of a card and the operator knows its identity and can demonstrate this knowledge in any fashion he pleases.

The ingenious principle used is this: On the second springing of the cards they are held at such an angle that the operator can see their faces. Watching the cards, he makes a mental note of the first card he can identify. It follows, reasonably enough, that this card will also be the first card that the spectator can select. If he chooses, the operator can also note any other card which he can distinguish, thus protecting himself in the event that the spectator has missed the first card and taken a second or third distinguishable card.

The trick again illustrates the great truth that presentation is vitally important to the success of any trick. Rosini so completely convinces his spectators that he is not in the least interested in which card they may think of that they are willing to concede that his gaze was averted at all times, the location thus becoming an absorbing mystery to them. Ample proof of this fact can be had by listening to laymen discuss Mr. Rosini's presentation of the trick.

THE WHEEL LOCATION

This trick might well have been titled "Do That Again," because of the spectators' insistence that it be repeated many times. When, under seemingly impossible conditions, the operator unerringly discovers the spectator's card, puzzlement changes to chagrin, chagrin to annoyance, and annoyance to complete and hopeless bewilderment. Little more can be asked for by any card man in the way of a satisfactory trick.

Effect. The deck, after being freely shuffled, is placed in the operator's left hand. Any person lifts up the right outer corner and glimpses the index of any card. Without any obvious mechanical moves, the operator transfers the pack to his right hand and forthwith makes a pressure fan, each card of which is in perfect alignment with its neighbors. The fan may be shown back and front; and yet the operator, without glancing at the faces, immediately withdraws the chosen card. If desired the fan is placed behind the back and the selected card is found without benefit of the sense of sight.

Working. The first part of the trick, utilizing the principle of the spectator peek, has surely been anticipated by the reader. The pack is held in the left hand, slightly fanned towards the right, with the left fingers on the right side. A spectator breaks open the pack at the outer right corner, the cards being held vertically for his convenience; after which, upon removal of the spectator's hand, the break is apparently closed in good order. Actually the left little finger, at the inner right corner of the pack, accepts and holds a tiny break under the sighted card.

The right hand covers the pack preparatory to making a pressure fan. The right second and third fingers take the pack at the outer end, near the right corner; the thumb is at the inner end, also near the right corner. The tip of the left little finger is inserted in the break and, pressing upward against the face of the spectator's card at the inner right corner, jogs it a fraction of an inch towards the right. This forces the card into a minutely diagonal position with the inner left

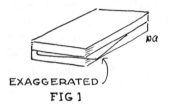

EXAGGERATED

FIG 1

corner also jogged from the end of the pack, Fig. 1. The left little finger is withdrawn from the break as soon as the jog is made.

When the right hand now removes the pack for fanning, the position of its grip is such that it does not affect the jogged card, and the pressure fan is made in the orthodox manner, the left hand holding the fanned cards.

To all appearances every card in the fan is in perfect alignment; the jog is so small that, at the outer end, no variation in the pattern of the fan can be discerned. If, however, the operator glances at the hub of the fan, under the left thumb, the position of the desired card is easily noted; for here the card is slightly out of line and may be found instantly although an unpracticed eye would never perceive the variation from the norm, Fig. 2.

The trick is so effective that, once performed, a repetition is invariably suggested. At this point it is wise to prove, apparently, that sight plays no part in the location. For this reason you locate the card while holding the fan behind the back.

The principle is precisely the same, save only that in this instance the chosen card is jogged a quarter of an inch out of the right side of the pack, diagonally; the inner end being well out of the pack while that corner of the card at the outer right end remains flush with the other cards. This extreme jog is nicely concealed by the back of the right hand and the angle at which the pack is held.

A pressure fan is made, after which the backs, but not the faces, of the cards are shown casually. The operator scarcely glances at the cards; clearly

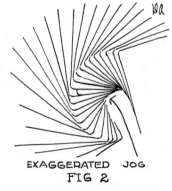

EXAGGERATED JOG

FIG 2

sight plays no part. The left hand carries the fan behind the back, or under the table; the right hand joins it and the first or second finger runs over the faces of the cards at the hub of the fan. The desired card is instantly located by feel alone, since it extends from the fan and cannot be mistaken. It is removed, brought forward in the right hand and, after the spectator has named his card, is turned face upwards.

Having thus proven, by conjurers' logic, that the sense of sight plays no part in the trick, the spectator is forced to seek other explanations and is at the operator's mercy.

It should be noted that the position of the right hand in grasping the pack prior to fanning the cards, conceals the jogged card but does not interfere with it. The pack may be handled loosely and apparently squared, the left thumb and forefinger actually pressing the pack on the sides at the outer corners, without interfering with the jogged card.

A Variation. Another method of performing this effect is to jog, with the tip of the left little finger, the entire packet above the peeked card a sixteenth of an inch diagonally to the right. The outer end of the pack remains in good order but a minute ledge is formed between the two packets at the left inner side. The pack is fanned faces downwards and the peeked card is found by looking for one card in the fan the left side of which parallels, for its length, the side of the card to its right. A quick glance at the hub of the fan suffices to locate this card. Remove the card to the right and display it; it is the spectator's peeked card.

This method does not permit placing the fan behind the back and removing the card without benefit of the sense of sight.

Wheels within Wheels. Having performed the wheel location as described above, the following ingenious method of performing the same trick makes an admirable variation. Based on an entirely different principle, the trick in good hands is absolutely indetectible.

1. Place the left little finger to the mouth and wet its tip copiously under cover of any natural action, as the pack is shuffled.

2. Hold the pack in the left hand as for the spectator peek holding the left little finger a little away from the deck. Request a spectator to peek at a card as in the first version.

3. Hold a break under the peeked card with the tip of the left little finger. Turn the pack down to a horizontal position and place the right hand over it, grasping it at the ends.

4. Draw the tip of the left little finger downwards against the side of the pack under the break. This action will scrape off a quantity of saliva upon the back of the card directly under the spectator's card.

5. Square the ends and the sides of the pack carefully, apparently tacitly proving that the card is lost, and in doing this turn it end for end so that the former inner end becomes the outer end.

6. Make a pressure fan with the cards faces downwards. Hold the fan so that the light, falling on the cards, strikes a highlight against the burnished surfaces. Glance at the outer left corners of all the cards until you find one card upon the corner of which moisture can be discerned.

7. Remove the card to the right of this card. It is the spectator's peeked card.

No more baffling quick location of a card could be desired than this since, under the imposed conditions of performance, the location of the card seems absolutely impossible to the layman. It is well, however, to alternate this method with the ones previously given when acceding to requests for continued performance, lest some acute person note the repeated movement of the left hand to the mouth. By thus changing methods the trick becomes wholly insolvable to the shrewdest of onlookers.

PSYCHO-INTELLIGENCE

In this pseudo-mindreading trick the spectator thinks of one of five cards. The operator places one of the five in his pocket and replaces the other four in the pack. The spectator names his card and the conjurer, removing the single card placed in his pocket, slowly turns it face outwards. It is the spectator's card.

Have the pack shuffled, then:

1. Take it and fan it for a free selection of five cards. Request the spectator to concentrate his thought upon one card of the five, after which he is to shuffle the packet.

2. Secretly bottom palm five cards in the left hand and then grasp the pack at the inner left corner between the thumb above and the fingers below.

3. Take the five cards from the spectator with your right hand, face upwards, fan them with that hand and, as you pretend to study them, memorize their denominations from left to right, as for instance, ace-three-queen-six-nine.

4. Turn the cards between the right first and second fingers, aided by the thumb, as the hand descends to rap the sides of the cards upon the table. The face of the packet is now to the right. At the same moment casually place the pack upon the table with the left hand.

5. With the thumb at the back of the packet, the fingers at the face,

once again fan the cards and request the spectator to glance at his card, the packet being face outwards. Close the fan, moving the wrist inward to the left and down, striking the lower sides of the cards against the side of the left first finger, the cards at right angles to the body, with their faces to the left. Drop the left thumb against the upper side and the packet is brought into the correct position for the hand to hand change. Both hands are directly in front of the body and the palmed cards in the left hand are at all times screened by the back of the left hand, which, after placing the pack on the table, has moved slowly upwards with the fingers naturally curved.

6. Make the palm to palm change* with a slow movement of both hands to the left. During the change excellent misdirection is afforded by vouchsafing some interesting or amusing information which, for the moment, will divert the spectators' thoughts. This can be done effectively by pausing after placing the hands in position for the exchange of packets, as though interrupting the trick while you digress. Make the change as a normal passing of the cards from one hand to the other, much as if you were toying with the cards during the momentary wandering into other topics.

7. After the exchange, the five cards, one of which is the spectator's card, are palmed in the right hand and the left hand holds five indifferent cards, backs outwards. Immediately transfer these to the right hand and fan them face inwards, thereby providing a natural cover for the palmed cards. As you study the cards again, apparently having resumed the trick, move them about in the fan so that the location of the chosen card cannot be followed by the spectator.

8. Retain the card farthest to the right in the fan between the right thumb and forefinger as the left hand removes the other four cards, drops them face downwards on the pack and buries them by cutting.

9. Transfer the single card in the right hand to a position between the thumb and finger tips and place it in the right trousers pocket together with the palmed cards.

10. Have the spectator grasp your left hand and request that he name his card. Knowing the sequence of the cards—ace-three-queen-six-eight—withdraw the spectator's card as you request him to name it again. Create the impression, if you can, that you failed to hear him the first time; thus, when he names the card a second time, you are holding it face downwards before him and can slowly turn it face upwards, proving that yours is truly a psychic intelligence.

---

* *Card Manipulations*, No. 2, page 25.

A good method of securing the spectator's card from amongst the other pocketed cards is to keep the right hand in the pocket as you recapitulate briefly what has been done so far. During this respite insert your fingers between the cards so that the moment the card is named the correct one can be gripped and the others released. The sixth card, the extra card openly placed in the pocket with the palmed five, plays no part in the action and, being nearest the body, is not in the way.

The five cards remaining in the pocket must be secretly palmed back onto the pack, or they can be used as the secret stock in that version of this trick in which the six cards are placed in the pocket, five indifferent cards are removed immediately and discarded, the spectator names his card and this is brought out by the operator.

THE PSYCHIC STOP!

This is one of the very finest card tricks it is possible to perform. It has been, practically, the exclusive property of a small clique of advanced card conjurers for a number of years.

The effect is this: A spectator's card is shuffled back into the pack and the expert deals cards one at a time upon the table, the spectator being requested to say "Stop!" on any dealt card. This is done and the designated card is turned face upwards; amazingly, it is the spectator's card.

Visualize, if you can, the effect upon the spectator, who has been given full freedom of choice and who, furthermore, is assured by the manner of the deal that sleight of hand could not conceivably have been brought into play. He can only conclude that you actually can perform the miracles you profess to be able to do; his surprise and perplexity make of the trick the very strongest kind of reputation builder.

As with all good tricks, the explanation is very simple, so simple that it is not until the conjurer has attempted it and noted the strong audience reaction that he can properly appreciate the ingenuity of the method.

The secret is this: The spectator's card is controlled upon its return to the pack and placed seventh from the top of the pack. The magician slowly, openly and honestly deals five cards face down upon the table, watching the cards as he deals and maintaining an absolute silence. After dealing the fifth card, he pauses, glances up at the spectator in surprise and in a tone which both urges him to make a choice and mildly reproaches him for his tardiness, says, "Say stop whenever you like."

The magician then deals two more cards upon the table, and on the second of these, the seventh card dealt, the spectator will inevitably call "Stop!"

This card, the spectator's card, is slowly turned face upwards and shown to be the desired card.

The trick is as simple as that and in good hands it is absolutely infallible. Success with the psychological gambit, which makes it possible, is dependent upon the curious frame of mind into which the operator must place the spectator. In the first place he deliberately refrains from explaining to the spectator that which he purposes to do as he deals the first five cards. The onlooker has no understanding of what is being done and therefore watches attentively but without comprehension. To him, the operator is dealing the cards for some unknown reason.

The magician, after dealing the first five cards, looks up at the spectator in surprise and requests him to stop the deal whenever he likes in a voice which expresses his supposed puzzlement at the spectator's failure to stop him previously on the deal.

The reaction of the spectator is this: Although he did not know before what was expected of him, the magician has contrived to make him feel that he has been negligent in failing to stop the deal. He now feels that the operator does not care where he calls stop, and more important, he feels that he is delaying the trick and should facilitate the dénouement by calling stop.

When the deal is resumed he lets the first card pass and calls stop on the next. He is certain he has been a free agent in stopping the deal—as indeed he has been—and subsequently will vehemently deny that he was influenced in any way. Nevertheless, if the magician's request is made in the correct tone and with the proper somewhat impatient (but not offensive) indifference, the spectator actually has no choice because of the peculiar psychological twist of the mind which forces him to stop the deal at the seventh.card.

There are few tricks of the self-working variety which are as gratifying to the operator or which produce such complete perplexity on the part of the onlookers.

ULTIMA THULE LOCATION

One of the most startling feats of the modern super-cardman is the discovery of a card which has been merely thought of by a spectator when the cards have been displayed before his eyes in a fan. We are not at liberty to divulge the method used by the most successful performers of this feat but the one which follows will be found to create the same effect. As with the original method it is not one hundred per cent effective but in the event of failure a plausible method of extricating oneself, without any loss of prestige, is provided.

Effect. After a pack of cards has been shuffled by a spectator, it is fanned before his eyes and he is requested to merely think of a card. The pack is closed, fanned again and the chosen card is found to be reversed in the deck.

Working. 1. After having had the pack shuffled by a spectator and having called particular attention to the fact, fan it in the left hand in a very tight formation with but half the index of each card showing.

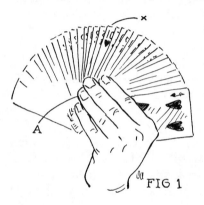

FIG 1

2. Place the tip of the left third finger at the hub of the fan, resting against the corner of a card midway in the fan, which we will call X, as at A in Fig. 1.

3. Move the finger to the right, shifting all the cards to the right of the finger tip approximately an eighth of an inch. Thus the entire index of a single card, X, in the middle of the fan will be exposed and the left third finger tip will rest upon its inner right corner, Fig. 1.

4. Present the fan to a spectator and request him to think of a card.

5. This done, turn the fan down and close it from right to left, pressing firmly on the corner of the X card with the left finger tip. This action automatically draws this card inwards together with all the cards above it, so that a break can be secured below them, the X card being the lowest card of the upper packet, Fig. 2.

6. Hold the pack vertically on its side, grip the upper packet between the right thumb and fingers, turn it to a horizontal position and slide it downwards so that the X card rests on the tips of the left fingers, Fig. 3; press them upwards against the face of this card, drawing it face upwards against the top of the lower packet and drop the upper packet upon it. The movement, which takes but a moment, should be done with your left side towards the front and be covered by brisk conversation.

7. Hold the pack before you, upright, squared and face outwards in the left hand; riffle the left upper corner with the left thumb, and sight

the index of the reversed card in the process. This can be done with certainty even in the course of a very fast riffle.

8. Ask the spectator to name his card. If you have succeeded in forcing the X card, again fan the deck and show that the card, freely thought of, has reversed itself in the deck.

9. If some other card is named, fan the deck back outwards and note the card on either side of the reversed card; if either of them is the chosen card, announce that you have reversed a card above or below the spectator's card and show that this is so.

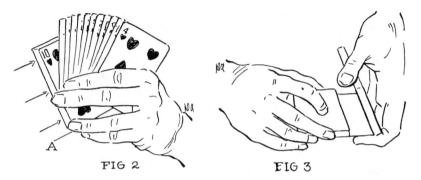

FIG 2   FIG 3

10. If this escape also fails, say, "Surely no choice of a card could be fairer than that"; fan the pack face upwards and have the spectator remove his card. With it perform any trick you please. Thus you do not have to acknowledge defeat, since you have not committed your-self to any particular trick. Disregard the reversed card and right it as opportunity offers or, possibly, use it as a locator card in the substitute trick.

This stratagem should not be attempted with magicians but with laymen there are several factors which work for its success. The spec-tator has shuffled the cards himself and you fan the cards immediately, thus he is sure you have no means of knowing the location of any par-ticular card. As the fan is presented to him you turn your head away to prove your complete indifference to the choice he may make so that if one card is slightly more exposed than its neighbors the fact does not arouse any suspicion in his mind. When in spite of all this guile, failure is the operator's reward, no one is any the wiser.

When the feat succeeds, however, as it does in most cases, it is con-sidered by the spectator to be a downright impossibility, which, as time passes, he will expand into an actual feat of magic as his imagination applies itself to the task of embroidering the trick. Having succeeded in performing his miracle, the wise performer will resolutely refuse to repeat the trick, lest his reputation be deflated by a subsequent failure.

AN INCREDIBLE LOCATION

When it is brought to a successful conclusion, no more baffling trick could be desired than the one about to be described. A spectator is handed the pack, requested to turn his back, cut the cards at any point he desires, note the face card of the upper packet and subsequently shuffle the pack thoroughly.

The operator, knowing the name of the card so chosen, divulges this knowledge in the most surprising manner at his command.

The trick is an old one in a new psychological dress. The expert, before placing the pack in the spectator's left hand, bridges the lower half lengthwise after first secretly noting the name of the face card of the upper packet. The deck is then placed in the spectator's hand as for dealing, so that he can cut only at the ends.

The spectator is then requested to turn his back, or leave the room; he is then to cut and note the face card of the upper packet. It is this apparent fairness, this apparent indifference to the manner in which the spectator may handle the pack, which disarms him and makes possible a surprising force. The spectator reasons that, under the conditions imposed, it is absolutely impossible for the operator to determine the card at which he will cut. Since the operator does not care where he cuts, then it is also a matter of indifference to the spectator. Thus, attaching no importance to the cut, he will, in the great majority of cases, cut directly into the bridge.

The psychological principle involved is the same as that which applies to the classic force: If a spectator suspects that a card is being forced on him, he will be chary in his choice. If he feels confident that no force is contemplated he will accept, as innocent, any card literally thrust into his hand.

While every expert will have his own method of glimpsing a card and bridging the deck, the following is given as an example for those unfamiliar with the technique employed in the trick.

After having allowed a spectator to shuffle the pack, take it back and:

1. Execute the Hindu shuffle in this manner: Pull off several small packets letting them fall into the left hand rather irregularly and square them by tapping the inner ends of these cards at right angles with the outer end of the packet held in the right hand, Fig. 1, thus naturally

bringing the bottom card of the latter packet into your line of vision and enabling you to note it. Done casually, this action passes quite unnoticed by the spectator.

2. Continue the shuffle by pulling off small packets until about half the pack remains in the right hand, then place this packet on top of the cards in the left hand so that its outer end projects a little. The card sighted is the bottom card of this packet, but the spectator can have no suspicion that you know any particular card.

3. Bring the right hand over the deck, pull down on the projecting end of the lower packet with the left little finger and insert its tip into the break thus made, at the same time square the ends of the pack with the right thumb and fingers.

FIG 1

4. Press the right thumb against the inner end of the upper packet, holding it, and squeeze the lower packet with the left little finger against the left palm at the base of the thumb, thus making its inner end slightly concave. This action is shown in Fig. 1, the Break from the Bridge, page 124.

5. Square the ends and the sides of the pack and place it crosswise on the spectator's hand as for dealing. Proceed with the trick as already explained.

This method leaves the upper packet perfectly flat and, since the spectator's attention is concentrated on its face card there is no likelihood of the bridge in the lower packet being noticed by him. Care, however, should be taken not to make the bend too pronounced. With cards in good order it is astonishing how small a bridge will govern a casual cut.

CRYSTAL THOUGHT

Many are the methods which have been devised to achieve the effect of the trick to be described; some have been good and some have been bad. The present method is not perfect but it can be very effective when introduced at a propitious moment.

Effect. A card is placed face downwards upon the table. A spectator is requested to think of any card. When the tabled card is turned face upwards, it is found to be the spectator's named card.

Requirements. A pack of cards which contains two sevens of hearts.

Preparation. Place both these cards at the top of the pack.

Method. 1. Shuffle the cards, retaining the sevens at the top. Place the pack upon the table, face downwards; remove the top card, a seven of hearts, and place it face downwards upon the table. Let it be noted that you have not glimpsed the face of this card.

2. Request the spectator to think of any card in the pack and, in an offhand manner, suggest that this might be any card at all, perhaps even his good luck card; he is to have an absolutely free choice, changing his mind as often as he desires.

3. Have him name his card. If, as will sometimes happen, the seven of hearts is named, you have been very fortunate and should make the most of your luck. If another card is named—say the nine of diamonds—remark that no one, not even yourself, can name the card on the table. "There is one curious aspect of this trick which at some time I hope to have explained to me," you observe, "and that is the frequence with which the seven of hearts is named." Make a pressure fan of the cards, faces inwards; locate the spectator's nine of diamonds, withdraw it from the fan and drop it at the top of the pack, directly above the duplicate seven of hearts. Make a double lift and turn the seven of hearts face upwards on the pack and tap its face with the right forefinger. "Under the present conditions, it was absolutely impossible for you to choose the seven of hearts; if you *had* thought of it, this seven of hearts, improbable as it sounds, would be the card on the table."

4. Turn the two cards down as one and remove the top card, the nine of diamonds. This is the spectator's card but he believes it to be the seven of hearts. "You thought of the nine of diamonds, you say, and that must be the card which, by purest chance, I placed on the table long before I asked you to think of a card."

5. Do the Mexican Turnover (page 128), leaving the nine of diamonds face upwards on the table and removing the seven of hearts with the right hand. Drop the seven of hearts on the table, face upwards, and make no further reference to it; let the spectators reach their own conclusions.

The trick definitely should not be repeated. Performed once, after a series of similar feats, it can be very surprising.

MENTAL SELECTIVITY

This is another impromptu trick which proves most effective when performed after other apparently impossible feats have placed the onlookers in a frame of mind in which they feel that no miracle would be beyond the performer's powers. It was created by Charles Miller.

Effect. A spectator thinks of one of five cards, the faces of which are concealed from the conjurer; it is produced in a manner apparently proving that the spectator's thought has been read.

Method. 1. Ribbon the cards face downwards across the table and invite an onlooker to withdraw any five cards. Request him to think of one of these and to shuffle it into the packet.

2. Fan the pack face downwards in the left hand, take the five cards face downwards and insert them at intervals in the fan. Do not give the spectators any reason for believing that you may have seen the faces of these cards.

3. Close the fan, squaring the pack with the five cards still extending beyond their outer end, and bring these cards to the top using the method described in sections 1 and 2 of the second phase of The Migratory Aces, page 252. False shuffle the cards, retaining the five cards at the top.

4. Hold the pack face upwards in the left hand and allow the first four cards to drop off the right thumb at the inner end. Palm these four cards in the left hand, using the Erdnase palm, the backs of the cards being toward the palm of the hand.

5. At the same moment move the right hand to the right, place the pack face upwards on the table, and cut it into four face upwards packets; A, B, C and D. The bottom card of A is one of the five cards. This action draws the eyes of the spectators and makes the palm an easy one, the left hand with the palmed cards dropping into the lap.

6. Note the card at the face of packet B. Place A upon B, both upon C, and all upon D. One of the five cards will be directly above the card noted at the face of packet B.

7. Spread the pack in a long ribbon of cards from right to left and ask the spectator if he sees his card. If he does, it must be the card to the left of the key card. Prove that you have divined his thought by producing this card in the most effective manner at your disposal.

8. If the spectator does not see his card, you know it is one of the four cards palmed in the left hand. Tell the spectator that it is only natural that he cannot find his card, since you have removed it from the pack. As you say this, move the left hand up under the coat on the right side, thrust the hand and the palmed cards into the inner coat pocket and spread the cards slightly so that the indexes may be noted, Fig. 1. Grasp the right coat lapel with the right hand and hold it away from the body, turning the body so that the onlookers may not see what is being done. Glance down openly and memorize the order of the four cards, viz: A 7 3 5. (If two cards of the same denomination are amongst the four,

remember the suit of the first card only.) This is the work of only a moment and should be done as apparently you reach into the pocket.

FIG 1

9. Pause in this action, as if for effect, glance up at the spectator and ask him to name his card, the intonation of the voice conveying the impression that, far from asking the name of his card, you are seeking a confirmation.

10. Knowing the order of the cards in the pocket, remove the spectator's card by counting to it; leave the remaining three cards in the pocket.

Glancing down into the pocket, the pretence under cover of which the conjurer memorizes the order of the cards, on first sight may seem to be dangerously open to suspicion on the part of the onlookers. On the contrary, lasting but a moment, the spectators do not regard it as unusual since they cannot know *why* the conjurer should need to look into the pocket.

PONSIN ON THOUGHT READING

Many a time has the modern magician hit upon a sleight or trick which has all the appearance of originality—only to learn later that he has been anticipated by his predecessors of a hundred years ago. It is discomfiting to the modern, but it is nonetheless a fact.

Here is a principle little known to the present-day magician which can be taken and, with practice, be developed into a sensational mystery. It comes from Ponsin (A.D. 1853), Section 19, and it is reprinted here in the words of the author to retain the full flavor of the original.

"There are some things which appear at first sight to be impossible; try them with close attention and you will soon change your opinion. This recalls to my mind a feat of which I was a witness not long ago. I saw a young prestidigitateur who, talking to four or five people, said to one of them: 'Think of a card and I will name it to you at once, but in order that all may be sure of the truth and that no one shall think that your acquiescence is dictated by mere complaisance, whisper the name of your card quietly to someone else while I am at a distance.' What he asked was done and in the eight or ten times that he repeated the experiment, he was not wrong once.

"He made no mystery of his secret. He made us note that the different movements of the lips in the pronunciation could be easily interpreted, that with a little practice and by paying close attention one could not make any mistake, but that it is necessary to place oneself in such a way as to be able to see the mouth of the person who names the card, without it being absolutely necessary to see it wholly.

"I found it hard to believe in perspicuity so prodigious; but I was soon convinced when I saw everyone present try the experiment and almost everyone succeed. The majority divined the card five times out of six."

So wrote Ponsin in 1853. A hundred years later some magician with the showmanship of a Dunninger will make of this an impenetrable mystery; it is passed on to the reader in the hope that he may be that man.

RISK LOCATION

This location is so named since it calls for boldness and the ability to make the most of favorable circumstances; it is the type of trick which is used by those experts who are willing to take a risk in order to achieve a great effect which can be had by no other means.

Effect. A spectator shuffles the pack, cuts freely, notes the card cut at and genuinely shuffles the cards. The conjurer, under these impossible conditions, discovers the card. As stated above, the trick is not without its element of risk.

Preparation. Prior to the exhibition, if it is at all possible, note which of those present shuffles with an even distribution of the cards of both packets.

Method. 1. Have the pack shuffled and request the spectator to cut freely and note the card at the cut. When he does this, estimate the depth of the cut.

2. Let us say that you have estimated the cut at twenty-one. After the first spectator shuffle the card will be at or near forty-one. After the second shuffle, it will be at or very near thirty. After this second shuffle extend your hand for the pack. If, however, a third shuffle is made you know that the card will be at or very near eight, as will be explained later.

3. Cut the pack at the point at which you estimate the spectator's card to be. Note the cards at or near this number, remembering four cards on each side of the number by memorizing the denominations as with a telephone number.

4. Have the card named and discover it by any method. For instance, palm four of the cards amongst which the chosen card may be into the

pocket and shift the other four to the center in preparedness for the Emergency Card Stabbing given on page 120. You are now prepared to produce the card as soon as it is named.

Again, when a spectator is of the type who will respond to leading questions, a casual remark or two often will tell you which of the cards under consideration is the desired card, before you request that it be named.

The rule for following the movement of the chosen card is this: In a perfect shuffle, a card always moves twice its own position, less one. Thus, if a card is at twenty-one and a single shuffle is made, the card will be at double twenty-one (forty-two) less one (forty-one). If this total should exceed fifty-two deduct fifty-two from the number. Thus, double forty-one (eighty-two) less fifty-two, tells you that the card will be at thirty.

In this trick you allow the spectator to shuffle but you depend upon the law of averages, plus a smooth spectator shuffle, to make the rule apply to a free shuffle as well as the perfect shuffle. To prove this, note the card eighteenth from the top and make two genuine riffle shuffles, cutting near twenty-six and allowing the cards to slip off the thumbs smoothly but without any effort to make a perfect shuffle. After two such shuffles, the card again will be at or near eighteen, this being largely due to the fact that errors in the first meshing riffle are compensated for by similar errors in the mesh of the second riffle.

As will be seen, the trick certainly is not dead certain of success, but the probabilities are favorable provided that the person who shuffles cuts naturally at or near twenty-six and shuffles fairly well. Moreover, you have allowed yourself a margin of error of eight cards, which is more than sixteen percent of the pack. With an erratic shuffler, who cuts once at twenty-six and next at fifteen, or who drops the cards in the shuffle in small batches, you have no chance of success.

The trick, when it comes off, is a reputation-maker. When it fails you can still extricate yourself by using the method given under the Lost Card, Method II. Once you have succeeded, rest on your laurels unless you have confidence in the shuffling of your spectator; remember that, as with the pseudo fortune-tellers, one remarkable success will be talked of and the spectators need never know that you are not infallible. Similarly, once you have failed, don't let your vanity goad you into trying again. Nothing is so respect-shattering to a spectator as to have a conjurer attempt a series of chancey locations and fail in each one. Better to accept your failure philosophically and pass on to another, and more certain, trick.

Chapter 10
REVERSES

~~~~~~

CAGLIOSTRO CUTS THE CARDS

HERE IS another example of ringing the changes with simple sleights to obtain an effective trick. A spectator replaces his chosen card in the deck, which is shuffled and placed face down before him with the request that he cut it. This he does, only to find that he has cut to his card, which rests face upwards on the lower packet.

To effect this surprising result proceed as follows:

1. Control the spectator's card to the top of the pack.

2. Reverse this card on the bottom during an overhand shuffle, using the method given on page 110.

3. Continue with the Hindu shuffle, running about half the pack into the left hand and then dropping the remaining cards, the bottom card of which is the reversed chosen card, upon the left hand packet, thus bringing the reversed card to the middle.

4. Place the pack face down upon the table with the ends towards the spectator, request him to name his card and make a quick cut. In nine cases out of ten he will cut to the reversed card, much to his surprise.

If, however, the trick fails, no harm is done as you have not said anything about what was to happen. In that case, complete the cut yourself and bring the card near the middle by a subsequent cut. Then cut to the card yourself or simply ribbon spread the cards backs upwards, the reversed card showing up immediately.

The trick is very effective and a welcome addition to the quick tricks.

A QUICK REVERSAL

A quick trick with the Two Card Turn-Up, *a*.

The following method for bringing about the discovery of a chosen card by finding it reversed in the deck is useful in a routine of discoveries since the action does not disturb the position of the remaining selected cards. It should not be despised but rather commended because of the simplicity of the means employed.

We will suppose that several selected cards have been returned to the pack, that you have brought them to the top and that you wish to produce the first card by showing it reversed amongst the others.

1. Execute a riffle shuffle and let the last card of the left hand packet fall underneath the top card, taking care to keep the remaining card stock intact.

2. Make the double lift and show the face of the indifferent card to the first spectator by means of the Two Card Turn-Up, *a*. Then ask him if it is his card, remarking that there is one chance in fifty-two that it might be. He disowns the card and you say that you propose to discover his card by making it turn over in the deck. "A simple way," you continue, "would be to have you name your card, take it like this and thrust it into the pack, face upwards." Suiting the action to the words, you turn half left, holding the pack vertically on its side, make a break about the middle with the left thumb and insert the two cards into this break, letting them project about an inch.

3. "That," you continue, "would be too simple. I shall do it by magic." With the right thumb on the face of the first card, draw it outwards and with the tip of the left forefinger behind it push the rear card (the chosen card) flush with the deck. Remove the indifferent card and replace it face downwards on the top of the pack.

4. Make a pressure fan, face outwards, and show the faces of the cards to the spectators; this action is quite safe, providing that cards with white margins on the backs are used, and reversed card tricks should only be done with such cards. Close the fan and place the pack face downwards on your outstretched left hand.

5. Continue, "I will not touch the cards again. Will you please name your card? The seven of spades? Very well. I take it out like this," make a pretence of taking a card from the middle of the pack, "I turn it over and replace it face upwards so," and you make the corresponding gestures. "Now, sir, your card is reversed in the deck. You don't believe it? Watch!" Make a pressure fan with the cards, backs outwards (or, if you prefer, ribbon the cards backs upwards on the table) and the card named at once shows up reversed.

FACED DECK REVERSE LOCATION

Here is an excellent example of the use of the faced deck and the bridge, two principles which are sadly neglected by modern card conjurers. Particular note should be made of the subtle use of the Charlier pass as a simple cut openly made.

1. As a preliminary preparation, bend the ends of the pack slightly upwards, making the backs of the cards concave, and then reverse thirteen cards on the bottom.

2. Spread the upper portion of the pack, being careful not to expose the reversed cards, and have a card chosen. As the spectator notes his card, openly cut about twenty cards from the top to the bottom, thus bringing the stack of reversed cards to the middle. Square the deck carefully, Fig. 1.

3. Invite the spectator to insert his card in the middle of the squared deck, ensuring that it goes in amongst the reversed cards. Push the card flush and square the pack by tapping its ends and sides on the table. This handling is so fair and open that it is impossible for the spectators to suspect the use of any subterfuges, such as crimps, breaks, jogs, etc., but no mention of these should be made. If anyone present is familiar with them, he can see that they are not used, so why suggest such possibilities to those who are unaware of them. This is a fault much too common amongst performers who think, wrongly, that it enhances the effect.

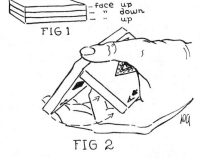

4. Hold the pack in the left hand as for the Charlier pass, and, by relaxing the pressure of the thumb, allow the pack to break open at the point where the lower face-down packet meets the bottom card of the face-up packet. Complete the Charlier pass quite slowly and openly, calling it a lazy man's way of cutting with one hand. The condition now is this: There are thirty-eight cards face down above thirteen cards face up and amongst these thirteen cards is the chosen card face down.

5. Again release the pressure of the left thumb, letting the face-up packet fall to the palm. Push this packet with the forefinger up against the thumb so that the two packets make an inverted V, Fig. 2, bend the left fingers inwards, pressing the two packets together and thus re-establishing the pack in regular order with the exception of the reversed chosen card.

6. This card is near the bottom of the pack so you repeat the slow motion Charlier pass, as an open one hand cut, first to bring the card near the middle, and again by letting the pack split open at that card, to bring it to the bottom. The chosen card can now be revealed in any way you wish.

Although the explanation is necessarily long, the action is remarkably rapid, the points at which the cuts are made being found automatically and instantly, thanks to the bridging of the cards. It should be needless to remark that this method must be used with white margined cards only.

REVERSE SUPREME

This effect has been a favorite of card men for many years but it has one great drawback in that doublebacked cards are necessary. The following Zingone sleight of hand method is a vast improvement since an ordinary pack of cards is used, the spectator has a free choice in his selection of cards, the cards can be shown on both sides, and above all the performer ends up cleanly with nothing to get rid of.

Effect. The cards are shuffled and spread face downwards on the table. A spectator pushes any four cards out of the spread. The performer picks up the remainder of the cards and turns his back while the spectator lifts one of the four cards, notes it and replaces it on the table. The performer turns, fans the pack face upwards and inserts the four cards face downwards into different parts of the fan. Squaring the deck he places it on the table to be cut by the spectator. Finally he spreads the cards on the table showing all the cards face upwards except one card which is face downwards in the middle of the spread. This card proves to be the selected card.

Requirement. A pack of cards with white margins on the backs.

Method. 1. Have cards shuffled, then spread them face downwards on the table and request a spectator to push any four cards out of the spread. Pick up the remainder of the cards and ask the spectator to take one of the four cards, note it and drop it back on the table while you turn away.

2. Make a mental picture of the positions of the four cards and turn your back. When the spectator has looked at a card and replaced it and you turn around it is an easy matter to discover the selected card as it is never replaced in exactly the same position.

3. In the meantime, while your back is turned, reverse the bottom card of the deck and then turn the top twelve to fifteen cards face upwards. Crimp the remainder of the cards by squeezing them with the left hand thus making a bridge between these face-down cards and the face-up cards above them.

4. Turn to the table, detect the selected card and then execute, right under the eyes of the spectators, the crucial and most disarming sleight in the entire effect. Hold the pack, apparently face upwards, in the left

hand and make a close but perfect fan, taking care that only the white margins of the bottom cards show. A subtle addition is to so arrange that the index pip of the bottom card which is face upwards shall be visible, Fig. 1. To the audience this is conclusive proof that the whole pack is face upwards.

5. Pick up one of the three odd cards and insert it face downwards between the bottom card and the remainder of the pack, bringing it almost halfway out of the pack on the bottom of the fan.

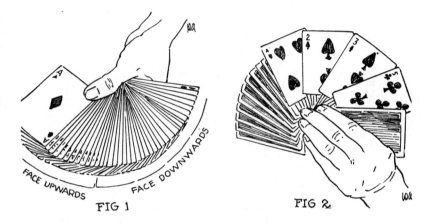

FIG 1   FIG 2

6. Place the other two odd cards amongst the face-down cards and bring them also about halfway out on the bottom of the fan. If the three cards are properly spaced they will completely hide the faces of the face down cards.

7. Pick up the selected card and insert it in the face-up section of the fan. Turn the fan of cards over and show that all four cards have been inserted in a reversed position, Fig. 2.

8. Turn the fan back to its original position. Push the protruding cards flush with the rest of the pack and square the cards. Under cover of this move reverse the bottom card and locate the break between the face-down and face-up cards.

9. Hold the break with the right thumb and, *in the act of placing the pack* before the spectator to be cut, turn over the entire group of face-down cards with the left hand under cover of the face-up cards held by the right hand. Place the pack down, face upwards, so that the face card which has been in view at all times is still seen by the spectators, negativing any idea that a pass might have been made.

10. Invite the spectator to cut the pack and complete the cut. Spread the cards in a straight line revealing all the cards face upwards except one card in the middle which is face downwards.

Have the selected card named and execute the flourish turnover of the entire spread (Fig. 1, page 174) revealing the chosen card face upwards amongst the face-down cards. This remarkably effective trick is by Mr. Luis Zingone.

Chapter 11
SPELLING

~~~~~~

MULTI-SPELLING TRICK
The Repeat Spelling of Mentally Selected Cards

EFFECT. A NUMBER OF CARDS are shown, spread fanwise, and several spectators are invited to select cards mentally. The cards are then replaced in the deck which is shuffled. Any one of the spectators names the card he thought of and it is spelled out from the top of the pack in the usual way, one card being dealt for each letter in its name, and the card itself is turned up on the last letter. The cards thus dealt are replaced in the pack, which is again shuffled, and the same procedure is carried through with each of the remaining selected cards.

Preparation. A set-up is used, the necessary cards being:

2C, 6S, 5H, 7S, 4D, QD.

If the reader is familiar with the Nikola system, the cards can be memorised by using this couplet:

A *can* of *soup* was cut in *half*
To *suit dear jeweleress* Pfalf.

The very absurdity of the rhyme serves to fix it in the mind. In any case, these six cards are arranged in the order given above and are placed on the top of the pack beforehand.

Working. Begin by undercutting the pack for an overhand shuffle, jog the first card and shuffle off. Cut at the jog and complete the cut, then take off the six cards in a casual manner to give the impression that the actual number is negligible. Spread them fanwise and show them to a number of spectators, asking each one to select any one card mentally.

This done, place the six cards on the top of the pack, undercut for an overhand shuffle, run nine cards, injog the next card and shuffle off. Form a break at the jog, shuffle to the break and throw the remainder on top. You can now spell off any one of the six cards. We will suppose that the two of clubs is called for. Spell it out, dealing a card for each letter and turn the two of clubs on the last.

Turn it face down on the top of the nine cards just dealt and pick up the packet of ten cards. Square it and insert it in a break made by the left thumb in the side of the pack, Fig. 1. Push the packet through diagonally so that the left little finger can secure and hold a break above the top card of the packet, the two of clubs.

Grip the right side of the deck between the right thumb at the inner right corner and the second finger at the outer right corner, pressing firmly with the thumb to hold the break. Withdraw the left little finger from the break, take hold of the left side of the pack with the left hand and press downwards so that the pack pivots into a vertical position ready for an overhand shuffle, Fig. 2.

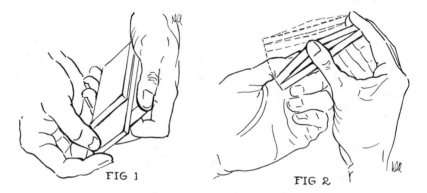

FIG 1   FIG 2

Undercut with the right hand at the break and run cards to the number of letters in the denomination of the card just spelled and include the word "of." In this case the first card has been taken to be the two of clubs, therefore you run cards for the letters t-w-o o-f, five in all. Injog the next card and shuffle off. Form a break at the injog, shuffle to the break and throw on top.

Again undercut about half the deck, run one card for each letter in the suit, clubs in this instance, injog the next card and shuffle off. Make a break at the injog, shuffle to the break and throw on top. The six set-up cards will be again in their original position with nine cards above them. You can now spell off the second card called for and repeat the spelling as many times as you please, using exactly the same formula given above but varying it, of course, according to the spelling of the different cards called for.

The same result can be obtained by dealing the cards face up when spelling and then replacing them on the pack without altering their order, but, almost inevitably, repetition of the effect would betray the fact that the six cards of the set-up do not change. A distinct clue would thus be given to any sharpwitted spectator.

The required cards, after each spelling, can be run off in one shuffle, but it is far better to use two as described. More than eight or nine cards should never be run off in one action.

Cards on Parade

Spelling tricks are always suitable for intimate exhibitions of card skill; here is a trick which makes use of the spelling principle to produce a chosen card.

Effect. A chosen card is found by spelling the names of twelve cards, the thirteenth and remaining card being the spectator's card.

Preparation. Place twelve cards at the top of the pack in the following order: Three, eight, seven, ace, queen, six, four, two, jack, ten, nine and five. The three is the first card. Any suits may be used. Place any three cards above this stock.

Method. 1. Insert the tip of the left little finger under the twelfth card —the jack—and riffle the outer end of the pack with the right fingers, inviting a spectator to remove any card. As he thrusts his forefinger into the pack open a fairly large break at the outer end to facilitate the removal of the card.

2. Have him show his card to all those present and, as he does so, hold the pack pointing obliquely downwards, drop the break being held at the point from which the card was removed and instead lift the twelve cards above the little finger break. Have the card replaced at this point. The spectators believe that the card is returned at the same position from which it was taken.

3. Reassemble the pack and square it carefully. Undercut half the pack, injog the first card and shuffle off. Undercut at the injog, run three cards (the extra cards above the twelve card stock) and throw. The twelve cards are once again at the top but the spectator's card now reposes between the jack and the ten.

Undercut about one-third of the deck, injog the first card and shuffle off. Cut at and including the jogged card, spread the cards face upwards and ask the spectator if he sees his card. On receiving a negative response, throw these cards on the table.

4. Remove the top thirteen cards (the set-up packet) from the remainder of the deck without changing their order, turn them face upwards, fan them and ask the spectator if he sees his card. It will be the card to the right of the jack; make a mental note of it.

5. Upon receiving an affirmative response square the packet and turn it face downwards. Spell a-c-e, placing one card from the top to the bottom for each of the three letters. Turn the next card face upwards, show that it is an ace and drop it to one side. Spell t-w-o, placing one card at the bottom for each letter, and turn up the next card. It is a two-spot; drop it upon the discarded ace. Continue in this fashion spelling the remainder of the cards from the three to the queen.

6. After spelling the queen one card remains in hand. "Since all the cards have been spelled by a curious mathematical oddity," you point out, "only the two of diamonds [name the spectator's card which you previously noted] remains in my hand. Therefore it must be your card." Turn the card face upwards, show that it is the spectator's card and obtain a confirmation from him.

The trick is practically self-working and makes an effective and easy discovery.

Chapter 12
DOUBLE-FACED CARDS

~~~~~~

HARDIN PLUS DEVANT

IN THIS FEAT we have an interesting example of the combination of two good tricks to produce a third, and new, mystery. The tricks thus combined are Henry Hardin's King's Cards, a description of which will be found in Theo Annemann's *Jinx 104*, and David Devant's Thirty Card Trick.

Effect. Thirty-three cards are counted, after which the performer retains eighteen and an assisting spec' 1tor holds fifteen. Three spectators each think of one of the eighteen held by the performer; the conjurer again counts his cards but now holds but fifteen, the spectators' cards having vanished. The assistant counts his cards and finds that they have magically increased to eighteen; the three extra cards are those of which the three spectators merely thought.

Requirements. Fifteen cards of any suit and denomination. Fifteen double-face cards, one face of which duplicates the cards in the first set of fifteen. Any three regular cards.

Preparation. Place the fifteen ordinary cards face upwards on the table. Place any three regular cards face upwards upon these. Finally place the fifteen double-face cards upon all, the indifferent faces being uppermost.

Method. 1. Take the packet of thirty-three cards and deal fourteen cards face down upon the table. Place these cards in front of an assisting spectator, inviting him to be their custodian. Four regular cards remain, face downwards, upon the top of the packet of cards remaining in your hands; under them are the fifteen double-face cards.

2. Turn this packet of nineteen face upwards and count the cards one upon another, bringing the four regular cards to the top. Remove the top card, one of the sequence of fifteen, and hand it to the assisting spectator as you point out that he now has fifteen cards and that you hold eighteen cards.

This deceptive manner of dealing the cards convinces the onlookers that they have seen the faces and backs of all the cards. Theo Annemann, quoting Mr. Rudy Reimer, writes as follows on this point: "The trick isn't worth a cent if anyone suspects that prepared cards are being used, and the subtle part which attracted [the late Nate] Leipzig is the manner in which both sides of the cards, back and front, are shown at the start."

3. Spread your cards face upwards on the table and request the assistant to do likewise; thirty-three different cards can be seen.

4. Gather your packet of cards and state that you are going to ask three spectators each to think of one card but that since, in prior performances, certain cynics have suggested that you watched the eyes of the spectators and thus determined which cards they had thought of, you will place the cards behind your back and have the selections made under conditions which would make impossible this subterfuge.

5. Place the cards behind your back as you speak and separate the fifteen double face from the three regular cards, reversing the former. You now hold eighteen cards behind your back, faces outwards, fifteen of which are duplicates of the cards held by the assistant, and three of which are any regular cards.

6. Turn your back and hold the cards with both hands close to the back, spreading them before three spectators in turn, requesting each to think of any card.

7. Close the spread, face forward again and immediately reverse the three regular cards, which are at the top of the packet, and palm them in the right hand, backs to palm. This is the work of but a moment but in making the move the arms must not be moved. At the same time request the assisting spectator to count his cards one at a time, slowly, and to drop them onto the table from a height of about a foot. This request is made ostensibly to prove to all that but one card at a time is dropped; it is actually made so that the cards will scatter on the table during the deal. Count the cards with the assistant and when he has dropped the fifteenth card reach forward and push the cards towards him with the request that he hold them tightly in his hands, adding the palmed cards in the action.

It is a curious fact that the replacement of the palmed cards in this action never is questioned and that later you can claim that never once did you touch the assistant's packet and the veracity of the statement will not be challenged.

8. During the foregoing the left hand has reversed its packet of double-face cards, bringing the indifferent faces uppermost, and has brought the cards in front of the body. You now claim that you will cause the three mentally chosen cards to pass to the packet of fifteen cards held by the assisting spectator.

9. Flick the packet of double-face cards and immediately count them,

face upwards, onto the table one at a time. You have but fifteen cards. Deal the cards again, or spread them on the table, asking each of the three spectators to name his card, thus securing the names of these cards, and request all those present to verify that the mentally chosen cards have vanished.

10. As you recapitulate what has been done, emphasize that never once have you touched the assistant's packet of cards (*sic!*) nor will you. Invite the assistant to count the cards in his hands one at a time onto the table, dealing exactly as in the first instance; he does so and finds that he has eighteen cards. Have him spread the cards face upwards on the table and, naming the three chosen cards, ask him to remove these cards and hand them to the spectators who chose them.

Second Method

This method is for those who may not desire to palm the cards onto the assistant's packet. The method follows that given above from 1 through 6.

7. Turn and gaze intently on each of the three spectators. Remove one of the three regular cards from behind the back, face downwards, drop it upon the assistant's packet and cut it. Repeat this action twice, in each case cutting the pack to disorder the cards.

8. Claim that the three cards which you placed in the assistant's packet are the three chosen cards. Count your cards after reversing them and show fifteen indifferent cards. Have the assistant's packet counted, showing eighteen cards, have the spectators name their cards, and show that they are indeed amongst the cards in the assistant's packet.

THE MECHANICAL FOUR ACES

The Four Ace trick, performed with double-face cards, is undoubtedly the most deceptive of all tricks of this genre. No sleight of hand can duplicate the effect when the aces vanish from their respective packets and gather clannishly in one pile. The effectiveness of the trick lies in using the cards so that the onlookers are satisfied that they have seen the faces and backs of all the cards, and this requirement is satisfied in this version.

Requirements. Three double-face cards showing on one face the aces of hearts, clubs and diamonds and on the other three indifferent cards. The genuine aces are scattered throughout the pack; the double-face cards are at the face, with the indifferent faces showing.

Presentation. 1. Turn the pack face up, deal four face-up packets of three cards, A, B, C, D, with the double-face packet at B. Run through the pack and remove the four aces, placing them face up before you.

2. Pick up the four aces, display them, and in so doing place the ace of spades at the top of the face-up packet. Deal these four aces face down, one at a time, the ace of spades being the last card dealt, each card overlapping a little to the right.

3. Pick up the right hand pile of three face-up cards, that at D, casually show the cards and deal them face up in an overlapping pile beside the face-down aces.

4. Pick up C, casually show the cards, and deal them face up in an overlapping pile.

5. Pick up B, the double-face cards, and deal these face up beside the other packets, the ace faces of these cards naturally being kept from view.

6. Place A beside B, face up. This arrangement of the cards, which should be on your right, is made so that the onlookers will note so many of the backs of the cards being exposed that later they will feel that they saw the backs of all the cards.

7. Pick up D and place its three cards face down on the natural ace pile, again with the cards overlapping one another.

8. Place A face down on C, overlapping the cards.

9. Remove the top four cards from the natural ace pile (the bottom card is the ace of spades) and place them face down upon B, the double-face pile. Square this packet.

10. Gather A on C, square them, turn them over, and deal the six cards face down on the natural ace pile. Because of the facing of these two packets, the deal further impresses upon the spectator that the backs of all the cards are shown, although never once in the entire routine is this fact commented upon.

11. Pick up the packet at the bottom of which the double-faced cards repose, place it in the left hand. With the right hand place the other packet of nine cards face down upon the left hand packet. At the bottom of the assembled packets are the double-face cards, with the aces at the face. Seventh, eighth and ninth from the top are the natural aces.

12. Turn the assembled packets face up in your hands and deal the first four cards from left to right. The first three will be double-faced cards, the ace face uppermost; the fourth will be the natural ace of spades. Consider these aces as A, B, C, D, the spade ace being at D.

13. Turn the packet in your hands face down. Count off the top three

cards, expose their faces briefly and drop them on A. Count off three more cards, expose their faces and drop them on B.

14. The next three cards are the natural aces, followed by three indifferent cards. Count off the first three cards, holding them in the right hand without exposing their faces. "Kindly notice," you say, "that not for one moment do I cover the faces of the aces upon the table. There is no trickery, no subterfuge." As if to demonstrate your meaning, cross the wrists and with the three cards held in the left hand slightly fanned cover the ace of spades at D, and with the cards held in the right hand similarly cover the ace at C.

15. Uncross the hands and immediately drop the right hand cards upon the ace of spades at D, at the same moment holding the three left hand cards face outward as if to show their faces before dropping them upon C.

The trick now is nearly done. Audacious as may seem the action in 12, in which the double-faced aces are dealt upon the table, not one person in a thousand will notice that the aces have moved out of position. This is due to the previous confusing movement of the cards which, although it may seem unnecessary, actually is vital to the successful performance of the trick.

16. Request a spectator to point to any pile. He chooses B. Remove the top indifferent card and, turning it face up, use it to scoop up the other three cards. If the four cards are spread slightly the top two cards are face down; the bottom two apparently are face up. In handing these to a spectator, or in placing them in his outer left handkerchief pocket, reverse them.

17. Repeat the actions in 16 with A and C, cautioning the assisting onlookers to hold the cards tightly.

18. Give D, the pile of natural aces, to any spectator.

19. Request spectator A to fan the cards in his hand. He will have three face-up cards, the top card being face down. Reach over and gently remove the three face-up cards. The card directly under the face-down card is the double-facer; drop this with a downward gesture of the right hand which, moving up again, takes one card in each hand and as it drops these cards to the right and left of the tabled double-facer makes certain that the backs of the cards are seen. Ask spectator A to look at the face-down card, which he believes to be an ace. It is an indifferent card.

20. Repeat the same procedure with B and C; thus, the three double-facers are gathered in the center pile on the table where they are available

for a repetition of the trick if it is so desired, or where they may be conveniently controlled for palming off the pack. Should any assistant inadvertently reverse the packet he holds, when the cards are fanned he will hold two face-down, two face-up cards, one of which is the double-face ace. In such a case, take the cards, reverse them in asking someone to blow upon them, and continue in the usual manner. It is a good idea, with at least one of the spectators, to show the ace still in the packet up to the last moment in this manner, for the impression made is a very strong one when the ace subsequently disappears.

21. The aces having disappeared, take D from the spectator's hands, make a magic incantation, spread the cards and show the aces.

Permitting the spectator to fan the four cards as in 19, one of which is a double-facer, may seem dangerous but in practice is perfectly safe since the three cards, including the faked card, are gently eased from his possession as his attention is concentrated on the face down card remaining there, which is taken to be the ace. It is not uncommon afterwards to hear onlookers claim that the ace vanished from amongst four cards, and that they then examined each of the four cards front and back.

The trick is most effective of all when the double-faced cards are palmed onto a borrowed pack.

The Radioactive Aces

This is another method of performing the four ace trick utilizing double-faced cards. Upon the table are four groups of three face-up cards, A, B, C, D, of which D consists of three double-faced cards, aces (C, H, D) on the under side and indifferent cards on the exposed upper faces.

1. Show the four natural aces and place them face down upon the table, jogging the top ace, which should be the spade ace, slightly to the right.

2. Drop D, the double-face packet, upon the ace pile with the indifferent faces uppermost.

3. Show A and place it face down in the left hand. Show B and place it face up upon A. Pick up the three double-faced cards and with them the top ace, the spade ace, and place these four cards upon the cards in the left hand.

4. Place the three remaining face-down aces, without showing their faces, upon the pile in the left hand. Square and drop the assembled packets upon C, which lies face up on the table. Square the complete packet of sixteen cards.

From the top down, the order is now this: At the top, three face-down aces; then three face-up double-faced cards, indifferent face exposed; then a single face-down card, the ace of spades; then three face-up cards; then three face-down cards; and finally three face-up cards.

5. Turn the complete packet of sixteen cards over in the left hand and deal the first three cards, which are face-down indifferent cards, face up on the table by pushing them off with the thumb and turning the left hand over, back upwards, as the cards are dropped, Fig. 1. Count, "One, two, three." With the right hand turn these cards face down.

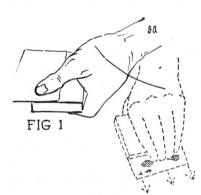

FIG 1

6. The next three cards lie face up. Push these off with the left thumb and drop them face up on the table, in this action turning the hand so that its back is uppermost as in the previous deal, which it exactly duplicates in appearance, Fig. 2. Turn these three cards face down with the right hand, counting, "Four, five, six."

7. Deal the next three cards, which are face down, face up on the table exactly as in 5, counting "Seven, eight, nine." With the right hand turn these cards face down.

8. If the cards in the left hand were now spread, seven face-up aces would be seen. Of these, the top card is the natural ace of spaces; the next three are double-faced aces; the final three the natural aces. Push off the first ace, the spade ace, with the left thumb and drop it face up in front of and to the right of the three face-down piles on the table; as it is pushed off, make a sweeping turning of the hand so that its back is uppermost, Fig. 2, this action wholly concealing the faces of the cards remaining in the left hand. Deal the next three cards, the double-faced aces, in the same manner, from right to left. These cards, dropping upon the table with their ace faces uppermost,

FIG 2

are taken to be the natural aces. As they fall, count, "Ten, eleven, twelve and thirteen."

9. With the back of the hand uppermost, Fig. 1, push the three aces one at a time out of the hand face down onto the right hand ace of the row of four, the spade ace. These natural aces fall face down as you count, "Fourteen, fifteen, sixteen. Sixteen cards, no more and no less!"

10. Drop a face-down packet upon each face-up ace, the natural aces falling on the spade ace. Place this latter packet of four cards aside to the right, or thrust it in the outer handkerchief pocket of an obliging spectator.

11. Emphasize at all times that only sixteen cards are used; assemble the three remaining packets, pointing out that an ace is each fourth card.

12. Square the packet of twelve cards in the left hand. Holding the cards face up, push the first card off with the left thumb and drop it face up on the table, turning the left hand back upwards in the action and thus turning the packet face downward, Fig. 2. Turn the hand back down, show the second card and repeat the deal with this card. Repeat the entire action with the third card, which is a double-faced card; it falls indifferent face upwards. Count, "One, two, three." With the back of the left hand up, Fig. 1, push the next indifferent card outward to the left with the thumb and let it drop face down some distance away on the table, saying, "And the fourth card, the ace."

13. Repeat the action in 12, counting "Five, six, seven and the eighth card, the ace." Repeat again, counting, "Nine, ten, eleven and the twelfth card, the ace." You now have a pile of three face-down cards at your left; actually they are indifferent cards although the spectators think them to be aces. The assisting spectator retains the ace of spades and the three remaining natural aces which are believed to be indifferent cards. Before you is a pile of nine face-up cards, three of which are double-faced.

14. Pick up the three face-up piles and deal them from left to right in three piles, counting from one to nine in so doing, and thus place the double-faced cards together in the right hand pile, available for a repetition of the trick or for palming off to the pocket.

15. "Nine cards here," you say, "and three aces here—" scattering the three supposed aces to the left "—and four cards in your pocket, sir. Nine and three and four, making a total of sixteen cards. And now, ladies and gentlemen, the miracle for which you have been breathlessly waiting. One by one I take each of the three aces in this little pile on

my left at the very tips of my thumb and forefinger; I hold it up before you so that you can see it. You can't? That's strange. . . . *I* can. I take it, I toss it like this, and as it strikes the gentleman holding the cards, which we know are one ace and three indifferent cards, one of those indifferent cards streaks across the table with the speed of lightning and takes the place of the ace I just showed you. Strange, isn't it? Twice more I repeat my awesome actions; watch me closely, for there's no deception at all, or at least very little deception. And yet . . . look!"

Turn over the three face-down cards at the left and show that they are indifferent cards. Have the spectator show his cards, the four aces.

This version of the classic is a very good one, suitable for the closest performance.

The Torn and Restored Card

This is a new version of the Torn and Restored Card trick, using a double-face card as the stranger card.

Effect. Two cards are chosen; one of these is replaced and magically flies to the performer's pocket. The second reverses itself in the pack; it is torn into small pieces; these vanish and the restored card is found in the pack, once again as good as new.

Requirements. A double-face card with, let us say, the nine of clubs on one side, the eight of hearts on the other. This card has been cut narrow. A thumb tip.

Preparation. Place the double-face card in the upper left vest pocket with the club face outwards. Place the thumb tip in the right trousers pocket.

Method. 1. Borrow any pack of cards and from it force the eight of hearts and the nine of clubs upon two spectators, using any method of forcing at which you are adept. Have the cards shown to all those present.

2. Advance to the spectator holding the nine of clubs and have him replace it in the pack. Give the pack a light overhand shuffle and hand it to the spectator for further shuffling. Take the pack back, riffle it once and, without showing the right hand empty, thrust it under the coat on the left side, holding the hand there as you request that the card be named. Immediately withdraw the double-face card, saying, "You took the lightning card!" Hold the card by the lower right corner, club face outwards, and shake it gently to emphasize your words.

3. Hold the remainder of the pack face upwards in the left hand and thrust the card into it, club face upwards, without exposing the other face of the card. Turn the pack face down.

4. Riffle with the left thumb to the narrow double-face card and cut it to the bottom. Request the spectator holding the eight of hearts to replace his card, undercutting the pack for its return, thus bringing the double-face card above it.

5. Fan the pack faces outward, tacitly demonstrating that there are no reversed cards. Have the card named by the spectator and run the cards, face downwards, from the left to the right hand. The heart face of the double-face card shows in the spread; apparently the eight of hearts has reversed itself.

6. Drop the card on the table, the heart face uppermost. The card directly below it is the genuine eight of hearts. Place the packet of which this is the top card on top of the packet held by the right hand in reassembling the pack, thus bringing the genuine eight of hearts to the top. Reverse this card, using the method given on page 110, and cut the pack, bringing the reversed eight of hearts to the middle. Hand the pack to a spectator, requesting that he place it in his coat pocket.

7. As this is done, secretly secure the thumb tip and palm it in the right hand. The nature of this palm is this: Place the rounded tip of the metal thumb in the crotch of the right second and third fingers, with the "nail" side nearest the flesh of the fingers. By curling the fingers inward naturally, the thumb tip is concealed and easily retained in the hand.

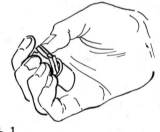

FIG 1

8. Pick up the double-face card, always being careful not to expose the club face, and tear it into two pieces, making as straight a tear as possible. Place these pieces together and tear again, making four pieces. Tear again, and again. You now hold sixteen pieces, approximately a half by three-fourths of an inch.

9. Hold these pieces between the tips of the right second and third fingers, with the thumb pressing against the back. Half the surface of the pieces extends beyond the tips of the fingers. Holding the packet firmly, so that the pieces remain a compact bundle, bend the second and third fingers, and the thumb, inward. It will be found that the inner end of the bundle can be lowered directly into the mouth of the thumb tip, Fig. 1. Once the inner ends are inserted in the thumb tip, shift the ball of the thumb to the outer end of the packet and press inward, forcing it well into the tip. Bend the thumb inward and force it into the thumb tip;

it will be found that the accessory will easily accommodate both the torn pieces and the thumb itself. All this is done as the hand is moved about, the fingers giving aid if necessary in pushing the torn pasteboard into the tip, the action being made to simulate the crumpling into nothingness of the torn pieces.

10. With the thumb firmly in the tip, make a throwing motion of the hand towards the spectator in whose pocket the pack reposes, opening the hand to show it empty. Request him to remove the pack. Have it spread on the table, showing that the eight of hearts has flown back to the pack, reversed itself, and become whole at one and the same time.

Get rid of the thumb tip at the earliest moment but do not make of this action a noticeable diving for the pocket.

Chapter 13
THE STRANGER CARD

~~~~~~

THE FIRST RECORDED application of the principle of introducing a card with a different back pattern into a borrowed pack to serve the purpose of a duplicate card is the trick entitled The Torn and Restored Card, as explained in *Card Manipulations*, No. 4.

It is a curious fact that, while a spectator may be only too quick to suspect the use of duplicate cards when the conjurer, using his own pack, produces with it an effect which could only be explained by the use of such a duplicate, he is utterly bewildered when the selfsame trick is performed with a borrowed pack of cards for which he knows that the conjurer could not conceivably have a duplicate card with a matching back.

By inserting a strange duplicate card in a borrowed pack and never permitting its back to be seen the card manipulator has a secret weapon with which he can achieve effects which cannot be had by any other means, which will be wholly incomprehensible to those who witness feats utilizing this ruse.

In order that the principle may be understood thoroughly we give a brief summary of the trick mentioned above:

THE TORN AND RESTORED CARD WITH A BORROWED DECK

Effect. A card, chosen from a borrowed deck, is torn to pieces and the fragments are vanished; it is then found to have returned to the pack which has been held by the spectator himself.

Requirements. An extra card with any back pattern and two small pieces of flash paper. Place the stranger card in your left trousers pocket, face inwards; one piece of flash paper crumpled into a ball and the other folded, in your outside right coat pocket.

Working. Suppose the stranger card is an eight of hearts; during some preliminary tricks get control of the regular eight of hearts.

1. Force this card on a spectator and have him show it to everyone as you turn away momentarily.

2. Seize the opportunity to palm the stranger in your left hand and add it to the bottom of the deck, face upwards.

3. Undercut half the pack, have the card replaced, drop the cut on it, square the cards in such a way that there cannot be the least suspicion that you can make any secret maneuver, and lay the pack on the table.

4. Order the chosen card to turn face upwards and, after suitable byplay, spread the pack face downwards on the table. The stranger eight of hearts shows up reversed and is naturally taken for the regular card.

5. Draw the stranger from the line towards yourself; assemble the pack bringing the regular eight of hearts to the top; secretly reverse it; pass or cut it to the middle and hand the pack to the spectator to place in his inside coat pocket.

6. Pick up the stranger card, holding it always face outwards, and, asking permission to mark it, accidentally tear it in half. The damage done, complete its destruction by tearing the pieces again and again, carefully keeping the face sides outwards.

7. Hold the fragments in your left hand and with the right take the folded piece of flash paper from your pocket, at the same time palming the balled piece. Wrap the pieces in the flash paper, crumpling it and, in doing this, add the palmed piece, squeezing the two tightly together so that they appear to be one packet only.

8. Take the empty packet in the left hand, leaving the other palmed in the right. Plunge this hand into your pocket for a match and leave the packet behind. Touch off the flash paper and toss it towards the spectator ordering the card restored and to return to the pack.

9. The spectator finds the card intact and again reversed.

Under appropriate conditions this is one of the most effective tricks that can possibly be done with cards. Some performers make a practice of always carrying two extra cards, one of bridge deck size, the other of poker deck size, so that they can do the trick with any deck at any time.

THE GHOST CARD

This trick devised by Mr. Theo Annemann again illustrates the excellent uses to which the stranger card can be placed.

Effect. A spectator chooses a card and, without looking at it, seals it in an envelope, which he retains. A second spectator selects another card from the pack, which is shown to the company; it is, say, the nine of spades. The pack is assembled and the cards counted one by one: There are only fifty-one cards, the nine of spades having vanished.

The envelope is torn open: In it is the missing nine of spades!

Preparation. A stranger, the nine of spades, is secretly added to the bottom of a borrowed pack. Place the regular nine of spades at the top.

Method. 1. Secretly slip the regular nine of spades to the middle by means of the slip cut, insert the little finger above it and, spreading the pack, force this card upon a spectator, requesting that, without looking at it, he seal it in an envelope which you hand him.

2. Secretly secure glycerine, or, wet your left second finger.

3. Bring the stranger nine of spades to the middle by means of an open cut, securing a little finger break under the card. Force this card by means of the knife force. Hold the packet up squarely with the right hand, letting everyone see the face of the stranger nine of spades.

4. Drop the right hand with its packet and draw the packet lengthwise upon the tip of the left second finger, thus applying moisture to the face of the stranger card. Replace the right packet, square the assembled pack and squeeze it tightly. The two cards will adhere firmly to one another.

5. Have the card named, deal the entire pack face upwards quickly to prove that the card is no longer there, counting the cards as you do so. Invite a spectator to open the envelope; in it he finds the nine of spades, as bizarre an enclosure as ever he found in an envelope.

6. As attention is centered upon the envelope, hold the pack face upwards and riffle to the double card. Palm out the stranger by means of the side slip and place the pack carelessly on the table available for inspection.

The plot presentation may be that of optical illusion, the unreliability of eye witnesses or as the individual reader desires.

As with all stranger card tricks, this trick is not worth two snaps of a finger done with the conjurer's own pack; done with a borrowed deck, it becomes a memorable feat.

WHERE IS IT?

We will suppose that you have a stranger card, the 2S, and that you have brought the regular 2S to the bottom of the pack. Add the stranger card and another from the pack to the bottom in the manner described at the end of this section. Take off the stranger card, keeping it face upwards and place it in a card box, preferably of the type made up as a cigarette case, and give this to a spectator to hold.

The regular 2S reposes next to the bottom card. Ask someone to name a number and proceed to deal to that number from the bottom of the pack. Show the face card, drop the left hand into the position for executing the glide, draw off the face card and deal it face upwards on the table.

Glide the two of spades back and continue to deal to the number named. Draw out the two of spades and place it aside face downwards.

Call attention to the impossible feat you are about to attempt, order the card to leave the cigarette case and take the place of the card on the table. Let the spectator open the case and show it empty, then turn the card on the table face upwards himself. It is the missing two of spades.

The execution of the trick is easy; the whole of the effect lies in the use of a borrowed deck.

Through the Tabletop

This is a good trick for impromptu intimate work when seated at a table.

Effect. A chosen card vanishes from the pack and is found to have passed through the tabletop.

Requirements. A stranger card, which we will say is the ten of diamonds; a small pellet of wax.

Preparation. Affix the stranger card, face upwards, to the under surface of the table under cover of any reasonable pretext, such as recovering a dropped serviette.

Method. 1. Locate the regular ten of diamonds and force this upon an onlooker. Have him show the card to the others present and, upon its return to the pack, control it to the bottom.

2. With your left side to the front, give the pack an overhand shuffle, retaining the ten of diamonds at the bottom, its face concealed from the company. Move the right hand to the left to place the pack in the left hand, and in the action palm the ten of diamonds by means of the one-hand top palm.

3. Place the pack face upwards on the table with the left hand and immediately show this hand on both sides, as if it were of great importance, at the same time tugging at the left sleeve with the right hand. Place the right hand with the palmed card well away to the right, resting it on the edge of the table.

4. Invite the spectator to place his hand on the pack and ask him to press downwards heavily. Show the left hand on both sides once again in a manner which musicians would describe as *mysterioso* and thrust it under the table. Request the spectator to strike the pack and his card will pass through the table top; but caution him not to strike too strongly, lest he pass the card also through your hand. He strikes the pack, spreads the cards, and finds that his card has vanished.

5. Bring up the left hand, holding the stranger ten of diamonds face upwards by the sides. In order again to show the left hand on both sides, take the stranger card by its ends with the right hand, adding the palmed card to it and holding the two cards as one.

6. In again taking the card with the left hand, execute the Hellis change; that is, push the lower card, the stranger card, into the right palm and draw away the visible card. As you hand this card to the spectator, rest the right finger tips on the edge of the table and let the palmed card drop into your lap, to be pocketed later as opportunity arises.

A Second Method

Requirements. A stranger card, say the two of diamonds, which has been cut narrow; a small pellet of wax.

Preparation. Secretly secure the regular two of diamonds from a borrowed pack and affix it, by means of the wax, to the under surface of the table at which you are seated under cover of any reasonable pretext, such as that used in the preceding method.

Method. Prior to performance, add the stranger two of diamonds to the bottom of the pack.

1. Give the pack a quick overhand shuffle with its back to the onlookers, retaining the stranger two of diamonds at the face. Hold the deck

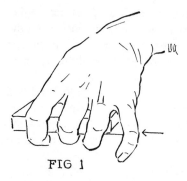

FIG 1

face downwards in the left hand in position for the glide, the thumb at the right side and the fingers at the left side, and draw back the stranger with the tip of the left second finger. Draw indifferent cards from the bottom one at a time, dropping them on the table. When about ten cards have been dealt in this manner, look up at a spectator and say, "Stop me whenever you like."

2. Upon being commanded to stop, push the stranger card outward flush with the pack with the left little finger, which has been pressed against its inner end, Fig. 1. Turn the pack up and show the face card, the stranger two of diamonds, requesting the onlookers to remember it.

3. Gather the cards dealt on the table and replace them at the bottom of the pack. Turn it face outwards and make an overhand shuffle, calling

attention to the fact that the cards are well mixed, a fact which is easily verified when the shuffle is made face outwards.

4. Hold the pack in the hands and make a series of cuts. On the last cut riffle to the narrow card with the left thumb at the side near the outer corner, allowing the stranger two of diamonds to spring off the thumb to the bottom of the upper packet; cut at this point, taking the stranger to the bottom.

5. Square the cards, backs towards the spectators, and in placing the pack in the left hand palm the bottom card, the stranger two of diamonds, by means of the one-hand top palm, page 177.

6. Place the pack face downwards on the table with the left hand and immediately show this hand on both sides, as if it were of great importance, at the same time tugging at the left sleeve with the right hand. Place the right hand with the palmed stranger well away to the right, resting on the edge of the table, as you place the left hand under the table.

7. Invite a spectator to slap the pack sharply, telling him that this will cause the chosen card to pass through the tabletop; but caution him not to strike too forcibly, lest he pass the card through the tabletop *and* your hand.

8. He strikes the pack, spreads the cards and finds that his two of diamonds has vanished.

9. Bring the regular two of diamonds, which you have removed from under the table, slowly above the table, face downwards. Extend it across the table and request the spectator to name his card for the first time. Slowly turn the card face upwards, at the same time placing the tips of the right fingers on the edge of the table, dropping the palmed stranger card in the lap as attention is centered on the card you are displaying.

10. Having shown that it is the two of diamonds, point to the tabletop and say, "You see that tiny crack? It went through there." Smile as you say this.

Everywhere and Nowhere with a Borrowed Deck

Attempts have been made to duplicate this trick using a borrowed deck without success, the many changes and manipulations required completely spoiling the cleancut effect of the original trick. This difficulty is overcome in the present method by the secret introduction of two stranger cards into the deck.

Effect. This is exactly the same as in the standard presentation of the feat: Three wrong cards change successively into the chosen card, every card in the pack is shown to be that card, then the pack is shown to be quite ordinary with no such card in it and, finally, the card is produced from the trousers pocket.

Preparation. We will suppose that the trick is to be done with the ten of spades. Take two tens of spades from any two packs of cards and apply a good roughing fluid to their backs. Place one in each of your lower vest pockets with the faces outwards.

Working. In the course of preliminary tricks get control of the ten of spades of the borrowed deck you are using. Force it on a spectator and for this we would suggest the table spread force explained on page 188. If the first spectator does not take the slightly exposed ten of spades, invite a second spectator to take a card, and, if necessary, a third and a fourth person. Perform quick tricks with the wrong cards, proceed as follows with the person who took the ten of spades:

1. Explain that you will turn your back, the spectator is then to show his freely selected card to everyone, cut the pack, replace the card completing the cut and shuffle the deck. Palm two cards in your right hand and place the pack on the table. Turn away and, with your elbows firmly pressed to your sides, first, put the two palmed cards in your left hand face outwards, with the right hand take the stranger ten of spades from the left vest pocket and press it on the face card of the two stolen cards; move the second stolen card to the front of the other two cards, take the stranger ten of spades No. 2 from the right vest pocket and put it on the face of the packet. Square the edges of the packet and squeeze the cards tightly. You now have two double cards showing the ten of spades on the face with borrowed cards at the back. Palm the two faked tens of spades face inwards in your left hand.

While making these operations, keep on talking to the spectator; insist that everyone see the card, the cut made, the replacement of the card and the final shuffle. There will be ample time for you to do what is necessary.

2. When the ready signal is given, turn, take the pack in your right hand and add the two palmed cards to the bottom in squaring it in your left hand. Announce that you will find the card by telepathic brain waves and ask everyone to think intently of it. Fan the deck with the faces towards you and proceed to take out cards tentatively, scrutinize them and replace them. In reality you are making necessary arrangements thus: Place the bottom double card on top, an indifferent card on it,

then find the regular ten of spades and place it on the top in its turn; finally move an indifferent card to the bottom covering the second double card. You now have the regular ten of spades on the top, followed by an indifferent card and next to that a faked ten of spades, while on the bottom there is an indifferent card with the second faked ten of spades above it.

3. Admit failure to find the cards by telepathy, accuse the spectators of not taking the experiment seriously and say you will fall back on magic, that in three attempts you will infallibly find the selected card. Make a false shuffle, double lift showing the second card. This is wrong, so you turn the cards down and thumb off the top card, the regular ten of spades onto the table.

Make a second attempt, hold the pack upright and claim that the bottom card is the chosen card. Wrong again, so you lower the pack, make the glide and put the faked ten of spades beside the real ten.

For your third choice, shuffle overhand, first running the top card to the bottom, then undercut half the cards, jog the first and shuffle off. Raise the pack level with your eyes, with the right thumb lift the inner end of the jogged card with the packet above it, push forward the second faked ten of spades with the card below it until they project about half their length. Keep the cards flush as if only one card and claim that the face card must be the correct card. Wrong again, so, dropping the left hand, with the right thumb and second finger pull the faked ten forward and with the left first finger push the indifferent card flush with the pack. Place this faked ten on the other side of the regular ten of spades.

4. Proceed as in the orthodox presentation. You are upset and flustered by your failure but finally pull yourself together and offer to change any one of the three cards on the table into the selected card. The middle card is generally chosen, so you have the selected card named, tap it with your finger uttering a mysterious formula, pick it up and show that it is the ten of spades.

5. Point out that there are two other cards on the table and turning towards the table make the top change and drop the indifferent card. Have one of the two cards chosen and go through with the same hocus-pocus, pick it up and show it also is the ten of spades. You have the pack in your left hand and you put the double card between the tips of the left thumb and second finger in order to show it to the folks on your left. Now place your right hand over the faked card, push the face card, the stranger ten of spades, into the right palm, take the indifferent card by the right corners and drop it on the table. In other words, you

make the Hellis change. Square the pack and with the left fingers pull the palmed stranger card onto the bottom of the pack.

6. Proceed in exactly the same way with the last of the three cards, showing it as a ten of spades, making the Hellis change, dropping the indifferent card onto the table and finally drawing the second stranger card onto the bottom of the pack.

7. Order the top card to change to the ten of spades, turn it up, show it, then replace it on top, face down. Make the slip or pass sending it to the bottom, then lift the pack and show it there. Drop the pack onto the left hand, pull off a packet with the left second finger and thumb as in the Hindu shuffle, lift the remaining cards in the right hand showing the ten of spades again. Make the same move again and proceed in like manner until three cards only remain in the left hand. Drop them on the top of the pack and turn the pack face up in your left hand, keeping the face towards your body.

8. Point to the three supposed tens of spades on the table and say that the whole thing has been an optical illusion. Turn the cards face upwards one by one, palm the three top cards of the pack in the left hand, take the pack in the right hand and spread the cards face upwards on the table in a wide sweep showing that there is not a single ten of spades amongst them. At the same moment slip the cards palmed in the left hand into the left trousers pocket.

9. Finally after you have allowed the surprise to register, you say that you knew the ten of spades to be an unlucky card for you and that you placed it in your pocket before beginning the experiment. Bring out the outside card, the regular ten of spades of the borrowed deck, leaving the two strange cards snugly concealed.

In displaying the cards as they are first set on the table the use of the matchbook easel idea is recommended, page 413.

A Stranger in the House

This cheerful deception is a good one to use when a pack is unexpectedly pressed into the conjurer's hands and the inevitable request is forthcoming: "Do us a card trick!" So long as the magician has that invaluable accessory on his person, the stranger card, he is prepared to present a workmanlike mystery.

Effect. A card is chosen from a borrowed deck, a hat is shown and placed at a distance, the card is marked, if desired, and replaced in the pack, from which it vanishes. It is found in the hat by the spectator, the magician never approaching the hat.

Preparation. Place a stranger ten of hearts face outwards in your right trousers pocket, have a pencil in your right vest pocket and a rubber band in your right trousers pocket.

Working. 1. Take the borrowed pack, locate the ten of hearts and force it upon a spectator. Take the card from him, show it to the company and toss it face downwards upon the table; drop the pack face downwards upon the card and walk away.

2. "May I borrow a *black* gentleman's soft felt hat?" you enquire. "That's the oldest word-play known to the honorable art of hanky-panky, that joke about the black gentleman's hat. That's why I use it; everybody expects magicians to use that little joke. You're not really a magician unless you do. . . . Thank you, sir, I'll make certain that your hat comes to no harm. There's nothing in it—no rabbits?" Hold the hat so that the company can see that it is empty, walk well away from the table, to your right, and place the hat, crown downwards, upon a convenient chair or side table.

3. During these peregrinations you have had ample time to thrust your right hand into your pocket and palm the stranger card, the ten of hearts, its face against the palm of the hand. Pick up the pack with the left hand, holding it face outwards; bring the right hand from the pocket and place the stranger card face outwards upon the pack by means of the one-hand replacement. A ten of hearts always remaining at the face of the pack, the expedient goes unnoticed. (Fours, sixes and tens should be used for this trick, since there are no odd pips on these cards which might, by reversal, betray the ruse.) "Tell me, sir, don't you always feel better when you pick a good-looking card such as the ten of hearts?" you remark during the preceding maneuvers. "I mean the black cards are so depressing. Don't you find it that way?"

4. Remove the pencil from the vest pocket with the left hand and offer it to the spectator. "Aren't magicians the oddest people, always asking people to mark something for them? This time it's a card," you ramble on. Turn the two cards face downwards by means of the double lift, thus exposing the back of the regular ten of hearts, and extend the pack for the spectator to initial it. "There. That wasn't so bad, was it?"

5. Gaze gravely at your audience and say: "Ladies and gentlemen, you are about to witness a masterpiece of modern miracle mongering, a feat never before attempted in this country, a mystery so amazing that it makes me shudder just to think of it. I am going to make certain cabalistic gestures, certain primitive and recondite movements of the

fingers known only to the inner circle; and although to you I may seem only to be wiggling my fingers, please preserve an intense silence. What I propose to do is to cause that initialed card to flash across the room with the speed of light and come to a resting place in the black gentleman's hat. You don't mind, sir? Thank you. Would you like the trick to be done visibly, so that you can see just what's going on, or would you prefer that I do it quickly and mysteriously, so that we're all of us in the dark? You want the trick done visibly? Very well. Watch!"

6. Take the two tens of hearts off the pack by their inner ends in the right hand, the tip of the thumb on the face, the tips of the three first fingers on the back, the face of the stranger card to the front. Walk over to the hat, holding the card always in the same position, drop the right hand over the mouth of the hat until the hand is almost hidden inside, release the rear card (the regular ten of hearts) and allow it to fall invisibly into the hat.

7. Immediately and quickly bring the hand up again, holding the stranger ten of hearts face outwards, as you say: "As you can see, it would be very easy to do this startling illusion visibly; you merely put the card in the hat. I prefer the invisible vanish; it's harder and in any event people don't think much of the visible version." Face the spectators, turn the pack face upwards in the left hand and push the stranger ten of hearts face outwards into the side of the deck. Tap it home slowly with the right hand and secure a break below it with the left little finger. As you do this move away from the hat as far as possible and call attention to the fact that the marked card is never removed from sight until it has been pushed squarely into the deck.

8. Square the cards with the right hand, push the stranger card into the right palm by means of the side slip but retain the pack in the right hand as, with your left hand, you search in your left trousers pocket for a rubber band. "Has anyone a rubber band?" you enquire somewhat plaintively. "I *should* have a rubber band. . . . I *always* carry one, right in that left trousers pocket, but tonight I don't seem to have one." Take the pack with the left hand and thrust your right hand into the right pocket, taking the palmed card with it; drop the palmed card and bring out the rubber band. Stretch this around the pack both ways and toss it to the spectator to hold.

9. "Will you please hold the pack above your head, with your right hand, and place your cupped left hand under your right elbow?" Illustrate what you want done by grasping your own right elbow with the left

hand. "You may not know it, sir, but you are now in the posture made famous by the whirling dervishes of Arabia. They sit like that when they're brooding, which is usually just after they've had an unusually invigorating whirl. You see, one of the great mysteries to a whirling dervish, even as to you and I, is why a whirling dervish should want to whirl. It's silly, when you stop to think of it, isn't it? Well, the dervish knows it's silly, too; that's why he broods. I beg your pardon, sir? . . . Oh, the *card* trick! Yes, we'll get right back to that."

10. It only remains for you to order the initialed ten of hearts to vanish, have the pack searched to prove that it has really gone and finally invite the drawer of the card to go to the hat and remove his marked card. "As I promised you, ladies and gentlemen, you have witnessed a mystery which you will remember as long as you live."

It is the use of the borrowed deck which turns the trick into a little miracle. Done with your own cards it would be just another card trick.

RED-BLACK TRANSMIGRATION

Here is another variation on the theme of two cards changing places. However, although the plot is a familiar one, the presentation and the use of a borrowed deck make the feat worthy of its name.

Effect. A spectator having selected a card and having named its color, a second spectator is asked to think of any card of the opposite color and this card he takes from the pack. Each person then holds his card tightly between his hands. The ends of a length of ribbon, one half of which is red, the other half black, are wound around the spectators' hands, the black end around those holding the black card, the red end around those holding the red card, the remainder of the ribbon being stretched taut between the two persons. A magical transposition of the two cards is ordered and the red card is found between the hands of the spectator who held the black card and vice versa.

Requirements. A stranger card, the ten of diamonds, for example, a coin, and a length of two inch ribbon, one half of which is red, the other half black. This ribbon can be prepared by dyeing black half the length of a red ribbon, or more simply by sewing together two pieces, one red, one black. In the black end sew a piece of a wooden match.

Preparation. Roll the ribbon tightly beginning at the red end, Fig. 1, and tuck it under your vest on the right side. Place the stranger ten of diamonds in your outside right coat pocket and the coin, a half-dollar, in your right trousers pocket.

Working. At any favorable opportunity steal a card from the deck and add it to the back of the stranger card in your coat pocket, the latter being face inwards, and get the ten of diamonds secretly to the top of the pack. Then proceed as follows:

1. You make use of two volunteer assistants and, for clarity, we will designate them A and B. Force the ten of diamonds on A and leave the card in his hands. Ask him, "Is your card a black one? No? Then by really transcendental powers of deduction I know it must be a red card. Since you have chanced upon a red card, I'll ask this gentleman (B) to

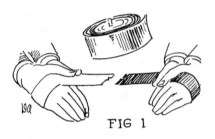

FIG 1

think of a black one. Will you do that, sir? Any black card at all. You have thought of one? Then please take the pack, remove the card and retain it. Nothing could be fairer than that, could it? You'll all agree that I could not possibly have known what cards these gentlemen would choose."

2. As you hand the pack to B with your right hand, your left hand, which has been at rest close to the bottom of your vest, quietly steals the roll of ribbon. You continue, "In my trick I shall make use of the invisible line of influence, but perhaps you would prefer to have it visible. There it is!" Turn half right, grip the free end of the ribbon and, with an outward and upward throw, release the roll so that it flashes out into the air to its full length. At the same moment drop the right hand into the right coat pocket and palm the two cards therein. Face front and grasp the middle of the ribbon with your right hand so that one half falls over the back of the hand.

3. Take the pack from B with your left hand, throw the ribbon over your left arm and take the pack in the right hand, adding the two palmed cards to the top.

4. Take the ten of diamonds from A, show it and place it face downwards on the top of the pack. Turn to B, take his card, let us say it is the jack of spades, show it and place it face downwards on the ten of diamonds. Pick up the black end of the ribbon and have B hold it in his right hand.

5. In squaring the pack make the top slide change (page 83) then double lift and turn the two cards face upwards so that the jack of spades shows on the top of the pack; keep the tip of the left little finger between the two cards and the pack. Request B to hold out his left hand, flat and palm upwards. Call attention to his card, the jack of spades, turn the two cards face downwards and with your left thumb slide the top card

(the ten of diamonds) onto his left hand. Take the ribbon from him and gently guide his right hand, palm downwards, onto his left hand as you tell him to hold his card tightly. "To make assurance doubly sure and remind you that your card is a black one, I'll wind this invisible, I mean visible, line of influence around your hands so. Now you must admit that no power on earth can get at that card without your consent." In winding the ribbon turn his hands over bringing his left hand uppermost, thus when, later on, he separates his hands, the ten of diamonds will lie face upwards.

6. Meantime you have prepared for a triple lift (page 7). Turn to A, make the triple lift showing the ten of diamonds (really the stranger card) and hold a break below the three cards as before. Place the red end of the ribbon in his right hand and have him hold his left hand flat and and palm upwards. Turn the three cards face downwards on the pack, slide off the top card, the jack of spades, onto his left hand. Guide his right hand, palm downwards onto his left hand and wind the red end of the ribbon around both hands, turning them over in the process. Adjust the winding of the ribbon so that it will be stretched taut between A and B, Fig. 1.

7. The stranger card is now the second card from the top of the pack. As you point out how securely the two cards are being held, slip the left little finger under the stranger card and side slip it into the right palm under cover of squaring the deck. Reach into your right trousers pocket, leave the card there and bring out the half-dollar. Place this on the ribbon at the junction of the two colors and impress on A and B that they must hold the ribbon taut and steady.

8. "Now for the miracle! I shall make the two cards flash across the invisible, I mean visible, line of influence so that you, sir (B), will have the red card and you, sir (A), will hold the black card, and that without even disturbing the coin. Ready? Go!"

9. Take off the coin, unwrap the black ribbon from B's hands, he lifts his left hand and finds the red card face up on the palm of his right hand. Go to A, unwrap the red end from his hands, he lifts his left hand and there is the black jack of spades staring him in the face.

In view of the fact that the trick is done with a borrowed deck it would be hard to find a more effective climax.

TOUCH AND GO

This is another trick of the "sell" variety. It has all the ingredients that go to the making of a good trick—a plot, amusing incidents and a very effective climax. The working is simple, the presentation is the thing.

Effect. After having shuffled a borrowed deck, a spectator chooses a card, returns it to the deck and again shuffles. The magician, claiming that by the use of a certain charm, a rabbit's foot, he can infallibly locate the selected card, makes three attempts but each of the cards he finds is wrong. These cards are removed each time from the pack by the spectator and, as he takes away the third, he sees the card he drew (as do all the other spectators) on the face of the deck. All are convinced that the magician has failed utterly. However, a mere touch of the charm transforms one of the three wrong cards into the selected card. A search of the pack reveals that there is no duplicate card.

Requirements. A stranger card, the king of hearts, for example, and a rabbit's foot, both in the outer right coat pocket.

Working. 1. Secretly get the king of hearts to the top of the pack, false shuffle retaining it there and palm it by means of the one-hand top palm in handing the pack to the spectator to shuffle. This done, hold out your left hand, have the spectator place the pack on it and make a cut. Pick up the cut with your right hand, adding the palmed card, take back the cut with your left hand and reassemble the deck.

2. Point out that the pack has not only been thoroughly shuffled but also cut, making it impossible for anyone to know the location of any particular card. Force the king of hearts by the Hindu shuffle force and ask the spectator who has drawn it to hold it up for all to see as you turn your back.

3. Turn away as this is done, holding the pack in your left hand behind your back. When everyone has seen the chosen card, have the spectator push it into the deck. Turn and face the audience, begin an overhand shuffle yourself, then ask the spectator to take the pack and shuffle it.

4. Turn around, bring out the rabbit's foot and extol its virtues as a magical charm asserting that it will enable you to detect, infallibly, the chosen card amongst the others. Rub the finger tips of your right hand with the rabbit's foot, then take it in your right hand as you receive the pack in your left. Replace the foot in your pocket and palm the stranger king of hearts. Bring your right hand over the pack and, in the action of squaring it, push the top card an inch over the side with the left thumb and slide the palmed card underneath it. The position now is this: Somewhere in the pack is the regular king of hearts, on the top is an indifferent card and next to it is the stranger king of hearts.

5. Fan the pack with the faces of the cards towards yourself, being

careful not to spread those near the top to avoid exposing the back of the stranger. Run the tips of your right fingers slowly over the cards, stop at anyone, pull it out, place it on the bottom of the pack and close the fan. Rub your finger tips over it again and say that you think you have found the card. Hold the pack in your left hand as for the glide, its face towards the spectators, and ask if the bottom card is the chosen card. The answer is no, so you draw the face card outwards about an inch, drop the left hand, bringing the pack face down a few inches above the table, and ask the spectator to place the card face downwards on the table.

6. Fan the pack again and again run the right finger tips over the cards, claiming you must have mistaken the signal, the charm itself being infallible. Spot the regular king of hearts, draw it out with an indifferent card in front of it, as one card, Fig. 1, place them on the face of the deck, close the fan and again rub the fingers on the bottom

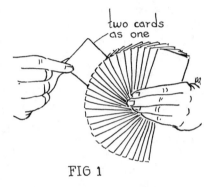

two cards as one

FIG 1

card. Confidently you claim to have succeeded and you lift the pack as before to show the bottom card to the spectators. Again you are told you have failed. Drop the left hand, glide the face card, draw out the king of hearts about an inch and have the spectator place it alongside the first card.

7. Take out the rabbit's foot and addressing it in mock seriousness say, "You know what the Chinese do to their joss when he fails them? They *wallop* him! Now, I'll give you one more chance. If you fail me this time . . . !" Replace it in your pocket.

8. Fan the deck, run your fingers over it and this time pull out the three top cards as one, place them on the face of the deck, thus bringing the stranger card second from the bottom. Close the fan, rub the bottom card as before saying, "Yes, this *must* be the card." Turn the pack face outwards showing the bottom card. "Wrong again? Well, my joss has certainly qualified for a walloping. Will you put the card with the other two?" As you say this draw the indifferent card upwards about an inch, still keeping the pack upright. Let the spectator take the card while you hold the pack in the same position for a moment or two so that everyone can see the stranger king of hearts.

9. Discoursing volubly about the walloping now to be administered to your rabbit's foot, cut the pack taking the stranger card to the middle with the left little finger under it, side slip it into the right palm and drop the pack onto the table. Take out the rabbit's foot, leaving the palmed card in the pocket. "Now for it," you say, making a gesture of striking the foot against the table. Hesitate and, addressing the charm, say, "I'll give you one more chance." Then, to the spectator, "Now, sir, you are sure that none of these cards is your card? Very well, please touch one." Most likely he will touch the middle one, the king of hearts. If so, tell him to keep his finger on it. Pick up and show the other two and place them on the pack. Again address the rabbit's foot, "This is your last chance!" To the spectator you say, "I'll rub the charm on the back of the card and it will at once change to your card. Please name your card. The king of hearts?" You rub the foot on the back of the card, it is turned face upwards and it is the king of hearts. "Aha," you say, "you have been playing a trick on me. Well, it was touch and go with you but you have saved your bacon," put the lucky charm to your lips and put it back in your pocket.

If the spectator touches one of the outside cards, simply remove it and ask him to place his hand on one of the two remaining cards. If he puts it on the king of hearts you say, "You want that one? Very well, keep your hand on it." If, however, he touches the indifferent card, you say, "I'm to take away that one too? Please place your hand on the card you have chosen." Then finish the trick as already described.

Leave the pack on the table. It is practically certain that someone will lose no time in examining it but you have left no clue.

The Run Around Aces

Here is a somewhat different application of the stranger card principle:

Effect. The four aces vanish from the pack and are found in various unexpected places about the conjurer's person.

Preparation. Place a stranger ace of clubs face outwards inside your shirt near the front opening.

Method. 1. At the conclusion of a four ace trick, push the four aces, the ace of clubs being the lowest, into the pack and strip them to the top as detailed on page 77.

2. Palm the aces in the right hand, riffle the pack lightly with the left thumb, plunge the right hand into the right trousers pocket, and push off the ace of clubs with the thumb, leaving it in the pocket.

3. Bring out the hand as if surprised at not finding a card there and thrust it under the left side of the coat. Push the three aces into the upper left vest pocket, then bring out one of them with an exclamation of gratification.

4. Let it be seen that your right hand is empty and again thrust it under your coat, pick up an ace and pretend to take it from the sleeve at the shoulder. Draw back the coat so that the shoulder is exposed and the onlookers can note that no other cards can be seen.

5. Produce a third ace exactly as in No. 4.

6. Name the aces thus produced, riffle the pack again and order the ace of clubs to pass up the sleeve. Fail to find it there and after a search open your shirt and produce the stranger ace of clubs, face outwards. Make the most of this untoward event.

7. Return the aces to the pack, faces upwards; shuffle and bring the ace of clubs, the stranger ace, to the bottom. Palm it in the left hand and offer the pack to a spectator.

8. Order the club ace to leave the pack and go to your trousers pocket.

9. Thrust your left hand into your left trousers pocket and leave the palmed stranger in the pocket. Withdraw the hand, professing failure.

10. Place both hands flat on the table and promise that, if the spectator will hand you the ace of clubs, you will make it vanish before his very eyes. A search of the pack discloses the fact that the card has already vanished. Remember that you failed to instruct the ace into which of the two trousers pockets it should fly; request a spectator to reach into your right trousers pocket and perhaps—just perhaps—he will find the ace.

11. He does.

Introducing the Stranger

An excellent method of adding a stranger card to the pack is this:

You have a stranger card, which we will say is the two of spades, face outwards in your pocket.

1. Palm any indifferent card from the borrowed pack at an opportune moment and place it, also face outwards, behind the stranger two of spades.

2. Force the two of spades from the pack and request the spectator to place it face downwards upon the table. Drop the pack face downwards upon the card. Place the right hand in the trousers pocket during this action and palm the two cards.

3. Pick up the pack with the left hand, turning its face to the onlookers

as you inform them what you purpose to do; the two of spades is naturally at the face of the pack.

4. Bring the right hand from the pocket with the two palmed cards and add these cards to the face of the pack by means of the one hand top replacement.

5. Prior to the replacement a two of spades could be seen at the face of the pack; a two of spades remains at the face after the replacement, but now this is the stranger card. Under it is an indifferent card, enabling the conjurer to remove the stranger two without disclosing the regular two of spades, which is third from the face.

Forcing a Stranger Card

When it is necessary to force a stranger card, the knife or locator card force, with the pack face upwards, will be found satisfactory. A good method is to have the required card face upwards on the bottom of the pack. Spread the cards on the table, face downwards, without exposing the reversed card and have a spectator touch any card. Push this card forward, gather the deck and, with the left hand, execute the Curry change.* This action leaves the stranger card face upwards ready to be dealt with as you may require for the effect you are about to produce.

Double-Faced Cards

This stranger card principle can also be applied to the introduction of double-faced cards into a borrowed deck. The field thus opened for startling effects is a wide one which has been barely touched. An excellent example of the possibilities will be found in *More Card Manipulations*, No. 3, entitled Married Couples and Bachelors.

Joker-Specimen Card

Akin to the stranger card principle is the use of the extra joker and specimen card which usually go with a deck. In this case you allow a perfectly free choice of a card and when it is returned you secretly add the joker to its back. Holding the two cards as one make the Hellis change, place the joker back out against a book or a glass and dispose of the palmed chosen card as may be necessary for the dénouement.

---

* *More Card Manipulations*, No. 2, Jean Hugard.

This working is not so strong as the first method since the back only of the supposed chosen card can be shown. As a camp fire trick the effect is all that one could wish since up to the moment of dropping the card into the fire you can show it both back and front. Of course, the rear card only is dropped, the face card being palmed and reproduced later in the most startling manner you can devise.

Chapter 14
SELF-WORKING TRICKS

IT MUST BE MAGIC

IT IS VERY DIFFICULT to obtain a really good effect with cards in which the spectator performs the whole of the necessary operations, without any clue being given to the modus operandi. There are various tricks of this kind which are not satisfactory from a magical point of view since they are too obviously dependent upon calculation. The following variation of the two pile system, one of the few really fine self-working tricks, gives a magical result which is astounding to the uninitiated.

Effect. A spectator selects a card from a shuffled deck and, after burying it in the deck, discovers that very card by spelling its name. From first to last the performer does not touch the cards.

Working. Let a spectator shuffle the deck, then turn your back and instruct him as follows:

1. Tell him to think of a small even number, such as 2, 4, 6, 8 or any such number; for convenience, request that it be not larger than twenty. Have the spectator deal this number of cards, cautioning him to deal so quietly that it will be impossible for you to follow the number by sound, face downward on the table; let us assume that he deals eighteen cards. "Now," you say, "I want you to deal your small pile of cards into two piles. Thank you, sir; obviously you are one of the better dealers. Will you now choose either packet, shuffle it, glance at and note the card at its face, and replace the packet upon the remainder of the pack? Accept my congratulations, sir," you continue expansively, "clearly you are not only one of the better dealers, but one of the better glancers-at and noters-of playing cards. You are *indeed* a fortunate person."

The assistant having dealt the original even number of cards into two piles, there must be the same number of cards in each of the secondary piles; this should be understood clearly for the success of the trick is dependent upon it.

2. "Now deal the cards," you continue, "starting with the top card, calling out red or black according to the varying colors. As you call the colors lay the cards face downwards in a pile. Are you ready?" You allow this deal and the calling of red or black cards to continue until

there are twelve cards on the table, and you feign to take particular note of the sequence of red and black cards. Stop the deal at twelve because you know by the two pile principle that when the second pile is placed on top of the reversed cards, the chosen card will be thirteenth, which is the position it must occupy for the purpose of the trick.

3. Instruct the spectator to place this packet upon the remainder of the deck; next to take the second small pile of cards, fan them before himself, and to inform you how many court cards there are in the packet. You receive this information gravely, as if it were very important, request him to shuffle these cards and drop them onto the pack. This done, turn around and continue: "I am sure you will agree that I cannot have any clue to the card you chose; you yourself could only find it by turning the pack face upwards and searching for it. That's right, isn't it? Very well; you are about to have the extraordinary privilege of discovering, for the first time in any gathering, your card by magic; and, to make it even more magical, I now pronounce that esoteric and potent word, abracadabra! Did you feel anything, sir? Ah, you see? An omen! Now square the deck and keep it in your own hands."

4. Pause for a moment, appear to cogitate and say, "Since I shall not touch the pack you can safely name your card. What was it? The seven of spades? Just give the cards a little shake to enable your card to move into its proper position. Thank you, sir; without a doubt you are a superb card shaker, which as we all know is a sadly neglected art. Now you have only to spell s-e-v-e-n o-f s-p-a-d-e-s, putting out one card for each letter, and your card will appear on the last letter. You don't believe it? Try it!"

The spectator spells and deals as instructed and his card turns up as stated. The result to him is astounding to say the least.

When it is recalled that any card in the pack can be spelled with either twelve or thirteen letters, the reason for reversing exactly twelve cards is manifest. In spades and hearts, the three, seven, eight and queen all spell with thirteen letters, therefore any one of them will be turned up on the last letter; the four, five, nine, jack and king take twelve letters, so you have the next card turned up after the spelling is completed. For ace, two, six and ten, prefix the word "t-h-e" to the value and have the suit spelled first, thus: "S-p-a-d-e-s, t-h-e t-w-o" and have the next card turned up.

For clubs, for the ace, two, six and ten, add "t-h-e"; for the four, five, nine, jack and king, spell the suit first and "t-h-e" before the value, thus: "C-l-u-b-s, t-h-e f-o-u-r" and turn the next card. For the three, seven, eight and queen, use the word "o-f" and turn the next card.

For diamonds, the ace, two, six and ten, spell: "D-i-a-m-o-n-d, t-h-e a-c-e," and the same with the other three cards; for the four, five, nine, jack and king, spell; "D-i-a-m-o-n-d-s, f-o-u-r" and the same with the other four cards; for the three, seven, eight and queen, spell the suit first, then the value and turn the last card.

TRICKY QUICKIE

Many very fine card feats are self-working tricks, extremely easy of execution. The following trick, simplicity itself, will be found effective.

Effect. A spectator notes a card at a certain number in the pack; it vanishes and is produced from the conjurer's pocket.

Method. 1. Request a spectator to think of any small number. Hand him the pack, invite him to shuffle it and note the card which lies at his number. Turn your back as he does this.

2. Take the pack, place it behind your back. Count off the top thirteen cards reversing their order and replace them on top of the pack.

3. Bring the pack forward and have the spectator name the number of which he thought. Let us say that he thought of seven. Count off cards beginning with the next unit—in this instance, eight—and at twelve place the counted cards on the bottom.

4. Hand the next card, the thirteenth, to the spectator. As he looks at it palm the next card, the spectator's card, by means of the one-hand top palm. Grasp the pack with the thumb at the back, the fingers at the face, as in Fig. 2, The Palm in Action, page 179.

5. The spectator disclaims the card you have handed him. "It's not your card?" Hold the pack upright with the right hand and tap the card at its face with the left second finger, calling attention to the card. At the same time note the name of the palmed card, which rests in the right hand. "I know that is not your card, nor is this card you are looking at your card. Your card was the [say] ten of clubs and I have it here in my pocket."

6. Thrust your hand into the right trousers pocket and bring out the palmed card, slowly turning it face outwards to show that it is the spectator's card.

The plot of this trick is similar to Williams' famous Card to Pocket but the manner of handling is entirely different. Sighting the spectator's card and naming it, when apparently it was impossible for you to have this information, gives the trick a twist which the older trick did not have. Beginning the count at the number following the spectator's number, which may at first sight appear to be a weakness, curiously enough never seems to be thought out of the way.

THE NUMEROLOGICAL CARD

This exceedingly easy self-working feat, presented as "proof" that numerology can foretell the future, makes an interesting close-up divertissement.

Effect. The conjurer writes a prediction on a slip of paper and places it to one side; a spectator selects a card and, without looking at it, puts it in

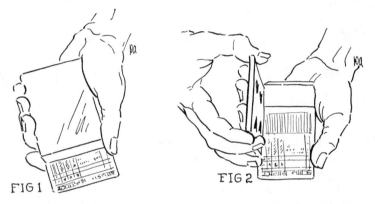

FIG 1

FIG 2

his pocket. A card is freely named, apparently, by means of a numerological computation; it is, say, the ten of hearts. The slip of paper is unfolded and upon it is written the name of this card. The spectator removes his chosen card from his pocket; it is the ten of hearts.

Preparation. Place an ace, two, three and four of hearts at the tenth, eleventh, twelfth and thirteenth place from the top of the pack. Place the ten of hearts on top of the pack. Have the score card of the pack at hand.

Working. 1. Write upon a piece of paper a message after this style: "It is ordained that at nine minutes past nine o'clock on Thursday, December 25th, the ten of hearts will be entrusted to your care." Refer to your watch during this ceremony, apparently making an abstruse calculation. Fold the paper and place it to one side.

2. Holding the pack in the left hand, give the score card to a designated person and request that he thrust it somewhere in the middle of the pack, leaving half the card projecting, Fig. 1. When he has done so lift, with the right hand, all the cards above the score card bookwise to the right so that the top card of this packet, the ten of hearts, rests against the left fingers in position for the regular back slip, Fig. 2. Execute this

sleight, pulling off the ten of hearts with the left fingers and folding it onto the top card of the portion which remains in the left hand. In this action both hands swing a little to the right and turn over so that, at the end of the movement, the right hand holds its packet face upwards, showing the face of the card that was above the score card and the left

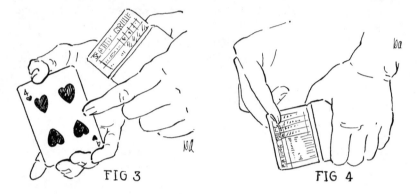

FIG 3   FIG 4

hand has its back uppermost, its forefinger pointing to the exposed card of the right hand packet. "Since everyone has seen this card, we cannot use it," you explain, Fig. 3.

Hold the right packet between the thumb and third finger at the ends, freeing the first and second fingers. Keep the left hand in the same position and with the tips of the right first and second fingers draw away the score card, Fig. 4. Turn the left hand over and show the packet lying face down on it. Tap its top card with the score card, saying, "Please take this card and, without looking at it, place it in your inner coat pocket."

Thus, in a perfectly deceptive manner and without disarranging the four card set-up near the top of the deck, the ten of hearts is forced.

3. Assemble the pack, the right hand packet being replaced at the top. Recapitulate briefly the theories of the numerologists. "If, for instance, a two-figure total is arrived at, these digits are added to ascertain the subject's key number," you conclude. "If, adding the digits of your birthdate the total is twelve, the numerologists add the one and the two, making your key number three. I shall follow exactly in the tracks of my distinguished colleagues. It's all very painless and scientific and you needn't be in the least alarmed, for although you may feel that you are the master of your fate, when, in a very few seconds, I ask you to name four figures, you will find it impossible to name

any other than those which govern your life at this particular moment—which happens to be nine minutes past nine o'clock of December 25th. Shall we start now or would you rather wait a few moments while you pull yourself together?"

4. Request the spectator to name a number between ten and nineteen. "Fifteen? Yes, of course. . . . I knew you'd name that number." Deal fifteen cards face downwards upon the table in a pile. Pick up the pile and say, "One and five added makes six, your first key number." Deal five cards face downwards upon the table and place the sixth card, one of the four card set-up, to one side face downwards. Drop the cards remaining in your hands upon the small packet of cards just dealt, square the assembled packet and drop it upon the pack proper.

5. Repeat the operations in No. 4 three times, thus placing the ace, two, three and four of hearts in a little face-down pile on the table. Recapitulate what has been done, saying, "I know that you don't believe in this sort of thing, and to be absolutely frank with you, neither do I. On the other hand, strange things do happen on occasion, and this may be one of those occasions, particularly as the experiment started at nine minutes past nine o'clock of December 25th, which obviously is a fateful moment in your life. You felt that queer creepy feeling move up your spine, didn't you, as though a ghost were caressing you? Then, sir, anything can happen."

6. Slowly turn the four cards face upwards. "The ace of hearts, the two, the three and the four of hearts. Did you ever hear of such a bizarre sequence of events?" Add the denominations of the four cards, totalling ten, and point out that, since all the cards are hearts, the chosen card must also be a heart. "It was ordained, sir, that at nine minutes past nine of December 25th you should choose the ten of hearts. Will you place the card you chose, which has remained in your pocket, face downwards beside the prediction which I wrote long before you chose it? Read aloud, now, what I predicted. You see—the ten of hearts! Ladies and gentlemen, witness a spectacular coördination of the factors of fate." Push the face-down ten of hearts across the table towards the spectator with the tip of the right forefinger; slide the finger tip under the edge of the card and, with a flourish, flip the card face upwards.

"Allow me to congratulate you, sir. Within a week, unexpected good fortune will be yours; I have never known it to fail; it is Kismet."

The trick should be done at a brisk tempo, with the deals made quickly in rapid succession to confuse the spectators and prevent them from analyzing their nature. The running fire of comment should not be permitted to slow down the pace, but rather should make emphatic what is being done. A tongue-in-cheek tone of voice can be very effective.

MATCHING THE PACKETS

This trick is almost self-working, since the only sleight used in it is made under the protection of misdirection which makes its accomplishment a very easy matter.

Preparation. Secretly place an ace at the top of the pack, with a two, three and four at the bottom, the two spot being the face card. Have a box of matches in your pocket.

Method. 1. Make several false riffle shuffles, retaining the stocked cards at top and bottom, and finish with a blind cut. Hand the pack to a spectator and invite him to deal any small number of cards face down upon the table, one upon the other.

2. Remove the matchbox from your pocket and hand it to the spectator, at the same time taking the pack from him. Request him to place one match upon the pile he has dealt. As he does this and audience attention is centered upon him, quietly side slip the bottom card, the two spot, to the top of the pack.

3. Take the matchbox from the spectator and hand him the pack. Have him deal a second pile of any small number of cards. When he has done this hand him the matchbox again and request that he place two matches on this pile. As he does this slip the bottom card, a three spot, to the top.

4. Give him the pack and take the matchbox. Have another pile dealt. Give him the matchbox so that he can place three matches upon the third pile and under cover of this misdirection slip the fourth card, the four spot, from bottom to top.

5. Have a fourth pile dealt and have four matches placed upon this pile.

6. Turn the first packet face upwards and show the ace at its face. Point to the single match and say, "That might be a coincidence . . . a single match, a single pip on the card."

Turn over the second pile and show the two spot. "And this might be another coincidence—two matches and the two of clubs."

Turn over the third pile and show the three. "Three matches and the three spot. It's a little uncanny, isn't it?"

Turn over the fourth pile, showing the four. "You must admit, ladies and gentlemen, that some mysterious force has been at work!"

The protective cover afforded by the exchange of the matchbox and the counting of matches is so perfect that almost the bottom card could be shifted openly from bottom to top in each case with no one the wiser.

For those who care to take a risk to obtain an added effect, let the stock be an ace at the top with a two, three and seven at the bottom, the seven being the third card from the face of the pack. Proceed exactly as above but, after the fourth pile has been dealt, turn to a feminine onlooker and invite her to name a number between one and ten. If seven, the usual response, is made, direct the first assistant to place seven matches upon the fourth pile. Thus, when the fourth pile is faced, the conjurer can claim that the number of matches placed upon this pile was chosen "by the purest chance," and the display of the seven comes as a surprise following the orderly sequence of one, two and three.

If the conjurer loses his gamble and another number is named, he can wriggle from his dilemma by some such remark as this: "You must remind me, later, to tell you what the numerologists claim that number means in your life." Tell the spectator to place seven matches on the last pile, giving any fanciful reason for the number or none at all, and finish the trick as above.

THE SEVENTH SON

This is a variation, and an effective one, of the preceding trick.

Effect. A spectator chooses a card and places it face down to one side. He deals three piles of cards, each of a number of cards determined by chance. The first card chosen, and the cards at the face of the three packets, all prove to be of the same denomination.

Preparation. Secretly gather the four sevens of the pack and place them at the top of the pack. Have a box of matches in the pocket.

Method. 1. Give the pack a false overhand shuffle, retaining the four sevens at the top. Undercut half the pack, injog the first card and shuffle off. Form a break under the injog and spread the cards, inviting a spectator to select one. Force one of the four sevens. (If preferred, the force can be made by other means.)

2. Request the spectator to place this card to one side without looking at it. As he does this, quietly square the pack, inserting the tip of the left little finger under two of the sevens. Make the pass, or cut the pack, taking two sevens to the bottom and one to the top.

3. Place the pack upon the table to your left and spread the cards in a long ribbon from left to right, inviting the spectator to remove any card and place it face upwards on the table. It is, let us say, a four spot.

Hand him the pack and request him to count four cards in a face-down pile beside this card.

4. Remove the box of matches from your right pocket and hand it to the spectator. Have him place a match on the packet, and as he does this side slip a seven from the bottom to the top.

5. Retake the matchbox and again spread the pack from left to right. Have another card selected, assemble the pack and have the spectator deal as many cards in a pile as there are pips on this second card. Give him the matchbox and request that he place two matches on this second pile.

6. As he does this, slip the third seven from bottom to top. Again spread the pack, have a card chosen, and have as many cards dealt from the pack as there are pips on the card. Have three matches placed on this last packet.

The condition is now this: A seven is the face card of each of the three packets dealt by the spectator. At a distance, face downward, is the seven forced at the start of the trick.

Have this card turned face upwards, regard it with benevolence, and intone the following mumbo-jumbo as glibly as possible: "I can hardly regard the fact that you chose the seven of diamonds with less than profound astonishment. As you may know, from the very earliest times seven has been regarded as a mystical number. Greece had her seven sages. There were the Seven Sleepers of Ephesus and the Seven Wonders of the Ancient World. In Holy Writ we have the seven seals, the seven stars, the seven lamps, the seven loaves, the seven mortal sins and the seven virtues. There are seven days in the week, seven notes in music and seven colors in the spectrum. A volume could be written on the number seven. To me, being the seventh son of a seventh son, it is peculiarly significant. I am sure that you will now understand why your choice of the seven of diamonds should have caused me to catch my breath in awe and amazement. Let me show you exactly why this should be."

Turn over the three piles, showing a seven at the face of each. Reverently make a low and dignified salaam to the cards.

The Hocus-Pocus Card

This is another of those excellent feats which, employing a psychological trap, appear wholly inexplicable to the onlookers.

Effect. The conjurer, attempting to find a chosen card, shows four cards, none of which is the desired card. A spectator points to any one of the cards. Although he has a free choice, this card is magically transformed into his chosen card.

Method. 1. Take the pack after it has been shuffled, place it in the left hand and lightly square the ends with the right fingers and thumb. Keep the thumb pressed against the inner end of the deck and push the pack forward in the action of squaring the sides with the left fingers and thumb, causing the bottom card to buckle and so bringing the inner left index into view, the actions being simultaneous and completely covered. (Fig. 2, Mercury's Card, page 303, although illustrating another sleight, also shows the nature of this glimpse.) Let us say that the sighted card is the queen of hearts.

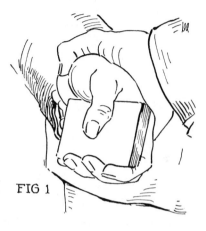

FIG 1

2. Bring the queen to the top in an overhand shuffle. Place both hands behind the back, palm the queen from the top in the right hand and rest the left hand, which holds the pack, upon the right palm, concealing the palmed card, Fig. 1.

3. Immediately turn your back and request the spectator to cut the pack. When he has done this turn to ask him if he is satisfied that his cut was a free cut and, as he affirms that it was, place the palmed queen upon the top of the packet remaining in the left hand. This action is concealed by the body and the arms must not be moved.

4. Again turn your back and push off the top card of the left hand packet, the queen. Request that the card be shown to those present, replaced upon the packet you hold, and that the cards previously cut from the pack then be replaced. At once ask that the deck be shuffled.

5. Face the spectators and point out that, under the circumstances, it is impossible for you to know which card was chosen; in this statement your audience will concur. Claim that you can find the chosen card but stipulate that you must be given four chances.

6. Fan the pack faces towards yourself and remove three cards distinctively different from the forced card. In this case, a queen of hearts having been forced, you will remove and place face downwards upon the table a two of spades, a four of clubs and a five of spades. If a black card were forced, you would remove red cards; if a spot card, you would remove court cards. You select cards which may be shown the spectators and which they will instantly perceive are not the chosen card.

7. Place the forced card, the queen of hearts, upon the three indifferent cards.

8. Hold the packet in the left hand in position for the glide. Tip it up and show the bottom indifferent card. Ask if this is the chosen card and upon receiving a negative response remove this card with the right hand and place it face downwards upon the table.

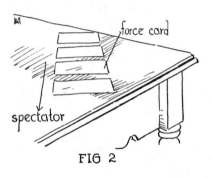

force card

spectator

FIG 2

9. Remove the card at the bottom and place it at the top. Show the card now at the bottom and upon being again informed that it is not the chosen card, turn the packet down, glide the indifferent card back with the left fingers and remove the next card, the queen of hearts. Place this upon the table behind the first card.

10. Remove the bottom card and place it on top. Tip up the packet and show the card now at the bottom; it is another indifferent card. Remove it and place it behind the first two.

11. Show the card remaining in the left hand. This card has already been shown and it is here that the reason for using cards dissimilar to the chosen card becomes clear. Because the onlookers could tell at a glance that the chosen card was not shown them, they have not bothered to remember the names of the cards. They glance now at the last card, at which you give them but a flash, and they affirm that it is not their chosen card without noting that it has been shown before.

12. The cards are now placed on the table, in relation to the spectator, as in Fig. 2; they extend in a row at right angles to him. Confess that you have failed to find the chosen card and invite the spectator to point to any card. Although he is given a free choice, he will point to the card second from his end of the row; this is his chosen card.

13. Remove the other three cards, show their faces briefly and replace them upon the pack. Request the spectator to name his card. He names the queen of hearts and you invite him to turn the tabled card face upwards. It is his chosen queen of hearts.

Although any manner of force may be used, it has been found that the force described is especially effective for this particular trick.

On very rare occasions a spectator will not point to the card second from his end of the tabled row. On these occasions the card is left on the table by the usual ruse of interpreting the spectator's instructions to fit the conjurer's needs, removing all cards but the chosen card. It will be found, however, that the use of the equivoque need not be resorted to more than once in a hundred trials, for this psychological force is almost unfailing. Indeed, it is the fairness of this final selection which makes of this a trick which is as effective as it is easy to perform.

Do As I Do

A New Presentation

This is one of the best of self-working feats, a trick which enjoyed phenomenal popularity in its heyday. In its present version a new presentation gives it an additional climax in the guise of a prediction effect which ensures for it a fresh lease on life.

Effect. A prediction is written and placed to one side. A spectator freely chooses any card from one pack and the conjurer selects a card from another. Each card is turned face upwards; they are identical. The pips of the two cards are added and the spectator is invited to remove the card at this number in one of the packs. It is the card named in the prediction which was written prior to the start of the trick.

Working. 1. Write the name of any card that can be found easily in the pack, such as a court card or an ace, seal the paper in an envelope and hand it to a spectator for safekeeping. Let us say that you have written "The ace of spades."

2. Offer the spectator the choice of one of two packs and request that he shuffle his pack while you shuffle the remaining one. Sight the bottom card of your deck, say the seven of diamonds, as you hand it to the spectator and take the pack he has just shuffled. "You have shuffled my pack thoroughly," you say in explanation of the exchange of packs. "I have shuffled the pack you now have. Clearly you cannot know the position of any given card in your pack, nor can I know where any particular card is in mine. I would like to show you now a most peculiar paradox with a pack of pasteboards, a curious concatenation of events which has puzzled our most erudite scientists. First of all, you must make your mind an absolute blank, so that you may receive the mental impulses which I shall presently hurl your way. Do you think you can do that, sir? You know during the middle ages the learned and bewhiskered scholars of that day made their minds a blank by contemplating how many angels could dance on the point of a needle. You might try that if you have trouble blanking your mind. The theory is that, like counting sheep jumping over a fence, thinking about angels dancing on the point of a

needle can grow very monotonous; after a time the mind is lulled into an almost hypnotic slumber, mainly because no one has yet thought of a good reason why any sensible angel should want to dance on the point of a needle. The entire project presently seems to be rather ridiculous and the first thing you know you're bored and your mind is a blank. . . . Can you visualize the point of a needle, sir? And now you're counting the angels? You *are?* Then, from now on, I should say that *anything* can happen."

3. Place your pack, squared, on your right and spread it in a long ribbon towards your left. Address the spectator: "I must ask you to do exactly as I do. First of all, spread your pack as I have spread mine." Extend your forefinger and run it back and forth over your spread pack, requesting the spectator to imitate your actions. Hold your hand poised over the cards; then say, "Now slide any card from your pack, any card at all, exactly as I am doing, look at it but do not allow anyone near you to see its face. Remember your card and I shall remember mine." Look at your card without letting anyone near you see what card it is, then place it at the left end of your spread pack, inviting the spectator to place his card similarly on his pack. Gather the cards, always insisting that the spectator's actions shall coincide with yours, and cut the deck several times. The condition now is that the spectator's chosen card is directly under the key seven of diamonds in his pack.

4. "Now we'll exchange packs," you say. Take the spectator's pack and hand him yours. Request him to remove his card and place it face downwards on the table as you remove the card you thought of. Run through the pack until you find the predicted card, the ace of spades, and cut this card to the top. Continue thumbing through the pack in apparent search for your card until you find the key card, the seven of diamonds, place the card under it, the chosen card, at the top of the pack above the predicted ace of spades. Let us assume that the chosen card was the eight of clubs. Double the number of pips and deduct one, in this case arriving at a total of fifteen. Run off fifteen cards from the face of the deck and cut them to the top. Fan the pack and remove the spectator's card, the eight of clubs, from amongst the top cards, placing it face downwards upon the table. Thus you have placed the predicted ace of spades sixteenth from the top during an apparent innocent search for your card. Almost invariably you can complete these preparations before the spectator will have found his card; it is good psychology to have your card on the table before he places his there, although it is not imperative.

5. When both cards are on the table, carefully place one above the

other, at right angles. Take the spectator's pack and put it on the table; then place your pack upon it also at right angles, doing all this gravely with an air of meticulous regard for detail. Recapitulate what has been done: "You remember I shuffled one pack, you shuffled the other. You chose a card at random from the face-down pack which I had shuffled: it was impossible therefore for you to know what card you would take. Similarly I took a card from the face-down pack you shuffled and could not conceivably have known beforehand which card L would draw. I have placed my card on the table and you have placed your card there. Now, would you be surprised, sir, if you found that we both have chosen the same card?" The spectator intimates that he would be surprised; you reach out gingerly and grasp both cards, still at right angles, and turn them face upwards on the table; they are two eights of clubs.

6. During the ensuing moment, in which your audience has the very natural desire to comment amongst themselves upon this strange coincidence, keep your hands well away from the packs still resting on the table. Then say, "There is a prediction written on the paper I gave you long before you chose your card, sir. It was plainly impossible for me to know at that time what card you would choose, or what card I would choose. I think you will grant that when I wrote the prediction it was impossible for me to know that sixteen would be the number at which we would finally arrive. Will you please take your pack [reach over and tap the upper pack of the two upon the table. Because of the several exchanges of the packs, and natural forgetfulness, this statement will go unchallenged] and count down to the sixteenth card. Place that card face down on the table."

7. When this has been done, request that the envelope be torn open and the prediction be read aloud. "The ace of spades!" you exclaim. "Gentlemen, let me show you what happens when you contemplate the number of angels dancing on the point of a needle!" Slowly turn the tabled card face upwards and show that it is the ace of spades.

CONTRARY DO AS I DO

This feat, with its surprise ending, serves equally well for intimate or platform work. It is a trick which has served Mr. Bert Allerton well in his performances before the luminaries of the motion picture colony in Hollywood, and it has helped, because of its effectiveness, to fill his scrapbook with glowing testimonials from many hundreds of the screen's celebrities.

Effect. A spectator is invited to be as contrary as he likes during a Do

As I Do trick. Nonetheless, spectator and conjurer twice deal matching cards, in the second instance in a manner which "sells" those present.

Requisites. Two glasses or goblets; a pack of ordinary cards.

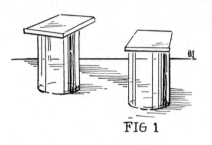

Preparation. Secretly place the ace of diamonds at the top of the pack, the queen of clubs under it. Place the ace of hearts second from the bottom, with the queen of spades at the bottom.

Method. 1. Make a riffle shuffle, retaining the set-up cards at top and bottom, and false cut.

FIG 1

2. Invite a spectator to choose which glass the pack shall be placed upon. When he has done so tell him that, to be contrary, you will place the pack on the other glass. (Note here that the use of the glasses as easels keeps the cards always in sight of those who might not be able to see the table top; it makes manipulation seem difficult or impossible, and makes the handling of the packets very open; and, even more important, it dresses the trick.)

3. Request the spectator to cut the pack freely, placing the top half upon the other glass, face downwards, Fig. 1. Note upon which glass this half, at the top of which are the ace and queen, is placed.

4. Tell the spectator that you are going to give him an absolutely free choice of one of the two packets. Whichever he selects, let him take this in his own hands.

5. *a.* Let us assume that you have the upper half, he has the lower half. Say, "Now you must designate my top or bottom card." If he signifies the top card, you are contrary and take the bottom card and bury it in the pack. He must then be contrary and, instead of burying the bottom card as you did, he must bury the top card.

Should he name the bottom card, bury this in the middle of your packet. Then tell him to be contrary and bury his top card. In either case, the ace and queen remain at the top of your packet, the ace and queen at the bottom of his.

b. But when the upper half is chosen by the spectator and you get the lower half, the procedure is reversed. If he signifies the top card, you bury it and contrarily have him bury his bottom card. If he chooses the bottom card, you are contrary and bury the top card, he buries the bottom card. The result is the same: the set-up cards remain in their proper places.

6. *a.* Again invite him to choose your top or bottom card. If you have the upper packet and he names the top card, place it at the bottom of your packet and have him, contrariwise, place the bottom card at the top. If he names the bottom card, be contrary and place your top card at the bottom of your packet and have him place his bottom card on top.

b. Once again, if you have the lower packet, the procedure is reversed exactly as in No. 5. Whichever packet is held, at the end of these actions each packet has an ace at its face, a queen as its first card.

7. Deal from the top of your packet face downwards onto your glass and invite the spectator to stop the deal whenever he likes. When he does so place the next card at the bottom of your packet openly, covering the ace now on the bottom; this is never commented upon. Invite the spectator to deal from his packet; when you tell him to stop, advise him to be contrary and deal a few more cards.

8. There is now a queen at the bottom of each packet, which lie on the glasses as in Fig. 1. Slowly turn over your packet and show the queen at the bottom. "Since I have the one black queen, you should have the other." Lift his packet cleanly and show the black queen at its face. Drop both of these packets to one side, out of the way.

9. Those present assume that this is the end of the trick. Wait a moment and then have the spectator place his packet face downwards on his glass. Show the bottom card of your packet, say an indifferent three of hearts, turn the pack down, make the glide and place the supposed three spot (actually the ace) face downwards on the glass. Place the remainder of your packet on top of it.

10. "My card is the three of hearts," you point out, naming the indifferent card. "Now, if you're not contrary you should have—what?" "The three of diamonds," chorus the spectators. Have the spectator turn his packet face upwards on the glass. It is the ace of hearts.

11. "You see, you really *were* contrary, so there's only one thing for me to do, and that is to be just as contrary as you are."

Turn over your packet and show the ace of diamonds at its face.

The Twenty-Sixth Location

This is not only a very subtle discovery of a chosen card but also a novel method of ascertaining the card at a certain number in the pack, which is to be used as a key card.

Effect. A card is chosen and returned to the pack; it is shuffled and the conjurer discovers the card in a manner which "sells" his onlookers. Another card is then freely chosen, replaced in the pack in such a way that to all appearances it is completely lost; yet on being spelled out it makes its appearance on the last letter.

Method. The second phase of the trick depends on the use of the twenty-sixth card as a key card and a knowledge of this card is obtained by working a get-ready trick, thus:

1. Force a card, say the four of spades, upon a member of the audience. Have this card shown to all those present and replaced in the pack at any place, contriving, however, to place this card somewhere amongst the top twenty-six cards by means of an overhand shuffle, an easy matter since the exact position of the card is of no importance.

2. Claim emphatically that you can find the card by the sense of touch alone and request the spectator to refrain from giving you any hint, by word or gesture, of the card he chose. Deal cards face upwards on the table in an overlapping ribbon, counting them silently as you do so. When the four of spades, the spectator's card, is dealt continue the deal in an orderly fashion; the spectators, with poorly repressed glee, jump to the conclusion that you have failed in your trick. Note the twenty-sixth card as it is dealt, for this card will be used as your key card in the trick for which this quick trick is merely a prelude. Let us say that the twenty-sixth card is the queen of diamonds.

3. Deal a few more cards and then push off the top card with the left thumb, pretend to feel its outer right index with the tip of the right second finger. Deal this card and repeat the action with the next card. Look up quickly and say, "Don't tell me the name of your card; there is no need, for the next card I turn over will be your card." Convey the impression that the card you refer to is the card at the top of the pack, without making a direct statement to this effect, and offer to wager any small sum that the next card you turn over will be the spectator's card.

The spectator usually looks back over the ribboned cards, notes his four of spades and, feeling safe in betting on a sure thing, accepts the wager.

4. Reach out slowly, remove the four of spades from the ribbon of cards and turn it over face downwards.

This old, old trick is the familiar Circus Card Trick, an ancient snare used by circus grifters against the gullible and the greedy. It is still a good trick and can be very amusing when used against the man from Missouri. It need hardly be added that the conjurer does not permit the spectator to pay his "loss" in the wager.

The magician now knows the name of the card at the twenty-sixth position in the pack, which we have said is the queen of diamonds. Replace the spectator's first card, the four of spades, amongst the top cards and reassemble the pack. You are now set for a surprising location.

1. Place the pack on the table and invite a spectator to cut it into three heaps about equal. Generally this will be done by his cutting about two-thirds of the pack to the right, then about half of this packet again to the right. We will call these packets A, B and C, A being originally the bottom portion of the pack, B the middle portion and C the top portion. The key card, therefore, will be in packet B.

2. Invite a spectator to touch one of the two outside packets. Suppose he touches C. Instruct him to shuffle it, take a card, note what it is and place it on top of the packet. If you now place C on B his card will be the twenty-sixth card above the key card. Instead of doing this at once, have the spectator cut off half of A and drop the cards on C, then lift all of C, placing the pile on B and finally take the remainder of A and placing these cards on top of all. The pack, thus reassembled, may be cut as often as desired provided that each cut is completed.

Even to the expert unacquainted with the method, there does not seem to be any possibility of discovering the card since the way in which the cuts were made and the pack reassembled precludes the use of the top or bottom cards as key cards. However, all you have to do is run through the pack, find the key card, the original twenty-sixth card, count to the twenty-sixth card above it—that is, to the left of it—and you have the selected card. If the top card of the pack is reached before you come to it, simply continue the count from the bottom card.

The mere discovery of the card is surprising enough but it is more satisfactory to finish the trick by spelling the card to produce it. To do this, when you reach the chosen card continue running the cards, spelling its name, a card for each letter up to the final *s*, and hold a break. Make the pass or a simple cut at that point.

Turn the pack face down, ask the spectator to think of his card and to spell it mentally one letter for each card you deal. Tell him to include the word *of* and to stop your deal when he comes to the last letter.

Deal the cards face downwards, keeping check on the spelling yourself. When he calls *Stop!*, place the card face down, have it named and let the spectator turn it up himself.

It is necessary to return for a moment to the three packets and the choice of a card. If packet A is chosen, let a card be taken from it and have it placed on C. It will then be the twenty-seventh card from the key card. Always count the key card as *one* in starting the count.

Although it requires an unconscionable number of words to explain it, the system will be found simple in actual practice.

The discovery is so perplexing that a repetition is usually demanded and, since the principle is so well disguised, the objection to instant repetition does not hold. To be prepared for this you have simply to replace the card just spelled on the top of the remainder of the deck and then drop these cards on top of those which were dealt face downward on the table in the process of the spelling. The original key card—the queen of diamonds—will again be the twenty-sixth card. A false shuffle and blind cut may be indulged in but are not absolutely necessary.

It should be noted that any method of discovering a card may, with a little ingenuity, be applied to the trick. For instance, on a repetition, the spectator's card may be brought to the top and six cards from the bottom be placed above it. The Psychic Stop trick may then be employed for the discovery. The extra six cards are replaced at the bottom of the pack, the chosen card replaced amongst the top twenty-six cards, and you are prepared for another demonstration. Other discoveries will suggest themselves to the reader.

It may further be added that, in making the count from the twenty-sixth card, it is an excellent practice to cut cards from the face to the top of the pack in small numbers. That is, count seven cards and transfer these to the top; count seven more and transfer these; count five more and transfer; count the final seven cards and upon transferring them the spectator's card is at the top. Transfer in like manner the number of cards needed to spell off the card; transfer similarly six cards if you are using the Stop trick.

The Unwitting Magician

In this amusing feat the conjurer invites a spectator to play the role of magician, which he does with a success surprising to himself.

Effect. An assisting spectator has three cards chosen by members of the audience. Although they are apparently lost in the pack, the assistant successfully locates the three cards.

Method. 1. Request the assistance of any member of the audience and tell him that the ability to perform hanky-panky is latent in all people; ask him if he has ever performed card tricks, to which his probable answer will be an affirmative. "You see? You're a potential magician!" you observe pleasedly. Hand him the pack and request that he do a trick. He will, in all likelihood, ask to be excused; but should he prepare to comply with your request, for goodness' sake stop him.

2. In either case, ask him to shuffle the pack and watch him as he does this, nodding approvingly. "A born magician!" you beam. "One little shuffle, and he knows the position of every card in the pack!" Invite the

assistant to take the pack to three spectators and to have each spectator select a card, and then to bring the pack back to you. Seat yourself comfortably to one side and look questioningly at the assistant. "So far, so good," you comment. "What do we do now?" Between you, decide that the return of the three cards to the pack is essential.

3. As the assistant collects the three cards upon the flat of his palm— "You really musn't peek at them, sir," you call out after he has taken the second card. "Magicians *never* do that. It's cheating!"—thumb count nine cards and hold a break with the left little finger.

4. Hold the pack well down in the left hand, riffle with the thumb and cut at the break. Request the assistant to drop the three chosen cards on the pack, replace the nine cards on top and square the pack openly and fairly.

5. Hand the deck to the assistant. Ask him what should be done next and immediately answer your own query by saying, "Somebody shuffles the cards. You'd better hand me the pack and ask me to shuffle it. Magicians always do that—don't you remember?" Take the pack, undercut the lower half, injog the first card and shuffle off. Form a break at the injog, shuffle to the break and throw on top. The stock of cards remains at the top.

6. Return the pack to the volunteer assistant, look at him blankly and say, "Well, what next?" Between you, decide that he shall ask the first spectator to name a number between ten and twenty. You have previously watched the order in which the assistant collected the cards and now you make certain that he approaches the proper person—i.e., the spectator who last placed a card on his palm.

7. The spectator names a number, say fourteen. Tell the assistant to deal that number of cards upon your left palm. When he has done this take the pack from him with your right hand, which then drops to your side, and hand him the cards he has dealt onto the left palm. Instruct him to add the two digits of the number—in this case, one and four, totaling five—and to deal to the card at that number from the packet of fourteen. He deals four cards upon your extended palm and the fifth card proves to be the spectator's card. Take this card from him, display it and place it to one side. During this part of the trick make it apparent that you are acting as an assistant only.

8. Place the small packet of cards remaining on your left palm—in this case, four—upon the pack held by the right hand; take the nine cards remaining in the assistant's hands and drop them on top. Give the pack a false shuffle.

9. Congratulate the assistant upon his first success and ask him if he feels strong enough to undertake a second location. Have him find the second card in the same manner, again placing it to one side with the first card; and have him find the last card again in the same manner.

10. Pick up the three cards which the dazzled assistant has located and, fanning them, show them to the audience and have the assistant accept his well-earned applause.

Through the locations you play the role of an approving assistant, leading the applause after each successful location and stressing the fact that the assistant is the magician and that you have taken no part in the trick.

The feat is almost wholly dependent upon the manner in which it is presented; if the reader will build into its presentation amusing incidents and comments which suit his particular personality and style, he will find that it can be very effective.

The Magic of Nine

A host of mathematical oddities are made possible by the curious properties of the number nine; magicians have made use of the principle since, in 1857, a section of *The Magician's Own Book* was devoted to innumerable divertissements made possible by the number. Since then any number of clever camouflages of the principle have been devised, of which this is one of the best.

Effect. A spectator removes a number of cards from a cut packet and places them in his pocket; he also makes a mental note of a card. The conjurer divines the number of cards in the pocket and discovers the noted card.

Method. 1. Have the pack shuffled by a spectator and, turning your back, invite him to cut a quantity of cards, count them secretly, add the digits and put aside cards to the sum so arrived at. (Thus, he cuts twenty-three cards; adds the two digits, totaling five; removes five cards and places them aside.)

2. Request him to think of any small number and to remove that number of cards from the packet in his hands, placing these in his pocket. (He thinks of the number seven, counts off seven cards and places them in his pocket.)

3. Tell him to count down to the card at this same number amongst the cards remaining in his hands and to make a mental note of the card. (He counts down seven cards and remembers this card.)

4. Turn around and take the packet of cards. Without glancing at

their faces, slowly pass the cards one by one before the spectator's eyes, secretly counting the cards as you request him to note that his card is still in the spread. There are eleven cards. Subtract this number from eighteen (if the number were less than nine, subtract it from nine) leaving a remainder of seven. This remainder is the number at which the noted card may be found from the top of the packet; it is also the number of cards the spectator placed in his pocket.

FIG 1

5. Again pass the cards before the spectator's eyes and this time sight the lower index of the spectator's card (in this case, the seventh card) by turning up the corner of the card with the left thumb, Fig. 1.

6. Drop the cards upon the pack and, in an overhand shuffle, run enough cards on top to spell out the name of the card you just sighted. (If it were the eight of diamonds, seventh card from the top, you would run eight cards.)

7. Tell the assisting spectator to spell one letter of the name of his card for each card you deal, including the "*of*." After fifteen cards have been dealt, the eight of diamonds is dealt on the final "*s*."

8. During the preceding spelling you have dealt the cards face upwards on the table. Watch them as they fall; should a seven spot be dealt secure it in gathering the cards and place it at the top of the pack. If a seven does not fall, it must be secured by one of the methods given in another part of this book. (Naturally, if you know three was the spectator's number, a three spot is secured.)

False shuffle the cards and force the seven upon another spectator. Claim that this card will infallibly reveal the number of cards freely cut from the pack by the first spectator and placed by him in his own pocket. The card is turned and shown to be a seven. The spectator removes and counts his cards; there are seven.

THE CERTAIN CARD TRICK

This is a new method of performing a very fine and puzzling feat devised by Mr. Percy Abbott, of Colon, Michigan.

Effect. The conjurer discovers a card noted under conditions which would seem to make this discovery impossible.

Method. 1. Hand the pack to a spectator and request him to shuffle it. If he is a careless shuffler, exposing the face of the bottom card of the pack, note it and request him to place the deck on the table. If he is more careful, note the card in taking the pack from him and placing it on the table yourself. This card is your key. Use 48 cards only.

2. Request him to cut the pack, note the face card of the cut packet, replace the cut and make as many complete cuts as he desires.

3. Estimate the depth of the cut. The spectator may lift twelve cards and your guess may be thirteen; or again you may guess sixteen. In either case, divide your estimate by six; for instance six into thirteen is *two* and one over, and six into sixteen is *two* and four over. Remember the *two* and discard the fraction, which in the cited cases would be one and four.

4. Take the pack after the spectator has cut freely and deal the cards face upwards into six piles, dealing the cards from left to right one card to each pile in turn. Watch for the key card and when it falls into a pile remember the number at which it falls. For instance, if it is the second card you deal into any one of the six piles, you will use the number *two;* if it is the sixth card dealt into a pile, *six* will be used in the later computation.

5. Let us say that your key card is the fourth card which you place in pile five. Add this number, *four*, to the number at which you arrived after the division in No. 3; in this case, add the *four* to the *two*, arriving at a new total of *six.*

6. Request the spectator to point at the pile in which his card rests. If this is to the right of the pile containing the key card, his chosen card will be at the number arrived at after the addition in No. 5; in the present case, it will be *six* from the top of the packet. If his card is to the left of the pile containing the key card, or if it is in the same pile, add *one* to the total arrived at in No. 5; in other words, in the present case, add *one* to *six*, obtaining a new total of *seven.* His card will be the seventh card from the top of the pile indicated. Should the number be more than eight begin the count at the top again.

7. Pick up this pile and turn it face downwards. Shuffle the cards in your hands, apparently idly, but contrive to place his card at the bottom of the packet, an easy matter.

8. Place the top card of the packet on the table and place the next card on the bottom; place the top card on the table and place the next card on the bottom. Continue this procedure until but one card remains in the hand. This will be the spectator's card.

Have him name his card and turn the last card face upwards, showing that you have discovered his card.

This method of handling provides a tacit reason for having the spectator point out the pile in which his card rests. The trick also is susceptible to many refinements, such as denting the key card with the thumbnail or applying daub, in which cases the deal may be made face downwards; or the cards may be spread in a ribbon and one card withdrawn and replaced; or the spectator may be invited to peek at a card. Although the same principle is employed, these minor deviations in presentation confuse the onlookers as to the procedure and make repetitions more entertaining and puzzling.

The trick is a very good one.

Part 5

MISCELLANY

HERE ARE GATHERED a number of odds and ends: Small conceits with accessories and the novel employment of familiar objects, hints, twists and quirks.

Although these have not been given the dignity of rigid classification, they will be found to be of value both in the presentation and in the performance of card conjuring.

Part 5

MISCELLANY

~~~~~~

PEELING CARDS

A DRY SPLIT is the best and quickest method of separating the three layers
of a playing card. Tap a corner of the card on the table to fray the edge,
then start either the front or the back layer, being careful not to include

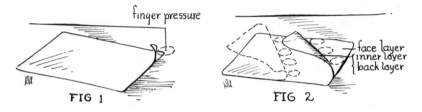

finger pressure

face layer
inner layer
back layer

FIG 1   FIG 2

the composition layer between. Hold the piece started down against the
table with the tips of the left fingers and peel the upper layers away,
Figs. 1 and 2.

The split should be made diagonally across the card. Once the corner
is started, the upper layers should be peeled back swiftly three quarters
of an inch or more at a time. The thin paper will not tear if the left fingers
move along with the peel and hold it down against the table top; this
very fast split does the least damage to the face of the card. If, on the
other hand, the split is made slowly and carefully the face layer will be
marred with tiny wrinkles. A card can and should be split in no more
than eight seconds.

It will be noted that in this method the face of a card is not peeled
from the other two layers; it is impossible to do this without tearing. The
secret is to peel the two upper layers from the face layer, as shown in
the illustrations.

MAKING DOUBLE-FACED CARDS

To make a double-face card of standard thickness, peel the face from
one card and the back from another. Scrape the rough surfaces of both
cards with a sharp knife to remove the fuzzy roughness. Draw the single
layer back and forth against the edge of a table, against the curl which the

peeling puts in the paper. Apply a very thin coating of rubber cement to the rough surface of the card with the composition layer and place this aside to dry. If the rubber cement is used too liberally and the card is assembled before the cement dries (it takes two or three minutes) the cement may stain through the thin single layer when the card is assembled. The cement may if desired be spread on both rough surfaces, but this is hardly necessary.

The various brands of rubber cement differ in formula; it may also be mentioned here that the product sold under the trade name De Voe is excellent for the purpose.

When the double-face (or double-back) card is assembled, rub both faces to remove any small air bubbles and dry under pressure. A satisfactory method is to place the card or cards in the center of a pack and to insert this into a flap card case, using enough cards to ensure a very tight fit.

Before using the cards, rub their edges with a clean cloth to remove any small particles of the cement which may have been forced from between the cards.

A very good double-face card is made by peeling the backs from the two cards to be used. Scrape the rough surfaces of both cards as smooth as possible, apply a thin coating of cement to each surface. Place the cemented surfaces together and rub the faces briskly. The cards need not be placed under pressure and may be used at once.

This card is a fraction of an inch thicker than an unfaked card, since it has two composition layers, and it is also a little heavier. These variations from the normal are scarcely perceptible and will pass unnoted. The cards manufactured by this method have the same elasticity as an unprepared card with both faces smooth and unmarked. Such a card may be made from the start to finish in approximately two minutes.

In both methods, the better the grade of card used, the better the resultant faked card.

A double-faced pack of cards is available at the magic depots and these specially manufactured cards are the very best to use in those feats for which they are suited. There are many other startling card feats, however, such as Sympathetic Clubs (*Jinx 53*) and The Married Couples and the Bachelors (*More Card Manipulations*, No. 3) which call for special double-face cards not procurable from the dealers. Many were deterred from using these tricks after attempting to make the cards by means of the old immersion method, which produced a very unsatisfactory faked card. Using the method given above, perfect faked cards can be made and those tricks dependent upon them added to the conjurer's repertoire.

SHINERS

The little metal disc which, attached to the forefinger, enables a card-worker to sight the index of a card in its bright surface, is at times an artful accomplice. If rubber cement is placed on its back, the lightest touch of the finger tip will affix the shiner firmly to the flesh with no danger of its dropping loose. When it is removed nothing sticky remains on the finger, since the cement can be rolled off in a moment.

THE SPECTATOR PEEK

When you have several persons select cards by peeking at the indices, it sometimes happens that a perverse person will lift the corners with a sharp riffle, giving you no chance to secure a break. To argue with him and get him to take another peek would be fatal. Simply ask him if he is sure he has seen a card and go on to the next person. Suppose you are dealing with five cards, you have four of them under control, the fifth you do not know. In making the discoveries use the slap color change to produce the third card, then go to the perverse person, lift your right hand as if about to slap the face card again and say sharply, "What was your card?" He names it expecting you to try to produce it, but you suddenly remember another card was selected and you produce the fourth card by fanning the deck and picking it out. Needless to say you seize the opportunity of locating the card just named and placing it in position for any method of discovery you please, the more startling the better.

ONE WILL MAKE SIX

Of general utility is the knowledge that a two spot will locate six cards if it be inserted in the deck within six of the desired card. For example:

Thrust into the pack, it locates:

1. The card above, or the card below.
2. Having two pips, you can plausibly count up or down two cards.
3. For the same reason, you can with seeming fairness remove two cards above or below, and display the next card.

The stratagem is strictly for emergency use.

AUDACITY PEEK

This can be used against a single spectator only.

Palm a card in the right hand after the spectator has shuffled the pack. Lay the back of your hand against the spectator's chest, high up, in gesturing to amplify a remark. Sight the card.

The move can be useful and surprisingly is not suspected if the gesture is kept in character.

Card to Pocket

This trick, one of the best, has only one small flaw. Too often spectators fail to understand the instructions as to the nature of the count in which they note the number at which a card lies from the top of the pack.

To obviate this, after the spectator has shuffled and your back is turned, instruct him to think of any number, then deal the cards one by one face up on the table, noting the card which falls on his number. He is then to continue dealing the cards, singly or in groups, until the deck is exhausted.

The spectator then squares the pack and hands it to you, and the trick is continued in the usual version. The simplification of the instructions given to the spectator prevents any "Which card do I look at—this one or that one?" queries which destroy the trick's illusion.

Svengali Shuffle

To shuffle a long-and-short pack without disturbing the set-up: Hold the pack between the right thumb at the inner end, second and third fingers at the outer end, forefinger resting lightly on the top. Place the

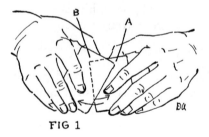

FIG 1

left hand in exactly the same position. Break the pack open and move the outer ends in contrary directions, the upper half to the right, the lower to the left, the packets pivoting on the thumbs, Fig. 1.

At the conclusion of the moves the packets will resemble a V.

With the thumbs, riffle corners A and B together. The shuffle is natural and easy of accomplishment.

The Charlier Shuffle

This easy and effective false shuffle is designed to keep the whole deck in a prearranged order. The deck is held in the left hand between the thumb, which rests on the top, and tips of the fingers, which are curled in against the face of the bottom card, Fig. 1. Several cards are pushed off with the left thumb and are taken in the right hand. Then the left fingers push a small packet from the bottom onto the top of the cards in the right hand. Next the left thumb pushes off several cards from the top of the pack and these are taken by the right fingers under the right hand portion. Again the left fingers push off some cards from the bottom onto those in the right hand and the moves are repeated until the whole pack is in the right hand.

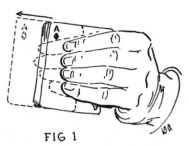

The shuffle leaves the pack in the same condition as if it had received a single complete cut. The sleight is all the more deceptive if it is done rather roughly or sloppily, in fact it is sometimes referred to as the "slop" shuffle.

FIG 1

When it is necessary to bring the whole pack back to the same order, the simplest method is this: Hold the pack in the left hand and ruffle the inner left corner upwards with the right thumb, the right forefinger pressing down rather strongly at the middle of the inner end, thus making a bridge at this end. Make the shuffle twice, cut at the bridge and the whole pack is back in its original order. The right thumb finds the bridge automatically in making the cut and the left hand takes out the bend in squaring the cards.

The Matchbook Easel

FIG 1

FIG 2

In the course of a series of tricks with cards it often becomes necessary to display a card, or cards, by standing it, or them, upright on the table. The difficulty is generally overcome by resting the card against a glass or a book, but the simplest solution and a most intriguing one, is to use a matchbook as a miniature easel. Lay the matchbook on its back on the table, open the flap and set it at right angles to the back, Fig. 1. Place the card on it as in Fig. 2, the flap forming a rest to keep the card upright and the ridge of the striking surface holding its lower end secure.

Matchbooks are obtainable everywhere and not only does their use add an engaging touch but the cards can be set upright instantly with no danger of their sliding away as is the case with a glass or book.

In such tricks as Everywhere and Nowhere, the Four Aces, etc., the extra matchbooks required should be produced from the first by magic and vanished when done with. These apparent impromptus add sparkle to the trick itself.

THE KAUFMAN CARD STAND

The recent popularity of the display of prowess in emulating the gamblers' ability to deal poker hands, etc., has created a demand for an easy and portable means for displaying the cards as they are dealt. This display rack, devised by Mr. Gerald Kaufman and first shown by him at the S.A.M. Parent Assembly, January 4, 1940, will be found ideal for the purpose.

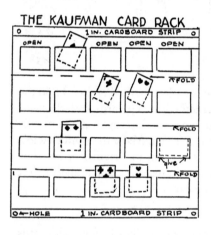

The rack is made of heavy brown wrapping paper, or white package paper, upon which has been glued four horizontal rows of cards, backs outwards.

Playing cards of a design and color to contrast with the backs of the pack used in the trick should be selected. Glue these to the wrapping paper with Le Page's or Duco transparent cement, *not* glue, liquid solder or rubber cement. Take care not to spread this in a strip more than a quarter of an inch in width, placing the cement on the faces of the cards so that the backs show outwards.

The dimensions of the paper are 20″×20″, with the cards and strips spaced as shown in the figure; thus the rack can be folded where indicated into a 5″×20″ package. By means of the strip of cardboard the rack can be hung on cords, thumbtacked or pinned to the back of a chair or any piece of furniture.

SECOND DEAL AID

Apply a small quantity of roughing fluid to the ball of the right thumb. It will be found that the abrasive action of the thumb against the card, in the strike method of second dealing, is greatly increased thereby and this aids greatly in expediting the withdrawal of the second card.

FALSE COUNTS AND DEALS

To Deal Four as Three

The preferred method of making such a deal is to deal one; deal two; push off two as one with the left thumb and deal these as the third card.

Another, easier method is to employ the double lift method given elsewhere in this book. Prepare by buckling the cards and inserting the tip of the little finger under the four top cards. Deal one; deal two; deal three, the little finger break making the push-off and deal of the last two as one an easy matter.

The best cover for the deal is the following gambling device: Deal the first card, deal the second upon it; take the third card (two cards) in the right hand and slide them, from the right, under the first two cards dealt.

The method is useful for four ace and other tricks.

A False Count

You wish, say, apparently to count off five cards from the deck, whereas actually you count off ten. Insert the left little finger under the six top cards. Push these off the pack with the left thumb exactly as in making a push-off for the double lift. The cards are pushed into the crotch of the right thumb, approaching to take them, and the thumb closes against the side of the palm, thus pinching the cards tightly. The outer left corner of the cards nestles between the fore and second fingers, at the second joints of both fingers; in this position the forefinger is at the outer end, the remaining three

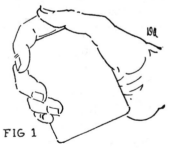

FIG 1

fingers at the left side, the thumb slanting diagonally across the outer right corner, its tip touching the flesh between the first and middle joints of the forefinger, Fig. 1.

The four remaining cards of the apparent five cards to be counted off the deck are drawn onto the original packet by the right thumb as it moves easily and smoothly to take them. The deal, a very simple one, is the very best of such counts, since at no time can the first deal of extra cards be betrayed by cards slipping out of line.

False Table Deal

You have a packet of 8 cards in the left hand and desire to deal these upon the table as 6. Hold the packet in the left hand, the four fingers at the right side, the thumb placed upon the top card. Push this card off the packet, counting one. Deal a second card, a third card and a fourth. On the 5th deal move the tips of the four left fingers under the face card and with them buckle this last card to the left, approximately a half-inch. The right thumb, first and second fingers take all the cards above the bottom buckled card at the outer right corner and deal them as one upon the four cards previously dealt. The last card, remaining in the left hand, is dealt upon the tabled packet.

It will be noted that the deal is an improvement of the old glide, applied to cards taken off the side of the pack rather than the end.

Magic Powder v. Rabbit's Foot

Decremps, the first modern writer on magic, said, in 1793, in explaining the accepted way of getting rid of the knot in the cut and restored cord:

"Place the knot in your pocket under the pretence of taking a handkerchief or some sympathetic powder."

The present day graduate of the mail order course, How to Become a Magician in Ten Lessons, when he wishes to dispose of a palmed object, puts his hand furtively in his coat pocket with a self-conscious smirk "to get some woofledust" and preens himself on being right up to the minute. If this atrocity must be used it would be well to have a little box, a pillbox for example, in the pocket and bring it out on other occasions when the hand is palpably empty in reaching for it. Thus when an article has to be disposed of in this fashion the action will arouse no suspicion.

A much better subterfuge is the use of a rabbit's foot. This lucky charm has been accepted so widely and for so long a time as a protective agency that even those who profess to scoff at such superstitious beliefs will accept it as a legitimate magician's accessory. By carrying it in the coat pocket and using it on occasion after the manner of a magic wand a palmed article can be disposed of or some other small article secured and palmed in the most natural way possible.

The Carbon Card

That ingenious device, the carbon card,* can be palmed onto the face of any borrowed pack, which is then handed to the spectator with a slip

---

* *Encyclopedia of Card Tricks*, edited by Jean Hugard, page 303.

of paper pressed upon its face. When the spectator mentally chooses any card and makes a notation of it, the conjurer has available a carbon imprint of the chosen card. Needless to say, the face card of the borrowed pack should correspond to the carbon card.

An excellent procedure when using this aid is apparently to forget the party who has "merely thought of" a card. When, later in the program, you are reminded of this fact, produce his card in some spectacular fashion and suppress any mention of the written slip of paper; many of the on-lookers will forget that such a notation was ever written and you will be credited with having performed a notable feat in thought-reading.

Daub

Water color in the silver shade, as supplied for a few cents by dealers in artists' supplies, makes an excellent daub and is used by many professional gamblers. Some of them use it unknowingly, since this product is sold by one of the leading purveyors of gamblers' supplies for two dollars and fifty cents. It is, however, neatly re-packaged.

Set-Ups

On those occasions when the conjurer is doing impromptu work with his own cards it is a good practice to use two packs of cards. If it is desired to do set-up tricks during the exhibition an excellent procedure is this: Make the set-up in one pack, place this pack to one side and, picking up the other pack, use it for other tricks. After an interval, pick up the first pack and perform the trick requiring the set-up. The time-lag will cause the spectators to forget even an open set-up openly arrived at.

The Card at Any Number

One of the earliest methods of placing a card at a chosen number is that of thumb counting to the desired number and then of back slipping the card from the top to this number.

Assume that the desired card is at the top of the pack. Thumb count seven cards and request the spectator to name any small number. If he names less than seven, release the cards and thumb count anew; if he gives a larger number, allow the additional cards needed to slip off the thumb.

If the number were thirteen, thumb count to this number and openly cut the pack, back slipping the top card onto the pack during the cut. Thus, when the righthand cards are returned, the desired card will be thirteen from the top.

Slap the cards cut by the right hand sharply onto the deck; cut the pack twice more indiscriminately and in each instance drop the packet sharply onto the deck. Explain that this is necessary to cause the card to rise to the proper position. The action affords an explanation of the cut which must be made to back slip the card into position and is accepted by the onlookers as in keeping with the hanky-panky nonsense which conjurers proverbially indulge in to "explain" their mysteries.

Moistening a Card

The fastidious performer who does not favor the gesture of placing the hand to the mouth may welcome an application of an idea, developed for another purpose, by Clayton Rawson, mentor of the Great Merlini.

Saturate a small ball of natural sponge or sponge rubber with water or glycerine and place it in a thumb tip, or preferably a wooden thimble, which is dropped in the right trousers pocket. The right second finger may be moistened at any moment by thrusting it into the receptacle; but it is advisable, in removing the hand, to brush the back of the finger against the cloth of the pocket, to remove any moisture from the back of the finger which might be noticed by the onlookers.

On occasion when this gimmick is not available, the best procedure when one has to moisten one's finger at the mouth, is to stand for a moment with the chin resting on the right hand, as one does when in a reflective mood. In this position it is easy, by turning aside ever so little, to effect the necessary moistening.

The Pass

This is a very fine cover for the pass when the conjurer is seated:
Prior to the pass push the chair back from the table at which you are

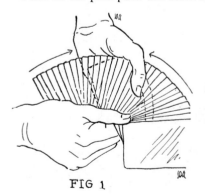

FIG 1

performing. When the pass is to be made lift up on the feet and shift the body until you are seated on the very edge of the chair. Under cover of this forward movement make the pass, the hands with the pack being held just above the lap. The larger movement of the body in shifting its position provides a natural distraction which serves to cover the pass perfectly.

LEFT HAND BOTTOM REPLACEMENT

With cards palmed in the left hand which must be replaced at the bottom of the pack, the following serves to cover the replacement:

Fan the cards in the right hand and turn this hand so that the periphery of the fan, which is held in a horizontal plane, is nearest the body. Bring the left hand with its palmed cards up to the fan, the hand behind held vertically, and place the fanned cards in the crotch of the left hand, the thumb of which rests on the backs of the cards. Hidden by the fan, turn the left hand into a horizontal position and close the fan with both hands, thus returning the palmed cards to the middle, Fig. 1.

Part 6

MISDIRECTION AND PRESENTATION

~~~~~~

THERE ARE SOME SLEIGHTS which are harder to conceal than others, for the hand has never been quicker than the eye. The first magician learned that if he could make those who watched look elsewhere momentarily, these sleights could be made with impunity. This practice is called *misdirection* by the present-day conjurer; successful, it represents a victory of the magician in a battle of wits for, purely through mental processes, he has forced the witness unknowingly to relax his vigilance and to turn his attention and his interest away from the conjurer at the vital moment, in the mistaken belief that the distraction offered him is of importance and hence should be considered attentively.

IN CONJURING there is but one real magic, and that is the presentation of magic, which will make an apparently unpretentious trick a minor miracle to those who see it. It is presentation which lifts the card trick from the level of the commonplace puzzle to the status of an unforgettable and inexplicable mystery; it is presentation, more important, which raises the conjurer in the esteem of his audiences, which prompts them to remember him when they have forgotten the tricks he performed.

BECAUSE BOTH presentation and misdirection are an integral part of all card tricks, as vital as the skill which makes them possible, there will be found on the following pages a summary of many of the factors which enter into the successful presentation of card magic, together with an outline of the methods employed by the conjurer in creating misdirection.

Chapter 1
MISDIRECTION

~~~~~~

To PRESENT SLEIGHT OF HAND with cards most effectively it is essential that the technique of manipulation should be complemented by an understanding of the laws of human interest and a knowledge of the manner in which they can best be put to use by the conjurer. "Misdirection" is the term which magicians have given to the application, for conjuring purposes, of certain of these laws of interest, and it is this misdirection which makes possible some amazing deceptions; it is as important as any sleight in card conjuring, for it makes possible the execution of many sleights under conditions which would otherwise make their use impossible.

It was Voltaire who said, "Define your subject, gentlemen!" and in approaching the subject of misdirection it may be well to observe this counsel, for there exists amongst conjurers a considerable difference of opinion as to the nature of misdirection and how it may be used to cloak their methods from prying eyes.

So, with Voltaire, let us define our subject:

Misdirection is arousing the absorbed interest of an audience in some object or person away from the conjurer during those moments in which the secret sleight (or subterfuge) is made, thus making possible its undetected execution.

The other devices used by the magician—the so-called mental-misdirection; feats based on the element of confusion of the spectator's mind, or by a deception of the senses; diversions created solely through the use of speech; the deception of an audience by causing it to make an incorrect inference—all these, which are often called misdirection, are not within the scope of this article.

The term misdirection as used in this article refers solely to the diversion of attention away from the performer in order to make possible the secret execution of a sleight, or the use of a subterfuge.

Although misdirection is as old as conjuring, once again it seems to have been that very shrewd and intelligent man, Robert-Houdin, who first gave examples of its actual workings. In his great book, *Secrets of Conjuring and Magic*, he has written:

"Some actions and movements of the performer are designed solely to facilitate what in conjuring is called a *temps*. A *temps* is the opportune moment for effecting a given disappearance, or the like, unknown to the spectators. In this case, the act or movement which constitutes the *temps* is specially designed to divert the attention of the spectators to some point more or less remote from that at which the trick is actually worked. For example, a conjurer will ostentatiously place some article on one corner of the table at which he is performing, while the left hand, finding its way behind the table, gets possession of some hidden object to be subsequently produced. Or, again, he will throw a ball in the air and catch it in the right hand, in order to gain an opportunity, during the same instant, of taking with the left hand another ball out of the *pochette*. Yet again, a mere tap with the wand on any spot, at the same time looking at it attentively, will infallibly draw the eyes of the whole company in the same direction.

"These modes of influencing the direction of the eyes of an audience seem very simple, and as though they could cause no deception, and yet they are never found to fail.

"Each trick has its own appropriate gestures, and its own special *temps*, combined with the *boniment*, or 'patter,' which supplies the pretext for them. We shall have occasion in the course of this work to describe sundry *temps* of extreme ingenuity, and the effect of which is such that even the most determined will cannot resist them."

It is a great loss that Robert-Houdin, out of his practical experience, did not write more fully of misdirection—or, as he called it, a *temps*—so contrived that "even the most determined will cannot resist [it]." For this man, whose every conscientiously-penned line shows that he knew thoroughly the subject which he discussed, could have saved later generations of conjurers much perplexity and bafflement. Robert-Houdin knew that misdirection exists in the *mind* of the spectator, that in order to misdirect him you must interest him, that you must turn his mind to new channels of thought through use of the laws of interest.

Because he knew this, because he was a thoughtful and intelligent man, he became the greatest magician of his day. He had an enquiring mind and he was something of a perfectionist, believing that what was done was worth doing well. He left nothing to chance; each trick had its appropriate gestures, its own special *temps* or misdirection, its own patter. In writing *Secrets of Conjuring and Magic*, Robert-Houdin wrote both with the authority of practical experience and the earnestness of an expert expounding the theory and practice of his craft, in which he took pride.

He knew what the reader already knows, or must some day learn, that each trick must have its special misdirection, in the use of which the element of chance plays no part. It is a fuller exposition of this art of misdirection with which this article concerns itself.

There is another point, a corollary of the first, which should be made clear before a number of examples of the use of misdirection can be given; this concerns the quality of the misdirection:

The distraction which is offered to the spectator in order to misdirect him must be of such a nature that he will concentrate his attention and thought upon it. It must pique his interest, or arouse his curiosity. It must pre-occupy his thoughts; it must be interesting and seem to him to be important.

In other words, the use of a gesture to divert attention, or the turning of the gaze in the hope that it will carry with it the gaze of *all* the spectators, is not enough. It may serve its purpose, and it may not; it is not certain. Similarly, making use of the "opportune moment" when this is left to chance may or may not afford the protection needed to cover the sleight. Our purpose here is to analyze misdirection so strong that it will divert the attention of all the spectators at the crucial moment, so that the reader, understanding its nature, may apply it to his own sleight of hand with cards.

Because it is used in all types of magic, let us examine several notably successful examples of misdirection, keeping in mind both its definition and the necessity for making the diversion offered of such a nature that it will capture the interest of those present. Note how, in the following examples, the absorbed interest of the spectator is turned away from the conjurer at the vital moment, how a new stimuli has claimed his attention which he can no more resist than the impulse to turn and see who has entered the room behind him.

a. The magician, wearing a hooded cloak, stands on the stage near the wings. A grotesque bear clambers on the stage and dances wierdly about. The spectator gazes at this strange apparition and for a few seconds his thoughts are concentrated upon it: *He wants to know why it dances so queerly and what part it takes in the illusion in hand.* He gives his undivided attention to the dancing bear and during these moments the magician steps back into the wings and an assistant, similarly garbed, takes his place.

No more perfect example of the principles of misdirection could be asked. A diversion is created away from the magician which catches and holds interest. Since it is impossible to concentrate on two ideas at once, the spectator dismisses the magician from his mind. The substitution of persons is made during these moments.

This misdirection has been used by Blackstone in a stage illusion over a period of twenty years. It works as efficiently today as it did two decades ago, because it is basically sound.

In card conjuring, with which this work is concerned, the misdirection which is used is in keeping with the type of magic being performed. The principle, however, is the same. Because of the wider range of vision on a full stage, illusion misdirection must be much stronger, the diversion of a more spectacular nature. In card conjuring, where it is necessary to shift the gaze of a spectator a few feet only, the diversion is of a more intimate, and logical, nature.

b. The Vanishing Pack of Cards: The conjurer arouses the interest of his onlookers by drawing an object from his rear right hip pocket. (*What will he take from his pocket?*) It proves to be a handkerchief. (*Oh, it's a handkerchief . . . well, what will he do with it?*) During the few seconds in which the spectator concentrates upon the handkerchief, the conjurer quietly drops the pack in his left coat pocket.

c. The magician has enticed a small boy upon the stage and the boy, under expert coaching, is providing that most amusing of human-interest spectacles: small boy *vs.* the magician. The conjurer turns away and the small boy lifts his coat tails and peers up under them, presumably in search of hidden rabbits. The audience rocks with laughter and for a few moments it is preoccupied with a never-failing source of audience interest, the revelation of human character. It knows that this is an exciting moment in the boy's life and it watches to see how he will react. In lifting the magician's tails he has acted with amusing audacity and the audience watches to see what the boy will do next; he has captured their absorbed interest, to the exclusion of all else. During these moments the magician pops the rabbit into the hat for later production.

d. The magician has placed one sponge ball in his own hand, one in the hand of a spectator. He asks the spectator if he, the magician, can remove the sponge ball in the former's tightly clenched hand. The spectator emphatically states that he can not. By making this query the conjurer has injected an element of doubt as to the issue of a conflict into his presentation, and an interest in the outcome of the trick. (*Can the magician remove the sponge ball from the spectator's hand? It doesn't seem possible . . . still, he seems very self-confident. . . .*)

The conjurer opens his hand and shows that his ball has vanished. The spectator opens his hand and therein finds not one, but two sponge balls.

As he opens his hand the interest of the spectators in the contents of his hand is at its peak. (*What will be in the hand? Has the sponge ball actually vanished?*) The magician, forgotten, steals another sponge ball, or a glass of liquid, or a small block of ice, from under his vest. His misdirection has been good.

e. A card has been chosen and returned to the pack. The conjurer promises that this card will be found at a named number. He deals to that number and places the card face downwards on the table. He reaches out to turn the card face upwards, and the spectator watches the card intently. (*Is it the chosen card, or isn't it?*) As the card is being faced the expert makes the glimpse, the one-hand shift, gets rid of a palmed card or performs any other sleight which must be made.

f. The sleight of hand artist wraps a glass in a piece of newsprint, places a coin on the table and promises to make it pass through the solid table top. He hits the table several times with the wrapped glass to emphasize its solidity and covers the coin with it. He announces that the coin has duly vanished and lifts the wrapped glass back to the edge of the table as the spectators watch intently. (*Is the coin under the glass, as it should be, or has it really disappeared?*) The conjurer drops the glass in his lap as the spectators, their thoughts on the coin and not the covering glass, note with satisfaction that the coin has not vanished.

The wizard re-covers the coin with the empty newsprint shell, which retains the form of the glass. He smashes the shell and makes the glass vanish, and makes the coin vanish; and both the coin and the glass are brought forth from under the table.

The evanishment of the glass is a complete mystery because it was made at a time when the thoughts of the spectator were upon the coin.

g. The card expert shows a card and requests a spectator to extend his hand. When a spectator offers his right hand, he is asked to use his left hand instead. He brings this up but he does not hold it in the correct position; the performer grasps it with his left hand, which holds the pack, and places it just so with meticulous care. He moves the left hand, with the pack, inwards towards his body and as he does this he says, "No, that's not quite right." Those present wonder why the hand must be placed with such care in exactly the proper position and they also speculate on when this proper position will be secured. They watch the spectator's hand. The conjurer top-changes the card being held in the right hand under cover of this misdirection and places the changed card on the outstretched hand. Later it is shown that the card has miraculously changed.

h. The magician places a blank square of paper in an envelope, has a card chosen (it is not looked at) and places the card on the envelope. He makes a mystic pass, cuts open the sealed envelope with a pen knife and removes the little square of paper resting on the flat knife blade. He places it on the table and requests the spectator to show his card. It is the ace of diamonds. The conjurer has folded the envelope (it is a faked double envelope) in half. He requests a spectator to turn the square of paper. The audience concentrates its attention upon the paper. (*What's on the under surface of that square of paper?*) It is turned over and on it is a miniature of the chosen ace of diamonds.

During the moments when the thought of those present was concentrated on the paper, the conjurer has thrust the folded double envelope into his right coat pocket and withdrawn an unprepared duplicate envelope which has been folded and cut as was the first envelope. He drops this on the table. When it is examined it affords no explanation of the mystery.

It is hoped that these few and varied examples of excellent misdirection will serve to show that in controlling the gaze of an audience you must interest it in that at which it is asked to look. This does not mean that the misdirection must be elaborate or lengthy. It may be a very simple action. You have, for instance, palmed cards from a packet of fifteen while performing the Three Cards Across and at the moment that the palm is made you request spectator A to hand the pack to spectator B on your left. The palm is completely covered since the spectators watch the pack of cards as it passes from assistant to assistant. You hand the packet of cards first dealt, minus the palmed cards, to spectator A and later the onlookers claim that they kept their eyes on this packet every moment, and that it contained the entire fifteen cards first dealt.

You request spectator B to deal fifteen cards onto your extended left hand and every eye in the audience watches the deal as the spectators count the cards one by one to make certain that no more than fifteen are dealt; they have been interested in the accuracy of the deal, and you have misdirected their attention from the right hand, which holds the palmed cards.

Misdirection can be built into the presentation of a card trick almost at will once a real understanding of its principles is had. This takes thought, more thought and still more thought, and after the misdirection has been conceived it must be tested before audiences to determine its effectiveness. But once a good misdirective device has been evolved, it is yours for all time and it will be as effective ten years hence as it is when first created. The very best conjurers, the ones who are esteemed by the general public, are the ones who have constructed their presentation so that, at the moment when the secret sleight is made, some logical stimuli will be presented which will interest and divert the spectator's attention. They have been willing to devote the sometimes exasperating thought to the problem of misdirection, knowing that the rewards are great.

On the other hand, many a card conjurer, especially in presenting intimate card feats, trusts to luck that his misdirection will be good. He never performs the same feat in the same manner twice in succession. He relies upon an "opportune moment" to provide the misdirection which he needs; and more often than not this moment does not materialize. Yet if he will take each feat in his repertoire, search out its weak spot and invent misdirection to cover this weakness, he will be enabled to present the trick successfully on all occasions and the trouble and time spent in inventing the misdirection will have more than repaid him.

It is always advisable to invent your own misdirection, for the ruses which are suitable for one personality are rarely natural when used by another, when it is not an inherent part of the trick itself. Cardini may secure perfect misdirection by allowing his monocle to drop from his eye, concentrating audience interest upon the monocle and its replacement as the suave deceiver quietly secures billiard balls, cards, or cigarettes with the other hand; but few of us can wear monocles and none of us can duplicate Cardini's superbly characterized ennuied man about town. Strive, rather, to create misdirection which will be individually your own; a product of your own thought, no one can use it so effectively as you.

The principles of misdirection which have been set down here have been proven psychologically sound by generations of conjurers. With a thorough understanding of the nature of misdirection and how it may be used, the reader can build into his own presentation this vital factor which makes possible so many surprising feats.

Chapter 2
PRESENTATION

~~~~~~

Mastery of the technique which makes his feats possible is an absolute essential to the card conjurer but it is not enough to make him a successful entertainer. Much as a jeweler mounts a diamond to bring out all the beauty of the stone, the conjurer must present his feats in the most entertaining manner of which he is capable. It is not enough merely to stand before an audience and do a card trick, no matter how great the technical expertness; the entertainer must employ all the tricks of the theatre to win for himself the approval of those present.

It is not the purpose of this book to expound the principles of presentation which, after all, are best learned through experience. Yet since good stagecraft is such a large part of the successful presentation of card magic it may not be inadvisable to point out some of the methods used by experienced artists in presenting their feats.

THE PRESENTATION OF MAGIC

It would be less than prudent to claim that the reader here will find infallible rules and regulations which will enable him overnight to become one of the greats of magic. Unfortunately, there is no magic road to success unless it be hard work and bitter experience. But you are a magician and you love magic; and, lacking experience, you are floundering about in all directions and you are getting a little discouraged. You present magic, but not very well, and you don't know what is wrong. You tell yourself that what you need is a new trick, something very new and amazing and impossible; but when you get this trick you are just where you were before and you decide that what you need is another new trick, also very amazing and impossible. And you don't know what is wrong.

It is to you that these words are addressed, and not to those others who have already learned from experience that which we hope to say here. We want to tell you about some very fine magicians, and what they did, and why they became famous.

They became famous because they knew how to present magic; or, to put it more concisely, they knew how to present themselves in an act of magic. After a great deal of hard work and thought they learned that there are three kinds of magicians. There is the conjurer who possesses the knack of creating spontaneous laughter; there is the wizard who is a mystic and who presents his feats in a more or less serious manner, implying that he has strange powers; and there is the magician who is a light-hearted and friendly fellow who somehow contrives to create the impression that his feats are the result of intellectual thimble-rigging; that his deceptions are successful because he thinks just a little faster than his audience.

If you are one of the first group, you will hardly be reading this chapter, for such men are the blessed of the gods and you will know it as surely as you know that the sun rises in the east, for this is a talent which cannot be concealed. Nothing will stop such a man from being what he is: an amusing zany.

But if you, in presenting your magic, are always casting about for something "funny" to say, if you borrow your contemporaries' clever lines and bits of business, then you are trying to be what you are not, and you should remember that not everyone can be a Frank van Hoven or a Russell Swann. You may be hurting yourself with your audiences by attempting this style of presentation.

Secondly there is the wizard who cloaks his mysteries in a pseudo-shroud of impenetrable darkness. He is the Merlin who nudges the occult in his performances, who wishes his audiences to believe, if ever so little, that he possesses powers not granted to the rest of the world—he is one of the pseudo-mentalists, soothsayers and pryers-into-the-future. Convincingly done, this sort of thing is an art in itself and, as in the case of the humorous magician, it is art in which no instruction can be given. If you possess the personal magnetism which would enable you to sell raccoon coats in Death Valley, you may be such a magician. This type of presentation does not readily lend itself to general magic of the type under discussion, and it is even more difficult to present card magic in this metier. Joseph Dunninger, apparently, is the only present day conjurer who can say "Take a card!" and still convince his spectators that fairies and goblins perch on his shoulder.

If you are not this type of magician, either, then you will undoubtedly adapt yourself very nicely to the remaining style; and a very good style it is. This is magic presented in the urbane, good-humored manner, with the tongue in the cheek.

This type of performer has enjoyed a steady popularity for decades; one thinks of Charles Bertram, Nate Leipzig, David Devant, Alexander

Herrmann, Howard Thurston, Max Malini and, currently, Blackstone, Cardini and Dante, international celebrities, all of whom played the suave and personable wizard of story-book tradition. In the more intimate night club field Paul Rosini is presently the leading exponent of this type of performance; in the field of society entertainment Luis Zingone dominates the field. In the case of each of these personalities it is worthy of comment that their audiences have gained the impression of a shrewd brain, a smooth tongue and an imperturbable nature capable of mastering any situation; in other words, a champion.

These men all have employed a type of humor little understood by the fraternity. This is situation humor stemming out of character, the ingratiating sort of amusing nonsense which the great American public so vastly enjoys. Nothing could be more absurdly rollicking than Blackstone, grey-haired, crinkle-eyed, struggling to defeat a dancing handkerchief which, for reasons of its own, perversely eludes his reaching hand. Rarely will you see a more deftly implausible sight than the immaculate Cardini, baffled by the cards, balls and cigarettes which swoop at him out of the nothingness. Rosini, too, is a master of the situation-character type of humor; it is tonic to watch him, nibbling a forefinger, as he enquires nebulously if the spectator is absolutely positive that the card is not his; to watch the magnificently comical manner in which, with a shrug, he passes off the failure as a matter of no importance—and a moment later discovers the missing card in his hand.

These things are amusing to an audience because it has been prepared to accept the performer as the type of person who, in such a situation, would react in exactly such a manner.

As an example familiar to all, consider Jack Benny, the radio comedian, and the character which he has evolved. Benny is the essentially timid man who, boasting and bragging, invariably is forced to eat his words; he is miserly, counting his pennies on every occasion; he is engaged in a constantly futile battle of wits with Rochester, his colored servant, in which the latter is always the winner; he is the roaring lion who, confronted by a really formidable adversary, forthwith turns into the woolly lamb. The radio audience has long accepted these characteristics of the radio Jack Benny and, when the comedian is thrust into a new situation, they sense long in advance what his reaction will be and can enjoy to the utmost his unhappy squirmings.

It is impossible for the magician, in the brief time at his disposal, to create so fully rounded a character as this; yet by short sharp strokes he can outline the character he is playing sufficiently to give background depth to the salient character traits, precisely as Cardini, by accentuating character traits of ennui and eccentricity, provides a perfect background for the production of objects which, apparently, harass and annoy him. This type of humor is more a created humor than any other; it is the result of the constant building of a character, of placing the character in a situation to which he reacts in a believable manner. It is the type of intellectual horseplay which never grows old.

It is not an easy humor to master, not nearly so easy as memorizing a few jokes and clever sayings and dropping these into your monologues; but it is a much safer humor, for the longer you live with the character you are creating, the more real that character becomes, very much like interest compounding in a bank.

It remains for you as an entertainer to decide upon the type of character you will portray, and this you alone can determine since, if you are plump and ruddy-cheeked, you can hardly play the sophisticated sorcerer. In most instances the character created is an accented and dramatized version of the performer's own character; Thurston built his character around a man very similar to the old country doctor, who was everyone's friend and whose heart was of gold; he managed to a surprising extent to make each spectator feel that this homey, comfortable-looking hanky-panky man was addressing him personally. Fred Keating made of his character a sharp-witted, sophisticated man of the world, a little above the miracles he peddled; Fulton Oursler has described the late Nate Leipzig as a laughing, mocking, triumphant mystic, the Paderewski of card manipulators and the Paganini of magicians; Charles Miller is a beaming young man struggling to be serious and, failing, moving with a certain implacability from trick to trick, always determined to do the next trick in a very grave mood and always happily failing. Dante, so Brooks Atkinson claims, is all grace, courtesy and insouciance; he is possibly a demi-god temporarily assuming human form, a man who acknowledges—and even encourages—applause by waving his arms in a proud salaam; who, as befits a man of his eminence, is waited on obsequiously by a staff of uniformed slaves, who keep turning up in turbans as the mysteries go deeper. After Dante has doffed a turban, the critic continues, a page waits on him with mirror and comb while he puts his silken hair in order again. "People of exalted station," Mr. Atkinson points out, "are accustomed to service."

The difference between these various men and the run of the mine conjurer is that each is a personality, distinctive and unlike any of his contemporaries. They are men whom audiences remember and of whom they speak when conjuring and magic is mentioned. There is nothing humdrum nor casual about them; it is not the tricks they perform that are important so much as the illusion they create about themselves.

Can anyone, having been told that Dante, with magnificent aplomb, combs his silken locks while the audience waits breathless for the next miracle, fail to understand and like such an extraordinary character? As with every great magician, he is selling not his magic but the character he has built around himself. Can anyone forget Paul Rosini in the spotlight, hand on heart, accepting the plaudits of the crowd? Or Thurston, Blackstone, Malini?

Not many may rise to great heights; but you, who may be one of these, must now inspect yourself to decide as an actor the role you will play; and then, like an actor, rehearse that role over and over again, building the character in word and action until it becomes an unforgettable reality. It will be difficult, but it will be worth the effort if you are one of the chosen few.

PATTER

Many men can think on their feet and often many of their best and most telling remarks are made on the spur of the moment. There are very few professional entertainers, however, who do not have a rough outline in their minds of the topic on which they are to speak before they appear before their audience. They may not know the exact words in which they will phrase their thought, but they do know the ideas those words will convey.

It is a mistake for the conjurer to feel that he can appear before an audience and clothe his feats with suitable patter which he will invent as he goes along. It is just as much of a mistake to learn your patter word for word, to be recited like a parrot.

A good method is first in private to think out the talk which you will use, keeping it in character with your own personality and style of presentation. Don't try to use another person's talk; it may be very good as he uses it and very bad as you do it; and, more to the point, in creating your own patter you will have evolved a presentation which you alone have. The temptation to adopt as your own a colleague's amusing remark or bit of business should be resisted; it is not good for either of you.

When your patter is written, memorize it word for word, by paragraphs. Talk out loud and use your voice as an actor uses his voice, making the inflections convey your smallest shade of meaning. Do your trick as you talk and coördinate your gestures and sleights with your patter. The more often you do this the more natural it will be.

When you have learned what you will say and how you will say it, put it out of your mind. You can learn your lines so well that your mind will grow weary, for memory can be strained. After several days go over your talk once more but this time make no attempt to repeat word for word what you have learned. Your memory will feed you the highlights and although you may clothe these thoughts in new words, you will gain spontaneity. You may not use the trick for which you have prepared in this manner for months on end, but when you do use it you will find that you will remember what to say and how to say it.

The next step is to find an audience on which to try your patter. Experiment with it; take out that which is weak and add that which you think will be strong. If you are a non-professional, beware of your family and your close friends. They know you too well and will either be too helpful or too critical; study instead the reaction of strangers; they are impartial and unbiased.

Whenever possible, attempt to remember the turn of the phrase of any remark which you make without premeditation, which may amuse your audience; these lines unconsciously uttered are often the very best and can be worked into your patter for continued use.

Good Humor

There is one quality alone which the great men of magic have had in common: all have radiated enjoyment of the work they do.

Good humor is contagious, exactly as gloom is pervasive. When a conjurer truly enjoys his work, when he radiates that uncounterfeitable pleasure he derives from doing his mysterious hoodwinkeries, no audience in the world can resist him.

May the reader have the good fortune to witness Charles Miller in an ebullient mood with fifty-two cards in his hands! Here is an expert for whom the pasteboards provide a series of brain-teasing mysteries, each a little more baffling than the last. So deftly does this card conjurer perform his chicaneries, with such huge enjoyment of his work apparent in his bland eyes, that the onlookers inevitably succumb to the spell he casts, for such good nature is irresistible.

If this performer were a dour man grudgingly performing his mysteries he would still be a superb card man, but he would not be one-hundredth the entertaining fellow he is. Good humor is a priceless ingredient which smooths the path in magic as in all other walks of life; let your audience see that you enjoy performing for them and they will respond to your efforts with greater appreciation.

THE FIRST TRICK

Let it be a good one which you know from experience will entertain those present. The first wave of laughter or applause will put you at your ease if you have reason to be at all nervous.

During the first trick the audience is sizing you up. If you fumble the trick or appear ill at ease it will feel that it can dominate you, that you are a suppliant asking for its favor. By using the trick that you can do well and that creates a maximum impression you should remove the cause of most nervousness, which is lack of confidence.

Relax to be natural and to be yourself. During the first trick look around you and find a friendly face; address your remarks to this man. Find another person and talk to him, and to still another. Meeting the gaze of these few interested and friendly people will remove any tenseness you may feel.

THE VOICE

Talk to the last row in a natural tone and your voice will reach it. Never shout to make yourself heard.

To determine how your voice sounds to others, go into a corner and cup your hands behind your ears. It will give you an idea. Better yet, have a phonograph record made. Watch particularly for faulty enunciation.

Actors know how to use their voices. One of their tricks is to recite the alphabet, letter for letter, putting into their voice all the emotions— love, anger, rage, contempt. Another trick is to make love to an inanimate object in honeyed tones, while using the most contemptuous language possible. Another is to change the meaning, by inflection, of a sentence. These things can be important to the magician who talks.

To learn to enunciate clearly, so that all may understand what you say: Place a cork between the lips, gripping it with the teeth, and read aloud from a book.

Old-time actors "packed their breath against the belt." Secure a good book on breath control and note how much more convincingly you speak your patter.

MAKING FRIENDS

An audience relishes being looked at.

It is an extremely fine presentation technique to pause for a moment in the course of a trick, glance about the company as you talk as though addressing your remarks to each individual whose glance meets yours. Each such person feels that his personality has been recognized by the performer, that he has been singled out from amongst many for a special attention. If the conjurer can smile sincerely both with his eyes and his lips upon such a person, he will create a bond which nine times out of ten will repay him in the rich dividends of applause and approval.

Opportunities in which this stratagem may be put to use without slowing the presentation are frequent. For instance, in shuffling the cards it is a good technique to pause with the cards in disorder in the left hand and make any remark which may be fitting, then continue the overhand shuffle as if resuming the trick. Never look at the cards during such a shuffle; look at the audience. This matter-of-factness and unconcern in the shuffle not only makes it appear very fair and innocent, but it permits the conjurer to establish an *entente cordiale* with members of the audience.

Robert-Houdin has phrased this phenomenon well: "Note the advance to the footlights of yonder artist, whose keen, intelligent, self-reliant glance goes straight to meet the eyes of the company. A relation of an almost mesmeric character is instantly established between all parties. The spectators are at their ease with the performer, they at once catch his eye, they listen to him with indulgence, and from this double relation there speedily arises a feeling of sympathy. Under such conditions success becomes an easy matter."

You Yourself

Put your weight on the balls of your feet, like a prize fighter. You can then move in any direction without stumbling or appearing awkward.

Concentrate upon the trick you are doing, and not upon yourself and what the audience thinks of you. When you are at your ease you can catch the "feel" of the audience and guide yourself accordingly.

You cannot ignore a distraction. When the show-off spectator attempts to spoil your trick you cannot ignore him nor can you fight him. If you ignore him he persists; if you fight him your audience will be against you. If possible, capitalize on him; look for the unoffensive remark which will cause laughter. Never under any conditions lose your temper; you will make yourself appear ridiculous.

If you have not secured the attention of your audience and a spectator is talking, don't attempt to out-talk him. To catch attention, lower your voice. A trick which will often prove effective with the rowdiest audience is to move your lips as though talking, or lower your voice to a near-whisper. Those who want to hear you will strain their ears for only so long; then they will demand that the person creating the disturbance come to order. *They* do the work for you.

Actors often read their opening lines in a low voice to stop audience restlessness and to focus attention. It is a good device.

Be sincere. Say what you have to say and believe both in it and in yourself. Never apologize, no matter what goes wrong or what you fear may go wrong. Audiences don't want apologies and they are not interested in your troubles. If you drop palmed cards, don't apologize; there is little you can say and you may only call attention to that which many failed to observe. When the four aces turn out to be four indifferent cards don't explain that it couldn't, or shouldn't, have happened. People will understand and overlook such a contretemps and will be with you if you pass over the matter lightly; if you apologize, they will be annoyed with you.

Never disparage yourself and mean it. When you make what should be a clever remark and no one is amused, don't show that the attempt at wittiness has failed. Don't pause and wait for the laughter which does not come.

Don't pluck at your clothes if you're nervous, straightening your tie or tugging at your coat.

THE ROUTINE

To present a trick most effectively, it is imperative that the conjurer should routine it so that the feat literally is at his finger tips. He should know what he will say, what he will do and, if the feat requires misdirection, what his method of diverting attention from himself at the vital moment will be.

Long ago David Devant pointed out that one trick, well done, is of greater value to the conjurer than a dozen tricks performed in a slipshod manner. A trick cannot be presented effectively if the magician must concentrate upon its mechanics, or grope for words to express his thought, or depend upon fortuitous circumstance to provide for him the misdirection he needs.

Routining a trick takes thought but it need not be drudgery. Paul Rosini will work for hours to achieve a natural presentation against a symphonic background of the *Meditation from Thaïs*, the music establishing for him the tempo and rhythm of the trick. Charles Miller, on the other hand, worries a trick like a dog a bone, doing each move over and over again, growling when he is balked in his search for simplicity and naturalness and purring when his effort is rewarded. Each professional conjurer has his own method of routining but a good one is to go through the actions as they would be made if you actually could perform magical feats. If you are routining the Cards to Pocket, go through the actions without attempting to palm the cards into the pocket; note how easily and cleanly the cards are handled. Strive to duplicate this handling when the cards are actually palmed. Again, note how directly the pack may be handed for shuffling, and duplicate these actions when cards are palmed.

Self-criticism is difficult but the great exponents of card conjuring have been men who could look at themselves from a distance and make their presentation conform exactly to the procedure which would be followed were sleights not attempted. All unnecessary actions should be rigidly suppressed; constant turning of the pack, or shifting it from hand to hand, is a disturbing element to the onlookers, exactly as constant riffling of the ends detracts from the effortless, silent handling you should strive to make your own. The pack should be held at all times almost at arm's length, well away from the body; it is amazing how this appears to make sleights impossible, as those who have seen Max Malini perform will testify. Unless you are a gifted raconteur, avoid long drawn-out "story" patter; remember that when performing minutes are hours. Provide misdirective cover for all sleights and include enough movement about the platform to give the appearance of action.

Routining the trick is the secret of successful card conjuring as every professional knows and which those who aspire to professional status, (and the casual performer as well), will do well to consider.

The Proof of the Pudding

In selecting the tricks which he will use to build a program, every conjurer attempts to select those which he is best equipped to perform and, theoretically at least, those which will give the greatest entertainment to those who witness them.

The best and only method of determining if a trick is entertaining, as performed by yourself, is to use it before an audience. The fact that a trick is a success in the hands of a contemporary does not mean that it will similarly be a success in your hands. Only by actual routining and performance can the conjurer discover the little bits of business which lift a trick out of the rut and which, fitting his temperament and personality, he alone can create for himself and without which a trick is merely a trick.

The quality of self-criticism stands the magician in good stead in selecting those tricks which he will place in his program. Without this ability to view one's self dispassionately, it is all too easy to be influenced by one's prejudices in favor of a trick. Theoretically any trick which is performed deceptively should be a good trick; in actual practice this is unfortunately not the case. A conjurer may have a magnificent—to him—method of locating and discovering a card of which he is exceedingly fond, but which induces only boredom in his audience. If he is not sensitive to audience reaction, the trick may stay in his program when it should be discarded.

On the other hand, feats which the magician holds in low esteem will often be received by an audience with gratifying enthusiasm; every card conjurer has had the experience of receiving high praise for a feat of which he expected little.

The reader is urged to study and to experiment with the old tricks which have proven themselves unfailingly welcome to audiences for decades. These may be found in Hoffmann's *Modern Magic*, *More Magic* and *Later Magic*, in Robert-Houdin's *Secrets of Conjuring and Magic*, in Sachs' *Sleight of Hand* and in other magic classics; modernized methods for many of these will be found in Jean Hugard's books and in *Greater Magic*. By taking such old-time tricks and enfusing them with his own personality, each individual performer will have, to all intents and purposes, a new trick, exactly as Nelson Eddy and John McCormack, both singing *Ave Maria*, actually sing two different songs since the mood they create by their differing techniques is wholly dissimilar. It is safe to say that any of the old masterpieces, capably performed, will be accepted warmly by any modern audience.

But the old axiom, that it is not what you do but the manner in which you do it, still remains operative. The feat which is a great success as performed by one conjurer is unsuited to another, and vice versa. The only manner in which you can determine which tricks are within your capabilities and which fit in with your style of presentation is to perform them and determine if they receive a favorable reception; the audience is always the final judge, and it is never—or hardly ever—wrong.

SOMETHING NEW

The neophyte in card magic has one overwhelming desire, one insatiable penchant, and that is to *do something new*. The excuse offered for this penchant is that, working before a limited circle of family and friends, new feats must be offered if the tyro is not to repeat himself.

Within reason, it is of course desirable to add new presentations to your repertoire. Too often, however, this desire for something new is merely a rationalization to explain a pell-mell desire to do tricks, tricks and more tricks, not for the entertainment of the spectators, but for the entertainment of the conjurer himself.

Those new to card conjuring would do well if, instead of attempting to learn a great number of tricks, they would instead concentrate upon a few good tricks and master them so that their technique and their presentation is so excellent that those who see them will want to see them again. The beginner fails to realize that, if he can do a trick really well, his own intimate circle will, far from growing tired of it, ask him to repeat it time and again.

One of the reasons that card tricks are sometimes looked upon with disfavor is that the beginner, attempting a trick which he cannot do well, bores and exasperates those upon whom he inflicts his unrehearsed trickeries. The professional card expert, who must please his audiences if he is to survive, never attempts always to be performing new tricks; He has a repertoire and uses it as the framework for his act; occasionally he interpolates a new feature, but always he has a smoothly planned and executed routine. Nate Leipzig, for instance, had four favorite tricks which he performed over a period of many years, and such was his skill and presentation that one never tired of the feats, any more than one would tire of Lawrence Tibbett singing *The Glory Road*.

This should not be read to imply that professionals can perform only a few tricks; actually they can perform a great many and, being experts, they can perform them well. In their working repertoires, however, they include only the feats which they can perform best.

The casual performer will do well to pattern his work in this mold; he will find that it is only when his own intimate group of their own volition request him to repeat a trick that he can feel sure that he is learning the skills of his avocation.

THE SPECTATOR PERSPECTIVE

There is a perfectly natural tendency amongst magicians to underrate the tricks which they perform; knowing the secret, it is little wonder that they often lose the viewpoint of the spectator, to whom a trick of which the conjurer thinks little may seem to be a little masterpiece.

Take, for instance, such a trick as the sadly maligned Four Ace trick, with its innumerable variations. Almost every magician has a method; it is one of the first tricks the neophyte attempts; the magical journals bourgeon with methods, and there is hardly a gathering of magicians in which the trick is not repeated two or three times. Little wonder that magicians are wearied of the very name of the trick! Familiarity breeds contempt, and this is as true of tricks as of men.

Unfortunately, this attitude towards a trick creeps into the presentation; it is presented half-heartedly, the conjurer going through the mechanical action in a perfunctory manner and making of the dénouement a climax as exciting as a slightly decrepit pancake.

Look at the Four Ace trick with the eyes of the onlooker. What could be more mysterious than the assembly of the aces if the trick is so performed as to preclude any possible explanation? The moment when the four cards are turned face upwards and shown to be aces is the very crux of the trick; it is the moment which calls for a blaring of brass. It is very decidedly not the moment to' face the aces lethargically with a let's-get-this-over-with manner; but this is exactly what the conjurer will do unless he believes in the trick, unless he can see it with the spectator's eyes.

A great part of the success of Charles Bertram lay in the fact that he had the happy faculty of visualizing his tricks in this manner. He too performed the Four Ace trick, and it was an old, old trick in his day. He made of it one of his most effective feats, a trick with which his name is linked; in his hands the flight of the aces was accentuated, dramatized, made odd and mysterious and amusing. He performed the feat as the spectators wanted to see a feat of magic performed, with an air.

It is axiomatic that knowing the secret of a trick destroys its charm; this is not only true of the layman, but of the conjurer himself. It is very difficult to visualize the effect of a trick when you know the method; if proof of this were needed consider the conjurer who reads a good trick in print and dismisses it as unimportant, only to see it performed by a colleague. It no longer seems to be the same trick; it is seen in a new light and only then is it evaluated properly.

The argument here is that your opinion of a trick is of little importance. The feat which you may feel to be a very fine one may be received apathetically by audiences; contrarily, the trick you hold lightly may bring forth a storm of applause. Look at every trick through the spectator's eyes and, once you are satisfied that a trick is a good one, pleasing to the onlookers, remember that although you may perform it a thousand times, and it may seem stale and old to you, it is new and surprising to the thousand and first person. Perform it always as though it were the very newest feat in card conjuring.

Sleight of Hand vs. Self-Working Feats

In considering the question of sleight of hand versus self-working tricks, it is well always to be guided not by your own personal prejudices, but by the effect any trick has upon those who see it. If, for instance, you double lift, showing the eight of spades, and remove the card above it, which is the seven of spades, thrusting this card into the end of the pack; and then show it as the eight by covering its index with the first finger so that it may be shown with impunity as the eight; and finally with a snap of the fingers apparently cause it to rise to the top—if you do this and those present think that the feat was the result of pure skill, you would be foolish to discard this method in favor of one depending upon sleight of hand.

One of America's finest sleight of hand artists is an adept at weaving self-working tricks into his routines; he performs a feat dependent upon remarkable sleight of hand and follows it with a self-working trick which could not conceivably be performed by sleight; yet his spectators gape in awe, mistakenly crediting him with incredible skill. To them, everything he does is made possible by the finest sleight of hand; he has an enormous reputation *and this reputation is justified*, for this expert is using not only his trained hands but he is using his brain as well. He is out-thinking and, in the vernacular, out-smarting those who watch him.

This conjurer will use any expedient available to the magician if it will assure him an effective trick. He will use prearrangement, double-face cards, mathematical principles, diachylon, stripper decks. In his hands, following hard on the heels of a series of tricks dependent upon sleights, Dai Vernon's Brain Wave deck is a veritable masterpiece of trickery which simply astounds those who witness his work.

At the same time, his presentation of such classics as Everywhere and Nowhere, Three Cards Across and similar feats leaves nothing to be desired.

His experience, and that of many another of the great names of card magic, is that, paradoxically, even the simplest self-working trick is made more effective when the performer has mastered pure sleight of hand. There is a stamp of authority which comes when the conjurer is master of all the artifice of card conjuring, and this transmits itself to the presentation of the self-working feat. It is like two pianists playing a simple but effective theme; the first, competent but pedestrian, gives an effective and creditable rendition; the second, a virtuoso, plays the same theme but there is a magic touch to his fingers; he imparts a new meaning to the tones and makes of it music in the finest sense. Behind the playing of the notes is skill, technique and the mysterious force of character which has brought this skill into being.

An expert in card magic imparts to the self-working feat the same background and technique which the virtuoso of the piano imparts to the simple theme. Because a trick works itself is no reason why it should not be done well. In performing self-working tricks, the reader is urged to give to them the same thought which must be given to tricks dependent upon skill. There is a right and a wrong way of performing even the simplest sleights. The expert makes the glide well; the dabbler does it as well as he can, with a wiggling of the fingers and perhaps a gratuitous glimpse of the card extending from the pack, which may or may not be well enough.

The expert studies to learn the manner in which the self-working feat may be performed with the fewest possible actions blending in a smooth continuity; the dabbler makes unnecessary actions, pauses to remember how the trick is done, picks up the wrong packet in the wrong hand, unnecessarily passes the packet from hand to hand and blunders merrily along his way.

It is well, also, in using self-working feats to use only those which experience has proven to be effective. The good self-working tricks, and the only ones worth bothering with, are those which apparently are not self-working; tricks in which cards are dealt interminably, in which the spectator must be watched like a hawk lest he disarrange the order of the cards, or in which complicated instructions must be given, should be tabu.

It is not a question of whether to perform tricks employing sleight of hand or of using tricks dependent upon self-working principles; the problem is to use the tricks which you can perform most effectively, and, if these include self-working tricks, to routine the trick smoothly and to use it with feats of skill, artfully, so that from them the maximum effect may be derived.

The Importance of the Inconsequential

Remember always that that which the performer appears to feel is of great importance will also be so regarded by the audience. Conversely, that which he treats as inconsequential will be given scant attention.

It is for this reason that, when you false count a number of cards, you should never look at them during the count. Instead avail yourself of the opportunity to gaze about you at the audience, making of the count a routine matter; the impression you give is that it is merely a formality and since those present have no reason to suspect chicanery they accept the count at face value. On the other hand, if the conjurer watches the cards closely, or shows nervousness, or counts each card as though it were breakable, he will give to the count an importance which the onlookers similarly attach to it.

Again, if you have anything to hide, place it in the most open position available. If it is a prearranged pack, hand it to a spectator and say, "Hold this for a moment," or place it on the table before another spectator. If you are using double-face cards for the Four Ace trick, drop them before a spectator rather than close to yourself; since there is no reason for him to handle them, the cards will be perfectly safe. Mr. Bert Allerton makes great use of this principle; whenever, in his table work, he has something he wishes to hide, he places it in the most (apparently) dangerous position; he knows that if a spectator suspects that he is trying to withhold an object, the spectator will want to see it desperately; if, on the other hand, it is placed directly before him, in ninety-nine cases out of a hundred he will regard it with indifference.

The same principle applies to all tricks in which you have gambled that a spectator will follow a certain set course of action; if you watch him like a hawk and attempt to guide him, he will fight you and ruin your trick. If, for instance, you want him to cut into a Bridge, place the pack before him, say, "Cut" and because he has no reason to suspect subterfuge he will cut into the bridge. If, again, you are performing a trick with a one-way pack in which the secret lies in the fact that a person will naturally place a card on the table in a certain manner, if you over-instruct the spectator he will suspect artifice and proceed to "improve" the handling in a manner which may spoil your trick.

Finally, never place too much importance in your sleights, lest you telegraph to the onlookers that the sleight is about to take place. If you are worried about making the top change you will almost instinctively become tense and hesitate before the action; nervousness is an intangible and can be felt by others. Learn the technique of your sleights perfectly, create a misdirection to cover them and, when they must be made, divest them of all importance in your own mind and you will avoid the danger of forewarning your spectators.

The rule, subject to the exception to which all rules are subject, is to treat as unimportant that which you really wish to conceal.

The Simple Way

The very best method of performing a given trick is the easiest method, and it is the method which should be used. The complication of a trick for complication's sake, a strange malady sometimes noted amongst conjurers, should be rigidly eschewed.

If, with a simple cut, you can secure the effect of transposing the packets, and do this undetected under cover of misdirection, the simple cut should by all means be used. To use the pass under such circumstances is unnecessary and unwise; the real card expert invariably employs the simplest sleight which will enable him to reach a given end, concentrating his attention upon doing the sleight well rather than expending energy in making difficult an easy move.

Remember always that it is not what you do, but what the spectator believes that you do which is important. One of the very finest of all card workers has, time and again, performed tricks which have appeared to be absolutely miraculous, by the simple expedient of looking at a chosen card carelessly held by the spectator. If you have the good fortune to be in the position where you can sight a chosen card, it would be foolish not to make the most of it.

The only demand that need be made of a method is that it shall deceive the onlookers; bluff, audacity, swindles and barefaced deceptions are all fair grist in the conjurer's mill. If it is effective, and it is simple in the bargain—so much the better.

The Audience Committee

Whenever possible in routining a trick make use of as many persons from the audience as possible. The use of a committee not only makes amusing by-play possible, but it affords excellent cover for secret sleights, such as that used by one card man in making a shift while passing behind an assistant, by another in making the one-hand pass behind the assistant's screening body in moving him into a desired position; or, less directly, by having a committeeman provide the misdirectional cover you need for the secret sleight.

More important still, the committee adds a more than welcomed dash of the element of drama and suspense to the program. With a committee close at hand, the magician's tricks seemingly become more difficult of performance, for the audience feels that the conjurer may be detected in his hocus-pocus at any moment; thus an element of wit-matching is injected into the presentation which is invaluable in creating atmosphere.

Lastly, a merit not to be overlooked is that any spectator who assists in a trick will surely, later on, tell his friends and acquaintances of the experience, creating invaluable word-of-mouth advertising.

Similarly, in impromptu work, have one man shuffle the pack, another choose the card, and a third make a second shuffle after the replacement of the card. Use as many of those present as you can; it makes them very happy, gives them a sense of importance, and makes the performance of the trick seem more difficult.

Plots for Tricks

There are very few good plots in magic and these the first magicians preëmpted for their own use; all that remains to be done by modern card experts is to improve, if they can, the method or the technique.

All good plots are direct and easily comprehended by the audience. Three cards leave one packet and fly to another; a dozen cards leave the left hand and wing their way to the right trousers pocket; a card of which the spectator thinks is found in some surprising manner or in some surprising place; two cards change places, or one card mysteriously disappears and another takes its place; or a pack of cards grows smaller and smaller until finally it disappears; or three selected cards rise from the pack. These are a few of the direct plots and they are all straightforward and without any elements which could confuse the audience.

Such a trick should never be complicated in its presentation. No single spectator, for instance, should be expected to remember three cards; almost invariably, stuttering and stammering, he will forget one of them and the climax shrivels and dies. If three cards are to fly from one packet to another, let the cards make their magical pilgrimage by a direct route; do not detour one of them into your coat pocket, produce it, vanish it and send it to complete its journey after, as a final fillip, having front-and back-palmed the card for several moments.

Never destroy the unity of a trick in such a manner. You would not enjoy a motion picture in which the hero, racing to rescue the heroine from the villain, stopped in at a confectioner's to partake of a milkshake and to exchange banter with the proprietor.

Confederacy

The use of confederates amongst the audience is a practice the use of which each conjurer must decide for himself. Some incredible results may be had by having a convenient confederate on hand to bolster a trick; but unfortunately the use of such secret agents is subject to very grave drawbacks.

In the first place, it is really surprising how quickly an audience can detect the use of such a person. The trick may be just a little too incredible; or the confederate may betray himself by his manner of playing the rôle of innocent assistant; or the conjurer himself may unconsciously expose the duplicity by his actions. Audiences, as someone has remarked, are intelligent animals; they seem to have an uncanny knack for ferreting out true conjuring from false, even though the conjurer may be blissfully unconscious of the fact that they see through him.

In the second place, the conjurer who depends upon confederates must always have the confederate with him, or use a series of confederates who as time passes will repeat as an amusing anecdote the story of their collaboration with the magician, to the inestimable hurt of the latter's reputation.

Thirdly, use of the confederate is the only exception to the rule that a deception may be effected by any means, no matter what, so long as it achieves its purpose of confounding the audience. This is because this practice is bad for the magician himself. He becomes a confederate-addict, and relies more and more upon such a secret assistant to make possible his miracles; he is utterly dependent upon the confederate and may at any time be made wholly ridiculous should the man fail him; and, finally, he loses some of his self-respect. He is accepting the applause of his audience under false pretences; he does not merit their approval, since he has done nothing, and he knows it. The conscience of men is a curious thing; the conjurer who uses a confederate sooner or later finds that the pride in his skill which he must have if he is to be successful has been eaten away by the knowledge that he is not as competent as his fellow craftsmen.

Yet it is, as we have said, for each individual to decide for himself the path he will follow.

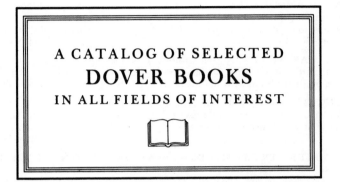

A CATALOG OF SELECTED
DOVER BOOKS
IN ALL FIELDS OF INTEREST

A CATALOG OF SELECTED DOVER
BOOKS IN ALL FIELDS OF INTEREST

THE ART NOUVEAU STYLE, edited by Roberta Waddell. 579 rare photographs of works in jewelry, metalwork, glass, ceramics, textiles, architecture and furniture by 175 artists—Mucha, Seguy, Lalique, Tiffany, many others. 288pp. 8⅜ × 11¼.
23515-7 Pa. $9.95

AMERICAN COUNTRY HOUSES OF THE GILDED AGE (Sheldon's "Artistic Country-Seats"), A. Lewis. All of Sheldon's fascinating and historically important photographs and plans. New text by Arnold Lewis. Approx. 200 illustrations. 128pp. 9⅜ × 12¼.
24301-X Pa. $7.95

THE WAY WE LIVE NOW, Anthony Trollope. Trollope's late masterpiece, marks shift to bitter satire. Character Melmotte "his greatest villain." Reproduced from original edition with 40 illustrations. 416pp. 6⅛ × 9¼.
24360-5 Pa. $7.95

BENCHLEY LOST AND FOUND, Robert Benchley. Finest humor from early 30's, about pet peeves, child psychologists, post office and others. Mostly unavailable elsewhere. 73 illustrations by Peter Arno and others. 183pp. 5⅜ × 8½.
22410-4 Pa. $3.50

ISOMETRIC PERSPECTIVE DESIGNS AND HOW TO CREATE THEM, John Locke. Isometric perspective is the picture of an object adrift in imaginary space. 75 mindboggling designs. 52pp. 8¼ × 11.
24123-8 Pa. $2.75

PERSPECTIVE FOR ARTISTS, Rex Vicat Cole. Depth, perspective of sky and sea, shadows, much more, not usually covered. 391 diagrams, 81 reproductions of drawings and paintings. 279pp. 5⅜ × 8½.
22487-2 Pa. $4.00

MOVIE-STAR PORTRAITS OF THE FORTIES, edited by John Kobal. 163 glamor, studio photos of 106 stars of the 1940s: Rita Hayworth, Ava Gardner, Marlon Brando, Clark Gable, many more. 176pp. 8⅜ × 11¼.
23546-7 Pa. $6.95

STARS OF THE BROADWAY STAGE, 1940-1967, Fred Fehl. Marlon Brando, Uta Hagen, John Kerr, John Gielgud, Jessica Tandy in great shows—*South Pacific, Galileo, West Side Story*, more. 240 black-and-white photos. 144pp. 8⅜ × 11¼.
24398-2 Pa. $8.95

ILLUSTRATED DICTIONARY OF HISTORIC ARCHITECTURE, edited by Cyril M. Harris. Extraordinary compendium of clear, concise definitions for over 5000 important architectural terms complemented by over 2000 line drawings. 592pp. 7½ × 9⅜.
24444-X Pa. $14.95

THE EARLY WORK OF FRANK LLOYD WRIGHT, F.L. Wright. 207 rare photos of Oak Park period, first great buildings: Unity Temple, Dana house, Larkin factory. Complete photos of Wasmuth edition. New Introduction. 160pp. 8⅜ × 11¼.
24381-8 Pa. $7.95

LIVING MY LIFE, Emma Goldman. Candid, no holds barred account by foremost American anarchist: her own life, anarchist movement, famous contemporaries, ideas and their impact. 944pp. 5⅜ × 8½. 22543-7, 22544-5 Pa., Two-vol. set $13.00

UNDERSTANDING THERMODYNAMICS, H.C. Van Ness. Clear, lucid treatment of first and second laws of thermodynamics. Excellent supplement to basic textbook in undergraduate science or engineering class. 103pp. 5⅜ × 8.
63277-6 Pa. $5.50

SMOCKING: TECHNIQUE, PROJECTS, AND DESIGNS, Dianne Durand. Foremost smocking designer provides complete instructions on how to smock. Over 10 projects, over 100 illustrations. 56pp. 8¼ × 11. 23788-5 Pa. $2.00

AUDUBON'S BIRDS IN COLOR FOR DECOUPAGE, edited by Eleanor H. Rawlings. 24 sheets, 37 most decorative birds, full color, on one side of paper. Instructions, including work under glass. 56pp. 8¼ × 11. 23492-4 Pa. $3.95

THE COMPLETE BOOK OF SILK SCREEN PRINTING PRODUCTION, J.I. Biegeleisen. For commercial user, teacher in advanced classes, serious hobbyist. Most modern techniques, materials, equipment for optimal results. 124 illustrations. 253pp. 5⅜ × 8½. 21100-2 Pa. $4.50

A TREASURY OF ART NOUVEAU DESIGN AND ORNAMENT, edited by Carol Belanger Grafton. 577 designs for the practicing artist. Full-page, spots, borders, bookplates by Klimt, Bradley, others. 144pp. 8⅜ × 11¼. 24001-0 Pa. $5.95

ART NOUVEAU TYPOGRAPHIC ORNAMENTS, Dan X. Solo. Over 800 Art Nouveau florals, swirls, women, animals, borders, scrolls, wreaths, spots and dingbats, copyright-free. 100pp. 8⅛ × 11. 24366-4 Pa. $4.00

HAND SHADOWS TO BE THROWN UPON THE WALL, Henry Bursill. Wonderful Victorian novelty tells how to make flying birds, dog, goose, deer, and 14 others, each explained by a full-page illustration. 32pp. 6½ × 9¼. 21779-5 Pa. $1.50

AUDUBON'S BIRDS OF AMERICA COLORING BOOK, John James Audubon. Rendered for coloring by Paul Kennedy. 46 of Audubon's noted illustrations: red-winged black-bird, cardinal, etc. Original plates reproduced in full-color on the covers. Captions. 48pp. 8¼ × 11. 23049-X Pa. $2.25

SILK SCREEN TECHNIQUES, J.I. Biegeleisen, M.A. Cohn. Clear, practical, modern, economical. Minimal equipment (self-built), materials, easy methods. For amateur, hobbyist, 1st book. 141 illustrations. 185pp. 6⅛ × 9¼. 20433-2 Pa. $3.95

101 PATCHWORK PATTERNS, Ruby S. McKim. 101 beautiful, immediately useable patterns, full-size, modern and traditional. Also general information, estimating, quilt lore. 140 illustrations. 124pp. 7⅞ × 10¾. 20773-0 Pa. $3.50

READY-TO-USE FLORAL DESIGNS, Ed Sibbett, Jr. Over 100 floral designs (most in three sizes) of popular individual blossoms as well as bouquets, sprays, garlands. 64pp. 8¼ × 11. 23976-4 Pa. $2.95

AMERICAN WILD FLOWERS COLORING BOOK, Paul Kennedy. Planned coverage of 46 most important wildflowers, from Rickett's collection; instructive as well as entertaining. Color versions on covers. Captions. 48pp. 8¼ × 11.
20095-7 Pa. $2.50

CARVING DUCK DECOYS, Harry V. Shourds and Anthony Hillman. Detailed instructions and full-size templates for constructing 16 beautiful, marvelously practical decoys according to time-honored South Jersey method. 70pp. 9¼ × 12¼.
24083-5 Pa. $4.95

TRADITIONAL PATCHWORK PATTERNS, Carol Belanger Grafton. Cardboard cut-out pieces for use as templates to make 12 quilts: Buttercup, Ribbon Border, Tree of Paradise, nine more. Full instructions. 57pp. 8¼ × 11.
23015-5 Pa. $3.50

25 KITES THAT FLY, Leslie Hunt. Full, easy-to-follow instructions for kites made from inexpensive materials. Many novelties. 70 illustrations. 110pp. 5⅜ × 8½.
22550-X Pa. $2.25

PIANO TUNING, J. Cree Fischer. Clearest, best book for beginner, amateur. Simple repairs, raising dropped notes, tuning by easy method of flattened fifths. No previous skills needed. 4 illustrations. 201pp. 5⅜ × 8½.
23267-0 Pa. $3.50

EARLY AMERICAN IRON-ON TRANSFER PATTERNS, edited by Rita Weiss. 75 designs, borders, alphabets, from traditional American sources. 48pp. 8¼ × 11.
23162-3 Pa. $1.95

CROCHETING EDGINGS, edited by Rita Weiss. Over 100 of the best designs for these lovely trims for a host of household items. Complete instructions, illustrations. 48pp. 8¼ × 11.
24031-2 Pa. $2.25

FINGER PLAYS FOR NURSERY AND KINDERGARTEN, Emilie Poulsson. 18 finger plays with music (voice and piano); entertaining, instructive. Counting, nature lore, etc. Victorian classic. 53 illustrations. 80pp. 6½ × 9¼. 22588-7 Pa. $1.95

BOSTON THEN AND NOW, Peter Vanderwarker. Here in 59 side-by-side views are photographic documentations of the city's past and present. 119 photographs. Full captions. 122pp. 8¼ × 11.
24312-5 Pa. $6.95

CROCHETING BEDSPREADS, edited by Rita Weiss. 22 patterns, originally published in three instruction books 1939-41. 39 photos, 8 charts. Instructions. 48pp. 8¼ × 11.
23610-2 Pa. $2.00

HAWTHORNE ON PAINTING, Charles W. Hawthorne. Collected from notes taken by students at famous Cape Cod School; hundreds of direct, personal *apercus*, ideas, suggestions. 91pp. 5⅜ × 8½.
20653-X Pa. $2.50

THERMODYNAMICS, Enrico Fermi. A classic of modern science. Clear, organized treatment of systems, first and second laws, entropy, thermodynamic potentials, etc. Calculus required. 160pp. 5⅜ × 8½.
60361-X Pa. $4.00

TEN BOOKS ON ARCHITECTURE, Vitruvius. The most important book ever written on architecture. Early Roman aesthetics, technology, classical orders, site selection, all other aspects. Morgan translation. 331pp. 5⅜ × 8½. 20645-9 Pa. $5.50

THE CORNELL BREAD BOOK, Clive M. McCay and Jeanette B. McCay. Famed high-protein recipe incorporated into breads, rolls, buns, coffee cakes, pizza, pie crusts, more. Nearly 50 illustrations. 48pp. 8¼ × 11.
23995-0 Pa. $2.00

THE CRAFTSMAN'S HANDBOOK, Cennino Cennini. 15th-century handbook, school of Giotto, explains applying gold, silver leaf; gesso; fresco painting, grinding pigments, etc. 142pp. 6⅛ × 9¼.
20054-X Pa. $3.50

FRANK LLOYD WRIGHT'S FALLINGWATER, Donald Hoffmann. Full story of Wright's masterwork at Bear Run, Pa. 100 photographs of site, construction, and details of completed structure. 112pp. 9¼ × 10.
23671-4 Pa. $6.95

OVAL STAINED GLASS PATTERN BOOK, C. Eaton. 60 new designs framed in shape of an oval. Greater complexity, challenge with sinuous cats, birds, mandalas framed in antique shape. 64pp. 8¼ × 11.
24519-5 Pa. $3.50

SOURCE BOOK OF MEDICAL HISTORY, edited by Logan Clendening, M.D. Original accounts ranging from Ancient Egypt and Greece to discovery of X-rays: Galen, Pasteur, Lavoisier, Harvey, Parkinson, others. 685pp. 5⅜ × 8½.
20621-1 Pa. $10.95

THE ROSE AND THE KEY, J.S. Lefanu. Superb mystery novel from Irish master. Dark doings among an ancient and aristocratic English family. Well-drawn characters; capital suspense. Introduction by N. Donaldson. 448pp. 5⅜ × 8½.
24377-X Pa. $6.95

SOUTH WIND, Norman Douglas. Witty, elegant novel of ideas set on languorous Mediterranean island of Nepenthe. Elegant prose, glittering epigrams, mordant satire. 1917 masterpiece. 416pp. 5⅜ × 8½. (Available in U.S. only)
24361-3 Pa. $5.95

RUSSELL'S CIVIL WAR PHOTOGRAPHS, Capt. A.J. Russell. 116 rare Civil War Photos: Bull Run, Virginia campaigns, bridges, railroads, Richmond, Lincoln's funeral car. Many never seen before. Captions. 128pp. 9⅜ × 12¼.
24283-8 Pa. $6.95

PHOTOGRAPHS BY MAN RAY: 105 Works, 1920-1934. Nudes, still lifes, landscapes, women's faces, celebrity portraits (Dali, Matisse, Picasso, others), rayographs. Reprinted from rare gravure edition. 128pp. 9⅜ × 12¼. (Available in U.S. only)
23842-3 Pa. $7.95

STAR NAMES: THEIR LORE AND MEANING, Richard H. Allen. Star names, the zodiac, constellations: folklore and literature associated with heavens. The basic book of its field, fascinating reading. 563pp. 5⅜ × 8½.
21079-0 Pa. $7.95

BURNHAM'S CELESTIAL HANDBOOK, Robert Burnham, Jr. Thorough guide to the stars beyond our solar system. Exhaustive treatment. Alphabetical by constellation: Andromeda to Cetus in Vol. 1; Chamaeleon to Orion in Vol. 2; and Pavo to Vulpecula in Vol. 3. Hundreds of illustrations. Index in Vol. 3. 2000pp. 6⅛ × 9¼.
23567-X, 23568-8, 23673-0 Pa. Three-vol. set $36.85

THE ART NOUVEAU STYLE BOOK OF ALPHONSE MUCHA, Alphonse Mucha. All 72 plates from *Documents Decoratifs* in original color. Stunning, essential work of Art Nouveau. 80pp. 9⅜ × 12¼.
24044-4 Pa. $7.95

DESIGNS BY ERTE; FASHION DRAWINGS AND ILLUSTRATIONS FROM "HARPER'S BAZAR," Erte. 310 fabulous line drawings and 14 *Harper's Bazar* covers, 8 in full color. Erte's exotic temptresses with tassels, fur muffs, long trains, coifs, more. 129pp. 9⅜ × 12¼.
23397-9 Pa. $6.95

HISTORY OF STRENGTH OF MATERIALS, Stephen P. Timoshenko. Excellent historical survey of the strength of materials with many references to the theories of elasticity and structure. 245 figures. 452pp. 5⅜ × 8½. 61187-6 Pa. $8.95

Prices subject to change without notice.

Available at your book dealer or write for free catalog to Dept. GI, Dover Publications, Inc., 31 East 2nd St. Mineola, N.Y. 11501. Dover publishes more than 175 books each year on science, elementary and advanced mathematics, biology, music, art, literary history, social sciences and other areas.